Spring MVC Cookbook

Over 40 recipes for creating cloud-ready Java web applications with Spring MVC

Alex Bretet

open source*
community experience distilled

BIRMINGHAM - MUMBAI

Spring MVC Cookbook

First published: February 2016

Production reference: 1220216

Published by Packt Publishing Ltd.
Livery Place
35 Livery Street
Birmingham B3 2PB, UK.

ISBN 978-1-78439-641-1

www.packtpub.com

Credits

Author
Alex Bretet

Reviewers
Bartosz Kielczewski
David Mendoza

Commissioning Editor
Amarabha Banerjee

Acquisition Editor
Manish Nainani

Content Development Editor
Mayur Pawanikar

Technical Editor
Pranjali Mistry

Copy Editor
Neha Vyas

Project Coordinator
Nikhil Nair

Proofreader
Safis Editing

Indexer
Monica Ajmera Mehta

Production Coordinator
Nilesh Mohite

Cover Work
Nilesh Mohite

About the Author

Alex Bretet is a certified Java and Spring Integration engineer. Currently working at Thunderhead, a pioneer company and global actor among SaaS providers, he has a rich developer background from different industries including energy, insurance, finance, and the Internet.

Captivated by the Internet's communication capabilities and by start-ups, he believes in skunk development outcomes (when groups of like-minded people together achieve unbelievable targets on tight deadlines).

He also defends a number of open source initiatives and indeed Spring technologies, whose pragmatism constantly disrupts the most established practices and offers valuable alternatives for the benefit of all.

You can contact him at `alex.bretet@gmail.com` or follow him on Twitter at `@abretet`

I would like first to thank all the people who have been directly related to this book, starting with all the reviewers, content development editors, technical and acquisition editors.

My thoughts go to my French engineering school and all the people I've met since then who have expressed and communicated their enthusiasm for the technology.

I am very grateful for being able to work in the IT industry nowadays. Thank you to all the elements around me that supported me going in this direction. When my interest for this topic grew, I couldn't imagine making a career out of it.

Writing this book has been a long project. I must mention my partner, Helena, for her patience and support throughout these months; my family and friends, who have been a source of encouragement; my dad, a source of inspiration.

My best regards go to Packt Publishing for producing this book and endorsing the project.

I acknowledge the expertise from the engineers at Pivotal Software, Inc. and the Spring community, their approachable set of documentation and their official references.

Finally, I want to thank you, who are reading these lines and have probably purchased this book. I hope it wil provide you help, spark, and Big Picture.

About the Reviewer

David Mendoza is a software engineer working on web development since 1999 with Java. He started his journey with JSPs and Servlets, creating a custom web framework to later find AppFuse, which introduced him to Spring and Struts. Then, he moved to Spring MVC and never looked back. David has worked as a Java consultant in Mexico, the United States, Canada, Venezuela, and Spain with companies such as ING Bank, Citi, and Telefonica. He is currently working for Southwestern Adventist University, a private university south of Dallas, Texas, where he's responsible for their entire web platform.

www.PacktPub.com

eBooks, discount offers, and more

Did you know that Packt offers eBook versions of every book published, with PDF and ePub files available? You can upgrade to the eBook version at www.PacktPub.com and as a print book customer, you are entitled to a discount on the eBook copy. Get in touch with us at customercare@packtpub.com for more details.

At www.PacktPub.com, you can also read a collection of free technical articles, sign up for a range of free newsletters and receive exclusive discounts and offers on Packt books and eBooks.

https://www2.packtpub.com/books/subscription/packtlib

Do you need instant solutions to your IT questions? PacktLib is Packt's online digital book library. Here, you can search, access, and read Packt's entire library of books.

Why Subscribe?

- ▶ Fully searchable across every book published by Packt
- ▶ Copy and paste, print, and bookmark content
- ▶ On demand and accessible via a web browser

Table of Contents

Preface

Welcome to the singular universe of *Spring MVC Cookbook*. We hope you are ready for this journey that will take you through modern Spring web development practices. We have been building the `cloudstreetmarket.com`, a stock exchange platform with social capabilities. We are about to take you through each step of its development process.

What this book covers

Chapter 1, Setup Routine for an Enterprise Spring Application, introduces a set of practices that are standard in the industry. From the configuration of an Eclipse IDE for optimized support of Java 8, Tomcat 8, GIT and Maven, to a proper understanding of Maven as a build automation tool and as a dependency management tool, you will learn how to deploy the Spring Framework on a sustainable base in this chapter.

Whether a project is meant to become a massively profitable product or to remain a rewarding experience, it should always begin with the same Enterprise-level patterns.

This chapter is more than a guide through the first development stage of the book's application, Cloud Street Market. A bunch of standard practices are presented here as a routine for developers toward enterprise Spring applications.

Chapter 2, Designing a Microservice Architecture with Spring MVC, is a slightly longer chapter. It covers the core principles of Spring MVC such as its request flow or the central role of DispatcherServlet. It is also about learning how to configure Spring MVC controllers and controller method-handlers with an extended source of information related to a controller's annotations.

In the path of a Microservice architecture, we install Spring and Spring MVC across modules and web projects to build functional units that are easy to deploy and easy to scale. In this perspective, we are going to shape our application with a web module that is responsible for serving a Twitter Bootstrap template along with another web module specialized in REST Web Services.

In this chapter, you also will learn how to transfer the model from controllers to JSP views using the JSTL and how to design a JavaScript MVC pattern with AngularJS.

Chapter 3, Working with Java Persistence and Entities, gives you a glimpse of . It is necessary at this stage to learn how persistent data can be handled in a Spring ecosystem and thus in a Spring MVC application. We will see how to configure, a JPA persistence provider (Hibernate) from dataSource and entityManagerFactory in Spring. You will learn how to build a beneficial JPA object-relational mapping from EJB3 Entities and then how to query repositories using Spring Data JPA.

Chapter 4, Building a REST API for a Stateless Architecture, provides insights into Spring MVC as a REST Web Services engine. We will see the amazing support the Framework provides, with several annotations acting as doorknobs on method-handlers to abstract web-related logic and thus only focus on the business. This principle appears with annotations for request binding (binding of parameters, URL paths, headers, and so on) and Response Marshalling and also for integrated support of Spring Data pagination.

This chapter also presents how to set up exception handling as part of Spring MVC to translate predefined exception-Types into generic error responses. You will understand how to configure the content negotiation, an important bit for REST APIs, and finally, how to expose and document REST Endpoints using Swagger and the Swagger UI.

Chapter 5, Authenticating with Spring MVC, presents how to configure an authentication on controllers and services from standard protocols such as HTTP BASIC and OAuth2. You will learn several concepts and practices related to Spring Security, such as the Filters chain, the <http> namespace, the Authentication Manager, or the management of roles and users. Our OAuth2 flow is a client implementation. We authenticate users in our application when they are first authenticated with a third-party provider: Yahoo! These Yahoo! authentications and connections are later used to pull fresh financial data from Yahoo! Finance. It will be very interesting to see how the OAuth2 flow can be entirely abstracted, in the backend, with the Spring Social library.

Chapter 6, Implementing HATEOAS, demonstrates how to take a RESTful Spring MVC API a step further. A Hypermedia-driven application provides links along with every single requested resource. These links reflect URLs of related resources. They provide to the user client (whatever type of client it may be) real-time navigation options—precious documentation that is also the actual implementation.

We will see how to build such links from JPA Entities associations or from the controller layer.

Chapter 7, Developing CRUD Operations and Validations, goes into the more advanced concepts of Spring MVC. Presenting the tools and techniques that support interactive HTTP methods (PUT, POST, and DELETE), we will lean on the HTTP1/1 specification (RFC 7231 Semantics and Content) to learn how to return the appropriate response status code or headers.

Our use of the Spring Validator together with the ValidationUtils utility class provides a compliant implementation of the validation-related JSR-303 and JSR-349 specifications.

The last recipe is the place where an internationalization (I18N) of messages and content happens. We also present a client-side implementation, with AngularJS, that relies on published internationalization web services.

Chapter 8, Communicating Through WebSockets and STOMP, focuses on the uprising WebSocket technology and on building Message-Oriented-Middleware for our application. This chapter provides a rare showcase that implements so much about WebSockets in Spring. From the use of the default embedded WebSocket message broker to a full-featured external broker (with STOMP and AMQP protocols), we will see how to broadcast messages to multiple clients and also how to defer the execution of time-consuming tasks with great scalability benefits.

You will learn how to dynamically create private queues and how to get authenticated clients to post and receive messages from these private queues.

To achieve a WebSocket authentication and an authentication of messages, we will make the API stateful. By stateful, understand that the API will use HTTP sessions to keep users authenticated between their requests. With the support of Spring Session and the highly clusterable Redis server, sessions will be shared across multiple web apps.

Chapter 9, Testing and Troubleshooting, introduces a set of tools and common practices to maintain, debug, and improve an application's state. As a way of finishing this journey, we will visit how to upgrade the database schema from one version of the application to another as part of the Maven builds with the Flyway Maven Plugin. We will also go through how to write and automate unit tests (with Maven Surefire and Mockito) and integration tests (using a set of libraries such as Cargo, Rest-assured, and Maven Failsafe).

The last recipe provides insightful guidelines in order to apply Log4j2 globally as a logging framework, as it is more than important to rely on a relevant logging solution to troubleshoot efficiently, whichever environment we may be on.

What you need for this book

The hardware and software list details the requirements for each chapter. Before everything, an Internet connection is necessary because many external references will be pointed out as links (URLs) and software will need to be downloaded.

Also, and even more importantly, you will see that we use the Git versioning system to manage (and work from) the codebase for each chapter. Your local Git repository will correspond to the remote repository for the project (on GitHub), and you will be required to reach out to this remote repository.

To rephrase the hardware and software list, we will support three operating systems throughout the book: MS Windows, Linux and Mac OS X.

For hardware, we recommend a modern, well-equipped workstation with at least 2 GB of RAM and 500 MB of free space on the hard drive.

Who this book is for

While writing this book, one of our objectives has been to remain as approachable as possible while providing the widest possible overview of modern web development practices.

We believed that most of you, with an interest in a cookbook about Spring MVC, are primarily looking for a starter kit and a toolbox to develop modern Spring-based web applications.

We also believed that most of you would tend to prefer conceptualizing from experience and not from theory. Nowadays, it is clear that people have different mindsets and learning preferences.

Under this light, chapters will have increasing exigence levels one after the other, from the intuitive *Chapter 1, Setup Routine for an Enterprise Spring Application,* to the more challenging *Chapter 8, Communicating Through WebSockets and STOMP.* The initial few chapters will definitely suit a broader audience of Java developers than the final ones.

Having said this, we have everything in this book! The prerequisites here are mostly pointing to external sources of information. And our showcase application is running and waiting for you to dive into it and understand how things work.

More generally, we assume you to be a Java developer with prior web experience. Beyond everything, we expect you to have a motivated interest in learning Spring web technologies.

Sections

In this book, you will find several headings that appear frequently (Getting ready, How to do it, How it works, There's more, and See also).

To give clear instructions on how to complete a recipe, we use these sections as follows:

Getting ready

This section tells you what to expect in the recipe, and describes how to set up any software or any preliminary settings required for the recipe.

How to do it...

This section contains the steps required to follow the recipe.

How it works...

This section usually consists of a detailed explanation of what happened in the previous section.

There's more...

This section consists of additional information about the recipe in order to make the reader more knowledgeable about the recipe.

See also

This section provides helpful links to other useful information for the recipe.

Conventions

In this book, you will find a number of text styles that distinguish between different kinds of information. Here are some examples of these styles and an explanation of their meaning.

Code words in text, database table names, folder names, filenames, file extensions, pathnames, dummy URLs, user input, and Twitter handles are shown as follows: "We are going to review the configuration changes applied to the `cloudstreetmarket-api` webapp in order to set up a type conversion".

A block of code is set as follows:

```
<bean id="conversionService" class="org.sfw.format.
  support.FormattingConversionServiceFactoryBean">
  <property name="converters">
    <list>
      <bean class="edu.zc.csm.core.
        converters.StringToStockProduct"/>
    </list>
  </property>
</bean>
```

New terms and **important words** are shown in bold. Words that you see on the screen, for example, in menus or dialog boxes, appear in the text like this: "Then select **Add and Remove...** from the right-click menu."

 Warnings or important notes appear in a box like this.

 Tips and tricks appear like this.

Reader feedback

Feedback from our readers is always welcome. Let us know what you think about this book—what you liked or disliked. Reader feedback is important for us as it helps us develop titles that you will really get the most out of.

To send us general feedback, simply e-mail `feedback@packtpub.com`, and mention the book's title in the subject of your message.

If there is a topic that you have expertise in and you are interested in either writing or contributing to a book, see our author guide at `www.packtpub.com/authors`.

The showcase application: CloudStreet Market

We enjoyed building `CloudStreet Market` for you. It will remain an OpenSource GPL v3 piece of software. `cloudstreetmarket.com` will serve to directly or indirectly promote the book.

The master branch will probably continue to evolve but the chapters' branches will always match the book.

Feel absolutely free to fork the repository for whichever reason you might have. We also welcome `Pull` Requests, if you feel things could be made differently. Also, a big amount of tests are yet to be added.

The Git repository is hosted on GitHub at the following address:

`https://github.com/alex-bretet/cloudstreetmarket.com`

Customer support

Now that you are the proud owner of a Packt book, we have a number of things to help you to get the most from your purchase.

Downloading the example code

You can download the example code files from your account at `http://www.packtpub.com` for all the Packt Publishing books you have purchased. If you purchased this book elsewhere, you can visit `http://www.packtpub.com/support` and register to have the files e-mailed directly to you.

Errata

Although we have taken every care to ensure the accuracy of our content, mistakes do happen. If you find a mistake in one of our books—maybe a mistake in the text or the code—we would be grateful if you could report this to us. By doing so, you can save other readers from frustration and help us improve subsequent versions of this book. If you find any errata, please report them by visiting http://www.packtpub.com/submit-errata, selecting your book, clicking on the **Errata Submission Form** link, and entering the details of your errata. Once your errata are verified, your submission will be accepted and the errata will be uploaded to our website or added to any list of existing errata under the Errata section of that title.

To view the previously submitted errata, go to https://www.packtpub.com/books/content/support and enter the name of the book in the search field. The required information will appear under the **Errata** section.

Piracy

Piracy of copyrighted material on the Internet is an ongoing problem across all media. At Packt, we take the protection of our copyright and licenses very seriously. If you come across any illegal copies of our works in any form on the Internet, please provide us with the location address or website name immediately so that we can pursue a remedy.

Please contact us at copyright@packtpub.com with a link to the suspected pirated material.

We appreciate your help in protecting our authors and our ability to bring you valuable content.

Questions

If you have a problem with any aspect of this book, you can contact us at questions@packtpub.com, and we will do our best to address the problem.

1

Setup Routine for an Enterprise Spring Application

The topics covered in this chapter correspond to this four-step routine:

- ▶ Installing Eclipse for JEE developers and Java SE 8
- ▶ Configuring Eclipse for Java SE 8, Maven 3, and Tomcat 8
- ▶ Defining the project structure with Maven
- ▶ Installing Spring, Spring MVC, and a web structure

Introduction

Before we dive into this routine for initializing the developments, we are going to answer, as an introduction, a couple of questions that should help you understand the routine better.

Remember that the result of this chapter will also constitute the minimal starting point for all the further chapters.

Let's do it with fun!

Throughout this book, we will be acting on behalf of the ZipCloud company. ZipCloud aims to build different products in the social and financial industry. We are going to build the first product of the company: `cloudstreetmarket.com` which will be a wonderful stock exchange platform with social capabilities. This project must be an optimal beginning for this little ZipCloud start-up!

Why such a routine?

Whatever your initial objectives may be, it is necessary to make sure that the design will not suffer from early stage failures. This routine should cover you against this risk.

The idea beyond the routine itself is to share a bootstrap methodology to kick off the project base that you need now and that will support your needs tomorrow. The routine is also a key to drive your product thoughts toward a sustainable architecture which will be easy to refactor and to maintain.

Setting up a new project for an enterprise-level architecture will not kill the excitement and creativity!

Why making use of the Eclipse IDE?

There is competition in the domain, but Eclipse is popular among the Java community for being an active open source solution; it is consequently accessible online to anyone with no restrictions. It also provides, among other usages, a very good support for web implementations and particularly to MVC web implementations.

Why making use of Maven?

Maven is a *software project management and comprehension tool*. It is an open source project supported by the Apache community and the Apache Software Foundation. For nearly 10 years, Maven has given massive benefits. It has also shaped a standard structure for Java projects. With its **Project Object Model** (**POM**) approach, it provides, to anyone and potentially to any third-party software, a uniform and radical way of understanding and building a Java project hierarchy with all its dependencies.

In early stage architectures, it is critical to consider the following decisions:

- Opening the project definition to potentially different development environments and continuous integration tools
- Monitoring the dependencies and maybe securing their access
- Imposing a uniform directory structure within the project hierarchy
- Building a self-tested software with self-tested components

Choosing Maven secures these points and fulfills our project's need to make our project reusable, secure, and testable (under automation).

What does the Spring Framework bri

The Spring Framework and its community have contributed to pulling forward the Java platform for more than a decade. Presenting the whole framework in detail would require us to write more than a book. However, the core functionality based on the princ ples of **Inversion of Control (IOC)** and **Dependency Injection (DI)** through a performant access to the bean repository allows considerable reusability. Staying lightweight, it secures great scaling capabilities and could probably suit all modern architectures.

Installing Eclipse for JEE Developers and Java SE 8

The following recipe is about downloading and installing the Eclipse IDE for JEE developers and downloading and installing JDK 8 Oracle Hotspot.

Getting ready

This first recipe could appear redundant or unnecessary in regard to your education or experience. However, having a uniform configuration all along this book will provide you with many benefits.

For instance, you will certainly avoid unidentified bugs (integration or development). You will also experience the same interfaces as seen in the presented screenshots. Also because the third-party products are living, you will not have the surprise of encountering unexpected screens or windows.

How to do it...

The whole first chapter in general requires a step by step cooperation. From the next chapter, we will be using GIT and your active involvement will be lightened.

1. Download a distribution of the Eclipse IDE for Java EE developers:
   - We will be using an Eclipse Luna distribution in this book. We recommend that you install this version in order to match our guidelines and screenshots completely. Download a Luna distribution for the OS and environment of your choice from `https://www.eclipse.org/downloads/packages/ eclipse-ide-java-ee-developers/lunasr1`.

   The product to download is not a compiled installer but a zip archive.

   - If you feel confident enough to use another version (more recent) of the Eclipse IDE for Java EE Developers, all of them can be found at `https://www.eclipse.org/downloads`.

For upcoming installations, on Windows, a few target locations are suggested to be in the root directory (`C:\`). To avoid permission-related issues, it would be better if your Windows user is configured to be a Local Administrator. If you can't be part of this group, feel free to target installation directories you have write access to.

2. Extract the downloaded archive into an `eclipse` directory from the steps:

    ❑ `C:\Users\{system.username}\eclipse`: Extract it here if you are on Windows

    ❑ `/home/usr/{system.username}/eclipse`: Extract it here if you are on Linux

    ❑ `/Users/{system.username}/eclipse`: Extract it here if you are on Mac OS X

3. Select and download JDK 8:

    ❑ We suggest that you download the Oracle Hotspot JDK. Hotspot is a performant JVM implementation originally built by Sun Microsystems. Now owned by Oracle, the Hotspot JRE and JDK are downloadable for free.

    ❑ Then, choose the product corresponding to your machine through the Oracle website's link `http://www.oracle.com/technetwork/java/javase/downloads/jdk8-downloads-2133151.html`.

To avoid a compatibility issue later on, do stay consistent with the architecture choice (32 or 64 bits) that you have made earlier for the Eclipse archive.

4. Install JDK 8 on the operating system of your choice using the following instructions:

    On Windows, this is a monitored installation initiated with an executable file:

    1. Execute the downloaded file and wait until you reach the next installation step

    2. On the installation-step window, pay attention to the destination directory and change it to `C:\java\jdk1.8.X_XX` (X_XX refers to the latest current version here. We will be using jdk1.8.0_25 in this book. Also, it won't be necessary to install an external JRE, so uncheck the public JRE feature.)

    On Linux/Mac, perform the following steps:

    1. Download the `tar.gz` archive corresponding to your environment

    2. Change the current directory to where you want to install Java. For easier instructions, let's agree on the `/usr/java` directory

    3. Move the downloaded `tar.gz` archive to this current directory

4. Unpack the archive with the following command line targeting the name of your archive: `tar zxvf jdk-8u25-linux-i586.tar.gz` (this example is for a binary archive corresponding to a Linux x86 machine)

You must end up with the `/usr/java/jdk1.8.0_25` directory structure that contains the `/bin`, `/db`, `/jre`, `/include` subdirectories.

How it works...

In this section we are going to provide more insights about the version of Eclipse we used and about how we chose this specific version of JVM.

Eclipse for Java EE developers

We have successfully installed the Eclipse IDE for Java EE developers here. Comparatively to Eclipse IDE for Java Developers, there are some additional packages coming along such as *Java EE Developer Tools*, *Data Tools Platform*, and *JavaScript Development Tools*. This version is appreciated for its ability to manage development servers as part of the IDE itself, its capability to customize project facets, and its ability to support JPA. The Luna version is officially Java SE 8 compatible; this has been a decisive factor at the time of writing.

Choosing a JVM

The choice of the JVM implementation could be discussed over performance, memory management, garbage collection, and optimization capabilities.

There are lots of different JVM implementations, including couple of open source solutions such as OpenJDK and IcedTea (RedHat). The choice of JVM really depends on the application's requirements. We have chosen *Oracle Hotspot* from experience and from reference implementations deployed in production; this JVM implementation can be trusted for a wide range of generic purposes. *Hotspot* also behaves very well if you have to run Java UI applications. Eclipse is one of them.

Java SE 8

If you haven't already played with Scala or Clojure, it is time that you took the functional programming train with Java! With Java SE 8, *Lambda expressions* reduce the amount of code dramatically providing improved *readability and maintainability*. We won't implement this Java 8 feature, but since it is probably the most popular, it must be highlighted as it has given a massive credit to the paradigm change. It is important, nowadays, to be familiar with these patterns.

Configuring Eclipse for Java 8, Maven 3, and Tomcat 8

This recipe entails configuration technics to develop efficiently on Eclipse with Java, Maven, and Tomcat.

Getting ready

Once the different products are installed, there are a couple of steps that we need to follow, mainly to make Eclipse work properly with Java SE 8, Maven 3, and Tomcat 8. In this recipe, we will also look at how to customize the Eclipse configuration file (`Eclipse.ini`) in order to make the most of the platform that runs Java and to make sure that it will cope with any significant growth of the application.

How to do it...

Let's take a look at the following steps to configure Eclipse on your desktop:

1. You can start by creating a shortcut on your desktop to point to the Eclipse executable:

   - On Windows, the executable file is `Eclipse.exe` and is located at the `eclipse` directory root

   - On Linux/Mac, the file is named `Eclipse` and is also is located at the `eclipse` directory root

2. Then, we need to customize the `eclipse.ini` file:

   In the Eclipse directory, where you have previously extracted the Eclipse archive, you can find the `eclipse.ini` file. *It is a text file that contains a few command-line options in order to control the Eclipse startup.*

   - The Eclipse community recommends to specify the path to our JVM here. Hence, depending on your system, add the following two lines at the top of the file:

   For Windows, add the following:

   ```
   -vm
   C:\java\jdk1.8.0_25\jre\bin\server\jvm.dll
   ```

   For Linux/Mac, add this:

   ```
   -vm
   /usr/java/jdk1.8.0_25/jre/lib/{your.architecture}/server/libjvm.so
   ```

   The following is an optional setting that you can consider:

   - If your development machine has at least 2 GB of RAM, you can enter the following options to make Eclipse run faster than the default settings. *This section is optional because Eclipse's default settings are already optimized to suit most users' environment*:

   ```
   -vmargs
   -Xms128m
   ```

```
-Xmx512m
-Xverify:none
-Dosgi.requiredJavaVersion=1.6
-XX:MaxGCPauseMillis=10
-XX:MaxHeapFreeRatio=70
-XX:+UseConcMarkSweepGC
-XX:+CMSIncrementalMode
-XX:+CMSIncrementalPacing
```

If your machine has less than 2 GB of RAM, you can still enter this set of options without overriding the default -Xms and -Xmx arguments.

All the options under -vmargs are arguments that will be passed to the JVM at startup. It is important not to mess up the Eclipse options (the top part of the file) with the VM arguments (the bottom part).

3. After this we will go through the following steps to start Eclipse and set the workspace:

Launch the executable described in the Step 2.

- For our project, specify the path: `<home-directory>/workspace`

This path is different for each Operating System:

- `C:\Users\{system.username}\workspace`: This is the path on Windows
- `/home/usr/{system.username}/workspace`: This is on Linux
- `/Users/{system.username}/workspace`: This is on Mac OS
- Click on **OK** and let the Eclipse program start

The workspace is the place from where you manage your Java projects. It can be specific to one application, but not necessarily.

4. Then, we need to check the JRE definitions:

Here, a couple of settings need to be verified in Eclipse:

1. Open the **Preferences** menu under **Window** (on Mac OS X the **Preference** menu is under the **Eclipse** menu).
2. In the navigation panel on the left-hand side, open the Java hierarchy and click on **Installed JREs** under **Java**.
3. On the central screen, remove any existing JREs that you may already have.
4. Click on the **Add...** button to add a standard JVM.

5. Enter `C:\java\jdk1.8.0_25` (or `/usr/java/...`) as **JRE home**.

6. And enter `jdk1.8.0_25` as **JRE name**.

 We tell Eclipse to use the Java Runtime Environment of JDK 8.

After completing these steps, you should end up with the following configuration:

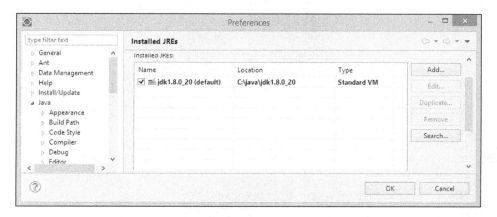

5. Now, we will check the compiler compliance level:

   1. In the navigation panel, click on **Compiler** under **Java**.

   2. Check that the **Compiler compliance level** is set to **1.8** in the drop-down list.

6. After this, we need to check the Maven configuration:

   1. Still in the navigation panel of the **Preferences** menu, open the Maven hierarchy and navigate to **Maven | Installations**.

   2. We will specify here which Maven installation we plan to use. For the purpose of this book, the embedded Maven will be perfect.

   3. Back in the navigation panel, go to **Maven | User Settings**.

   4. Set the local repository to `<home-directory>/.m2/repository`.

 In this local repository, our local cached versions of the required artefacts will reside. It will prevent our environment from having to download them on each build.

   5. For the **User Settings** field, create a `settings.xml` file in the `.m2` directory: `<home-directory>/.m2/settings.xml`.

6. Edit the `settings.xml` file and add the following block:

(You can also copy/paste it from the `chapter_1/source_code/.m2` directory):

```
<settings xmlns="http://maven.apache.org/SETTINGS/1.1.0"
  xmlns:xsi="http://www.w3.org/2001/XMLSchema-instance"
  xsi:schemaLocation="http://maven.apache.org/SETTINGS/1.1.0
    http://maven.apache.org/xsd/settings-1.1.0.xsd">
  <profiles>
    <profile>
      <id>compiler</id>
        <properties>
          <JAVA_HOME>C:\java\jdk1.8.0_25</JAVA_HOME>
        </properties>
    </profile>
  </profiles>
  <activeProfiles>
  <activeProfile>compiler</activeProfile>
  </activeProfiles>
</settings>
```

 If you are *not* on a Windows machine, change `JAVA_HOME` in this file to your JDK installation directory (`/usr/java/jdk1.8.0_25`).

7. Go back to the navigation panel and click on **Maven**. Follow the configuration given in this screenshot:

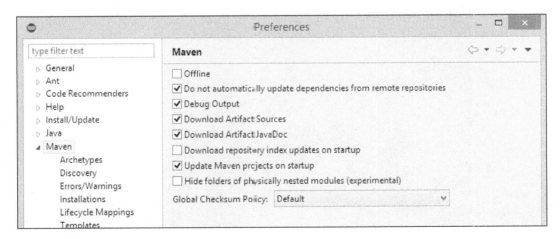

8. Click on **OK** to save these configuration changes.

7. Now we will install Tomcat 8 in the Eclipse IDE. For this, go through these steps:

1. Download a ZIP archive for the latest Core version of Tomcat8 from the Tomcat website: `http://tomcat.apache.org/download-80.cgi`.

2. Extract the downloaded archive to the following directory:

❑ On Windows, extract the archive at `C:\tomcat8`

❑ On Linux, extract the archive at `/home/usr/{system.username}/tomcat8`

❑ On Mac OS X, extract the archive at `/Users/{system.username}/tomcat8`

 Depending on your system, you must be able to access the bin directory from the hierarchy: `C:\tomcat8\bin`, `/home/usr/{system.username}/tomcat8/bin` or `/Users/{system.username}/tomcat8/bin`.

3. In Eclipse, select the **Preferences** menu under **Windows**, and in the navigation panel on the left-hand side, open the **Server** hierarchy and then select **Runtime Environments**.

4. On the central window, click on the **Add...** button.

5. In the next step (the **New Server** environment window), navigate to **Apache | Apache Tomcat v8.0**.

6. Also, check this option: **Create a New Local Server**.

7. Click on the **Next** button.

8. Fill in the details in the window as shown in the following screenshot:

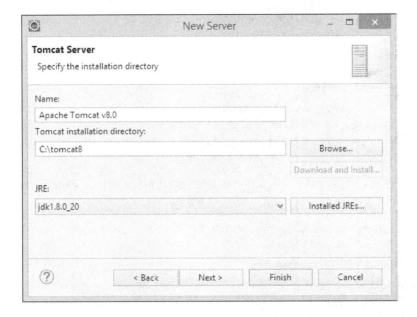

 If you are on Linux (or Mac OS X), replace `C:\tomcat8` with your Tomcat installation directory.

How it works...

We are going to review in this section the different elements and concepts that this recipe took us through.

The eclipse.ini file

As we've already seen, the `eclipse.ini` file controls the Eclipse startup. It is an extra component that makes the Eclipse platform very configurable. You can find the list of command-line arguments that can be used in their documentation at

`http://help.eclipse.org/luna/topic/org.eclipse.platform.doc.isv/reference/misc/runtime-options html`

It is important to acknowledge the following warnings that this documentation mentions:

► All lines after `-vmargs` are passed as arguments to the JVM; all arguments and options for Eclipse must be specified before `-vmargs` (just like when you use arguments on the command line

 This explains why we have inserted the –vm option at the top of the file.

> ▸ Any use of -vmargs on the command line replaces all -vmargs settings in the .ini file unless --launcher.appendVmargs is specified either in the .ini file or on the command line

Setting the –vm option

Setting the -vm option allows us to be sure of the JVM implementation on which Eclipse runs as a program. You might have noticed that we've targeted the JVM as a library (*.dll / *.so). It has better performance on startup and also identifies the program process as the Eclipse executable and not just as the Java executable.

If you wonder which JVM Eclipse uses when a –vm option is not set, be aware that Eclipse *DOES NOT* consult the JAVA_HOME environment variable. (Eclipse wiki).

Instead, Eclipse executes the Java command that parses your path environment variable.

Customizing JVM arguments

The suggested JVM argument list comes from Piotr Gabryanczyk's work on the Java memory management model. Initially, for JetBRAINS IntelliJ settings, this configuration is also useful for an Eclipse environment. It helps in the following tasks:

> ▸ Preventing the garbage collector from pausing the application for more than 10 ms (-XX:MaxGCPauseMillis=10)
> ▸ Lowering the level from which the garbage collector starts to 30% of the occupied memory (-XX:MaxHeapFreeRatio=70)
> ▸ Imposing the garbage collector to run as a parallel thread, lowering its interference with the application (-XX:+UseConcMarkSweepGC)
> ▸ Choosing the incremental pacing mode for the garbage collector, which generates breaks in the GC job so that the application can definitely stop freezing (-XX:+CMSIncrementalPacing)

The instantiated objects throughout the program's life cycle are stored in the Heap memory. The suggested parameters define a JVM startup Heap space of 128 mb (-Xms) and an overall 512 mb maximum heap space (–Xmx). The heap is divided in two subspaces, which are as follows:

> ▸ **Young generation**: New objects are stored in this area. For the leading Hotspot or OpenJDK JVMs, the young memory space is divided in two:
>> ❑ Eden: New objects are stored in this subdivision area. Objects with short lives will be deallocated from here.
>> ❑ Survivor: This is a buffer between the young and old generation. The survivor space is smaller than the Eden and it is also divided in two (the FROM and TO areas). You can adjust the ratio between Eden and Survivor objects with -XX:SurvivorRatio (here, -XX: SurvivorRatio=10 means YOUNG = 12, EDEN = 10, FROM = 1 and TO =1).

The minimum size of the young area can be adjusted with
`-XX:NewSize`. The maximum size can be adjusted with
`-XX:MaxNewSize`.

▶ **Old generation**: When objects in `Eden` or `Survivor` spaces are still referenced after enough garbage collections, they are moved here. It is possible to set the `Young` area size as a ratio of the `Old` area size with `-XX:NewRatio`. (That is, `-XX:NewRatio=2` means `HEAP = 3, YOUNG = 1` and `OLD =2`).

 The maximum size for the new generation space `-XX:MaxNewSize` must always remain smaller than half the heap space (`-Xmx/2`) because the garbage collector may move all the `Young` space to the `Old` space.

With Hotspot or OpenJDK, the permanent generation space was used to store information related to the classes' definition (structure fields, methods, and so on.). You may have already encountered a `PermGen space OutOfMemoryError` exception when the loaded structure becomes too big. In this situation, the solution is to increase the `-XX:MaxPermSize` argument. *It is no longer necessary with JDK8.*

For this purpose, the **Permanent Generation (PermGen)** space has been replaced by a metadata space that is not part of the heap but of the native memory. The default maximum size of this space is unlimited. However, we can still restrict it with `-XX:MetaspaceSize` or `-XX:MaxMetaspaceSize`.

Changing the JDK compliance level

Downgrading a compliance level allows us to run a lower version of a Java compiler than the one the JDK is natively identified to. It impacts the Eclipse builds, errors, and warnings and also the JavaDocs. It is obviously not possible to set a higher compilation version than the native version of a compiler.

Configuring Maven

Inside Eclipse, most of the Maven configuration comes from the `m2eclipse` plugin (also called Maven integration for Eclipse). This plugin is included, by default, in Eclipse Luna. It is then not necessary to download it manually. After the Maven configuration that we went through, m2eclipse is also very helpful to trigger Maven operations from the IDE context and to provide assistance to create Java Maven projects. You will learn more about m2eclipse in the next section.

We then installed a basic `settings.xml` file. This file is used to configure Maven without being bound directly to any projects. The most common uses of `settings.xml` are probably profile definition and credential storage to access the repository manager(s).

With Maven profiles, you have the possibility to run a build for a specific environment and to match a specific configuration (variable values, set of dependencies, and so on.). Maven profiles can be cumulated with each other. They can be activated through a command line, declaratively in the Maven settings or from the environment configuration such as files being present or missing on the filesystem, the used JDK, and so on.

In our `settings.xml` file, we have defined a compiler profile with its own `JAVA_HOME` property. The compiler profile is activated by default to be declaratively defined in the `<activeProfiles>` section. Maven will consult the `settings.xml` file before looking up the system variables.

A repository manager

A repository manager is a third-party application that manages all the required binaries and dependencies that a developed application may need. Acting as a buffering proxy between development environments and public repositories, a repository manager provides control of critical parameters such as build time, availability of dependencies, visibility and access restriction, and so on.

Famous solutions include *Apache Archiva, Artifactory, Sonatype Nexus*. In the context of our application, we won't make use of a repository manager.

Tomcat 8 inside Eclipse

Eclipse for JEE developers allows the integration of Tomcat with other application servers within the development environment. This is made possible through the provided **Web Tools Platform** (**WTP**) plugins that can manage web artefacts, their compilation, and their deployment into the web server.

In the `servers` tab (made visible earlier), double-clicking on the created Tomcat v8.0 server, opens a configuration window and enables the possibility of setting up parameters that are normally defined in the `server.xml` Tomcat file, which is located in the `tomcat8\conf` directory.

By default, WTP abstracts this configuration and doesn't impact the genuine `server.xml` file. This behavior can be changed by activating the **Publish module contexts to separate XML files** option in the **Server configuration** window.

There's more...

> ▶ Find out more about the Eclipse installation at `http://wiki.eclipse.org/Eclipse/Installation`

> ▶ Learn more about the `Eclipse.ini` file at `http://wiki.eclipse.org/Eclipse.ini`

> ▶ Learn more about the m2eclipse plugin at `https://maven.apache.org/plugins/maven-eclipse-plugin/`

> ▶ To understand how to use a repository manager, refer to `http://maven.apache.org/repository-management.html`

> ▶ The Piotr Gabryanczyk article about the garbage collection optimization for IDEs can be found at `http://piotrga.wordpress.com/2006/12/12/intellij-and-garbage-collection`

> ▶ You can know more about memory optimization in general at `http://pubs.vmware.com/vfabric52/topic/com.vmware.vfabric.em4j.1.2/em4j/conf-heap-management.html` and `https://blog.codecentric.de/en/2012/08/useful-jvm-flags-part-5-young-generation-garbage-collection`

Defining the project structure with Maven

In this recipe, we will focus on defining, with Maven, the project structure we need for our application.

Getting ready

We will initially create two Eclipse projects: one for the application and one for the components that ZipCloud as a company could share later on with other projects. Take a look at the following image which presents the project components that we are going to build:

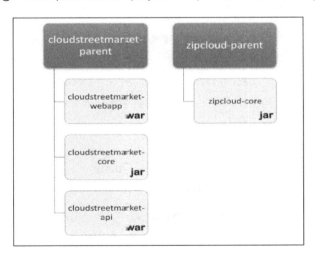

The application project **cloudstreetmarket-parent** will have three modules. Two of them will be packaged as web archives (**war**): the main web application and the REST API. One of them will be packaged as a **jar** dependency (cloudstreetmarket-core).

The company-specific project **zipcloud-parent** will have only one submodule—**zipcloud-core**, which will be packaged as **jar**.

How to do it...

The following steps will help us create a Maven parent project:

1. From Eclipse, navigate to **File | New | Other**.

2. A **New** wizard opens up wherein you can select the type of project within a hierarchy. Then, open the **Maven** category, select **Maven Project**, and click on **Next**.

   The New Maven Project wizard opens as shown in the following screenshot:

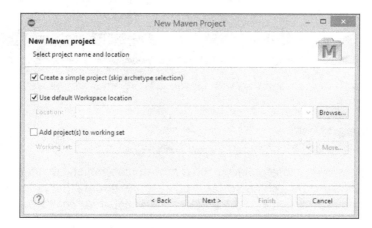

3. Make sure to check the **Create a simple project** option. Click on **Next**.

4. Fill up the next wizard as follows:

   ❑ edu.zipcloud.cloudstreetmarket as **Group Id**

   ❑ cloudstreetmarket-parent as **Artifact Id**

   ❑ 0.0.1-SNAPSHOT as **Version**

   ❑ pom as **Packaging**

   ❑ CloudStreetMarket Parent as **Name**

   ❑ Then, click on the **Finish** button

   The parent project must appear in the package explorer on the left-hand side of the dashboard.

We now have to tell m2eclipse which Java compiler version you plan to use in this project so that it automatically adds the right JRE system library to the submodules we are about to create. This is done through the pom.xml file.

5. Edit pom.xml file to specify the Java compiler version:

- ❏ Double-click on the **pom.xml** file. The **m2eclipse Overview** tab shows up by default. You have to click on the last tab, **pom.xml**, to access the full XML definition.

- ❏ In this definition, add the following block at the end but still as part of the **<project>** node. (*You can also copy/paste this piece of code from the cloudstreetmarket-parent's* pom.xml *of the* chapter_1 *source code):*

```xml
<build>
  <plugins>
    <plugin>
      <groupId>org.apache.maven.plugins</groupId>
      <artifactId>maven-compiler-plugin</artifactId>
      <version>3.1</version>
      <configuration>
          <source>1.8</source>
          <target>1.8</target>
          <verbose>true</verbose>
          <fork>true</fork>
          <executable>${JAVA_HOME}/bin/javac</executable>
          <compilerVersion>1.8</compilerVersion>
      </configuration>
    </plugin>
    <plugin>
      <groupId>org.apache.maven.plugins</groupId>
      <artifactId>maven-surefire-plugin</artifactId>
      <version>2.4.2</version>
      <configuration>
        <jvm>${JAVA_HOME}/bin/java</jvm>
        <forkMode>once</forkMode>
      </configuration>
    </plugin>
  </plugins>
</build>
```

 You have probably noticed the **maven-surefire-plugin** declaration as well. We will review it soon; it allows us to run unit tests during the build.

6. Now, we will create submodules:

As submodules of the Parent project, we have seen that we needed one web module to handle and render the site's screens, one web module for the REST API, and one other module that will be used to package all the business logic (services, data access, and so on.) specific to the first product `cloudstreetmarket.com`:

1. From the main Webapp module:in Eclipse, navigate to **File | New | Other**. A **New** wizard opens up through which you can select the type of project within a hierarchy. Open the **Maven** category, select **Maven Module**, and click on **Next**.

2. The New Maven Module wizard opens up after this; fill it up as follows:

   Check Create a simple project.

   Enter `cloudstreetmarket-webapp` as **Module Name**.

   Enter `cloudstreetmarket-parent` as **Parent project**.

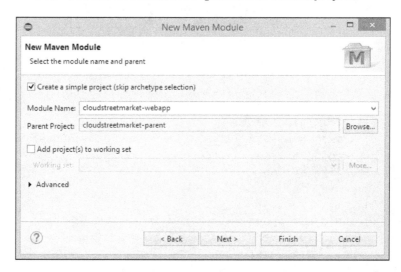

3. Click on the **Next** button after which the next step shows up. Enter the following entries in that new window:

   Enter `edu.zipcloud.cloudstreetmarket` as **Group Id**.

   Enter `0.0.1-SNAPSHOT` as **Version**.

   Select **war** as **Packaging**.

   Enter `CloudStreetMarket Webapp` as **Name**.

   Then click on the **Finish** button.

7. Now we will go ahead to create and REST API module:

    We are going to repeat the previous operation with different parameters.

    1. From Eclipse, navigate to **File | New | Other**. The selection wizard pops up when you go there. After this, open the **Maven** category, select **Maven Module**, and click on **Next**:

    2. In the **New Maven Module** wizard, enter the following entries:

        Check the **Create a simple project** option.

        Enter `cloudstreetmarket-api` as **Module Name**.

        Enter `cloudstreetmarket-parent` as **Parent project**.

    3. Click on the **Next** button to proceed to the next step. Enter the following entries in that window:

        Enter `edu.zipcloud.cloudstreetmarket` as **Group Id**.

        Enter `0.0.1-SNAPSHOT` as **Version**.

        Select **war** as **Packaging**.

        Enter `CloudStreetMarket API` as **Name**.

        Then click on the Finish button.

8. Now, we will create the core module:

    For this, navigate to **File | New | Other**. The selection wizard pops up when you do so. Open the **Maven** category, select **Maven Module**, and click on **Next**.

    1. In the **New Maven Module** wizard, enter the following entries:

        Check the **Create a simple project** option.

        Enter `cloudstreetmarket-core` as **Module Name**.

        Enter `cloudstreetmarket-parent` as **Parent project**.

    2. Click on the **Next** button to go to the next step. Fill in the fields with the following:

        Enter `edu.zipcloud.cloudstreetmarket` as **Group Id**.

        Enter `0.0.1-SNAPSHOT` as **Version**.

        This time, select **jar** as **Packaging**.

        Enter `CloudStreetMarket Core` as **Name**.

        Then click on the Finish button.

If you have the Java perspective activated (in the top-right corner), you should see the overall created structure matching the screenshot here:

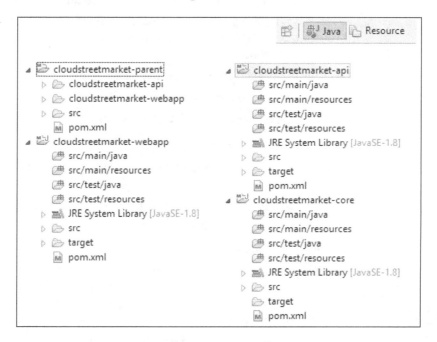

9. Now, we will create a company-specific project and its module(s):

Let's assume that many different categories of dependencies (core, messaging, reporting, and so on...) will be part of the company-business project later.

1. We need a parent project, so from Eclipse, navigate to **File | New | Other**. The selection wizard pops up. Open the Maven category, select Maven Project, and click on Next.

2. In the first step of the New Maven Project wizard, as for the Parent project we created earlier, only check the **Create a simple Project** and **Use default workspace location** options.

3. Click on the **Next** button and fill in the next wizard as follows:

   Enter edu.zipcloud as **Group Id**.

   Enter zipcloud-parent as **Artifact Id**.

   Enter 0.0.1-SNAPSHOT as **Version**.

   Select **pom** as **Packaging**.

   Enter ZipCloud Factory Business Parent as **Name**.

Again, in the created `pom.xml` file, add the following block inside the `<project>` node to create the underlying modules properly and to enable automatic test execution. (*You can also copy/paste this piece of code from the zipcloud-parent's pom.xml file of the chapter_1 source code*):

```
<build>
  <plugins>
    <plugin>
    <groupId>org.apache.maven.plugins</groupId>
      <artifactId>maven-compiler-plugin</artifactId>
      <version>3.1</version>
      <configuration>
        <source>1.8</source>
        <target>1.8</target>
          <verbose>true</verbose>
          <fork>true</fork>
        <executable>${JAVA_HOME}/bin/javac</executable>
      <compilerVersion>1.8</compilerVersion>
      </configuration>
    </plugin>
    <plugin>
    <groupId>org.apache.maven.plugins</groupId>
      <artifactId>maven-surefire-plugin</artifactId>
        <version>2.4.2</version>
        <configuration>
        <jvm>${JAVA_HOME}/bin/java</jvm>
        <forkMode>once</forkMode>
      </configuration>
    </plugin>
  </plugins>
</build>
```

Now, we are going to create one company-business core module, which will be a sub module of the parent project we just created.

For this, navigate to **File** | **New** | **Other**. The selection wizard pops up. Open the **Maven** category, select **Maven Module**, and click on **Next**.

1. In the **New Maven Module** wizard, enter the following details:

   Check the **Create a simple project** option.

   Enter `zipcloud-core` as **Module Name**.

   Enter `zipcloud-parent` as **Parent project**.

2. Click on the **Next** button and go to the next step. Here, enter the following details:

Enter `edu.zipcloud` as **Group Id**.

Enter `0.0.1-SNAPSHOT` as **Version**.

Select **jar** as **Packaging**.

Select `ZipCloud Factory Core Business` as **Name**.

10. Now, build the two projects:

If the structure is correct, the following Maven command could be successfully run:

```
mvn clean install
```

 This command can be launched in the terminal if Maven is installed on the development machine.

In our study case, we will, for now, launch it using the m2eclipse modified **Run As** menu: Right click on the zipcloud-parent project and click on **Run As | Maven Clean**.

 In the Maven console, you should now see this beautiful line at the bottom:
[INFO] BUILD SUCCESS

Now, repeat the operation for the install build phase. You should now see the following output in the console:

```
[INFO] ZipCloud Parent ......................SUCCESS [  0.313 s]
[INFO] ZipCloud Core ........................SUCCESS [  1.100 s]
[INFO] ------------------------------------------------------------
[INFO] BUILD SUCCESS
[INFO] ------------------------------------------------------------
```

Ok, now you should be able to build `cloudstreetmarket-parent` as well.

For this, right-click on the **cloudstreetmarket -parent** project and click on **Run As | Maven Clean**. The Maven console should print the following after this step:

```
[INFO] BUILD SUCCESS
```

Again, right-click on the **cloudstreetmarket** -parent project and click on **Run As | Maven Install**. The Maven console should now print the following:

```
[INFO] CloudStreetMarket Parent ..............SUCCESS [  0.313 s]
[INFO] CloudStreetMarket Webapp ..............SUCCESS [  6.129 s]
```

```
[INFO] CloudStreetMarket Core ................SUCCESS [  0.922 s]
[INFO] CloudStreetMarket API .................SUCCESS [  7.163 s]
[INFO] -----------------------------------------------------------
[INFO] BUILD SUCCESS
[INFO] -----------------------------------------------------------
```

Scrolling up a bit should display the following trace:

```
-----------------------------------------------------------
 T E S T S
-----------------------------------------------------------
There are no tests to run.
Results :
Tests run: 0, Failures: 0, Errors: 0, Skipped: 0
```

> Maven here, with the help of the maven-surefire-plugin, which we manually added, parses all the classes encountered in the `src/test/java` directories. Again, this path can be customized.
>
> In the detected test classes, Maven will also run the methods annotated with the JUnit `@Test` annotation. A JUnit dependency is required in the project.

How it works...

In this section, we are going through quite a few concepts about Maven so that you can better understand its standards

New Maven project, new Maven module

The project creation screens we just went through also come from the m2eclipse plugin. These screens are used to initialize a Java project with a preconfigured `pom.xml` file and a standard directory structure.

The m2eclipse plugin also provides a set of shortcuts to run Maven build phases and some handy tabs (already seen) to manage project dependencies and visualize the `pom.xml` configuration.

The standard project hierarchy

Navigating through the created projects, you should be able to notice a recurring hierarchy made of the following directories: `src/main/java`, `src/main/resource`, `src/test/java`, and `src/test/resource`. This structure is the default structure that Maven drives us through. *This model has become a standard nowadays*. But, we can still override it (in the `pom.xml` files) and create our own hierarchy.

If you remember the **maven-compiler-plugin** definition added in the pom.xml files of the parent projects, there were the following four lines of code that we used:

```
<verbose>true</verbose>
<fork>true</fork>
<executable>${JAVA_HOME}/bin/javac</executable>
<compilerVersion>1.8</compilerVersion>
```

These lines allow Maven to use an external JDK for the compiler. It is better to have control over which compiler Maven uses, especially when managing different environments.

Also, there were the following two lines that might look like an over configuration:

```
<source>1.8</source>
<target>1.8</target>
```

From a strict Maven point of view, these lines are optional when an external JDK is defined with a specified compilerVersion. Initially, with these two lines, we can control which Java version we want the default code to be compiled in. When maintaining older systems, the existing code might still compile in a previous version of Java.

Actually, m2eclipse specifically expects these two lines in order to add JRE System Library [JavaSE-1.8] to the build path of the jar and war modules. Now, with these lines, Eclipse compiles these projects in the same way Maven does: in Java SE 8.

 If this dependency still shows up as a different version of Java, you may need to right-click on the module and then navigate to **Maven | Update Project**.

The project's structure in the IDE

About the parent projects in the Eclipse project hierarchy; did you notice that the created submodules seem duplicated as standalone projects and as direct children of the parent? This is due to the fact that Eclipse doesn't handle hierarchies of projects yet in Luna. For this reason, the modules appear as separated projects. It might be slightly confusing because the source code appears to be located beside the parent projects. *This is not the case in reality, it is only the way they are rendered, so we can have all the tools normally bound to the project level.*

 At this time, JetBRAINS IntelliJ IDEA already supports visual hierarchies of the projects.

Finally, if you open a parent project's pom.xml file, you should see the <modules> node populated with the created submodules. This has been done automatically as well by m2eclipse. We recommend that you keep an eye on this feature because m2eclipse doesn't always update these <modules> nodes depending on which way you alter the project hierarchy.

Maven's build life cycles

A build life cycle in Maven is a specific sequence (and a group) of predefined operations called phases. There are three existing life cycles in Maven: default, clean, and site.

Let's have a look at all the phases that include the default and clean life cycles (probably the life cycles the most commonly used by developers).

The clean life cycle

The Maven **clean** phase plays a central role. It resets a project build from Maven's perspective. It is usually about deleting the target directory that is created by Maven during the build process. Here are some details about the phases included in the **clean** life cycle. These details come from the Maven documentation:

Phases	Description
pre-clean	This executes processes that are needed prior to the actual project cleaning
clean	This removes all files generated by the previous build
post-clean	This executes processes that are needed to finalize the project cleaning

The default life cycle

In the default life cycle, you can find the most interesting build phases that deal with source generation, compilation, resource handling, tests, integration tests, and artefact deployment. Here are some details about the phases included in the default life cycle:

Phases	Descriptions
validate	This validates whether the project is correct and all necessary information is available.
initialize	This initializes the build state, for example, setting properties or creating directories.
generate-sources	This generates source code for inclusion in compilation.
process-sources	This processes the source code, for example, to filter any values.
generate-resources	This generates resources to be included in the package.
process-resources	This copies and processes the resources into the destination directory, which is ready for packaging.
compile	This compiles the source code of the project.
process-classes	This post processes the generated files from compilation, for example, to perform bytecode enhancement on Java classes.
generate-test-sources	This generates any test source code to be included in compilation.

Phases	Descriptions
process-test-sources	This processes the test source code, for example, to filter any values.
generate-test-resources	This creates resources for testing.
process-test-resources	This copies and processes the resources into the test destination directory.
test-compile	This compiles the test source code into the test destination directory.
process-test-classes	This post processes the generated files from test compilation, for example, to perform bytecode enhancement on Java classes. For Maven 2.0.5 and above.
test	This runs tests using a suitable unit testing framework. These tests should not require the code to be packaged or deployed.
prepare-package	This performs the operations necessary to prepare a package before the actual packaging. This often results in an unpacked, processed version of the package. (Maven 2.1 and above)
package	This takes the compiled code and packages it in its distributable format, such as JAR.
pre-integration-test	This performs actions required before integration tests are executed. This may involve things such as setting up the required environment.
integration-test	This processes and deploys the package if necessary into an environment where integration tests can be run.
post-integration-test	This performs the actions required after integration tests have been executed. This may include cleaning up the environment.
verify	This runs checks to verify that the package is valid and meets the quality criteria.
install	This installs the package into the local repository to be used as a dependency in other projects locally.
deploy	This copies the final package to the remote repository to share it with other developers and projects (done in an integration or release environment).

Plugin goals

With the concept of plugins, Maven acquires a much wider dimension. Maven natively provides built-in plugins, but external plugins can be introduced just as other dependencies (identified by groupIds and artefactIds).

Each build phase can be attached to zero, one, or more plugin goals. A goal represents a specific and concrete task responsible for building or handling a project in a certain manner. Some phases have goals bound to them, by default, through native plugins.

Built-in life cycle bindings

Now that we have seen the purpose of each phase in the presented two life cycles, we must say that, for the default life cycle, depending upon which module packaging type we are choosing, only some of these phases are potentially activated for goal execution.

Let's see the phases that we skipped in the default life cycle for different packaging types:

Packaging type	Default life cycle			
	jar/war/ejb/ejb3/ear	ear	maven-plugin	pom
Activated phases		generate-resources	generate-resources	
	process-resources	process-resources	process-resources	
	compile		compile	
	process-test-resources		process-test-resources	
	test-compile		test-compile	
	test		test	
	package	package	package	package
	install	install	install	install
	deploy	deploy	deploy	deploy

 In *Chapter 9, Testing and Troubleshooting*, we will practically bind external plugins goals to identified build phases.

In summary, calling: mvn clean install on a jar packaged-module will result in executing the following phases: clean, process-resources, compile, process-test-resources, test-compile, test, package, and install.

About Maven commands

When Maven is told to execute one or more phases targeting a specific project's pom.xml file, it will execute the requested phase(s) for each of its modules.

Then, for every single requested phase, Maven will do the following:

- ▸ Identify which life cycle the phase belongs to
- ▸ Look for the packaging of the current module and identify the right life cycle binding
- ▸ Execute all the phases in the hierarchy of the identified life cycle bindings, which are located before the requested phase in the hierarchy

By the term execute all the phases, we mean execute all the underlying detected and attached plugin goals (native plugins or not).

In summary, calling `mvn clean install` on a `jar` packaged module will execute the following phases: `clean`, `process-resources`, `compile`, `process-test-resources`, `test-compile`, `test`, `package`, and `install`.

There's more...

You may wonder why we have created these projects and modules in regard to our application.

How did we choose the jar module's name?

About the Maven structure, the best names for nondeployable modules often emphasize a functional purpose, a specific concept created by the business, or are driven by the product (cloudstreetmarket-chat, cloudstreetmarket-reporting, cloudstreetmarket-user-management, and so on.). This strategy makes the dependency management easier because we can infer whether a new module requires another module or not. Thinking about controllers, services, and DAO layers at a macro scale doesn't really make sense at this stage, and it could lead to design interference or circular dependencies. These technical subcomponents (service, DAO, and so on) will be present or not, as needed, in each functional module as Java packages but not as JAR-packaged dependencies.

How did we choose the names for deployable modules?

Choosing a name for a deployable module (`war`) is a bit different different from choosing a name for a JAR-packaged module. The deployable archive must be thought of as scalable and potentially load balanced. It is fair to assume that the requests that will target the application to retrieve HTML contents can be distinguished from the ones that will return REST contents.

With this assumption, in our case it has been our wish to split the `war` into two. Doing so may raise the question of how the *web sessions* are maintained between the two webapps. We will answer this point later on.

Why did we create core modules?

We created the core modules, firstly, because it is certain that, in the `cloudstreetmarket` application and also in the company-shared project, we will have POJOs, exceptions, constants, enums, and some services that will be used horizontally by almost all the modules or applications. If a concept is specific to a created functional module, it must not be part of core modules.

Then, it is probably better to *start big grained* to *refine later* rather than thinking about modules that may be implemented differently or even not implemented at all. In our case, we are a start-up, and it is not silly to say that the 5 to 10 features we are going to implement can constitute the core business of this application.

See also...

> ▶ We also recommend that you install **Code Style Formatters**. Triggered from the **Save Event**, we have, with these formatters, the ability to restyle our code automatically with a uniform predefinition. Having such formatters in a team is much appreciated since it guarantees the same rendering while comparing two files with a versioning tool.

Installing Spring, Spring MVC, and a web structure

In this recipe, we will add third-party dependencies to our `pom.xml` files using inheritance. We will load `Spring application contexts` and create the first controller of our application. Finally, we will deploy and start the web app in Tomcat.

Getting ready

Now that we have Eclipse ready and Maven configured properly, the fun can begin. We need to specify all the necessary Spring dependencies in our `pom.xml` files, and we need to set up Spring so that it loads and retrieves its context for every module.

We also need to organize and optionally expose web resources, such as JSPs, JavaScript files, CSS files, and so on. If you've completed this configuration, we should end up with a static welcome page provided by the Tomcat server, started without exceptions!

How to do it...

Our first set of changes relate to the parent projects:

1. We will define dependencies and build options for those parent projects. Let's do it with the following steps:

   1. Open the cloudstreetmarket-parent `pom.xml` from the chapter_1 source code directory and select the **pom.xml** tab (underneath the main window).

      Copy and paste into the cloudstreetmarket-parent's **pom.xml** file the `<properties>`, `<dependencyManagement>`, and `<build>` blocks.

      Now, repeat the operation for zipcloud-parent.

   2. Open the zipcloud-parent's `pom.xml` file from the **chapter_1** source code and click on the **pom.xml** tab.

3. Copy and paste into your zipcloud-parent's **pom.xml** the `<properties>` and `<dependencyManagement>` blocks. You should already have copied over the `<build>` section in the *third recipe*.

2. Now, we will define dependencies and build options for web modules:

    1. Open the cloudstreetmarket-api's `pom.xml` from the **chapter_1** source code and select the **pom.xml** tab.

    2. Copy and paste into your cloudstreetmarket-api's `pom.xml` the `<build>` and `<dependencies>` blocks.

    3. Now, repeat the operation for cloustreetmarket-webapp.

    4. Open the cloudstreetmarket-webapp's `pom.xml` from the **chapter_1** source code directory and click on the **pom.xml** tab.

    5. Copy and paste into your cloudstreetmarket-webapp's **pom.xml** file the `<build>` and `<dependencies>` blocks.

3. After this, we define dependencies for jar modules:

    1. Open the cloudstreetmarket-core's `pom.xml` from the **chapter_1** source code and click on the **pom.xml** tab.

    2. Copy and paste into your cloudstreetmarket-core's **pom.xml** the entire `<dependencies>` block.

4. Then, we place the web resources:

    1. From the **chapter_1** source code, copy and paste the entire **src/main/webapp/*** directory into your **cloudstreetmarket-webapp** project. You need to end up with the same **webapp** directory structure as the **chapter_1** source code:

2. Now, perform the same operation for **cloudstreetmarket-api**. Copy and paste from the **chapter_1** source code the entire **src/main/webapp/*** branch into your **cloudstreetmarket-api** project. You need to end up with the same webapp node and children as the **chapter_1** source code:

5. Now, we target a runtime for the web modules:

   1. In Eclipse, right-click on the **cloudmarket-api** project.
   2. Select the **Properties** menu.
   3. On the navigation panel select **Targeted Runtimes**.
   4. On the central window, check the **Server Apache Tomcat v8.0** option.
   5. Click on **OK** and repeat the fifth operation on **cloudstreetmarket-webapp**.

> A few Eclipse warnings in the **index.jsp** files must have disappeared after this.

If you still have Warnings in the project, your Eclipse Maven configuration may be out of synchronization with the local repository

6. This step should clean your existing project warnings (if any):

In this case, perform the following steps:

1. Select all the projects in the project hierarchy, except the servers, as follows:

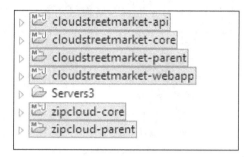

2. Right-click somewhere in the selection and click on **Update Project** under **Maven**. The **Warnings** window at this stage should disappear!

7. Let's deploy the `wars` and start Tomcat:

    Add the **servers** view in Eclipse. To do so, perform the following operations:

    1. Navigate to **Window | Show view | Other**.

    2. Open the **Server** directory and select servers. You should see the following tab created on your dashboard:

8. To deploy the web archives, go through the following operations:

    1. Inside the view we just created, right-click on the **Tomcat v8.0 Server at localhost** server and select **Add and Remove...**.

    2. In the next step, which is the **Add and Remove** window, select the two available archives and click on **Add** and then on **Finish**.

9. To start the application in Tomcat, we need to complete these steps:

    1. In the **Servers** view, right-click on the **Tomcat v8.0 Server at localhost** server and click on **Start**.

    2. In the **Console** view, you should have the following at the end:

```
INFO: Starting ProtocolHandler ["http-nio-8080"]
Oct 20, 2014 11:43:44 AM org.apache.coyote.AbstractProtocol start
INFO: Starting ProtocolHandler ["ajp-nio-8009"]
Oct 20, 2014 11:43:44 AM org.apache.catalina.startup.Cata.. start
INFO: Server startup in 6898 ms
```

If you scroll up through these logs, you shouldn't have any exceptions!

Finally, if you try to reach `http://localhost:8080/portal/index.html` with your browser, you should receive the following HTML content:

 A static access to an HTML page remains a modest visual achievement for this chapter. All along this book, you will discover that we haven't diminished the importance of the environment and the context Spring MVC acts in.

How it works...

Through this recipe, we have been moving across web resources and Maven dependencies related to Spring, Spring MVC, and the web environment. Now, we will go through the way that Maven dependency and plugin management are performed. We will then talk about the Spring web application context and finally about the organization and packaging of web resources.

Inheritance of Maven dependencies

There are two strategies concerning the inheritance of dependencies between parent projects and children modules. They both are implemented from the parent project. On the one hand, we can choose to define these dependencies directly from the <dependencies> node, shaping a basic inheritance in this way. On the other hand, to set up a managed inheritance, we can define the <dependencies> node as a child node of <dependencyManagement>. Let's have a look at the differences between the two.

Basic inheritance

With a basic inheritance, all the dependencies specified in the parent's `pom.xml` file are automatically inherited into the child module with the same attributes (scope, version, packaging type, and so on) unless you override them (redefining these dependencies with the same couple `groupId/artifactId`).

On the one hand, it provides the option of using the versions of the dependencies we want in the modules we want. On the other hand, we can end up with a very complex dependencies schema and huge `pom.xml` files in the children modules. Also, managing version conflicts with external transitive dependencies can be a pain.

A transitive dependency is a required dependency with the needed dependency. Transitive dependencies have been automatically imported since Maven 2.0.

There are no standards in this inheritance type for external dependencies.

Managed inheritance

With the `<dependencyManagement>` mechanism, dependencies defined in the parent `pom.xml` are not automatically inherited in children modules. However, the dependency attributes (scope, version, packaging type, and so on) are pulled from the parent dependency's definition, and therefore, the redefinition of these attributes is made optional.

This process drives us towards a centralized dependency definition where all the children modules use the same versions of dependencies unless a specific dependency requires a custom one.

Including third-party dependencies

Among the dependencies copied over, you might have noticed a few Spring modules, some test, web, logging, and utility dependencies.

The idea has been to start with a basic web development tool box, which is enhanced with all the Spring modules. We will visit most of the dependencies actually included when we face a particular situation.

The Spring Framework dependency model

As presented in the following diagram taken from the `spring.io` website, these days, the Spring Framework is currently made of 20 modules that are grouped in different areas:

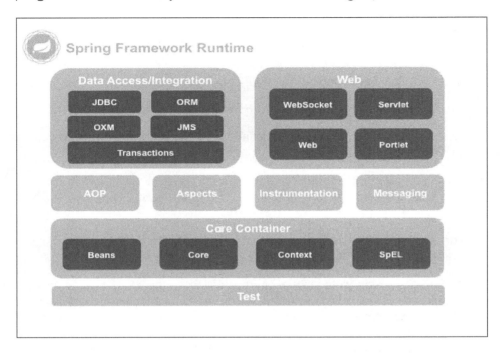

These modules have been included in the parent POMs as managed dependencies. This will allow us, later on, to quickly cherry-pick the needed ones, narrowing down a selection for our `wars`.

The Spring MVC dependency

The Spring MVC module is self-contained in the `spring-webmvc` jar. Spring MVC in a web application is a fundamental element, as it handles incoming client requests and smoothly monitors the business operations from controllers. It finally offers a number of tools and interfaces capable of preparing responses in the format the clients expect them in.

All this workflow comes along with the spring-webmvc jar output HTML content or web services.

Spring MVC is entirely integrated in the Spring Framework, and all its components are standard with regard to the Spring architecture choices.

Using Maven properties

In each parent `pom.xml` file, we have defined a `<properties>` block as part of the `<project>` section. These properties are user-defined properties bound to a project, but we can also define such properties within a **Maven Profile** option. Like variables, properties are referenced in the POMs with their name surrounded by **${...}**.

There is a standard on defining property names using periods as word separators. More than a standard, it is a uniform notation to access both user-defined variables and attributes of objects that constitute the Maven model. The Maven model is the public interface of Maven and starts from the project level.

The POM **XML Schema Definition** (**xsd**) is generated from this Maven model. It can sound abstract but in the end, the Maven model is only a set of POJOs with getters and setters. Have a look at the JavaDoc of the Maven model from the URL below, to identify concepts, specific to pom.xml files (Build, Dependency, Plugin, and so on.):

`http://maven.apache.org/ref/3.0.3/maven-model/apidocs/index.html`

To summarize, we can retrieve a node value defined in a POM and navigate the Maven model hierarchy using a period-based expression language that targets the getters.

For example, `${project.name}` references the current `project.getName()`, `${project.parent.groupId}`, the current `project.getParent().getGroupId()`, and so on.

Defining user properties that match an existing path of the Maven model is a way of overriding its value. That's what we have done for `project.build.sourceEncoding`.

Maven also offers the possibility to reach properties defined in the `settings.xml` files such as `${settings.localRepository}`; but also environment variables such as `${env.JAVA_HOME}`; and Java System properties such as `${java.class.path}`, `${java.version}`, `${user.home}`, or `${user.name}`.

The web resources

If you remember, we copied/pasted the entire `src/main/webapp` directory from the `chapter_1` source code. The `webapp` directory name is a Maven standard. The `webapp` folder in Eclipse doesn't need to be tagged as a source folder for the build path, as it would create a complex and useless package hierarchy for static files. Preferably, it appears as a plain directory tree.

The `webapp` directory must be seen as the document root of the application and positioned at the root level of the WAR. The public static web resources under `webapp`, such as HTML files, Javascript, CSS, and image files, can be placed in the subdirectories and structure of our choice. However, as described in the *Servlet 3.0 Specification*, the `WEB-INF` directory is a special directory within the application hierarchy. All its contents can never be reached from outside the application; its content is accessible from the servlet code calling for `getResource` or `getResourceAsStream` on `ServletContext`. The specification also tells us that the content of a `WEB-INF` directory is made up of the following:

▶ The `/WEB-INF/web.xml` deployment descriptor.

▶ The `/WEB-INF/classes/` directory for servlet and utility classes. The classes in this directory must be available to the application class loader.

▶ The /WEB-INF/lib/*.jar area for Java ARchive files. These files contain servlets, beans, static resources, and JSPs packaged in a JAR file and other utility classes useful to the web application. The web application class loader must be able to load classes from any of these archive files.

It is good practice to create a jsp directory inside the WEB-INF folder so that the jsp files cannot be directly targeted without passing through an explicitly defined controller.

JSP applications do exist, and by definition they will not follow this practice. These type of applications may be suited to certain needs, but they also don't specifically promote the use of an MVC pattern nor a great separation of concerns.

To use JSPs in a web application, the feature must be enabled in web.xml with the definition of a servlet of the org.apache.jasper.servlet.JspServlet type mapped to the JSP files location.

The target runtime environment

We have experienced warnings in the index.jsp files. We have sorted them out by adding a target runtime to our projects. We also saw that Tomcat comes with the Eclipse Compilator for Java as a JAR library. To perform the JSP compilation, the tomcat8\lib directory must include the following JAR libraries: jsp-api, servlet-api and el-api, and so on. Specifying a target runtime for a project in Eclipse emulates and anticipates situation where the application will be run from an external Tomcat container (setup with those libraries). This also explains why the jsp-api and el-api dependencies are defined in the parent POMs with a *provided* scope.

The Spring web application context

In the web.xml files, we defined a special type of Servlet, the Spring MVC DispatcherServlet, and we named it spring. This servlet covers the widest /* URL pattern. We will revisit the DispatcherServlet in the next chapter.

A DispatcherServlet has its own discovery algorithm that builds up WebApplicationContext. An optional contextConfigLocation initialization parameter is provided that points to a dispatcher-context.xml file. This parameter overrides the default expected filename and path (/WEB-INF/{servletName}-servlet.xml) for the WebApplicationContext defined in the DispatcherServlet discovery logic.

With the load-on-startup attribute set to 1, as soon as the servlet container gets ready, a new WebApplicationContext gets loaded and scoped only for the starting servlet. Now, *we don't wait for the first client request to load WebApplicationContext*.

A Spring WebApplicationContext file usually defines or overrides the configuration and beans that Spring MVC offers to the web application.

Still in the web.xml file, an org.sfw.web.context.ContextLoaderListener listener is set up. The purpose of this listener is to start and shut down another Spring ApplicationContext, which will be the root one following the container's life cycle.

To load more than one spring context file easily, the trick here is to use the classpath notation (which is relative) and the star (*) character in the resource path:

```
<context-param>
  <param-name>contextConfigLocation</param-name>
  <param-value>classpath*:/META-INF/spring/*-config.xml</param-value>
</context-param>
```

Doing so allows us to *load all the context files encountered in the classpath that match a standard notation and location*. This approach is appreciated for the consistency it imposes but also for the way it targets context files in underlying jars.

The aggregation of all the matching context files creates an `ApplicationContext` root with a much broader scope, and the `WebApplicationContext` inherits it. The beans we define in the root context become visible to the `WebApplicationContext` context. We can override them if needed. However, the `DispatcherServlet` context's beans are not visible to the root context.

Plugins

Maven is, above all, a plugin's execution framework. Every task run by Maven corresponds to a plugin. A plugin has one or more goals that are associated individually to life cycle phases. Like the dependencies, the plugins are also identified by a `groupId`, an `artifactId`, and a version. When Maven encounters a plugin that is not in the local repository, it downloads it. Also, a specific version of Maven targets, by default, a number of plugins that match the life cycle phases. These plugins are frozen on fixed versions and therefore on a defined behavior—you need to override their definition to get a more recent version or to alter their default behavior.

The Maven compiler plugin

The maven-compiler-plugin is a Maven core plugin. The core plugins are named as such because their goals are triggered on Maven core phases (clean, compile, test, and so on.). Noncore plugins relate to packaging, reporting, utilities, and so on. It is good practice to redefine the maven-compiler-plugin to control which version of the compiler is to be used or to trigger some external tools' actions (the m2eclipse project management tool, actually).

As its name suggests, the maven compiler plugin compiles the Java sources. For that, it uses the `javax.tools.JavaCompiler` class and has two goals: `compiler:compile` (triggered as part of the compile phase to compile the `java/main` source classes) and `compiler:testCompile` (triggered as part of the test-compile phase to compile the `java/test` source classes).

The Maven surefire plugin

The maven-surefire-plugin is also a Maven core plugin that has only one goal: `surefire:test`. This is invoked as part of the default life cycle (the test phase) to run unit tests defined in the application. It generates reports (`*.txt` or `*.xml`), by default, under the `${basedir}/target/surefire-reports` location.

The Maven enforcer plugin

The maven-enforcer-plugin is very useful to define environmental conditions as *critical* for the project. It has two goals: enforcer:enforce (bound, by default, to the validate phase, where it executes each defined rule once per module) and enforcer:display-info (it displays the detected information on execution of the rules).

The most interesting standard rule is probably DependencyConvergence: it analyzes all the used dependencies (direct and transitive) for us. In case of divergence of a version, it highlights it and stops the build. When we face this kind of conflict, it is amazingly easy to decide between the following:

  ▸ Excluding the lowest version from the classpath

  ▸ Not upgrading the dependency

We also quickly talked about the <pluginManagement> section, which was associated to the maven-enforcer-plugin. In this case, this is because m2eclipse doesn't support this plugin. Thus, to avoid a warning in Eclipse, it is necessary to add this section so that m2eclipse skips the enforce goal.

The Maven war plugin

Using the maven-war-plugin, we redefined in our web POMs. We have again overridden the default behavior of this plugin that is used to package web modules. This is definitely necessary if you have a non-Maven standard project structure.

We may want to package our web resources in a different way that how it is organized in our IDE. We may need, for some reason, to exclude some resources from the war packaging or we may even want to give a name to the built war so that it can be used by the servlet container that matches a specific context path in the application URLs (/api, /app, and so on). Filtering, moving web resources around, and managing the generated war is the purpose of this plugin.

 By default, the web resources are copied to the WAR root. To override the default destination directory, specify the target path *.

There's more...

This has been quite a broad overview about concepts that naturally require deeper interest:

  ▸ About the way Maven manages its dependencies, we would suggest you to go through the Maven documentation on this topic at:

    http://maven.apache.org/guides/introduction/introduction-to-dependency-mechanism.html

- The Sonatype ebook talks nicely about Maven properties. You can find this ebook at: `https://books.sonatype.com/mvnref-book/reference/resource-filtering-sect-properties.html#resource-filtering-sect-settings-properties`

- The Maven model API documentation can again be found at:

  `http://maven.apache.org/ref/3.0.3/maven-model/apidocs/index.html`

- Concerning the servlet 3.0 specification that we mentioned earlier, more information can be found about the `web.xml` file definition and about the structure of a WebArchive at: `http://download.oracle.com/otn-pub/jcp/servlet-3.0-fr-eval-oth-JSpec/servlet-3_0-final-spec.pdf`

- Finally, for more information about Maven plugins; we absolutely recommend you visit the Maven listing at `http://maven.apache.org/plugins`

See also

- The `spring.io` website from Pivotal, and especially the Spring Framework overview page, can also refresh, or introduce a few key concepts. Follow the address: `http://docs.spring.io/spring-framework/docs/current/spring-framework-reference/html/overview.html`

The Maven checkstyle plugin

One other interesting enough plugin which could also be highlighted here is the maven-checkstyle-plugin. When a team is growing, we sometimes need to guarantee the maintenance of certain development practices or we may need to maintain specific security-related coding practices. Like the maven-enforcer-plugin, the maven-checkstyle-plugin makes our builds assertive against this type of violation.

Find out more about this plugin, again in the Maven documentation, at: `http://maven.apache.org/plugins/maven-checkstyle-plugin`.

2

Designing a Microservice Architecture with Spring MVC

In this chapter, we will cover the following topics:

- ▸ Configuring a controller with simple URL mapping
- ▸ Configuring a fallback controller using the ViewResolver
- ▸ Setting up and customizing a responsive single page webdesign with Bootstrap
- ▸ Displaying a model in the View using the JSTL
- ▸ Defining a common WebContentInterceptor
- ▸ Designing a client-side MVC pattern with AngularJS

Introduction

You need to complete the first chapter before starting this new one. The first chapter installs the basics for the trading platform we are building. It also creates a modular toolkit that every recipe will be using.

This second chapter sets the product on an acceleration ramp. It will shape the whole chain of responsibilities and draft the big picture of the Microservice architecture. Once more, we will establish a necessary structure for the chapters to come, but on another level.

The User eXperience paradigm

For a couple of years now, we've assisted an amazingly active frontend revolution. Since the rise of HTML 5 and CSS3, with the common development platforms for mobile (iOS, Android, and so on), and with the amount of connected devices, so many doors and opportunities have been opened to the developer communities. The frequency of new JavaScript libraries popping-up in the open source field has made it quite difficult to follow.

But it's a revolution for good! It targets the customer and user experience. The customer nowadays wants to interact with a brand or a product from the desktop, laptop, TV, tablet, mobile, and soon the car. Network connection speeds vary as well from more than 150 megabytes per second to very few bytes per second. The customer can also expect offline features or at least a decent user experience. It's obvious that new challenges have come out of this complexity to improve the user experience.

As our reachability through different means has largely increased, our level of exposure to spam, direct solicitations, advertising, and marketing in general has never been higher. Interestingly, we are now far more sensitive and assertive to every single message that retains our attention online. As it takes us a fraction of second to decide whether something is worth it or not, we reject a poor design for the same reason. We are more demanding and saturated targets, and every brand has to follow the latest UX standards to make us interact with them.

Microservice architectures

We have seen already the massive benefits in terms of communication, image, and development that Internet organizations have generated by opening their APIs to the public (Facebook, Twitter, Amazon, and so on). Such radical changes in IT infrastructures are now becoming the norm for smaller companies and start-ups.

Modern architectures provide documented Public APIs and device-specific installation packages for their clients: mobile apps or responsive HTML contents delivered under specific shots. REST APIs are also a navigable dimension for more autonomous modules of the **Internet of Things (IoT)**.

Maybe the main concern remains how to handle the load on the server side, but more computation is transferred to client devices and REST architectures are by definition stateless and consequently a good support for scalability.

Configuring a controller with simple URL mapping

This recipe introduces the Spring MVC controller with its simplest implementation.

Getting ready

We will discover later on, and especially in *Chapter 3*, *Working with Java Persistence and Entities,* that Spring MVC is a great tool to build a REST API. Here, we will focus on how to create a controller that prints some content in the response.

Starting with this recipe, we will be using GIT to follow each iteration that has been made to develop the `cloudstreetmarket` application. After the initial setup, you will appreciate how smoothly you can upgrade.

How to do it...

This recipe comes with two initial sections for installing and configuring GIT.

Downloading and installing GIT

1. To download GIT, go to the GIT download page at `https://git-scm.com/download`. Select the right product corresponding to your environment _Mac OS X, Windows, Linux, or Solaris).

2. To install GIT for Linux and Solaris, execute the suggested installation commands using the system's native package manager.

For Mac OS X, double-click on the downloaded `dmg` file to extract the package on your hard drive. Navigate to the extracted directory and double-click on the `pkg` file. Select all the default options, one step after an other, up to the **Successful Installation** screen. Close the screen.

For Windows, execute the downloaded program and follow the default options for every step up to these screens:

- **Adjusting your PATH environment**: Select the **Use Git from the Windows Command Prompt** option
- **Choosing the SSH executable**: Select the **Use OpenSSH** option
- **Configuring the line endings conversions**: Select the **Checkout Windows-style** *and* **commit Unix-style line endings** options
- **Configuring the terminal emulator to use Git Bash**: Select **Use Windows' default console window**
- **Configuring experimental performance tweaks**: Don't tick the **Enable file system caching** checkbox

Let the installation finish and click on the **Finish** button.

For verification, open your terminal and enter the following command:

```
git -version
```

This command should display the installed version. The presented installation guidelines were associated with GIT 2.6.3.

Configuring GIT in Eclipse

1. We will first initialize the local repository from the terminal. Go to your workspace location: `cd <home-directory>/workspace`.

    Replace `<home-directory>` with your own home path.

2. Enter the following command to create a local Git repository at this location:

    ```
    git init
    ```

3. Enter the following command:

    ```
    git remote add origin https://github.com/alex-bretet/
    cloudstreetmarket.com
    ```

4. Then, enter the `git fetch` command.

5. Select both your parent projects and right-click on one of them. Go to **Team | Add to index**:

6. From the top-right panel, click on the **Git perspective**:

    Add this perspective with the ⊞ button if you don't have it yet.

7. From the left hierarchy (the **Git** perspective), select **Add an existing local Git repository**.

8. A contextual window opens. Target the location of the local Git repository we just created (it should be the current workspace directory).

9. A new repository should now appear in **Git** perspective.

10. As shown in the following screenshot, right-click and select **Checkout** to see the latest version of the branch **origin/v1.x.x**.

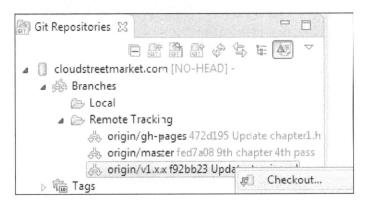

11. When prompted, Checkout as **New Local Branch**:

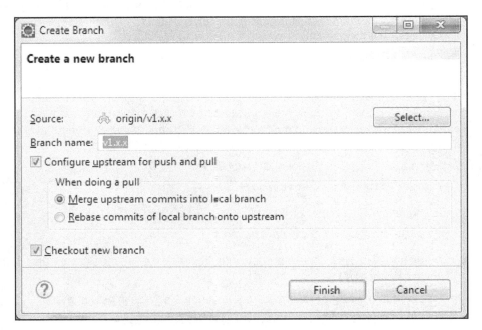

12. The actual workspace should now be synchronized with the branch v1.x.x. This branch reflects the state of the environment at the end of *Chapter 1*, Setup *Routine for an Enterprise Spring Application.*

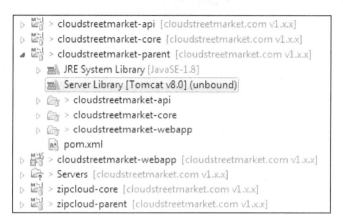

13. Right-click on **zipcloud-parent** to execute **Run as | Maven clean** and **Run as | Maven install**. Then, do the same operation on cloudstreetmarket-parent. You will observe BUILD SUCCESS each time.

14. Finally, right-click on one project and go to **Maven | Update Project**. Select all the projects of the workspace and click on **OK**.

15. If you still have a red warning in one of your projects (as shown in the previous screenshot), you will probably have to reattach a target runtime environment to **cloudstreetmarket-api** and **cloustreetmarket-webapp** (as per *Chapter 1 , Setup Routine for an Enterprise Spring Application, 2nd recipe, 7th step*).

16. From the terminal, go to the local GIT repository:

```
cd <home-directory>/workspace
```

17. Enter the following command:

```
git pull origin v2.2.1
```

18. Reiterate steps 13 and 14. (Be prepared to repeat these two steps every time after pulling new changes.)

19. In the **cloudstreetmarket-webapp** module, a new package is now present:

```
edu.zipcloud.cloudstreetmarket.portal.controllers.
```

20. Inside this package, an InfoTagController class has been created:

```
@Controller
@RequestMapping("/info")
public class InfoTagController {
  @RequestMapping("/helloHandler")
```

```
  @ResponseBody
  public String helloController(){
    return "hello";
  }
}
```

21. Make sure the two `wars` are deployed in the Tomcat server. Start the Tomcat server and access the `http://localhost:8080/portal/info/helloHandler` URL with your browser.

 You should see a simple hello displayed as HTML content.

22. In the `cloudstreetmarket-webapp/src/main/webapp/WEB-INF/` `dispatcher-context.xml` file, the following bean definition is added:

```
<bean id="webAppVersion" class="java.lang.String">
  <constructor-arg value='1.0.0'/>
</bean>
```

23. The following method and members in the `InfoTagController` class are also added:

```
@Autowired
private WebApplicationContext webAppContext;
private final static LocalDateTime startDateTime =
  LocalDateTime.now();
private final static DateTimeFormatter DT_FORMATTER =
  DateTimeFormatter.ofPattern("EEE, d MMM yyyy h:mm a");
@RequestMapping("/server")
@ResponseBody
public String infoTagServer(){
  return new StringJoiner "<br>")
    .add("-----------------------------------")
    .add(" Server: "+
    webAppContext.getServletContext().getServerInfo())
    .add(" Start date: "+
    startDateTime.format(DT_FORMATTER))
    .add(" Version: " +
    webAppContext.getBean "webAppVersion"))
    .add("-----------------------------------")
    .toString();
}
```

24. Now, access the `http://localhost:8080/portal/info/server` URL with your browser.

You should see the following content rendered as an HTML document:

Server: Apache Tomcat/8.0.14
Start date: Sun, 16 Nov 2014 12:10 AM
Version: 1.0.0

How it works...

We are going to draft an overview of Spring MVC as a Framework. We will then review how a Controller is configured from the `DispatcherServlet`, the controller-level annotations, and from the method-handler signatures.

Spring MVC overview

Spring MVC implements two common design patterns: the front controller design pattern and the MVC design pattern.

Front controller

A system designed as a Front controller exposes a single entry point for all incoming requests. In Java Web environments, this entry point is usually a servlet—a unique servlet that dispatches and delegates to other components.

In the case of Spring MVC, this unique servlet is the `DispatcherServlet`.

Servlets are standards in the Java web. They are associated to predefined URL paths and are registered in deployment descriptors (the `web.xml` files). Parsing deployment descriptors, the servlet-container (such as Apache Tomcat) identifies the declared servlets and their URL mapping. At runtime, the servlet-container intercepts every HTTP client request and creates a new Thread for each one of them. Those Threads will call the matching relevant servlets with Java-converted request and response objects.

MVC design pattern

The MVC design pattern is more of an arch tectural style. It describes the application as a whole. It encourages a clear separation of concerns between three different layers that the request thread has to pass through: the **Model**, the **View**, and the **Controller**—the Controller, the Model, and then the View to be accurate.

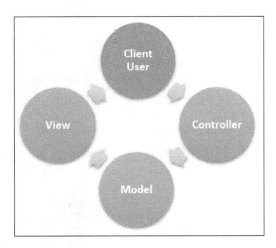

When a client request is intercepted by the servlet-container, it is routed to the `DispatcherServlet`. The `DispatcherServlet` sends the request to one Controller (one controller method-handler), which has a configuration matching the request state (if a match is found).

The Controller orchestrates the business logic, the model generation and ultimately chooses a View for the model and the response. In this perspective, the model represents a populated data structure handled by the controller and given to the view for visualization purposes.

But the three components (Model, View, and Controller) can also be visualized at a Macro scale as independent static layers. Each of these components is a layer and a placeholder for every individual constituent, part of the category. The **Controller layer** contains all the registered controllers as well as the Web Interceptors and converters; the Model generation layer (and Business logic layer) contains the business services and data access components. The View layer encloses the templates (JSPs for example) and other web client-side components.

Spring MVC flow

The Spring MVC flow can be represented with the following diagram:

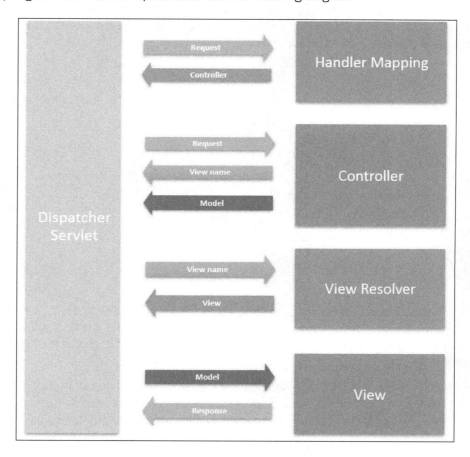

We previously mentioned that Spring MVC implements a front controller pattern. The entry point is the `DispatcherServlet`. This `DispatcherServlet` relies on a `HandlerMapping` implementation. With different strategies and specificities, the `HandlerMapping` resolves a Controller method-handler for the request.

Once the `DispatcherServlet` has a Controller method-handler, it dispatches the request to it. The method-handler returns a View name (or directly the View itself) and also the populated model object to the `DispatcherServlet`.

With a View name, the `DispatcherServlet` asks a `ViewResolver` implementation to find and select a View.

With the request, a View, and a Model, the `DispatcherServlet` has everything to build the client response. The view is processed with all these elements and the response is finally returned to the servlet-container.

DispatcherServlet – the Spring MVC entrypoint

As explained, the `DispatcherServlet` is quite a central piece in Spring MVC. It intercepts the client requests that target predefined URL paths for the application. It maps them to handlers that belong to business logic operators (Controllers, Interceptors, Filters, and so on). It also provides a set of tools, available as beans for solving recurring web development issues and techniques such as serving a centralized and modular View layer, handling internationalisation, themes, handing exceptions, and so on.

Before everything, the `DispatcherServlet` is a servlet and is defined as such in the `web.xml` file with a servlet configuration and its servlet-mapping. The code is as follows:

```
<servlet>
  <servlet-name>spring</servlet-name>
   <servlet-class>
       org.springframework.web.servlet.DispatcherServlet
   </servlet-class>
   <load-on-startup>1</load-on-startup>
</servlet>
<servlet-mapping>
    <servlet-name>spring</servlet-name>
    <url-pattern>/*</url-pattern>
</servlet-mapping>
```

In our application, in the **cloudstreetmarket-webapp**, the `DispatcherServlet` is named spring and covers the full context-path of the application: `/*`.

We have already seen that each `DispatcherServlet` has a restricted-scope `WebApplicationContext` that inherits the beans from the root `ApplicationContext`.

By default, for the `WebApplicationContext`, Spring MVC looks in the `/WEB-INF` directory for a configuration file named `{servletName}-servlet.xml`. We have, however, overridden this default name and location through the initialization parameter `contextConfigLocation`:

```
<servlet>
 <servlet-name>spring</servlet-name>
   <servlet-class>
    org.springframework.web.servlet.DispatcherServlet
  </servlet-class>
   <init-param>
    <param-name>contextConfigLocation</param-name>
    <param-value>/WEB-INF/dispatcher-context.xml</param-value>
   </init-param>
   <load-on-startup>1</load-on-startup>
</servlet>
<servlet-mapping>
```

```
    <servlet-name>spring</servlet-name>
    <url-pattern>/*</url-pattern>
</servlet-mapping>
```

Still in the `web.xml`, you can see that the root application context (`classpath*:/META-INF/spring/*-config.xml`) starts with the `ContextLoaderListener`:

```
<listener>
  <listener-class>
    org.springframework.web.context.ContextLoaderListener
  </listener-class>
</listener>
```

Annotation-defined controllers

Spring MVC controllers are the place where client requests really start to be processed by the business-specific code. Since *Spring 2.5*, we have been able to use annotations on controllers so we don't have to explicitly declare them as beans in configuration. This makes their implementation much easier to extend and understand.

@Controller

A `@Controller` annotation tags a class as a Web controller. It remains a Spring Stereotype for presentation layers. The main purpose of defining a Spring Stereotype is to make a target type or method discoverable during the Spring classpath scanning which is activated by package with the following command:

```
<context:component-scan base-package="edu.zipcloud.cloudstreetmarket.
portal"/>
```

There is not much custom logic related to this annotation. We could run a Controller with other Stereotype annotations (`@Component` or `@Service`) if we don't bother making the application a cleaner place.

@RequestMapping

The `@RequestMapping` annotations define handlers onto Controller classes and/or onto controller methods. These annotations are looked-up among stereotyped classes by the `DispatcherServlet`. The main idea behind the `@RequestMapping` annotations is to define a primary path mapping on the class-level and to narrow HTTP request methods, headers, parameters, and media-types on the methods.

To implement this narrowing, the `@RequestMapping` annotation accepts comma-separated parameters within parentheses.

Consider the following example:

```
@RequestMapping(value="/server", method=RequestMethod.GET)
```

Available parameters for @RequestMapping are summarized in the following table:

Parameter and type	Use/description (from JavaDoc)
name (String)	Assign a name to the mapping.
value (String[])	The path mapping URIs (for example, /myPath.do). Ant-style path patterns are also supported (for example, /myPath/*.do).
	Path mapping URIs may contain placeholders (for example, /${connect}) against local properties and/or system properties and environment variables.
	A path implements URI templates that give access to selected parts of a URL through patterns, variables, placeholders, and matrix variables (see section URI Templates).
	At the method level, relative paths (for example, edit.do) are supported within the primary mapping expressed at the type level.
method (RequestMethod[])	GET, POST, HEAD, OPTIONS, PUT, PATCH, DELETE, TRACE.
params (String[])	A sequence of myParam=myValue style expressions.
	Expressions can be negated using the != operator, as in myParam!=myValue.
headers (String[])	A sequence of My-Header=myValue style expressions.
	Specifying only the header name (for example, My-Header) is supported (allowed to have any value).
	Negating a header name (for example, "!My-Header") is also supported (the specified header is not supposed to be present in the request).
	Also supports media type wildcards (*), for headers such as Accept and Content-Type.
consumes (String[])	The consumable media types of the mapped request.
	Only mapped if the {@code Content-Type} matches one of these media types.
	Negating an expression (for example, !text/xml) is also supported.
produces (String[])	The producible media types of the mapped request.
	Only mapped if the {@code Accept} matches one of these media types.
	Negating an expression (for example, !text/plain) is also supported. It matches all requests with a {@code Accept} other than "text/plain".

All these parameters can be used both at the type and method level. When used at the type level, all method-level parameters inherit the parent-level narrowing.

Controller method-handler signatures

Several constituents make a Controller method-handler. Here's another example of such a handler with Spring MVC:

```
@RequestMapping(value="/index")
public ModelAndView getRequestExample(ServletRequest request){
    ModelAndView mav = new ModelAndView();
    mav.setViewName("index");
    mav.addObject("variable1", new ArrayList<String>());
    return mav;
}
```

We have just talked about how to use the `@RequestMapping` annotation. With regard to the method signature, this annotation can only be placed before the return-type.

Supported method arguments types

Declaring specific types of arguments for handler methods can get Spring to automatically inject in them references to external objects. Objects related to the request lifecycle, the session, or to the application configuration. With the benefit of being scoped for the method, those argument types are presented in the following table:

Supported arguments	Use/description	Packages
`ServletRequest / HttpServletRequest`	Injects the servlet request/response.	`javax.servlet. http.*`
`ServletResponse / HttpServletResponse`		
`HttpSession`	Injects the HTTP session bound to the servlet request. If null, Spring creates a new one. `synchronizeOnSession` must be set on an `AbstractController` or in `RequestMappingHandlerAdapter` if sessions should be shared concurrently across multiple requests.	
`WebRequest / NativeWebRequest`	Injects a wrapper for access to request parameters and request/session attributes only.	`org. springframework. web.context. request.*`
`Locale`	Injects the local e of the request using the configured `LocaleResolver`.	`java.util.*`

Supported arguments	Use/description	Packages
InputStream / Reader OutputStream / Writer	Provides a direct access to the request/ response payload.	java.io.*
HttpMethod	Injects the current method of the request.	org. springframework. http.*
Principal	Using the Spring security context, it injects the authenticated account.	java.security.*
HttpEntity<?>	Spring converts and injects the inbound request to a custom type using HttpMessageConverter. It also provides access to the request headers.	org. springframework. http.*
Map	Instantiates for us a BindingAwareModelMap to be used in the view	java.util.*
Model ModelMap		org. springframework. ui.*
RedirectAttributes	Injects and repopulates a map of attributes and flash attributes maintained over request redirection	org. springframework. web.servlet.mvc. support.*
Errors BindingResult	Injects the validation results of the argument located just before in the argument list.	org. springframework. validation.*
SessionStatus	Allows tagging with setComplete(Boolean), the completion of a session. This method clears the session attributes defined at the type level with @SessionAttributes.	org. springframework. web.bind. support.*
UriComponentsBuilder	Injects a Spring URL builder UriComponentsBuilder.	org. springframework. web.util.*

Supported annotations for method arguments

A set of native annotations for method-handler arguments has been designed. They must be seen as handles that configure the web behavior of controller methods in regard to incoming requests or the response yet to be built.

They identify abstractions for handy Spring MVC functions such as request parameter binding, URI path variable binding, injection-to-argument of request payloads, HTML form-parameter binding, and so on.

Supported annotation arguments	Use/description	Package
`@PathVariable`	Injects an URI Template variable into an argument.	`org. springframework. web.bind. annotation.*`
`@ MatrixVariable`	Injects name-value pairs located in URI path segments into an argument.	
`@RequestParam`	Injects a specific request parameter into an argument.	
`@RequestHeader`	Injects a specific request HTTP Header into an argument.	
`@RequestBody`	Allows direct access to the request payload injecting it into an argument.	
`@RequestPart`	Injects the content of a specific part (meta-data, file-data...) of a multipart/form-data encoded request into an argument of the matching type (MetaData, MultipartFile...)	
`@ ModelAttribute`	Populates automatically an attribute of the Model using the URI template. This binding is operated before the method handler processing.	

These annotations have to be placed just before the method argument to be populated:

```
@RequestMapping(value="/index")
public ModelAndView getRequestExample(@RequestParam("exP1") String
  exP1){
  ModelAndView mav = new ModelAndView();
  mav.setViewName("index");
  mav.addObject("exP1", exP1);
  return mav;
}
```

Supported return Types

Spring MVC, with different possible controller method return Types, allows us to specify either the response sent back to the client or the necessary configuration for targeting or populating with variables an intermediate View layer. Depending upon what we want to do or the actual application state, we have the choice among the following:

Supported return Types	Use/description	Packages
Model	Spring MVC creates an implementation of the Model Interface for the handler method. The Model objects are populated manually within the handler- method or with @ModelAttribute. The view to render needs to be mapped to the request with RequestToViewNameTranslator.	org. springframework. ui.*
ModelAndView	A wrapper object for the Model with a View and a view name. If a view name is provided, Spring MVC will attempt to resolve the associated View. Otherwise, the embedded View is rendered. The Model objects are populated manually within the method or with @ModelAttribute.	
Map	Allows a custom Model implementation. The view to render needs to be mapped to the request with RequestToViewNameTranslator.	java.util.*
View	Allows the rendering of a custom View object. Spring MVC creates an implementation of the Model interface for the handler method. The objects of the model are populated manually within the method or with the help of @ModelAttribute.	org. springframework. web.servlet.*
String	If a @ResponseBody annotation is not specified on the handler method, the returned String is processed as a View name (View identifier).	java.lang.*
HttpEntity<?> / ResponseEntity<?>	Two wrapper objects to easily manage the response headers and converted-by-Spring body (with HttpMessageConverters).	org. springframework. http.*
HttpHeaders	Provides a wrapper object for HEAD responses.	org. springframework. http .*

Supported return Types	Use/description	Packages
`Callable<?>`	Can produce asynchronously a typed object when the Thread is controlled by Spring MVC.	`java.util.concurrent.*`
`DeferredResult<?>`	Can produce asynchronously a Typed object when the Thread is not controlled by Spring MVC.	`org.springframework.web.context.request.async.*`
`ListenableFuture<?>`		`org.springframework.util.concurrent.*`
`void`	When the view is externally resolved with `RequestToViewNameTranslator` or when the method prints directly in the response.	

There's more...

In the `InfoTagController.infoTagServer()` method-handler, we have used the `@ResponseBody` annotation before the return Type. This annotation has been borrowed from the REST-specific tools. When you don't need to process a View, the `@ResponseBody` directive will use the registered Spring converters to marshal the returned object into the expected format (XML, JSON, and so on). It will then write the marshalled content to the Response body (as the Response payload).

In the case of a String object with no more configurations, it is printed out as such in the Response body. We could have used the `ResponseEntity<String>` return Type to achieve the same goal.

Configuring a fallback controller using ViewResolver

This recipe introduces some more advanced concepts and tools related to Controllers such as `ViewResolvers`, URI Template Patterns, and Spring MVC's injection-as-argument. The recipe is quite simple but there is more to talk about.

Getting ready

We will keep working from the same codebase state as the previous recipe where we have pulled the v2.2.1 tag from the remote repository. It will only be about creating one Controller with its handler method.

How to do it...

1. In the **cloudstreetmarket-webapp** module and in the package `edu.zipcloud.cloudstreetmarket.portal.controllers`, the following `DefaultController` has been created:

```
@Controller
public class DefaultController {
  @RequestMapping(value="/*",
    method={RequestMethod.GET,RequestMethod.HEAD})
  public String fallback() {
    return "index";
  }
}
```

 We will explain in detail how this method-handler serves as a fallback interceptor.

2. Access the `http://localhost:8080/portal/whatever` or `http://localhost:8080/portal/index` URL with your browser.

   You should also receive the HTML content we saw earlier:

How it works...

This second recipe revisits the use of the `@RequestMapping` annotation. With no longer a fixed URI as a path value but with an opened-pattern (fallback). The recipe also makes use of the configured View resolver that we didn't use before.

URI template patterns

The template word is recurring in the Spring terminology. It usually refers to generic support Spring APIs to be instantiated in order to fill specific implementations or customisations (REST template to make REST HTTP requests, JMS template to send JMS messages, WS template to make SOAP webservices requests, JDBC template, and so on). They are bridge the developer needs to Spring core features.

Under this light, URI templates allow configuring generic URIs with patterns and variables for controller end points. It is possible to instantiate URI builders that will implement URI templates but developers probably mostly use URI templates in the support they provide to @ `RequestMapping` annotations.

Ant-style path patterns

We have made use of these types of pattern to define the path value for our fallback handler method:

```
@RequestMapping(value="/*", ...)
```

This specific case, with the * wildcard, allows whichever request URI starts with a / after the application display name to be eligible for being handled by this method.

The wildcard can match a character, a word, or a sequence of words. Consider the following example:

```
/portal/1, /portal/foo, /portal/foo-bar
```

A limitation would be to use another slash in the last sequence:

```
/portal/foo/bar
```

Remember the difference with the table here:

/*	All resources and directories at the level
/**	All resources and directories at the level and sublevels

We have been using the single wildcard on purpose in the `cloudstreetmarket-webapp` application. It might be more suited for other types of applications to redirect every unmatched URI to a default one. In our case of a single page application that will be strongly REST oriented, it is nicer to inform the client with a `404` error when a resource hasn't been found.

It is not the only option to use wildcards at the end of path patterns. We could have implemented the following type of pattern if needed:

```
/portal/**/foo/*/bar
```

(not for fallback purposes, though).

We will see that Spring MVC, to select one handler compares, all the matching Path patterns and selects the most specific of them.

 At the Controller type-level, we haven't specified a @RequestMapping. f we had done so, the specified path for the method-level woulc have been concatenated to type- evel one (implementing a narrowing).

For example, the following definition would have defined the path pattern /portal/ default/* for our fallback controller:

```
@RequestMapping(value="/default"...)
@Controller
public class DefaultController...{
        @RequestMapping(value="/*"...)
        public String fallback(Model model) {...}
}
```

Path pattern comparison

A pathpattern comparison is done by Spring MVC when a given URL matches more than one registered path-pattern, to choose which handler the request will be mapped to.

 The pattern considered the most specific will be selected.

The first criterion is the number of countec variables and wildcards in the compared path patterns: the pattern having the lowest number of variables and wildcards is cons dered the most specific.

To discriminate two path-patterns that have the same cumulated number cf variables and wildcards, remember that the one with the lowest number of wildcards will be the most specific and then the longest path will be the most specific.

Finally a pattern with double wildcards is always less specific than a pattern without any.

To illustrate this selection, let's consider the following hierarchy going from the most to the least specific:

/portal/foo

/portal/{foo}

/portal/*

/portal/{foo}/{bar}

/portal/default/*/{foo}

```
/portal/{foo}/*
/portal/**/*
/portal/**
```

ViewResolvers

In `dispatcher-context.xml` of **cloudstreetmarket-webapp**, we have defined the `viewResolver` bean:

```
<bean id="viewResolver" class="org.springframework.web.servlet.view.
InternalResourceViewResolver">
  <property name="viewClass" value="org.springframework.web.servlet.
  view.JstlView" />
  <property name="prefix" value="/WEB-INF/jsp/" />
  <property name="suffix" value=".jsp" />
</bean>
```

A `viewResolver` bean is a specific instance of a predefined class used to serve an organized and uniform set of view layers. In the case that we have configured, the `viewResolver` bean is an instance of `InternalResourceViewResolver`, which can serve JSP pages, handle the JSTL and tiles. This class also inherits `UrlBasedViewResolver` that can navigate the application resources and can bind a logical view name to a View resource file. This capability prevents the creation of extramappings.

In our configuration, we have defined the view repository (`/WEB-INF/jsp/*.jsp`) and we can directly refer to `index.jsp` with the String `index`.

It is better practice to set up the JSP repository under `/WEB-INF` so those JSPs cannot be targeted publicly. Rather than a JSP templating, we could have used Velocity or Freemarker respectively using the view resolvers `VelocityViewResolver` or `FreeMarkerViewResolver`.

Also, we will talk about the `ContentNegotiatingViewResolver` later on when we build the REST API.

There's more...

This section highlights particularly the @PathVariable annotation. This annotation is an annotation for controller method-handler arguments (we have introduced all of them in the previous recipe).

@PathVariable to read variables in URI template patterns

You will find later, on several examples, the method-level `@RequestMapping` annotations . Those annotations will sometimes be related to `@PathVariable` annotations or the method-handler arguments. For now, let's consider the following example:

```
@RequestMapping(value="/example/{param}")
public HttpEntity<String> example(@PathVariable("param") String
  parameter) {
  return new HttpEntity<>(parameter);
}
```

As announced before, `@PathVariable` tells Spring MVC where and how to realize its injection-as-argument from the request URI. The framework will parse the current URI Template pattern to extract the variable named `param` and will inject the matching value in the current URI into the targeted method-argument.

We also declare an `HTTPEntity` to be returned as a response. This `HTTPEntity` will be a wrapper of a String generic type. Inside the method-handler, we instantiate this wrapper with the necessary String element.

If we would call for the `/portal/example/foo` URI, it would be displayed as a response from the body of the returned `HTTPEntity`: the String `foo`.

With another interesting feature, we could have built this last scenario with the following declaration for `@PathVariable`:

```
@RequestMapping(value="/example/{param}")
public HttpEntity<String> example(@PathVariable String param) {
  return new HttpEntity<>(param);
}
```

> Not providing a value to the annotation, Spring MVC will by default look in the URI Template pattern for a variable of the same name as the targeted argument.

We will explore other features with regard to `@RequestMapping` and `@PathVariable`.

Setting up and customizing a responsive single page webdesign with Bootstrap

Bootstrap is a UI Framework initially created by Mark Otto and Jacob Thornton at Twitter. It is an amazing source of styles, icons, and behaviors, abstracted to define and enrich components. Bootstrap offers an easy, rational, and unified set of patterns for defining styles. It had no equivalent before. If you have never used it, you will be excited to get so much visual feedback from a quick definition of the DOM.

In June 2014 it was the number 1 project on GitHub with over 73,000 stars and more than 27,000 forks. Their documentation is very fluid and easy to go through.

Getting ready

In this recipe, we will use Bootstrap to set up the web-design basics for our CloudStreet Market project from an existing Bootstrap theme. We will remake the `index.jsp` page to render a better looking welcome page that can be previewed with the following screenshot.

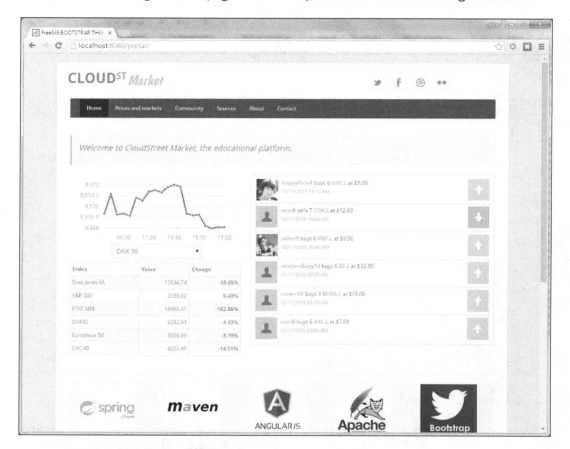

How to do it...

There are three major steps in this recipe:

- ▶ Installing a Bootstrap theme
- ▶ Customizing a Bootstrap theme
- ▶ Creating responsive content

From the Git Perspective in Eclipse, checkout the latest version of the branch v2.x.x:

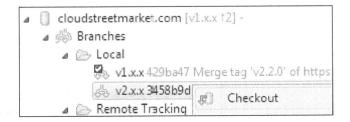

Installing a Bootstrap theme

1. In the chapter_2 directory, you can find a freeme.zip archive. It is a responsive Bootstrap template downloadable for free. This zip comes from the bootstrapmaster.com website

2. Inside this archive, you'll see a css directory, a js directory, an img directory, and finally an index.html file. Opening the index.html file with a web browser should render the following home page:

We are using this template as a base for the webapp module.

3. All the JavaScript files located in the freeme/js directory have been copied over to the /cloudstreetmarket-webapp/src/main/webapp/js directory.

4. All the CSS files located in the freeme/css directory have been copied over to the /cloudstreetmarket-webapp/src/main/webapp/css directory.

5. All the pictures located in `freeme/img` have been copied over to the `/cloudstreetmarket-webapp/src/main/webapp/img` directory.

6. The content of the `freeme/index.html` file has been copied and pasted into the `/cloudstreetmarket-webapp/src/main/webapp/WEB-INF/jsp/index.jsp` file, as UTF-8.

7. Also, the `freeme/licence.txt` has been copied and pasted to the `/cloudstreetmarket-webapp/src/main/webapp/WEB-INF/jsp` directory.

8. At this point, calling `http://localhost:8080/portal/index` with a web browser displayed exactly the same visual you saw earlier, but served by our application.

Customising a Bootstrap theme

We will detail in this section what has been done in order to adapt the downloaded template to our use case.

1. All the images previously located in `cloudstreetmarket-webapp\src\main\webapp\img\logos` have been removed and replaced with six new images representing brands of technical products that we have been using through out this application and this book.

2. In the `index.jsp` file located in the `cloudstreetmarket-webapp` module has been implemented the following changes:

    1. The following two lines have been added to the top:

```
<%@ page contentType="text/html;charset=UTF-8" language="java" %>
<%@ page isELIgnored="false" %>
```

    2. The `<!-- start: Meta -->` section has been replaced with the following:

```
<!-- start: Meta -->
<meta charset="utf-8">
<title>Spring MVC: CloudST Market</title>
<meta name="description" content="Spring MVC CookBook: Cloud
Street Market"/>
<meta name="keywords" content="spring mvc, cookbook, packt
publishing, microservices, angular.js" />
<meta name="author" content="Your name"/>
<!-- end: Meta -->
```

    3. The `<!--start: Logo -->` section has been replaced with the following:

```
<!--start: Logo -->
<div class="logo span4">
  CLOUD<span class="sub">ST</span><span>Market</span>
</div>
<!--end: Logo -->
```

4. The navigation menu definition has been changed:

```
<ul class="nav">
  <li class="active"><a href="index">Home</a></li>
  <li><a href="markets">Prices and markets</a></li>
  <li><a href="community">Community</a></li>
  <li><a href="sources">Sources</a></li>
  <li><a href="about">About</a></li>
  <li><a href="contact">Contact</a></li>
</ul>
```

5. The `<!-- start: Hero Unit -->` and `<!-- start: Flexslider -->` sections have been removed and `<div class="row">` coming after the navigation menu (`<!--end: Navigation-->`) has been emptied:

```
<!-- start: Row -->
<div class="row"></div>
<!-- end: Row -->
```

6. The `<!-- start: Row -->` section to the `<!-- end: Row -->` section, which is located after the `<!-- end Clients List -->`, has been removed along with the `<hr>` just after it.

7. The footer section `<!-- start: Footer Menu -->` to `<!-- end: Footer Menu -->` has been replaced with the following content:

```
<!-- start: Footer Menu -->
<div id="footer-menu" class="hidden-tablet hidden-phone">
  <!-- start: Container -->
  <div class="container">
    <!-- start: Row -->
    <div class="row">
      <!-- start: Footer Menu Logo -->
      <div class="span1">
      <div class="logoSmall">CLOUD<span
      class="sub">ST</span><span>M!</span>
        </div>
        </div>
      <!-- end: Footer Menu Logo -->
      <!-- start: Footer Menu Links-->
      <div class="span10" >
      <div id="footer-menu-links">
      <ul id="footer-nav" style="margin-
        left:35pt;'>
        <li><a href="index">Home</a></li>
        <li><a href="markets">Prices and
        markets</a></li>
        <li><a
        href="community">Community</a></li>
```

```
<li><a href="sources">Sources</a></li>
<li><a href="about">About</a></li>
<li><a href="contact">Contact</a></li>
</ul>
</div>
</div>
<!-- end: Footer Menu Links-->
<!-- start: Footer Menu Back To Top -->
<div class="span1">
<div id="footer-menu-back-to-top">
  <a href="#"></a>
  </div>
</div>
<!-- end: Footer Menu Back To Top -->
  </div>
  <!-- end: Row -->
  </div>
 <!-- end: Container   -->
</div>
<!-- end: Footer Menu -->
```

8. The section: `<!-- start: Photo Stream -->` to `<!-- end: Photo Stream -->` has been replaced with:

```
<!-- start: Leaderboard -->
<div class="span3">
  <h3>Leaderboard</h3>
  <div class="flickr-widget">
    <script type="text/javascript" src=""></script>
    <div class="clear"></div>
  </div>
</div>
<!-- end: Leaderboard -->
```

9. As a last change in the `index.jsp` file, the copyright section has been adapted.

3. In the previously copied `cloudstreetmarket-webapp/src/main/webapp/css/style.css` file, the following classes have been added:

```
.logo{
  font-family: 'Droid Sans';      font-size: 24pt; color:     #666;
  width:157pt; font-weight:bold; margin-top:18pt;     margin-
  left:10pt; height:30pt;
}
.logo span{
```

```
    position:relative;float:right; margin-top: 3pt;        font-
  weight:normal; font-family: 'Boogaloo'; font
  -     style:italic;color: #89C236; padding-right: 3pt;
}
.logo .sub {
  vertical-align: super;   font-style:normal;font-size: 16pt;
  font-family: 'Droid Sans';       font-weight:bold; position:
  absolute;   color: #888; margin:-4pt 0 -4pt 0;
}
.logoSmall{
  font-family: 'Droid Sans';       font-size: 16pt; color:
  #888;width:80pt;   font-weight:bold; margin-top:10pt;
  height:20pt; margin-right:30pt;
}
.logoSmall span{
  position:relative;          float:right; margin-top: 3pt;
  font-weight:normal;font-family: 'Boogaloo';   font-
  style:italic;color: #89C236;
}
.logoSmall .sub {
  vertical-align: super;
  font-style:normal;          font-size: 10pt;font-family: 'Droid
  Sans';font-weight:bold;position: absolute; color: #666;
  margin:-2pt 0 -4pt 0;
}
```

4. At this point, after all these changes, restarting Tomcat and calling the same URL `http://localhost:8080/portal/index` resulted in the following state:

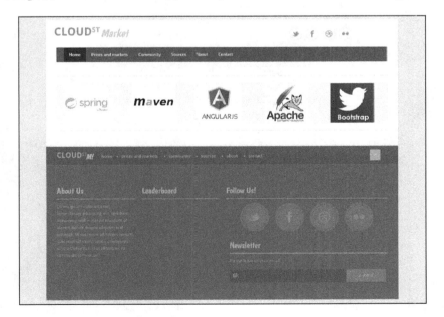

Creating responsive content

We will focus in this section on the changes that have been made to fill the welcome page with responsive content. By responsive, understand that the content will be rendered under a style appropriate for the device size and orientation.

1. In the `index.jsp` file:

    1. The `<div class="row">` has been added the following content:

```
<div class='span12'>
   <div class="hero-unit hidden-phone"><p>Welcome to
   CloudStreet Market, the educational platform.</p></div>
</div>
<div class='span5'>
    <div id='landingGraphContainer'></div>
    <div id='tableMarketPrices'>
      <table class="table table-hover table-condensed
      table-bordered table-striped">
        <thead>
          <tr>
            <th>Index</th>
            <th>Value</th>
            <th>Change</th>
          </tr>
        </thead>
        <tbody>
        <tr>
            <td>Dow Jones-IA</td><td>17,634.74</td>
            <td class='text-success'><b>-
              18.05</b></td>
            </tr>
            ...
            <tr>
              <td>FTSE MIB</td><td>18,965.41</td>
              <td class='text-error'><b>-
                182.86</b></td>
            </tr>
            ...
        </tbody>
        </table>
      </div>
</div>
<div id="containerCommunity" class='span7'>
    <div id="divRss3"></div>
</div>
```

In the previously added *landingGraphContainer*, we have inserted a generated graph that renders the evolution of specific markets during the last opened day. The graph uses the `morris.js` library (`http://morris.s.github.io/morris.js`), which also relies on the `raphael.js` library (`http://raphaeljs.com`).

2. At the bottom of the file, the `<!-- start: Java Script -->` section to the `<!-- end: Java Script -->` section has been added the following content:

```html
<script src="js/jquery-1.8.2.js"></script>
<script src="js/bootstrap.js"></script>
<script src="js/flexslider.js"></script>
<script src="js/carousel.js"></script>
<script def src="js/custom.js"></script>
<script src="js/FeedEk.js"></script>
<script src="js/raphael.js"></script>
<script src="js/morris.min.js"></script>
<script>
$(function () {
    var financial_data = [
      {"period": "08:00", "index": 66},{"period": "09:00",
        "index": 62},
      {"period": "10:00", "index": 61},{"period": "11:00",
        "index": 66},
      {"period": "12:00", "index": 67},{"period": "13:00",
        "index": 68},
      {"period": "14:00", "index": 62},{"period": "15:00",
        "index": 61},
      {"period": "16:00", "index": 61},{"period": "17:00",
        "index": 54}
    ];
    Morris.Line({
      element: 'landingGraphContainer',
      hideHover: 'auto', data: financial_data,
      ymax: 70, ymin: 50,
      pointSize: 3, hideHover:'always',
      xkey: 'period', xLabels: 'month',
      ykeys: ['index'], postUnits: '',
      parseTime: false, labels: ['Index'],
      resize: true, smooth: false,
      lineColors: ['#A52A2A']
    });
});
</script>
```

2. In the `cloudstreetmarket-webapp\src\main\webapp\js` directory, the `morris.min.js` and `raphael.js` libraries have been copied and pasted from their respective websites.

3. Back to the `index.jsp` file:

   1. The previously created `<div id='containerCommunity'>` has been filled with the following content:

```
<div id="divRss3">
  <ul class="feedEkList">
    <li>
    <div class="itemTitle">
      <div class="listUserIco">
        <img src='img/young-        lad.jpg'>
      </div>
      <span class="ico-white ico-up-arrow
      listActionIco        actionBuy"></span>
        <a href="#">happyFace8</a> buys 6 <a
        href="#">NXT.L</a> at $3.00
        <p class="itemDate">15/11/2014 11:12
        AM</p>
    </div>
    </li>
    <li>
    <div class="itemTitle">
      <div class="ico-user listUserIco"></div>
      <span class="ico-white ico-down-arrow
        listActionIco actionSell"></span>
      <a href="#">actionMan9</a> sells 6 <a
    href="#">CCH.L</a> at $12.00
        <p class="itemDate">15/11/2014 10:46        AM</p>
    </div>
    </li>
      . . .
  </ul>
</div>
```

   2. The section here uses the feedEk jQuery plugin. It comes with its own CSS and JavaScript file.

4. The `cloudstreetmarket-webapp\src\main\webapp\js` directory includes the `FeedEk.js` file related to the feedEk jQuery plugin. This plugin can be found online (`http://jquery-plugins.net/FeedEk/FeedEk.html`).

5. The `cloudstreetmarket-webapp\src\main\webapp\css` directory also has the related `FeedEk.css` file.

6. Still in `index.jsp`, under the `<!-- start: CSS -->` comment, the `FeedEk` css document has been added:

```
<link href="css/FeedEk.css" rel="stylesheet">
```

7. In the `style.css` file, before the first media query definition (`@media only screen and (min-width: 960px)`), the following style definitions have been added:

```
.listUserIco {
    background-color:#bbb;
    float:left;
    margin:0 7px 0 0;
}
.listActionIco {
    float:right;
    margin-top:-3px;
}
.actionSell {
    background-color:#FC9030;
}
.actionBuy {
    background-color:#8CDBA0;
}
#landingGraphContainer{
    height:160px;
    padding: 0px 13px 0 10px;
}
.tableMarketPrices{
    padding: 13px 13px 0 15px;
}
```

8. Finally, two new images (profile pictures) have been added to `cloudstreetmarket-webapp\src\main\webapp\img`.

9. Try to dynamically resize a browser window that renders: `http://localhost:8080/ portal/index`. You should observe a responsive and adaptive style as in the following picture:

How it works...

To understand our Bootstrap deployment, we are going to review now how it has been installed as a predesigned theme. We will then discover some key features of the Bootstrap Framework—not only the implemented features because, logically enough, only a few features of the Framework can visually be used on one single page example.

The theme installation

The theme we have obtained is no more than a classical static theme, as you can find thousands of them over the Internet. They are made by web designers and distributed for free or commercially. This one is made with the basic structure of HTML files, a JS directory, a CSS directory, and an IMG directory.

The theme installation is quite straightforward to understand, since we have just placed the JavaScript files, CSS files, and images in their expected locations for our application.

> The Bootstrap core features are self-contained in `bootstrap.js`, `bootstrap.css`, and `bootstrap-responsive.css`. You should not really have to tweak these files directly.

Bootstrap highlights

The implemented theme (FreeME) uses Bootstrap 2. We are going to review a couple of features that have been implemented in the template and for the needs of our project.

Bootstrap scaffolding

The Bootstrap scaffolding helps with designing the HTML structure usually built from a grid model. The Bootstrap strategy on this topic is described in the following sections.

Grid system and responsive design

Bootstrap offers a styleframe to handle a page-specific grid system. The key point is in the default grid-system made up of 12 columns and designed for a 940px wide nonresponsive container.

The Bootstrap responsive features are activated with the use of `<meta name="viewport"...>` tag and with the import of the `boostrap-responsive.css` file. The container width can extend from 724px to 1170px in that case.

> Also, below 767px, the columns become fluid and stack vertically.

These Bootstrap specifications define quite a drastic set of constraints but Bootstrap somehow creates an easy-to-understand design uniformity for its implementations.

In the case of our template, the viewport metatag is the following:

```
<meta name="viewport" content="width=device-width, initial-scale=1,
maximum-scale=1">
```

If you are not familiar with this tag, its main purpose is to define device-specific sizes in the document. From these sizes, rules are defined for orientation-specific and device-specific rendering. These rules that are bound to style definitions are called mediaqueries. You can find an example of a mediaquery in the style.css file:

```
/* Higher than 960 (desktop devices)
==========================================================
============= */
@media only screen and (min-width: 960px) {

. . .

    #footer-menu {
        padding-left: 30px;
        padding-right: 30px;
        margin-left: -30px;
        margin-right: -30px;
    }

. . .

}
```

This media query overrides the style that is specific to the id footer menu only where the device presents a width greater than 960px.

Defining columns

To define columns within the grid system, Bootstrap drives us towards the use of a `row` div tagged as a `row` class element. Then, the idea is to define subdivs marked with custom `span*` class elements where the * characters represents subdivisions of the 12-column grid we have to deal with.

For example, consider the following two possible designs:

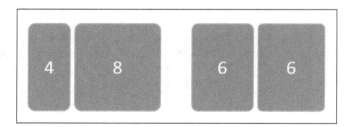

The two columns on the left example can be rendered from the DOM definition:

```
<div class="row">
  <div class="span4">...</div>
  <div class="span8">...</div>
</div>
```

The two columns on the right example can be rendered from the DOM definition:

```
<div class="row">
  <div class="span6">...</div>
  <div class="span6">...</div>
</div>
```

With this in mind, the grid of our welcome page is actually the following:

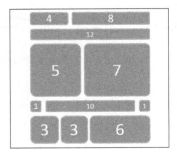

Offsetting and nesting

Offsetting a column allows you to create a fixed-sized decay corresponding to one or more invisible columns. For example, consider the following snippet:

```
<div class="row">
    <div class="span6">...</div>
    <div class="span4 offset2">...</div>
</div>
```

This DOM definition will correspond to the following columns:

A column can also be nested inside another column redefining a new row. The sum of the newly created columns must correspond to the parent's size:

```
<div class="row">
  <div class="span6">
    <div class="row">
      <div class="span2">...</div>
```

```
        <div class="span4">...</div>
      </div>
    </div>
</div>
```

Fluid gridding

We were saying earlier that, with Boostrap2, below 767px *the columns become fluid and stack vertically*. The template gridding can be changed from static to fluid turning `.row` classes to `.row-fluid`. Rather than fixed pixels sized columns, this system will use percentages.

Bootstrap CSS utilities

Bootstrap also provides a few pre-designed elements such as buttons, icons, tables, forms and also utilities to support typography or images.

Uniform Buttons

Default styled buttons can be created from the `<a>` and `<button>` tags with only addition of the `.btn` class element. The created default gray button with a gradient can then be declined in different colour variations. For example, **by default**, the following classes combination:

- ▶ `.btn` `.btn-primary`: This produces an intense ultramarine blue button to identify the primary action among other buttons
- ▶ `.btn` `.btn-info`: This produces a moderate turquoise blue button
- ▶ `.btn` `.btn-success`: This produces a positive green button
- ▶ `.btn` `.btn-warning`: This produces a warning orange button
- ▶ `.btn` `.btn-danger`: This produces a dangerous red button
- ▶ `.btn` `.btn-inverse`: This produces a black button with white text
- ▶ `.btn` `.btn-link`: This produces a link while maintaining a button behavior

These buttons are also resizable declaratively by adding a `.btn-large` class, adding a `.btn-small` class, or adding a `.btn-mini` class:

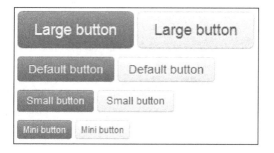

A button can be disabled by adding it as a **disabled** attribute. Similarly, a `<a>` tagged button can be disabled with the addition of a `.disabled` class. We didn't make use of buttons yet, but it is a great feature to be presented at this point.

Icons

Bootstrap 2 comes with an impressive set of 140 dark gray icons available as sprites and provided by Glyphicons:

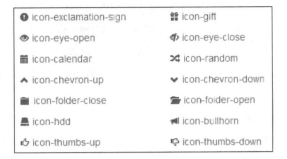

 These icons are normally available commercially but they are also usable for free as part of the Bootstrap product. However Bootstrap asks us to provide an optional backlink to `http://glyphicons.com`.

All these icons can be pulled from the DOM with a simple class within a `<i>` tag such as `<i class="icon-search"></i>`.

The amazing thing is that you can actually embed these icons in every suitable Bootstrap component. For example, the button definition: `<a class="btn btn-mini" href="#"><i class="icon-star"></i> Star</a>`, produces the following:

Tables

We have implemented a Bootstrap table for the market activity overview. We have basically shaped the following table:

```
<table class="table table-hover table-condensed table-bordered
  table-striped">
  <thead>
    <tr><th>Index</th>
        <th>Value</th>
        <th>Change</th></tr>
  </thead>
  <tbody>
      <tr><td>...</td>
        <td>...</td>
        <td>...</td>
    </tr>
  </tbody>
</table>
```

In the same way as we can define a button class overridden with customization classes, we have defined a generic Bootstrap table with the class `.table`, and then we have made use of the following customization classes:

▶ `.table` `.table-hover`: This enables a hover state on table rows within a `<tbody>`

▶ `.table` `.table-condensed`: This makes tables more compact

▶ `.table` `.table-bordered`: This adds borders and rounded corners to the table

▶ `.table` `.table-striped`: This adds zebra-striping to any table row within the `<tbody>`

Bootstrap components

The framework has other pre-designed elements identified as Components. Among them, dropdowns, button groups, breadcrumbs, pagination, Navbars, labels and badges, thumbnails, alerts, progress bars, and so on. Here we only present some of them:

Navbars

The Bootstrap navigation bars provide support for a basic navigation menu. They are not by default fixed to the top of the page; they must be included in a `.container`. The code is as follows:

```
<div class="navbar navbar-inverse">
  <div class="navbar-inner">
  . . .
  <ul class="nav">
    <li class="active"><a href="index">Home</a></li>
    <li><a href="markets">Prices and markets</a></li>
    <li><a href="community">Community</a></li>
    <li><a href="sources">Sources</a></li>
    <li><a href="about">About</a></li>
    <li><a href="contact">Contact</a></li>
  </ul>
. . .
```

The most basic feature in the navbar is the activable link:

The example above can be designed from the following DOM definition:

```
<ul class="nav">
    <li class="active"><a href="#">Home</a></li>
    <li><a href="#">Link</a></li>
</ul>
```

We strongly recommend reading the Bootstrap documentation. More details can be found on how to implement other features. For example, Bootstrap provides tools for:

- Form elements such as input texts, search fields, and submit buttons.
- Different positioning variations such as fixed-to-top (with `.navbar-fixed-top`), fixed-to-bottom (with `.navbar-fixed-bottom`), at the opposite of the full-width navbar that scrolls away with the page (with `.navbar-static-top`).
- Collapsible responsive navbars (`.nav-collapse.collapse`) that allow significant space savings. With the use of the data-toggle HTML5 attribute, dynamic handling is performed with no extra JavaScript configuration.

Hero units

There was a hero unit defined in the provided template. We've just moved it a bit to suit our responsive needs.

It is a lightweight, flexible component to showcase key content on your site.

> *Welcome to CloudStreet Market, the educational platform.*

The example above can be designed from the following DOM definition:

```
<div class="hero-unit"><p>Welcome to CloudStreet Market, the
educational platform.</p></div>
```

Alerts

Bootstrap alerts are great to quickly generate a predefined style for a warning message or another contextual message. A Bootstrap alert comes with an **optional** dismiss button (which will hide the alert with no extraJavaScript configuration). The code is as follows:

```
<div class="alert">
    <button type="button" class="close" data-dismiss="alert">&times;</
    button>
    <strong>Warning!</strong> Best check yo self, you're not looking
    too good.
</div>
```

This definition produces the output presented here:

> Warning! Best check yo self, you're not looking too good   ✕

An Alert is defined with the class `.alert` on a `<div>` tag, from which contextual color variations can be set up, providing extra overriding classes such as `.alert-success`, `.alert-info`, or `.alert-error`.

Badges and labels

Bootstrap labels are very nice for enriching content. They render particularly well in list or in tables. Find here an overview of the possible contextual variations:

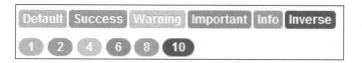

The labels here would be defined with:

```
<span class="label">Default</span>
<span class="label label-success">Success</span>
<span class="label label-important">Important</span>
...
```

The badges would be defined with:

```
<span class="badge">1</span>
<span class="badge badge-warning">4</span>
<span class="badge badge-important">6</span>
...
```

There's more...

There is much more to Bootstrap than this *tiny* overview for enriching official documentation. Again, the official documentation is very well done and very comprehensible.

Visit `http://getbootstrap.com` for the documentation related to the latest supported version of the framework. Go to `http://getbootstrap.com/2.3.2` for the documentation related to the version we use in our project.

We will implement more features in the coming chapters and care will be taken to highlight them wherever possible.

See also

If you like Bootstrap and feel you want to use it in your projects, you must consider Version 3.

 Bootstrap 3 is not directly retro-compatible with Bootstrap 2 but it implements a very similar gridding system and slightly different markups.

  ▸ **Bootstrap 3 new features**: Here's a preview of important changes from Bootstrap 2 to Bootstrap 3.

▸ **New flat-styled design**: The new design is easily noticeable with the end of 3D and textures on buttons, navbars and other menus. They have now gone for a new flat style with no gradients. It certainly goes along with the actual global design trend.

▸ **Column naming span* renamed to col-***: In addition to the row-fluid class that is no longer available as such (all rows are now fluid automatically) for less confusion, the column naming pattern has been rethought for more consistency.

▸ **Mobile-first**: The responsive features of the framework are now natively included in the `bootstrap.js` and `bootstrap.css` files (there is no more `bootstrap-responsive.js` or `bootstrap-responsive.css`). It is now possible to drive media-query duties directly from the DOM using a set of new device-specific classes.

Displaying a model in the View, using the JSTL

This recipe shows how to populate the Spring MVC View with data and how to render this data within the View.

Getting ready

At this point, we don't have any real data to be displayed in our View. For this purpose, we have created three DTOs and two service layers that are injected from the r Interface into the controller.

There are two dummy service implementations that are designed to produce a fake set of data. We will use the **Java Server Tags Library** (**JSTL**) and the **JSP Expression Language** (**JSP EL**) to render the server data in the right places in our JSP.

How to do it...

1. After checking out the `v2.x.x` branch (in the previous recipe), a couple of new components are now showing-up in the **cloudstreetmarket-core** module: two interfaces, two implementations, one enum, and three DTOs. The code is as follows:

```
public interface IMarketService {
  DailyMarketActivityDTO getLastDayMarketActivity(String
    string);
  List<MarketOverviewDTO> getLastDayMarketsOverview();
}
    public interface ICommunityService {
    List<UserActivityDTO> getLastUserPublicActivity(int
      number);
}
```

As you can see they refer to the three created DTOs:

```
public class DailyMarketActivityDTO {
  String marketShortName;
  String marketId;
  Map<String, BigDecimal> values;
  Date dateSnapshot;
  ... //and constructors, getters and setters
}
public class MarketOverviewDTO {
  private String marketShortName;
  private String marketId;
  private BigDecimal latestValue;
  private BigDecimal latestChange;
  ... //and constructors, getters and setters
}
public class UserActivityDTO {
  private String userName;
  private String urlProfilePicture;
  private Action userAction;
  private String valueShortId;
  private int amount;
  private BigDecimal price;
  private Date date;
  ... //and constructors, getters and setters
}
```

This last DTO refers to the `Action` enum:

```
public enum Action {
  BUY("buys"), SELL("sells");
  private String presentTense;
    Action(String present){
  presentTense = present;
  }
    public String getPresentTense(){
    return presentTense;
  }
}
```

Also, the previously created `DefaultController` in `cloudstreetmarket-webapp` has been altered to look like:

```
@Controller
public class DefaultController {
  @Autowired
  private IMarketService marketService;
```

```
@Autowired
private ICommunityService communityService;
@RequestMapping(value="/*",
method={RequestMethod.GET,RequestMethod.HEAD})
public String fallback(Model model) {
  model.addAttribute("dailyMarketActivity",
    marketService.getLastDayMarketActivity("GDAXI"));
  model.addAttribute("dailyMarketsActivity",
    marketService.getLastDayMarketsOverview());
  model.addAttribute("recentUserActivity",
    communityService.getLastUserPublicActivity(10));
  return "index";
  }
}
```

And there are the two dummy implementations:

```
@Service
public class DummyMarketServiceImpl implements
  IMarketService {
    private DateTimeFormatter formatter =
    DateTimeFormatter.ofPattern("yyyy-MM-dd HH:mm");
    public DailyMarketActivityDTO
    getLastDayMarketActivity(String string){
    Map<String, BigDecimal> map = new HashMap<>();
    map.put("08:00", new BigDecimal(9523));
    map.put("08:30", new BigDecimal(9556));
    ...
    map.put("18:30", new BigDecimal(9758));
    LocalDateTime ldt = LocalDateTime.parse("2015-04-10
        17:00", formatter);
    return new DailyMarketActivityDTO("DAX 30","GDAXI",
      map, Date.from(ldt.toInstant(ZoneOffset.UTC)));
  }
    @Override
  public List<MarketOverviewDTO>
    getLastDayMarketsOverview() {
      List<MarketOverviewDTO> result = Arrays.asList(
      new MarketOverviewDTO("Dow Jones-IA", "DJI", new
        BigDecimal(17810.06), new BigDecimal(0.0051)),
      ...
      new MarketOverviewDTO("CAC 40", "FCHI", new
        BigDecimal(4347.23), new BigDecimal(0.0267))
    );
    return result;
  }
```

```
}
  @Service
public class DummyCommunityServiceImpl implements
    ICommunityService {
  private DateTimeFormatter formatter =
  DateTimeFormatter.ofPattern("yyyy-MM-dd HH:mm");
    public List<UserActivityDTO>
    getLastUserPublicActivity(int number){
      List<UserActivityDTO> result = Arrays.asList(
      new UserActivityDTO("happyFace8", "img/young-
        lad.jpg", Action.BUY, "NXT.L", 6, new
        BigDecimal(3), LocalDateTime.parse("2015-04-10
        11:12", formatter)),

      ...
       new UserActivityDTO("userB", null, Action.BUY,
         "AAL.L", 7, new BigDecimal(7),
         LocalDateTime.parse("2015-04-10 13:29",
         formatter))
      );
    return result;
  }
}
```

The index.jsp has been altered with the addition of the following section below the graph container:

```
<div class='morrisTitle'>
  <fmt:formatDate
    value="${dailyMarketActivity.dateSnapshot}"
    pattern="yyyy-MM-dd"/>
</div>
<select class="form-control centeredElementBox">
  <option value="${dailyMarketActivity.marketId}">
    ${dailyMarketActivity.marketShortName}
  </option>
</select>
```

The market overview table, especially the body, has been added:

```
<c:forEach var="market" items="${dailyMarketsActivity}">
  <tr>
    <td>${market.marketShortName}</td>
    <td style='text-align: right'>
      <fmt:formatNumber type="number" maxFractionDigits="3"
        value="${market.latestValue}"/>
    </td>
     <c:choose>
        <c:when test="${market.latestChange >= 0}">
```

```
          <c:set var="textStyle" scope="page" value="text-success"/>
        </c:when>
        <c:otherwise>
          <c:set var="textStyle" scope="page"
            value="text-error"/>
        </c:otherwise>
      </c:choose>
        <td class='${textStyle}' style='text-align: right'>
          <b><fmt:formatNumber type="percent" maxFractionDigits="2"
          value="${market.latestChange}"/>
      </b>
    </td>
    </tr>
</c:forEach>
```

The container for the community activity has been added:

```
<c:forEach var="activity" items="${recentUserActivity}">
    <c:choose>
        <c:when test="${activity.userAction == 'BUY'}">
          <c:set var="icoUpDown" scope="page" value="ico-up-arrow
            actionBuy"/>
        </c:when>
        <c:otherwise>
          <c:set var="icoUpDown" scope="page" value="ico-down- arrow
            actionSell"/>
        </c:otherwise>
      </c:choose>
      <c:set var="defaultProfileImage" scope="page" value=""/>
      <c:if test="${activity.urlProfilePicture == null}">
      <c:set var="defaultProfileImage" scope="page"
        value="ico-user"/>
      </c:if>
    <li>
    <div class="itemTitle">
      <div class="listUserIco ${defaultProfileImage}">
        <c:if test="${activity.urlProfilePicture !=    null}">
        <img src='${activity.urlProfilePicture}'>
</c:if>
</div>
  <span class="ico-white ${icoUpDown}
    listActionIco"></span>
<a href="#">${activity.userName}</a>
${activity.userAction.presentTense} ${activity.amount}
  <a href="#">${activity.valueShortId}</a>
  at $${activity.price}
```

```
      <p class="itemDate">
        <fmt:formatDate value="${activity.date}" pattern="dd/MM/yyyy
        hh:mm aaa"/>
      </p>
      </div>
    </li>
</c:forEach>
```

At the bottom of the file, a hardcoded set of JavaScript data is now populated from the server:

```
<script>
  var financial_data = [];
  <c:forEach var="dailySnapshot"
    items="${dailyMarketActivity.values}">
  financial_data.push({"period": '<c:out
    value="${dailySnapshot.key}"/>', "index": <c:out
    value='${dailySnapshot.value}'/>});
  </c:forEach>
</script>
<script>
  $(function () {
    Morris.Line({
      element: 'landingGraphContainer',
      hideHover: 'auto', data: financial_data,
      ymax: <c:out
        value="${dailyMarketActivity.maxValue}"/>,
      ymin: <c:out
        value="${dailyMarketActivity.minValue}"/>,
      pointSize: 3, hideHover:'always',
      xkey: 'period', xLabels: 'month',
      ykeys: ['index'], postUnits: '',
      parseTime: false, labels: ['Index'],
      resize: true, smooth: false,
      lineColors: ['#A52A2A']
    });
  });
</script>
```

How it works...

These changes don't produce fundamental UI improvements but they shape the data supply for our View layer.

The approach to handle our data

We are going to review here the server side of the data-supply implementation.

Injection of services via interfaces

Forecasting application needs to feed the frontpage in dynamic data, the choice has been made to inject two service layers `marketService` and `communityService` into the controller. The problem was that we don't yet have a proper Data Access layer. (This will be covered in *Chapter 4, Building a REST API for a Stateless Architecture*!). We need the controller to be wired to render the front page though.

Wiring the controller needs to be loosely coupled to its service layers. With the idea of creating dummy Service implementations in this chapter, the wiring has been designed using interfaces. We then rely on Spring to inject the expected implementations in the service dependencies, typed with the relevant Interfaces.

```
@Autowired
private IMarketService marketService;
@Autowired
private ICommunityService communityService;
```

Note the types `IMarketService` and `ICommunityService`, which are not `DummyCommunityServiceImpl` nor `DummyMarketServiceImpl`. Otherwise, we would be tied to these types when switching to real implementations.

How does Spring choose the dummy implementations?

It chooses these implementations in the **cloudstreetmarket-core** Spring context file: `csmcore-config.xml`. We have defined the beans earlier:

```
<context:annotation-config/>
<context:component-scan base-package="edu.zipcloud.cloudstreetmarket.
core" />
```

Spring scans all the types matching the root package `edu.zipcloud. cloudstreetmarket.core` to find stereotypes and configuration annotations.

In the same way that `DefaultController` is marked with the `@Controller` annotation, our two dummy implementation classes are marked with `@Service`, which is a Spring Stereotype. Among the detected stereotypes and beans, the dummy implementations are the only ones available for the injection configuration:

```
@Autowired
private IMarketService marketService;

@Autowired
private ICommunityService communityService;
```

With only one respective match per field, Spring picks them up without any extra-configuration.

DTOs to be used in View layer

We have made use of DTOs for the variables fetched in our JSPs. Exposed DTOs can be particularly useful in web services when it comes to maintaining several versions simultaneously. More generally, DTOs are implemented when the target and destination objects differ significantly.

We will implement **Entities** later. It is better not to make use of these **Entities** in the rendering or version-specific logic, but instead defer them to a layer dedicated to this purpose.

Although, it must be specified that creating a DTO layer produces a fair amount of boilerplate code related to type conversion (impacting both sides, other layers, tests, and so on).

Dummy service implementations

The `DummyMarketServiceImpl` implementation with the `getLastDayMarketActivity` method builds an activity map (made of static daily times associated to values for the market, the index). It returns a new `DailyMarketActivityDTO` instance (built from this map), it is in the end a wrapper carrying the daily activity for one single market or Index such as DAX 30.

The `getLastDayMarketsOverview` method returns a list of `MarketOverviewDTOs` also constructed from hardcoded data. It emulates an overview of daily activities for a couple of markets (indices).

The `DummyCommunityServiceImpl` implementation with its `getLastUserPublicActivity` method returns a list of instantiated `UserActivityDTO`, which simulates the last six logged user activities.

Populating the Model in the controller

Presenting the possible method-handler arguments in the first recipe of this chapter, we have seen that it can be injected-as-argument a Model. This Model can be populated with data within the method and it will be transparently passed to the expected View.

That is what we have done in the `fallback` method-handler. We have passed the three results from the Service layers into three variables `dailyMarketActivity`, `dailyMarketsActivity`, and `recentUserActivity` so they can be available in the View.

Rendering variables with the JSP EL

The JSP Expression Language allows us to access application data stored in **JavaBeans components**. The notation `${...}` used to access variables such as `${recentUserActivity}` or `${dailyMarketActivity.marketShortName}` is typically a JSP EL notation.

An important point to remember when we want to access the attributes of an object (like `marketShortName` for `dailyMarketActivity`) is that the object class must offer JavaBeans standard getters for the targeted attributes.

In other words, `dailyMarketActivity.marketShortName` refers in the `MarketOverviewDTO` class to an expected:

```
public String getMarketShortName() {
    return marketShortName;
}
```

Implicit objects

The JSP EL also offers implicit objects, usable as shortcuts in the JSP without any declaration or prepopulation in the model. Among these implicit objects, the different scopes pageScope, requestScope, sessionScope, and applicationScope reflect maps of attributes in the related scope.

For example, consider the following attributes:

```
request.setAttribute("currentMarket", "DAX 30");
request.getSession().setAttribute("userName", "UserA");
request.getServletContext().setAttribute("applicationState", "FINE");
```

These could respectively be accessed in the JSP with:

```
${requestScope["currentMarket"]}
${sessionScope["username"]}
${applicationScope["applicationState"]}
```

Other useful implicit objects are the map of request headers: `header` (that is, `${header["Accept-Encoding"]}`), the map of request cookies: `cookies` (that is, `${cookie["SESSIONID"].value}`), the map of request parameters: `param` (that is, `${param["paramName"]}`) or the map of context initialization parameters (from `web.xml`) `initParam` (that is, `${initParam["ApplicationID"]}`).

Finally, the JSP EL provides a couple of basic operators:

- **Arithmetic**: +, - (binary), *, / and `div`, % and `mod`, - (unary).
- **Logical**: and, &&, or, ||, not, !
- **Relational**: ==, eq, !=, ne, <, lt, >, gt, <=, ge, >=, le.

Comparisons can be made against other values, or against Boolean, String, integer, or floating point literals.

- **Empty**: The empty operator is a prefix operation that can be used to determine whether a value is null or empty.
- **Conditional**: A ? B : C.

Evaluate B or C, depending on the result of the evaluation of A.

This description of operators comes from the JavaEE 5 tutorial.

Rendering variables with the JSTL

The **JSP Standard Tag Library** (**JSTL**) is a collection of tools for JSP pages. It is not really a brand new feature of Java web but it is still used.

The tags the most used are probably Core and I18N when we need a display logic, or when we need to format data or to build a hierarchy in the View layer.

Area	Function	Tags	Description
Core	Variable support	`c:set` `c:remove`	Set/unset a variable from a scope.

	Flow control	`c:choose`
		`c:when`
		`c:otherwise`
			Implements a conditional block IF/THEN/ELSE.

		`c:if`	Implements a conditional IF block.
		`c:forEach`	Iterates over collection types.
		`c:forTokens`	Iterates over tokens, separated by provided delimiters.
	URL management	`c:import` `c:param`	Resolves a URL, imports its content into a page, a variable (var) or a variable reader (varReader). Can pass parameters to the underlying resource with param.
		`c:redirect` `c:param`	Redirects to a URL. Can pass parameters.
		`c:url` `c:param`	Creates a URL. Can assign parameters.
	Miscellaneous	`c:catch`	Catches any throwable that happens in its block.
		`c:out`	Fetches an expression or a variable.

I18N	Setting Locale	`fmt:setLocale`	Stores a Locale in a specific scope.
		`fmt:requestEncoding`	Sets the Encoding type for the HTTP requests of the page.
	Messaging	`fmt:bundle` `fmt:message` `fmt:param` `fmt:setBundle`	Sets bundles for a specific tag or scope. Retreives a message, output its content, pass optional parameters.
	Number and Date Formatting	`fmt:formatNumber` `fmt:formatDate` `fmt:parseDate` `fmt:parseNumber` `fmt:setTimeZone` `fmt:timeZone`	Outputs different contents in different formats. Parse dates and number. Sets timezone for a specific tag or scope.

These presented tags are not the only capabilities of the JSTL, visit the Java EE tutorial for more details:

http://docs.oracle.com/javaee/5/tutorial/doc/bnakc.html

Taglib directives in JSPs

If we plan to make use of one or the other of the above tags, we first need to include the suited directive(s) in the JSP page:

```
<%@ taglib uri="http://java.sun.com/jsp/jstl/core" prefix="c" %>
<%@ taglib uri="http://java.sun.com/jsp/jstl/fmt" prefix="fmt" %>
```

There's more...

More about JSP EL

There is more features covered by the JSP EL. Feel free to read the Oracle tutorials such as http://docs.oracle.com/javaee/5/tutorial/doc/bnahq.html.

More about the JavaBeans standard

We have talked about the expected JavaBean standard when using the JSP EL. More information about JavaBeans can be found in the Oracle tutorial again:

`http://docs.oracle.com/javaee/5/tutorial/doc/bnair.html`

More about the JSTL

As announced, you can discover more modules of the JSTL on the Java EE tutorial:

`http://docs.oracle.com/javaee/5/tutorial/doc/bnakc.html`

Defining a common WebContentInterceptor

In this recipe, we will highlight how we have implemented a `WebContentInterceptor` superclass for Controllers.

Getting ready

We are about to present a Controller superclass having the specificity of being registered as a `WebContentInterceptor`. This superclass allows us to globally control sessions and to manage caching options.

It will help us understanding the request lifecycle throughout the Framework and through other potential interceptors.

How to do it...

1. Registering a default `WebContentInterceptor` with its specific configuration can be done entirely with the configuration approach:

```
<mvc:interceptors>
  <bean id="webContentInterceptor"
  class="org.sfw.web.servlet.mvc.WebContentInterc     eptor">
    <property name="cacheSeconds" value="0"/>
    <property name="requireSession" value="false"/>
    ...
  </bean>
<mvc:interceptors>
```

 In our application, we have registered custom `WebContentInterceptors` to override the behaviors of the default one.

2. In the codebase, still from the previously checked-out v2.x.x branch, a new cloudstreetApiWCI class can be found in cloudstreetmarket-api:

```java
public class CloudstreetApiWCI extends
  WebContentInterceptor {
  public CloudstreetApiWCI(){
    setRequireSession(false);
    setCacheSeconds(0);
  }
  @Override
  public boolean preHandle(HttpServletRequest request,
    HttpServletResponse response, Object handler) throws
    ServletException {
      super.preHandle(request, response, handler);
      return true;
  }
  @Override
  public void postHandle(HttpServletRequest request,
    HttpServletResponse response, Object handler,     ModelAndView
    modelAndView) throws Exception {
  }
  @Override
  public void afterCompletion(HttpServletRequest request,
    HttpServletResponse response, Object handler, Exception
    ex) throws Exception {
  }
}
```

3. A similar CloudstreetWebAppWCI is also present in **cloudstreetmarket-webapp**:

```java
public class CloudstreetWebAppWCI extends
  WebContentInterceptor {
  public CloudstreetWebAppWCI(){
    setRequireSession(false);
    setCacheSeconds(120);
    setSupportedMethods("GET","POST", "OPTIONS", "HEAD");
  }
  @Override
  public boolean preHandle(HttpServletRequest request,
    HttpServletResponse  response, Object handler) throws
    ServletException {
      super.preHandle(request, response, handler);
      return true;
  }
  @Override
  public void postHandle(HttpServletRequest request,
    HttpServletResponse response, Object handler,
    ModelAndView    modelAndView) throws Exception {
```

```
    }
    @Override
    public void afterCompletion(HttpServletRequest request,
    HttpServletResponse response, Object handler, Exception
ex) throws Exception {
    }
}
```

4. In **cloudstreetmarket-webapp**, `DefaultController` and `InfoTagController` now both inherit `CloudstreetWebAppWCI`:

```
public class InfoTagController extends CloudstreetWebAppWCI {
...
}
public class DefaultController extends CloudstreetWebAppWCI {
...
}
```

5. In **cloudstreetmarket-webapp** the `dispatcher-context.xml` context file registers the interceptor:

```
<mvc:interceptors>
    <bean        class="edu.zc...controllers.CloudstreetWebAppWCI">
        <property name="cacheMappings">
          <props>
            <prop key="/**/*.js">86400</prop>
            <prop key="/**/*.css">86400</prop>
            <prop key="/**/*.png">86400</prop>
            <prop key="/**/*.jpg">86400</prop>
          </props>
        </property>
    </bean>
</mvc:interceptors>
```

6. In the **cloudstreetmarket-api**, `dispatcher-context.xml`, the other interceptor has also been registered:

```
<mvc:interceptors>
    <bean class="edu.zc...controllers.CloudstreetApiWCI"/>
</mvc:interceptors>
```

7. Finally, in both `dispatcher-context.xml`, the `RequestMappingHandlerAdapter` bean has been given the `synchronizeOnSession` property:

```
<bean
class="org.sfw...annotation.RequestMappingHandlerAdapter">
    <property name="synchronizeOnSession" value="true"/>
    </bean>
```

How it works...

In each web module, we have created a superclass for Controllers. In the **cloudstreetmarket-webapp** module for example, both `InfoTagController` and `DefaultController` now inherit the `CloudstreetWebAppWCI` superclass.

Common behaviors for Controllers

Beyond the `WebContentInterceptor` capabilities, it is more than a good practice to share common logic and attributes between controllers if they relate to configuration (application or business); the idea is to avoid creating another service layer. We will see with further implementations that it is a good place for defining user contexts.

A `WebContentInterceptor` through its `WebContentGenerator` superclass offers useful request and session management tools that we are going to present now. As an interceptor, it must be registered declaratively. This is the reason why we have added two `<mvc:interceptors>` entries in our context files.

Global session control

A `WebContentInterceptor`, handling requests provides the ability to control how the application should react with HTTP sessions.

Requiring sessions

The `WebContentInterceptor` through `WebContentGenerator` offers the `setRequireSession(boolean)` method. This allows defining whether or not a session should be required when handling a request.

If there is no session bound to the request (if the session has expired for example), the controller will throw a `SessionRequiredException` method. In such cases, it is good to have a global `ExceptionHandler` defined. We will set up a global exception mapper when we will build the REST API. By default, the sessions are not required.

Synchronizing sessions

Another interesting feature comes with the `synchronizeOnSession` property that we have set to true in the `RequestMappingHandlerAdapter` definition. When set it to true, the session object is serialized and access to it is made in a synchronized block. This allows concurrent access to identical sessions and avoids issues that sometimes occur when using multiple browser windows or tabs.

Cache-header management

With the `setCacheSeconds(int)` method that we have used in the constructors of `CloudstreetWebAppWCI` and `CloudstreetApiWCI`; the `WebContentInterceptor` with `WebContentGenerator` can manage a couple of HTTP response headers related to caching.

Set to zero, it adds the extra headers in the response such as Pragma, Expires, Cache-control, and so on.

We have also defined custom caching for static files at the configuration level:

```
<props>
  <prop key="/**/*.js">86400</prop>
  <prop key="/**/*.css">86400</prop>
  <prop key="/**/*.png">86400</prop>
  <prop key="/**/*.jpg">86400</prop>
</props>
```

All our static resources are cached in this way for 24 hours, thanks to the native `WebContentInterceptor.preHandle` method.

HTTP method support

We have also defined a high-level restriction for HTTP methods. It can be narrowed down by the `@RequestMapping` method attribute at the Controller level. Accessing a disallowed method will result in `405 HTTP error: Method not supported`.

A high-level interceptor

In the Interceptor registration in `dispatcher-context.xml`, we haven't defined a path mapping for the interceptor to operate on. It is because by default Spring applies the double wildcard operator `/**` on such standalone interceptor definitions.

It is not because we have made `DefaultController`, extending an interceptor, that the interceptor is acting on the Controller `@RequestMapping` path. The interceptor's registration is only made through configuration. If the covered path mapping needs to be modified, we could override our registration in the following way:

```
<mvc:interceptors>
  <mvc:interceptor>
  <mvc:mapping path="/**"/>
  <bean class="edu.zc.csm.portal...CloudstreetWebAppWCI">
  <property name="cacheMappings">
    <props>
    <prop key="/**/*.js">86400</prop>
    <prop key="/**/*.css">86400</prop>
    <prop key="/**/*.png">86400</prop>
    <prop key="/**/*.jpg">86400</prop>
    </props>
  </property>
  </bean>
  </mvc:interceptor>
</mvc:interceptors>
```

We have also overridden the `WebContentInterceptor` method's `preHandle`, `pcstHandle`, and `afterCompletion`. It will allow us later to define common business related operations before and after the Controller request handling.

Request lifecycle

Throughout the interceptor(s), each request is processed according to the following lifecycle:

- ▸ Prepare the request's context
- ▸ Locate the Controller's handler
- ▸ Execute interceptor's preHandle methods
- ▸ Invoke the Controller's handler
- ▸ Execute interceptor's postHandle methods
- ▸ Handle the Exceptions
- ▸ Process the View
- ▸ Execute interceptor's afterCompletion methods

To better understand the sequence, especially when Exceptions occur, the following workflow is very useful:

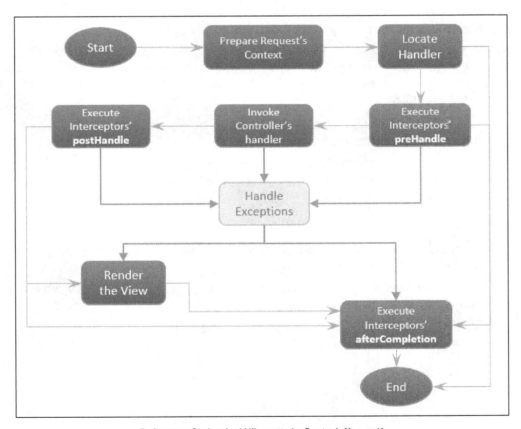

Reference: Spring And Hibernate by Santosh Kumar K.

From this diagram, you can see that:

▸ The controller handler is invoked, unless one of the interceptors' `preHandle` methods throws an exception.

▸ An interceptor's `postHandle` method is called when the controller's handler finishes without throwing an exception and if no preceding `postHandler` method has thrown an exception.

▸ An interceptor's `afterCompletion` is always called, unless a preceding `afterCompletion` throws an exception.

Obviously, if no Interceptor is registered, the same sequence applies, skipping the interceptors' steps.

There is more...

There is more to say about the `WebContentGenerator` class.

More features offered by WebContentGenerator

Again, `WebContentGenerator` is a superclass of `WebContentInterceptor`. From its JavaDoc page: `http://docs.spring.io/spring/docs/current/javadoc-api/org/springframework/web/servlet/support/WebContentGenerator.html` you can find the following for example:

▸ Three constants (String) `METHOD_GET`, `METHOD_POST`, and `METHOD_HEAD` refer to the values `GET`, `POST`, and `HEAD`

▸ Some caching specific methods such as `setUseExpiresHeader`, `setUseCacheControlHeader`, `setUseCacheControlNoStore`, `setAlwaysMustRevalidate`, and `preventCaching`

Also, with `WebApplicationObjectSupport`, `WebContentGenerator` provides:

▸ Access to `ServletContext` out of the request or response object through `getServletContext()`.

▸ Access to the temporary directory for the current web application, as provided by the servlet container through `getTempDir()`.

▸ Access to the `WebApplicationContext` through `getWebApplicationContext()`.

▶ Also, a couple of tools to set and initialize the `ServletContext` and the `WebApplicationContext`, even if these tools are initially intended for use within the Framework itself.

See also...

We quickly passed through web caching. There are a lot of customizations and standards in this domain. Also, a new `RequestMappingHandlerAdapter` has been created with Spring MVC 3.1. It will be helpful to understand the change.

Web caching

Find out more about web caching through this very complete caching tutorial:

```
https://www.mnot.net/cache_docs
```

New support classes for @RequestMapping since Spring MVC 3.1

We have used the `RequestMappingHandlerAdapter` with its bean definition in `dispatcher-context.xml`. This bean is a new feature with Spring MVC 3.1 and has replaced the former `AnnotationMethodHandlerAdapter`. Also, the support class `DefaultAnnotationHandlerMapping` has now been replaced by `RequestMappingHandlerMapping`.

We will go deeper into `RequestMappingHandlerAdapter` in *Chapter 4, Building a REST API for a Stateless Architecture*.

In the meantime, you can read the official change note:

```
http://docs.spring.io/spring-framework/docs/3.1.x/spring-framework-
reference/html/mvc.html#mvc-ann-requestmapping-31-vs-30
```

Designing a client-side MVC pattern with AngularJS

This recipe explains the installation and the configuration of AngularJS to manage a single-page web application.

Getting ready

In this recipe, we explain how we got rid of the rendering logic introduced previously in the JSPs to build the DOM. We will now rely on AngularJS for this job.

Even if we don't have yet a REST API that our frontend could query, we will temporarily make the JSP build the needed JavaScript objects as if they were provided by the API.

AngularJS is an open source Web application Framework. It provides support for building single-page applications that can directly accommodate microservice architecture requirements. The first version of AngularJS was released in 2009. It is now maintained by Google and an open source community.

AngularJS is a whole topic in itself. As a Framework, it's deep and wide at the same time. Trying to present it as a whole would take us beyond the scope of this book and wouldn't really suit our approach.

For this reason, we are going to highlight details, features, and characteristics of the Framework that we can use to our advantage for the application.

How to do it...

Setting up the DOM and creating modules

1. Still from the previously checked-out `v2.x.x` branch, the `index.jsp` file has been added an Angular directive to the HTML tag:

```
<HTML ng-app="cloudStreetMarketApp">
```

2. The AngularJS JavaScript library (angular.min.js from `https://angularjs.org`) has been placed in the `cloudstreetmarket-webapp/src/main/webapp/js` directory.

The `index.jsp` file has been added a wrapper `landingGraphContainerAndTools` div around `landingGraphContainer`, a select box and an `ng-controller="homeFinancialGraphController"`:

```
<div id='landingGraphContainer' ng-
  controller="homeFinancialGraphController">
    <select class="form-control centeredElementBox">
      <option value="${dailyMarketActivity.marketId}">
      ${dailyMarketActivity.marketShortName}</option>
    </select>
  </div>
```

The whole tableMarketPrices div has been reshaped in the following way:

```
<div id='tableMarketPrices'>
    <script>
      var dailyMarketsActivity = [];
      var market;
    </script>
    <c:forEach var="market"
      items="${dailyMarketsActivity}">
      <script>
```

```
        market = {};
        market.marketShortName = '${market.marketShortName}';
        market.latestValue =
          (${market.latestValue}).toFixed(2);
        market.latestChange =
          (${market.latestChange}*100).toFixed(2);
        dailyMarketsActivity.push(market);
      </script>
      </c:forEach>
  <div>
  <table class="table table-hover table-condensed table-
    bordered table-striped" data-ng-
    controller='homeFinancialTableController'>
      <thead>
        <tr>
          <th>Index</th>
          <th>Value</th>
          <th>Change</th>
        </tr>
      </thead>
      <tbody>
          <tr data-ng-repeat="value in financialMarkets">
          <td>{{value.marketShortName}}</td>
          <td style="text-
            align:right">{{value.latestValue}}</td>
          <td class='{{value.style}}' style="text-
          align:right">
          <strong>{{value.latestChange}}%</strong>
          </td>
        </tr>
      </tbody>
      </table>
      </div>
  </div>
```

Then, the `<div id="divRss3">` div has received significant refactoring:

```
<div id="divRss3">
  <ul class="feedEkList" data-ng-
    controller='homeCommunityActivityController'>
    <script>
      var userActivities = [];
      var userActivity;
     </script>
      <c:forEach var="activity"
        items="${recentUserActivity}">
```

```
      <script>
        userActivity = {};
        userActivity.userAction = '
         ${activity.userAction}';
         userActivity.urlProfilePicture =
            '${activity.urlProfilePicture}';
            userActivity.userName = '${activity.userName}';
            userActivity.urlProfilePicture =
               '${activity.urlProfilePicture}';
        userActivity.date = '<fmt:formatDate
          ="${activity.date}"
          pattern="dd/MM/yyyy hh:mm aaa"/>';
        userActivity.userActionPresentTense =
           '${activity.userAction.presentTense}';
        userActivity.amount = ${activity.amount};
        userActivity.valueShortId =
           '${activity.valueShortId}';
        userActivity.price =
           (${activity.price}).toFixed(2);
        userActivities.push(userActivity);
      </script>
       </c:forEach>
    <li data-ng-repeat="value in communityActivities">
    <div class="itemTitle">
    <div class="listUserIco
      {{value.defaultProfileImage}}">
      <img ng-if="value.urlProfilePicture"
        src='{{value.urlProfilePicture}}'>
    </div>
    <span class="ico-white {{value.iconDirection}}
      listActionIco"></span>
      <a href="#">{{value.userName}}</a>
      {{value.userActionPresentTense}} {{value.amount}}
      <a href="#">{{value.valueShortId}}</a> at
        {{value.price}}
      <p class="itemDate">{{value.date}}</p>
      </div>
    </li>
  </ul>
</div>
```

The graph generation section has disappeared, and it is now replaced with:

```
<script>
  var cloudStreetMarketApp =
    angular.module('cloudStreetMarketApp', []);
  var tmpYmax = <c:out
```

```
    value="${dailyMarketActivity.maxValue}"/>;
  var tmpYmin = <c:out
    value="${dailyMarketActivity.minValue}"/>;
</script>
```

This graph generation has been externalized in one of the three custom JavaScript files, included with the declarations:

```
<script src="js/angular.min.js"></script>

<script src="js/home_financial_graph.js"></script>
<script src="js/home_financial_table.js"></script>
<script src="js/home_community_activity.js"></script>
```

We are going to see those three custom JavaScript files next.

Defining the module's components

1. As introduced, three custom JavaScript files are located in the `cloudstreetmarket-webapp/src/main/webapp/js` directory.

2. The first one, `home_financial_graph.js`, relates to the graph. It creates a factory whose ultimate role is to pull and provide data:

```
cloudStreetMarketApp.factory("financialDataFactory",
  function () {
    return {
       getData: function (market) {
         return financial_data;
       },
       getMax: function (market) {
         return tmpYmax;
       },
       getMin: function (market) {
         return tmpYmin;
       }
    }
});
```

This same file also creates a controller:

```
cloudStreetMarketApp.controller('homeFinancialGraphControll
  er', function ($scope, financialDataFactory){
  readSelectValue();
  drawGraph();
  $('.form-control').on('change', function (elem) {
    $('#landingGraphContainer').html('');
    readSelectValue()
    drawGraph();
```

```
    });
    function readSelectValue(){
    $scope.currentMarket = $('.form-control').val();
    }
    function drawGraph(){
      Morris.Line({
        element: 'landingGraphContainer',
          hideHover: 'auto',
          data:
            financialDataFactory.
            getData($scope.currentMarket),
          ymax:
            financialDataFactory.getMax($scope.currentMarket),
          ymin:
            financialDataFactory.getMin($scope.currentMarket),
          pointSize: 3,
          hideHover:'always',
          xkey: 'period', xLabels: 'time',
          ykeys: ['index'], postUnits: '',
          parseTime: false, labels: ['Index'],
          resize: true, smooth: false,
          lineColors: ['#A52A2A']
        });
    }
});
```

The second file: `home_financial_table.js` relates to the markets overview table. Just like `home_financial_graph.js`, it creates a factory:

```
cloudStreetMarketApp.factory("financialMarketsFactory",
  function () {
  var data=[];
    return {
        fetchData: function () {
          return data;
        },
        pull: function () {
        $.each( dailyMarketsActivity, function(index, el ) {
          if(el.latestChange >=0){
            dailyMarketsActivity[index].style='text-success';
          }
          else{
            dailyMarketsActivity[index].style='text-error';
          }
        });
        data = dailyMarketsActivity;
```

```
        }
      }
});
```

The `home_financial_table.js` file also have its own controller:

```
cloudStreetMarketApp.controller('homeFinancialTableController',
function ($scope, financialMarketsFactory){

    financialMarketsFactory.pull();

    $scope.financialMarkets =
      financialMarketsFactory.fetchData();

});
```

3. The third and last file, `home_community_activity.js` relates to the community activity table. It defines a factory:

```
cloudStreetMarketApp.factory("communityFactory", function
   () {
  var data=[];
    return {
        fetchData: function () {
          return data;
        },
        pull: function () {

        $.each( userActivities, function(index, el ) {
        if(el.userAction =='BUY'){
          userActivities[index].iconDirection='ico-up-arrow
            actionBuy';
          }
          else{
          userActivities[index].iconDirection='ico-down-
            arrow actionSell';
        }
        userActivities[index].defaultProfileImage='';
        if(!el.urlProfilePicture){
          userActivities[index].defaultProfileImage='ico-
            user';
        }
        userActivities[index].price='$'+el.price;
        });
        data = userActivities;
        }
    }
});
```

And its controller:

```
cloudStreetMarketApp.controller('homeCommunityActivityContr
  oller', function ($scope, communityFactory){
   communityFactory.pull();
   $scope.communityActivities =
    communityFactory.fetchData();
});
```

How it works...

To understand better how our AngularJS deployment works, we will see how AngularJS is started and how our Angular module (app) is started. Then, we will discover the AngularJS Controllers and factories and finally the implemented Angular directives.

One app per HTML document

AngularJS is automatically initialized when the DOM is loaded.

 The **Document Object Model** (**DOM**) is the cross-platform convention for interacting with HTML, XHTML objects. When the browser loads a web page, it creates a Document Object Model of this page.

AngularJS looks up the DOM for an ng-app declaration in order to bind a module against a DOM element and start (autobootstrap) this module. Only one application (or module) can be autobootstrapped per HTML document.

We can still define more than one application per document and bootstrap them manually, though, if required. But the AngularJS community drives us towards binding an app to an HTML or BODY tag.

Module autobootstrap

Our application is autobootstrapped because it's referenced in the HTML tag:

```
<HTML ng-app="cloudStreetMarketApp">
```

Also, because the module has been created (directly in a <script> element of the HTML document):

```
var cloudStreetMarketApp= angular.module('cloudStreetMarketApp', []);
```

 Note the empty array in the module creation; it allows the injection of dependencies into the module. We will detail the AngularJS dependency injection shortly.

Manual module bootstrap

As introduced before, we can bootstrap an app manually, especially if we want to control the initialization flow, or if we have more than one app per document. The code is as follows:

```
angular.element(document).ready(function() {
    angular.bootstrap(document, ['myApp']);

});
```

AngularJS Controllers

AngularJS controllers are the central piece of the Framework. They monitor all the data changes occurring on the frontend. A controller is bound to a DOM element and corresponds to a functional and visual area of the screen.

At the moment, we have defined three controllers for the market graph, the markets list, and for the community activity feed. We will also need controllers for the menus and for the footer elements.

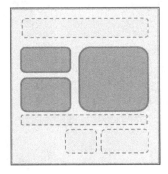

The DOM binding is operated with the directive's ng-controller:

```
<div ng-controller="homeFinancialGraphController">
  <table data-ng-controller='homeFinancialTableController'>
  <ul data-ng-controller='homeCommunityActivityController'>
```

Each controller has a scope and this scope is being passed as a function-argument on the controller's declaration. We can read and alter it as an object:

```
cloudStreetMarketApp.controller('homeCommunityActivityController',
function ($scope, communityFactory){

    ...
    $scope.communityActivities = communityFactory.fetchData();
    $scope.example = 123;
}
```

Bidirectional DOM-scope binding

The scope is synchronized with the DOM area the controller is bound to. AngularJS manages a bidirectional data-binding between the DOM and the controller's scope. This is probably the most important AngularJS feature to understand.

 The AngularJS model is the controller's scope object. Unlike Backbone.js, for example, there is not really a view layer in Angular since the model is directly reflected in the DOM.

The content of a scope variable can be rendered in the DOM using the {{...}} notation. For example, the $scope.example variable can be fetched in the DOM with {{example}}.

AngularJS directives

The directives are also a famous feature of AngularJS. They provide the ability of attaching directly to the DOM some. We can create our own directives or use built-in ones.

We will try to visit as many directives as we can along this book. For the moment, we have used the following.

ng-repeat

In order to iterate the communityActivities and financialMarkets collections, we define a local variable name as part of the loop and each item is accessed individually with the {{...}} notation. The code is as follows:

```
<li data-ng-repeat="value in communityActivities">
  <div class="itemTitle">
    <div class="listUserIco {{value.defaultProfileImage}}">
     <img ng-if="value.urlProfilePicture"
       src='{{value.urlProfilePicture}}'>
    </div>
    ...
  </div>
</li>
```

ng-if

This directive allows removing, creating, or recreating an entire DOM element or DOM hierarchy depending on a condition.

In the next example, the {{value.defaultProfileImage}} variable only renders the CSS class ".ico-user" when the user doesn't have a custom profile image (in order to display a default generic profile picture).

When the user has a profile picture, the `value.urlProfilePicture` variable is therefore populated, the `ng-if` condition is satisfied, and the `<img>` element is created in the DOM. The code is as follows:

```
<div class="listUserIco {{value.defaultProfileImage}}">
  <img ng-if="value.urlProfilePicture"
    src='{{value.urlProfilePicture}}'>
</div>
```

AngularJS factories

Factories are used to obtain new object instances. We have used factories as data generator. We will also use them as services coordinator and intermediate layer between the services and Controller. The Services will pull the data from the server APIs. The code is as follows:

```
cloudStreetMarketApp.factory("communityFactory", function () {
  var data=[];
    return {
        fetchData: function () {
        return data;
        },
        pull: function () {
        $.each( userActivities, function(index, el ) {
          if(el.userAction =='BUY'){
            userActivities[index].iconDirection='ico-up-arrow
              actionBuy';
          }
          else{
          userActivities[index].iconDirection='ico-down-
            arrow actionSell';
          }
          userActivities[index].defaultProfileImage='';
          if(!el.urlProfilePicture){
          userActivities[index].defaultProfileImage='ico-
          user';
          }
          userActivities[index].price='$'+el.price;
        });
        data = userActivities;
        }
    }
});
```

In this factory, we define two functions: `pull()` and `fetchData()` that populate and retrieve the data:

```
cloudStreetMarketApp.controller('homeCommunityActivityController',
   function ($scope, communityFactory){
     communityFactory.pull();
     $scope.communityActivities = communityFactory.fetchData();
});
```

Once the controller is loaded, it will `pull()` and `fetchData()` into the `$scope.communityActivities`. These operations are in this case executed only once.

> Our factories are injected as dependencies into our controller declarations:
>
> cloudStreetMarketApp.controller('homeCommunityActivityC ontroller', function ($scope, communityFactory)

Dependency injection

In our factories, controllers, and module definitions, we use AngularJS Dependency Injection to handle the components' lifecycle and their dependencies.

AngularJS uses an injector to perform the configured injections. There are three ways of annotating dependencies to make them eligible for injection:

- ► Using the inline array annotation:

```
cloudStreetMarketApp.controller('homeCommunityActivityControll
er', ['$scope', 'communityFactory', function ($scope,
communityFactory){
   communityFactory.pull();
   $scope.communityActivities =
     communityFactory.fetchData();
}]);
```

- ► Using the `$inject` property annotation:

```
var homeCommunityActivityController = function ($scope,
communityFactory){
   communityFactory.pull();
   $scope.communityActivities =
     communityFactory.fetchData();
}
homeCommunityActivityController.$inject = ['$scope',
   'communityFactory'];
cloudStreetMarketApp.controller('homeCommunityActivityControll
er', homeCommunityActivityController);
```

► Using the implicit annotation mode from the function parameter names:

```
cloudStreetMarketApp.controller('homeCommunityActivityContr
  oller', function ($scope, communityFactory){
    communityFactory.pull();
    $scope.communityActivities =
      communityFactory.fetchData();
});
```

While we have been using mostly the implicit annotation style and the inline array annotation style, we have to highlight the fact that the implicit annotation dependency injection will not work using JavaScript minification.

There's more...

As you may imagine, this has been a quick introduction of AngularJS. We will discover more of it in-situ when we have a REST API and more features in our application.

AngularJS is becoming very popular and an active community is supporting it. Its core idea and implementation, based on an explicit DOM, provide a radical and simplified way of getting in touch with an application.

The documentation is very detailed: `https://docs.angularjs.org`.

There are loads of tutorials and videos on the web:

► `http://www.w3schools.com/angular`

► `http://tutorials.jenkov.com/angularjs`

► `https://egghead.io`

3

Working with Java Persistence and Entities

In this chapter, we will develop the following recipes:

- ► Configuring the **Java Persistence API** (**JPA**) in Spring
- ► Defining useful EJB3 entities and relationships
- ► Making use of the JPA and Spring Data JPA

Introduction

The **Java Persistence API** (**JPA**) is a specification that has been produced in different releases from 2006 (JPA 1.0) to 2013 (JPA 2.1) by a group of various experts. Historically, it is one of the three pieces of the EJB 3.0 specification, which has come along with JEE5.

More than an upgrade of **Enterprise JavaBeans** (**EJB**), JPA was pretty much a complete redesign. At the time, the leading providers of Object Relational Mapping solution (such as Hibernate) and of J2EE application servers (such as WebSphere, JBoss) have been involved, and the global result has been unarguably simpler. All the types of EJBs (stateful, stateless, and entities) are now simple **Plain Old Java Objects** (**POJOs**) that are enriched with specific metadata that is nicely presented as annotations.

The Entities' benefits

Entities play a key role in the EJB3 model. As simple POJOs, they can be used in every single layer of the application.

Ideally, an entity represents an identifiable functional unit within a business domain. The norm is to make an entity representing a database table row. As simple POJOs, entities can rely on inheritance (the IS-A relationship) and can have attributes (the HAS-A relationship), just as a database schema is normally be described with. Through these relationships, an entity establishes connections with other Entities. These connections are described with @Annotations, which make the entity metadata.

An entity must be seen as the application-equivalent element of a database table row. JPA allows to operate this element and its whole ecosystem as a Java object hierarchy and to persist it as such.

Entities have brought an amazing radicalization of the persistence layer (by decreasing the number of hardcoded SQL queries to be maintained), and also the simplification of the service and transformation layers. Being able to pass through all the levels (they are used even in views), they dramatically drive the domain-specific names and concepts used within the application (methods, classes, and attributes). They indirectly focus on the essentials, and impose consistency between application concepts and database concepts.

It is obviously a plus to have a solid and well-thought schema from the beginning.

 JPA brings amazing performance and maintainability results on UI applications. However, it may not always suit performance expectations if it is used to accomplish batches or bulk database operations. It can sometimes be sensible to instead consider direct JDBC accesses.

The Entity manager and its persistence context

We have seen that an entity can have relations with other entities. In order for us to be able to operate on an entity (read from a database, update, delete, and persist), there is a background API that generates the preparation of SQL queries. This API in a persistence provider (Hibernate, Toplink, and so on) is the EntityManager. Once it loads the object for the purpose of the application, we can trust it to manage its life cycle.

There are a couple of concepts attached to the EntityManager that we need to review before moving forward. An entity is managed once the EntityManager gets an instance of it from a database read (explicit or implicit). The JPA persistence context is formed by the conceptual aggregation of the whole set of managed entities. A persistence context will always carry no more than one instance of an entity discriminated by its identifier (@Id or a unique ID class).

If, for some reason, an entity is not managed, it is said to be detached (understand detached from the persistence context).

Configuring the Java Persistence API in Spring

Now that we have introduced JPA, its role, and the benefits of using Entities, we can now focus on how to configure our Spring application to handle them.

Getting ready

As we said earlier, the JPA is a specification. Choosing a persistence provider (Hibernate, OpenJPA, TopLink, and so on) or a database provider for an application won't be a commitment as long as they match the standards.

We will see that our JPA configuration in Spring is done by defining two beans: **datasource** and **entityManagerFactory**. Then, the optional `Spring Data JPA` library offers a JPA repository abstraction that is able to surprisingly simplify some database operations.

How to do it...

1. From the **Git Perspective** in Eclipse, check out the latest version of the `v3.x.x` branch.

2. As previously introduced, we have added a couple of beans to the Spring configuration file (in the core module) `csmcore-config.xml`:

```
<jpa:repositories base-package="edu.zc.csm.core.daos" />
<bean id="dataSource" class="org.sfw.jdbc.datasource.
DriverManagerDataSource>
  <property name="driverClassName">
  <value>org.hsqldb.jdbcDriver</value>
  </property>
  <property name="url">
  <value>jdbc:hsqldb:mem:csm</value>
  </property>
  <property name="username">
  <value>sa</value>
  </property>
</bean>

<bean id="entityManagerFactory" class="org.sfw.orm.jpa.
LocalContainerEntityManagerFactoryBean">
```

```xml
        <property name="persistenceUnitName"
          value="jpaData"/>
        <property name="dataSource" ref="dataSource" />
        <property name="jpaVendorAdapter">
        <beanclass="org.sfw.orm.jpa.vendor.
          HibernateJpaVendorAdapter"/>
        </property>
        <property name="jpaProperties">
        <props>
            <prop key="hibernate.dialect">
              org.hibernate.dialect.HSQLDialect
            </prop>
            <prop key="hibernate.show_sql">true</prop>
            <prop key="hibernate.format_sql">false</prop>
            <prop key="hibernate.hbm2ddl.auto">create-drop</prop>
            <prop key="hibernate.default_schema">public</prop>
        </props>
      </property>
    </bean>
```

3. Finally, the following dependencies have been added to the parent and core projects:

   ❏ `org.springframework.data:spring-data-jpa` (1.0.2.RELEASE)

   ❏ `org.hibernate.javax.persistence:hibernate-jpa-2.0-api` (1.0.1.Final)

   ❏ `org.hibernate:hibernate-core` (4.1.5.SP1)

Adding this dependency causes the Maven enforcer plugin to raise a version conflict with `jboss-logging`. This is why jboss-logging has been excluded from this third-party library and referenced as a dependency on its own:

   ❏ `org.hibernate:hibernate-entitymanager` (4.1.5.SP1)

`jboss-logging` has also been excluded from this third-party library because, it is now referenced as a dependency on its own:

   ❏ `org.jboss.logging:jboss-logging` (3.1.0.CR1)

   ❏ `org.hsqldb:hsqldb` (2.3.2)

   ❏ `org.javassist:javassist` (3.18.2-GA)

   ❏ `org.apache.commons:commons-dbcp2` (2.0.1)

How it works...

We are going to review these three configuration points: the **dataSource** bean, the **entityManagerFactory** bean, and Spring Data JPA.

The Spring-managed DataSource bean

Because creating a database connection is time consuming, especially through the network layers, and because it is sensible to share and reuse an opened connection or a connection pool, a **datasource** has the duty of optimizing the use of these connections. It is a scalability indicator and also a highly configurable interface between the database and the application.

In our example, Spring manages the datasource just as for any other bean. The datasource can be created through the application or can be accessed remotely from a JNDI lookup (if the choice is made of giving up the connection management to the container). In both cases, Spring will manage the configured bean, providing the proxy that our application needs.

Also in our example, we are making use of the Apache Common DBCP 2 datasource (released in 2014).

In a production environment, it might be a good idea to switch to a JNDI-based datasource, such as the native Tomcat JDBC pool.

The Tomcat website clearly suggests a significant gain in performance when using the Tomcat JDBC pool instead of DBCP1.x on highly concurrent systems.

The EntityManagerFactory bean and its persistence unit

As its name suggests, the `EntityManagerFactory` bean produces entity managers. The configuration of `EntityManagerFactory` conditions the entity manager behavior.

The configuration of the `EntityManagerFactory` bean reflects the configuration of one persistence unit. In a Java EE environment, one or more persistent units can be defined and configured inside a `persistence.xml` file, which is unique in the application archive.

In a Java SE environment (our case), the presence of a `persistence.xml` file is made optional with Spring. The configuration of the `EntityManagerFactory` bean almost completely overrides the configuration of the persistence unit.

The configuration of a persistence unit, and, therefore, of an `EntityManagerFactory` bean, can either declare the covered Entities individually or scan packages to find them.

A persistence unit can be seen as a subarea among the horizontal scaling ecosystem. A product can be broken down into wars (web archives) for each the functional area. Functional areas can be represented with a selection of Entities that are delimited by a persistence unit.

The main point is to avoid creating Entities that overlap different persistence units.

The Spring Data JPA configuration

We are about to use some very useful tools from the Spring Data JPA project. These tools aim to simplify the development (and maintenance) of the persistence layers. The most interesting tool is probably the repository abstraction. You will see that providing implementations for some database queries can be optional. An implementation of the repository interface will be generated at runtime from the method signatures if they match a standard in their declarations.

For example, Spring will infer the implementation of the following method `signature` (if the `User` entity has a `String userName` field):

```
List<User> findByUserName(String username);
```

A more extended example of our bean configuration on Spring Data JPA could be the following:

```
<jpa:repositories base-package="edu.zipcloud.cloudstreetmarket.core.
  daos"
    entity-manager-factory-ref="entityManagerFactory"
    transaction-manager-ref="transactionManager"/>
```

As you can see, Spring Data JPA contains a custom namespace that allows us to define the following repository beans. This namespace can be configured as follow:

▶ Providing a `base-package` attribute in this namespace is mandatory to restrict the lookup for Spring Data repositories.

▶ Providing an `entity-manager-factory-ref` attribute is optional if you have only one `EntityManagerFactory` bean configured in `ApplicationContext`. It explicitly wires `EntityManagerFactory`, which is to be used with the detected repositories.

▶ Providing a `transaction-manager-ref` attribute is also optional if you have only one `PlatformTransactionManager` bean configured in `ApplicationContext`. It explicitly wires `PlatformTransactionManager`, which is to be used with the detected repositories.

More details can be found about this configuration on the project website at:

http://docs.spring.io/spring-data/jpa/docs/1.4.3.RELEASE/reference/html/jpa.repositories.html.

▶ **HikariCP DataSource**: HikariCP (from its BoneCP ancestor) is an open source Apache v2 licensed project. It appears to perform better in speed and reliability than any other DataSource. This product should probably be considered considered when choosing a datasource nowadays. Refer to `https://brettwooldridge.github.io/HikariCP` for more information on this.

Defining useful EJB3 entities and relationships

This topic is critical because a well-designed mapping prevents errors, saves a lot of time and has a big impact on performance.

Getting ready

In this section, we are going to present most of the Entities that we needed for the application. A couple of implementation techniques (from inheritance types to relationship cases) have been chosen here and highlighted for example purposes.

The *How it works...* section will explain why and how things are defined in the way they are and what were the thoughts that drove us toward the Entities' definitions we made.

How to do it...

The following steps will help you create Entities in the application:

1. All the changes from this recipe are located in the new package `edu.zipcloud.cloudstreetmarket.core.entities`. First, created three simple entities as shown here:

   ❑ The `User` entity:

```
@Entity
@Table(name="user")
public class User implements Serializable{
    private static final long serialVersionUID =
    1990856213905768044L;
    @Id
    @Column(nullable = false)
    private String loginName;
    private String password;
    private String profileImg;

    @OneToMany(mappedBy="user", cascade = {CascadeType.ALL},
```

```
      fetch = FetchType.LAZY)
  @OrderBy("id desc")
  private Set<Transaction> transactions = new
    LinkedHashSet< >();
  ...
  }
```

❏   The `Transaction` entity:

```
@Entity
@Table(name="transaction")
public class Transaction implements Serializable{
  private static final long serialVersionUID =
    -6433721069248439324L;
  @Id
  @GeneratedValue
  private int id;

  @ManyToOne(fetch = FetchType.EAGER)
  @JoinColumn(name = "user_name")
  private User user;

  @Enumerated(EnumType.STRING)
  private Action type;

  @OneToOne(fetch = FetchType.EAGER)
  @JoinColumn(name = "stock_quote_id")
  private StockQuote quote;
  private int quantity;
...
}
```

❏   And the `Market` entity:

```
@Entity
@Table(name="market")
public class Market implements Serializable {
  private static final long serialVersionUID = -
    6433721069248439324L;
  @Id
private String id;
private String name;

@OneToMany(mappedBy = "market", cascade = { CascadeType.ALL
  }, fetch = FetchType.EAGER)
private Set<Index> indices = new LinkedHashSet<>();
  ...
  }
```

2. Then, we have created some more complex entity Types such as the abstract
   Historic entity:

```
@Entity
@Inheritance(strategy = InheritanceType.SINGLE_TABLE)
@DiscriminatorColumn(name = "historic_type")
@Table(name="historic")
public abstract class Historic {

    private static final long serialVersionUID = -
      8023063919159565678L;

    @Id
    @GeneratedValue
    private int id;

    private double open;

    private double high;

    private double low;

    private double close;

    private double volume;

    @Column(name="adj_close")
    private double adjClose;

    @Column(name="change_percent")
    private double changePercent;

    @Temporal(TemporalType.TIMESTAMP)
    @Column(name="from_date")
    private Date fromDate;

    @Temporal(TemporalType.TIMESTAMP)
    @Column(name="to_date")
    private Date toDate;

    @Enumerated(EnumType.STRING)
    @Column(name="interval")
    private QuotesInterval interval;
    ...
    }
```

We have also created the two Historic subtypes, `HistoricalIndex` and `HistoricalStock`:

```
@Entity
@DiscriminatorValue("idx")
public class HistoricalIndex extends Historic implements
Serializable {

  private static final long serialVersionUID =
    -802306391915956578L;

  @ManyToOne(fetch = FetchType.EAGER)
  @JoinColumn(name = "index_code")
  private Index index;
...
}
@Entity
@DiscriminatorValue("stk")
public class HistoricalStock extends Historic implements
  Serializable {

  private static final long serialVersionUID =
    -802306391915956578L;

  @ManyToOne(fetch = FetchType.LAZY)
  @JoinColumn(name = "stock_code")
  private StockProduct stock;

  private double bid;
  private double ask;
  ...
  }
```

3. Then, we also created the `Product` entity with its StockProduct subtypes:

```
@Entity
@Inheritance(strategy = InheritanceType.TABLE_PER_CLASS)
public abstract class Product {
  private static final long serialVersionUID = -
    802306391915956578L;
  @Id
  private String code;
  private String name;
  ...
}

@Entity
```

```
@Table(name="stock")
public class StockProduct extends Product implements
Serializable{
  private static final long serialVersionUID =
     1620238240796817290L;
  private String currency;
  @ManyToOne(fetch = FetchType.EAGER)
  @JoinColumn(name = "market_id")
  private Market market;
  ...
}
```

4. In reality, in the financial world, an index (S&P 500 or NASDAQ) cannot be bought as such; therefore, indices haven't been considered as products:

```
@Entity
@Table(name="index_value")
public class Index implements Serializable{
  private static final long serialVersionUID = -
     2919348303931939346L;
  @Id
  private String code;
  private String name;

  @ManyToOne(fetch = FetchType.EAGER)
  @JoinColumn(name = "market_id", nullable=true)
  private Market market;

  @ManyToMany(fetch = FetchType.LAZY)
  @JoinTable(name = "stock_indices",
     joinColumns={@JoinColumn(name = "index_code")},
     inverseJoinColumns={@JoinColumn(name ="stock_code")})
  private Set<StockProduct> stocks = new LinkedHashSet<>();
  ...
}
```

5. Finally, the Quote abstract entity with its two subtypes, StockQuote and IndexQuote, have created (indices are not products, but we can still get instant snapshots from them, and the Yahoo! financial data provider will later be called to get these instant quotes):

```
@Entity
@Inheritance(strategy = InheritanceType.TABLE_PER_CLASS)
public abstract class Quote {
  @Id
  @GeneratedValue(strategy = GenerationType.TABLE)
  protected Integer id;
  private Date date;
```

```
    private double open;

    @Column(name = "previous_close")
    private double previousClose;
    private double last;
    ...
}

@Entity
@Table(name="stock_quote")
public class StockQuote extends Quote implements
    Serializable{
    private static final long serialVersionUID = -
        8175317254623555447L;
    @ManyToOne(fetch = FetchType.EAGER)
    @JoinColumn(name = "stock_code")
    private StockProduct stock;
    private double bid;
    private double ask;
    ...
}

@Entity
@Table(name="index_quote")
public class IndexQuote extends Quote implements
    Serializable{
    private static final long serialVersionUID = -
        8175317254623555447L;

    @ManyToOne(fetch = FetchType.EAGER)
    @JoinColumn(name = "index_code")
    private Index index;
    ...
}
```

How it works...

We are going to go through some basic and more advanced concepts that we have used to build our relational mapping.

Entity requirements

An entity, to be considered as such by the API requires the following conditions:

▶   It has to be annotated on The type level with the `@Entity` annotation.

- It needs to have a defined **identifier** with either a basic or a complex type. In most cases, a basic identifier is sufficient (the @Id annotation on a specific entity field).

- It must be defined as public and not declared as final.

- It needs to have a default constructor (implicit or not).

Mapping the schema

Both databases and Java objects have specific concepts. The metadata annotations for Entities, along with the configuration by default, describe the relational mapping.

Mapping tables

An entity class maps a table. Not specifying a @Table(name="xxx") annotation on the Type level will map the entity class to the table named with the entity name (this is the default naming).

> The Java's class-naming standard is CamelCased with a capital case for the first letter. This naming scheme doesn't really match the database table-naming standards. For this reason, the @Table annotation is often used.

The @Table annotation also has an optional schema attribute, which allows us to bind the table to a schema in the SQL queries (for example public.user.ID). This schema attribute will override the default schema JPA property, which can be defined on the persistence unit.

Mapping columns

As with the table names, the column name to map a field to is specified with the @Column(name="xxx") annotation. Again, this annotation is optional, and not specifying it will make the mapping fall back to the default naming scheme, which is literally the cased name of the field (in case of single words it is often a good option).

The fields of an entity class must not be defined as public. Also keep in mind that you can almost persist all the standard Java Types (primitive Types, wrappers, Strings, Bytes or Character arrays, and enumerated) and large numeric Types, such as BigDecimals or BigIntegers, but also JDBC temporal types (java.sql.Date, java.sql.TimeStamp) and even serializable objects.

Annotating fields or getters

The fields of an entity (if not tagged as @Transient) correspond to the values that the database row will have for each column. A column mapping can also be defined from a getter (without necessarily having a corresponding field).

The @Id annotation defines the entity identifier. Also, defining this @Id annotation on a field or getter defines whether the table columns should be mapped by a field or on a by getters.

When using a getter access mode, and when a `@Column` annotation is not specified, the default naming scheme for the column name uses the JavaBeans property naming standard (for example, the `getUser()` getter would correspond to the `user` column).

Mapping primary keys

As we have seen already, the `@Id` annotation defines the entity's identifier. A persistence context will always manage no more than one instance of an entity with a single identifier.

The `@Id` annotation on an entity class must map the persistent identifier for a table, which is the primary key.

Identifier generation

A `@GeneratedValue` annotation allows ID generation from the JPA level. This value may not be populated until the object is persisted.

A `@GeneratedValue` annotation has a `strategy` attribute that is used to configure the generation method (to rely, for example, on existing database sequences).

Defining inheritance

We have defined entity inheritance for subtypes of `Products`, `Historics`, and `Quotes`. When two Entities are close enough to be grouped into a single concept, and if they actually can be associated with a parent entity in the application, it is worth using the JPA inheritance.

Depending upon the persistence strategy for specific data, different storage options can be considered for inheritance mapping.

The JPA allows us to configure an inheritance model from different strategies.

The single-table strategy

This strategy expects or creates one big table with a discriminator field on the schema. This table hosts the parent-entity fields; these are common to all subentities. It also hosts all the fields of subentity classes. Consequently, if an entity corresponds to one subtype or another, it will populate the specific fields and leave the others blank.

The following table represents the `Historic` table with its `HISTORIC_TYPE` discriminator:

ID	OPEN	HIGH	LOW	CLOSE	VOL.	ADJ_CLOSE	CHANGE_PERC.	FROM_DATE	TO_DATE	INTERVAL	INDEX_CODE	STOCK_CODE	BID	ASK	HISTORIC_TYPE
3	10046.58	3042.9	9813.99	9813.99		9813.99	-2.37	15/11/2014 08:00	15/11/2014 08:30	MINUTE_30	GDAXI				idx
4	9813.99	9813.99	9813.99	9823.65		9823.65	-0.24	15/11/2014 09:00	15/11/2014 09:30	MINUTE_30	GDAXI				idx
5	9823.65	9823.65	9823.65	9832.74		9832.74	-0.15	15/11/2014 09:30	15/11/2014 10:00	MINUTE_30	GDAXI				idx
6	2.76	2.8	2.76	2.8		2.8	1.2	15/11/2014 11:30	15/11/2014 12:00	MINUTE_30		NXT.L	2.8	2.9	stk
7	2.8	2.86	2.8	2.86		2.86	1.2	15/11/2014 12:00	15/11/2014 12:30	MINUTE_30		NXT.L	2.86	2.95	stk

The table-per-class strategy

This strategy uses specific tables for concrete Entities. There is no discriminator involved here, just specific tables for subtypes. These tables carry both common and specific fields.

We have, for example, implemented this strategy for the `Quote` entity and its concrete `StockQuote` and `IndexQuote` Entities:

ID	DATE	LAST	OPEN	PREVIOUS_CLOSE	ASK	BID	STOCK_CODE
1	15/11/2014 11:12	3	2.9	2.8	3	2.9	NXT.L
2	15/11/2014 10:46	13	12	12	13	12	CCH.L
3	15/11/2014 10:46	9.5	9	9	9.5	9	KGF.L
4	15/11/2014 09:55	32	30	30	32	30	III.L
5	15/11/2014 09:50	15	14	14	15	14	BLND.L
6	15/11/2014 09:46	7	6	6	7	6	AA.L

ID	DATE	LAST	OPEN	PREVIOUS_CLOSE	INDEX_CODE
1	15/11/2014 09:46	6796.63	6797	6796.63	^FTSE
2	13/11/2014 10:46	6547.8	6548	6547.8	^FTSE

Defining relationships

Entities have the capability to reflect database foreign keys and table to table relationships in their class attributes.

On the application side, because these relationships are built transparently by the entity managers, a huge amount of developments are bypassed.

How relationships between entities have been chosen

Before talking about relationships between entities, it is necessary to understand what we plan to do in the *cloudstreet-market* application.

As introduced in *Chapter 1*, Setup *Routine for an Enterprise Spring Application*, we will pull financial data from providers that open their APIs (Yahoo! actually). To do so, there are always limitations to keep in mind in terms of call frequency per IP or per authenticated user. Our application will also have its community inside of which financial data will be shared. For financial data providers, when talking about a given stock, the historical view of a stock and an instant quote of a stock are two different things. We had to deal with these two concepts to build our own data set.

In our application, `Users` will be able to buy and sell `Products` (stock, fund, option, and so on) by executing `Transactions`:

▸ First, let's consider the User(s)/Transaction(s) relationship with the following screenshot:

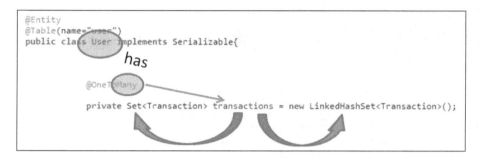

▸ A `User` entity can have many `Transactions` Entities.

In the User class, the second part of the `@OneToMany` relationship annotation (the `Many` element) drives the Type of attribute we are creating. Specifying `Many` as the second part declares that the origin entity (`User`) can have several target Entities (`Transactions`). These targets will have to be wrapped in a collection type. If the origin entity cannot have several targets, then the second part of the relationship has to be `One`.

▸ A `Transaction` can have only one `User` entity.

Still in the User class, the first part of the `@OneToMany` relationship (the `@One` element) is the second part of the relationship annotation defined in the target entity (if defined). It is necessary to know whether the target entity can have several origins or not, in order to complete the annotation in the origin.

▸ We can then deduce the two annotations: `@OneToMany` in `User` and `@ManyToOne` in `Transactions`.

▸ If we are not in the case of a `@ManyToMany` relationship, we are talking about a unidirectional relationships. From a database's point of view, this means that one of the two tables having a join column that targets the other table. In the JPA, the table that has this join column is the relationship's **owner**.

> The entity, which is the relationship's owner has to be specified by a `@JoinColumn` annotation on the relationship. The entity that is not the owner, has to provide for its relationship annotation a `mappedBy` attribute that targets the corresponding Java field name in the opposite entity.

▶ This can now explain the relationship in `Transaction`:

```
@ManyToOne(fetch = FetchType.EAGER)
@JoinColumn(name = "user_name")
private User user;
```

The `user_name` column is expected (or automatically added) in the transaction table. We will talk about the fetch type later in the *There's more... section*.

▶ The relationship in the `User` entity is defined as follows:

```
@OneToMany(mappedBy="user", cascade ={CascadeType.ALL},
fetch = FetchType.LAZY)
@OrderBy("id desc")
private Set<Transaction> transactions = new
LinkedHashSet<>();
```

> The `@OrderBy` annotation tells the JPA implementation to add an `ORDER BY` clause to its SQL query.

An `Index` entity has one `Market` entity. We have decided that a market is the geographical area (Europe, the US, Asia, and so on). A market has several concrete indices.

This looks like a `@OneToMany`/`@ManyToOne` relation again. The relationship's owner is the `Index` entity because we expect to have a `Market` column in the `Index` table (and not an `Index` column in the `Market` table).

It is the same story between the concrete `Product` (such as `StockProduct`) and `Market` entities, except that, since it doesn't look mandatory in the application to retrieve stocks directly from `Market`, the relationship has not been declared on the `Market` entity side. We have kept only the owner side.

About the concrete `Quotes` entity (such as `StockQuote`) and the concrete `Products` entity (such as `StockProduct`), one quote will have one product. If we were interested in retrieving `Quote` from a `Product` entity, one product would have many quotes. The owner of the relationship is the concrete `Quote` entity.

It is the same logic as the previous point for `IndexQuote` and `Index`.

Between `Index` and `StockProduct`, in reality, indices (S&P 500, NASDAQ, and so on) have constituents, and the sum of the constituents' values makes the index value. Thus, one `Index` entity has several potential `StockProduct` entities. Also one `StockProduct` can belong to several `Indices`. This looks like a bidirectional relationship. We present here the `Index` side:

```
@ManyToMany(fetch = FetchType.LAZY)
@JoinTable(name = "stock_indices", joinColumns={@JoinColumn(name =
"index_code")}, inverseJoinColumns={@JoinColumn(name ="stock_code")})
private Set<StockProduct> stocks = new LinkedHashSet<>();
```

This relationship is specified an extra join table (expected or generated by the JPA). It is basically a table with two join columns pointing to the `@Ids` fields of the respective entities.

There's more...

We are going to visit two metadata attributes that we didn't explain yet: the `FetchType` attribute and the `Cascade` attribute.

The FetchType attribute

We have seen that the relationship annotations `@OneToOne`, `@OneToMany`, and `@ManyToMany` can be specified in a fetch attribute, which can either be `FetchType.EAGER` or `FetchType.LAZY`.

When a `FetchType.EAGER` attribute is chosen, relationships are automatically loaded by the `entityManager` when the entity gets managed. The overall amount of SQL queries executed by JPA is significantly increased, especially because some related entities that may not be required each time are loaded anyway. If we have two, three, or more levels of entities bound to a root entity, we should probably consider switching some fields locally to `FetchType.LAZY`.

A `FetchType.LAZY` attribute specifies the JPA implementation not to populate a field value on the entity-loading SQL query. The JPA implementation generates extra-asynchronous SQL queries to populate the `LAZY` fields when the program specifically asks for it (for example, when `getStock()` is called in the case of a `HistoricalStock` entity). When using Hibernate as an implementation, `FetchType.LAZY` is taken as the default fetch type for relationships.

It is important to think about lightening the relationship loading, especially on collections.

The Cascade attribute

Another attribute to be mentioned in relationship annotations is the Cascade attribute. This attribute can take the values `CascadeType.DETACH`, `CascadeType.MERGE`, `CascadeType.PERSIST`, `CascadeType.REFRESH`, `CascadeType.REMOVE`, and `CascadeType.ALL`.

This attribute specifies how the JPA implementation should process the related Entities when asked to perform an operation (such as persist, update, delete, find, and so on.) on the main Entity. It is an optional attribute which is usually defaulted to **no-cascaded operations**.

See also

There is a third strategy to define Entity inheritance:

▸ **The joined-table inheritance strategy**: We haven't implemented it yet, but this strategy is a bit similar to the table-per-class strategy. It differs from it in the fact that, instead of repeating the parent-entity fields (columns) in the concrete tables, the JPA creates or expects an extra table with only the parent-entity columns and manages the joins transparently with this table.

Making use of the JPA and Spring Data JPA

In this section, we are going to wire the business logic we need for our application.

Because we have set up the configuration for the JPA and Spring Data JPA, and because we have defined our entities and their relationships, we can now use this model for time and energy-saving.

How to do it...

The following steps will guide you through the changes:

1. In the `edu.zipcloud.cloudstreetmarket.core.daos` package, we can find the following two interfaces:

```java
public interface HistoricalIndexRepository {
  Iterable<HistoricalIndex> findIntraDay(String code, Date
    of);
  Iterable<HistoricalIndex> findLastIntraDay(String code);
  HistoricalIndex findLastHistoric(String code);
}
public interface TransactionRepository {
  Iterable<Transaction> findAll();
  Iterable<Transaction> findByUser(User user);
  Iterable<Transaction> findRecentTransactions(Date from);
  Iterable<Transaction> findRecentTransactions(int nb);
}
```

2. These two interfaces come with their respective implementations. The
   HistoricalIndexRepositoryImpl implementation out of the two is defined
   as follows:

```
@Repository
public class HistoricalIndexRepositoryImpl implements
  HistoricalIndexRepository{

  @PersistenceContext
  private EntityManager em;

  @Override
  public Iterable<HistoricalIndex> findIntraDay(String
  code,Date of){
    TypedQuery<HistoricalIndex> sqlQuery = em.createQuery("from
    HistoricalIndex h where h.index.code = ? and h.fromDate
      >= ? and h.toDate <= ? ORDER BY h.toDate asc",
      HistoricalIndex.class);

    sqlQuery.setParameter(1, code);
    sqlQuery.setParameter(2, DateUtil.getStartOfDay(of));
    sqlQuery.setParameter(3, DateUtil.getEndOfDay(of));

    return sqlQuery.getResultList();
  }

  @Override
  public Iterable<HistoricalIndex> findLastIntraDay(String
    code) {
    return findIntraDay(code,
      findLastHistoric(code).getToDate());
  }

  @Override
  public HistoricalIndex findLastHistoric(String code){
    TypedQuery<HistoricalIndex> sqlQuery =
    em.createQuery("from
    HistoricalIndex h where h.index.code = ? ORDER BY
    h.toDate desc", HistoricalIndex.class);

  sqlQuery.setParameter(1, code);

    return sqlQuery.setMaxResults(1).getSingleResult();
  }
}
```

And the `TransactionRepositoryImpl` implementation is as follows:

```
@Repository
public class TransactionRepositoryImpl implements
  TransactionRepository{
  @PersistenceContext
  private EntityManager em;
  @Autowired
  private TransactionRepositoryJpa repo;
  @Override
  public Iterable<Transaction> findByUser(User user) {
    TypedQuery<Transaction> sqlQuery = em.createQuery("from
    Transaction where user = ?", Transaction.class);
    return sqlQuery.setParameter(1, user).getResultList();
  }
  @Override
  public Iterable<Transaction> findRecentTransactions(Date
    from) {
    TypedQuery<Transaction> sqlQuery = em.createQuery("from
    Transaction t where t.quote.date >= ?",
    Transaction.class);
    return sqlQuery.setParameter(1, from).getResultList();
  }
  @Override
  public Iterable<Transaction> findRecentTransactions(int
    nb) {
  TypedQuery<Transaction> sqlQuery = em.createQuery("from
    Transaction t ORDER BY t.quote.date desc",
    Transaction.class);
    return sqlQuery.setMaxResults(nb).getResultList();
  }
  @Override
  public Iterable<Transaction> findAll() {
    return repo.findAll();
  }
}
```

3. All the other interfaces in the `dao` package don't have explicitly defined implementations.

4. The following bean has been added to the Spring configuration file:

    ```
    <jdbc:initialize-database data-source="dataSource">
        <jdbc:script location="classpath:/META-
        INF/db/init.sql"/>
    </jdbc:initialize-database>
    ```

5. This last configuration allows the application to execute the created `init.sql` file **on startup**.

6. You will notice that the `cloudstreetmarket-core` module has been added in its `pom.xml` file, a dependency to `zipcloud-core` for the `DateUtil` class that we created.

7. To replace the two dummy implementations that we created in *Chapter 2, Designing a Microservice Architecture with Spring MVC*, the `CommunityServiceImpl` and `MarketServiceImpl` implementations have been created.

> We have injected repository dependencies in these implementations using `@Autowired` annotations.
>
> Also,we have tagged these two implementations with the Spring `@Service` annotations using a declared `value` identifier:
>
> ```
> @Service(value="marketServiceImpl")
> @Service(value="communityServiceImpl")
> ```

8. In the `cloudstreetmarket-webapp` module, the `DefaultController` has been modified in its `@Autowired` field to target these new implementations and no longer the dummy ones. This is achieved by specifying the `@Qualifier` annotations on the `@Autowired` fields.

9. Starting the server and calling the home page URL, `http://localhost:8080/portal/index`, should log a couple of SQL queries into the console:

```
Markers   Properties   Console ⌧   Servers   Data Source Explorer   Snippets   Search   History   Call Hierarchy

Tomcat v8.0 Server at localhost [Apache Tomcat] C:\th\apps\java\jdk8\bin\javaw.exe (26 Jan 2015 08:37:02)
Hibernate: select historical0_.id as id2_, historical0_.adj_close as adj3_2_, historical0_.change_percent as change4_2_,
Hibernate: select index0_.code as code7_1_, index0_.market_id as market3_7_1_, index0_.name as name7_1_, market1_.id as i
Hibernate: select indices0_.market_id as market3_3_1_, indices0_.code as code1_, indices0_.code as code7_0_, indices0_.ma
Hibernate: select historical0_.id as id2_, historical0_.adj_close as adj3_2_, historical0_.change_percent as change4_2_,
Hibernate: select index0_.code as code7_1_, index0_.market_id as market3_7_1_, index0_.name as name7_1_, market1_.id as i
Hibernate: select indices0_.market_id as market3_3_1_, indices0_.code as code1_, indices0_.code as code7_0_, indices0_.ma
Hibernate: select transactio0_.id as id9_, transactio0_.quantity as quantity9_, transactio0_.stock_quote_id as stock4_9_,
Hibernate: select stockquote0_.id as id0_3_, stockquote0_.date as date0_3_, stockquote0_.last as last0_3_, stockquote0_.d
Hibernate: select user0_.loginName as loginName6_0_, user0_.password as password6_0_, user0_.profileImg as profileImg6_0_
Hibernate: select stockquote0_.id as id0_3_, stockquote0_.date as date0_3_, stockquote0_.last as last0_3_, stockquote0_.d
Hibernate: select user0_.loginName as loginName6_0_, user0_.password as password6_0_, user0_.profileImg as profileImg6_0_
Hibernate: select stockquote0_.id as id0_3_, stockquote0_.date as date0_3_, stockquote0_.last as last0_3_, stockquote0_.d
Hibernate: select user0_.loginName as loginName6_0_, user0_.password as password6_0_, user0_.profileImg as profileImg6_0_
Hibernate: select stockquote0_.id as id0_3_, stockquote0_.date as date0_3_, stockquote0_.last as last0_3_, stockquote0_.d
Hibernate: select user0_.loginName as loginName6_0_, user0_.password as password6_0_, user0_.profileImg as profileImg6_0_
Hibernate: select stockquote0_.id as id0_3_, stockquote0_.date as date0_3_, stockquote0_.last as last0_3_, stockquote0_.d
Hibernate: select user0_.loginName as loginName6_0_, user0_.password as password6_0_, user0_.profileImg as profileImg6_0_
Hibernate: select stockquote0_.id as id0_3_, stockquote0_.date as date0_3_, stockquote0_.last as last0_3_, stockquote0_.d
Hibernate: select user0_.loginName as loginName6_0_, user0_.password as password6_0_, user0_.profileImg as profileImg6_0_
```

Also, the **Welcome** page should remain the same.

How it works...

Let's see the breakdown of this recipe with the following sections.

Injecting an EntityManager instance

We saw in the first recipe of this chapter that the configuration of the `entityManagerFactory` bean reflects the persistence unit's configuration.

Historically created by the container, EntityManagers need to handle transactions (user or container-manager transactions).

The `@PersistenceContext` annotation is a JPA annotation. It allows us to inject an instance of EntityManager, whose lifecycle is managed by the container. In our case, Spring handles this role. With an EntityManager, we can interact with the persistence context, get managed or detached entities, and indirectly query the database.

Using JPQL

Using **Java Persistence Query Language** (**JPQL**) is a standardized way of querying the persistence context and, indirectly, the database. JPQL looks like SQL in the syntax, but operates on the JPA-managed entities.

You must have noticed the following query n the repositories:

```
from Transaction where user = ?
```

The select part of the query is optional. Parameters can be injected into the query and this step is managed by the persistence providers' implementation. Those implementations offer protections against SQL injection (using Prepared Statements) With the example here, take a look at how practical it is to filter a subentity attribute:

```
from Transaction t where t.quote.date >= ?
```

It avoids declaring a join when the situation is appropriate. We can still declare a `JOIN` though:

```
from HistoricalIndex h where h.index.code = ? ORDER BY h.toDate desc
```

A couple of keywords (such as `ORDER`) can be used as part of JPQL to operate functions that are usually available in SQL. Find the full list of keywords in the JPQL grammar from the JavaEE 6 tutorial at `http://docs.oracle.com/javaee/6/tutorial/doc/bnbuf.html`.

JPQL has been inspired from the earlier-created **Hibernate Query Language** (**HQL**).

Reducing boilerplate code with Spring Data JPA

We have discussed in the *How to do it...* section that some of our repository interfaces don't have explicitly defined implementations. This is a very powerful feature of Spring Data JPA.

Query creation

Our `UserRepository` interface is defined as follows:

```
@Repository
public interface UserRepository extends JpaRepository<User, String>{
  User findByUserName(String username);
  User findByUserNameAndPassword(String username, String
  password);
}
```

We have made it extend the `JpaRepository` interface, passing through the generic types `User` (the entity type this repository will relate to) and `String` (the type of the user's identifier field).

By extending `JpaRepository`, `UserRepository` gets from Spring Data JPA capability to define query methods from Spring Data JPA by simply declaring their method signature. We have done this with the methods `findByUserName` and `findByUserNameAndPassword`.

Spring Data JPA transparently creates an implementation of our `UserRepository` interface at runtime. It infers the JPA queries from the way we have named our methods in the interface. Keywords and field names are used for this inference.

Find the following keywords table from the Spring Data JPA doc:

Keyword	Sample	JPQL snippet
And	findByLastnameAndFirstname	... where x.lastname = ?1 and x.firstname = ?2
Or	findByLastnameOrFirstname	... where x.lastname = ?1 or x.firstname = ?2
Between	findByStartDateBetween	... where x.startDate between 1? and ?2
LessThan	findByAgeLessThan	... where x.age < ?1
GreaterThan	findByAgeGreaterThan	... where x.age > ?1
After	findByStartDateAfter	... where x.startDate > ?1
Before	findByStartDateBefore	... where x.startDate < ?1
IsNull	findByAgeIsNull	... where x.age is null
IsNotNull,NotNull	findByAge(Is)NotNull	... where x.age not null
Like	findByFirstnameLike	... where x.firstname like ?1
NotLike	findByFirstnameNotLike	... where x.firstname not like ?1
StartingWith	findByFirstnameStartingWith	... where x.firstname like ?1 (parameter bound with appended %)
EndingWith	findByFirstnameEndingWith	... where x.firstname like ?1 (parameter bound with prepended %)
Containing	findByFirstnameContaining	... where x.firstname like ?1 (parameter bound wrapped in %)
OrderBy	findByAgeOrderByLastnameDesc	... where x.age = ?1 order by x.lastname desc
Not	findByLastnameNot	... where x.lastname <> ?1
In	findByAgeIn(Collection<Age> ages)	... where x.age in ?1
NotIn	findByAgeNotIn(Collection<Age> age)	... where x.age not in ?1
TRUE	findByActiveTrue()	... where x.active = true
FALSE	findByActiveFalse()	... where x.active = false

Without specifying anything in the configuration, we have fallen back to the configuration by default for JPA repositories, which injects an instance of our single `EntityManagerFactory` bean and of our single `TransactionManager` bean.

Our custom `TransactionRepositoryImpl` is an example that uses both custom JPQL queries and a `JpaRepository` implementation. As you might guess, the `TransactionRepositoryJpa` implementation , which is autowired in `TransactionRepositoryImpl`, inherits several methods for saving, deleting, and finding, `Transaction` Entities.

We will also use interesting paging features offered with these methods. The `findAll()` method, which we have pulled, is one of them.

Persisting Entities

Spring Data JPA also specifies the following:

Saving an entity can be performed via the `CrudRepository.save(...)` method. It will persist or merge the given entity using the underlying JPA EntityManager. If the entity has not been persisted yet, Spring Data JPA will save the entity via a call to the `entityManager.persist(...)` method; otherwise, the `entityManager.merge(...)` will be called.

This is interesting behavior that we will use to prevent again, a significant amount of boilerplate code.

There's more...

There are more aspects that can be explored around this topic.

Using native SQL queries

We haven't made use of native SQL queries yet, but we will. It is important to know how to implement them because bypassing the JPA layer can sometimes be a better option performance-wise.

The following link points to an article from the Oracle website, which is interesting as it relates to native SQL queries:

`http://www.oracle.com/technetwork/articles/vasiliev-jpql-087123.html`

Transactions

We haven't applied any specific transaction configuration to our repository implementations. Refer to *Chapter 7*, *Developing CRUD Operations and Validations*, for more details about transactions.

See also

- ▶ **Custom implementations for Spring Data repositories**: With the `TransactionRepositoryImpl` example, by redefining the methods we need from `TransactionRepositoryJpa`, we present a pattern for creating custom implementations of data repositories. It somehow forces us to maintain an intermediate proxy. The related Spring document proposes a different technique
- that solves this issue. This technique is detailed online at `http://docs.spring. io/spring-data/jpa/docs/current/reference/html/#repositories. custom-implementations`.

4

Building a REST API for a Stateless Architecture

This chapter will present the following recipes:

- ▸ Binding requests and marshalling responses
- ▸ Configuring the content-negotiation (json, xml, and so on)
- ▸ Adding pagination, filters, and sorting capabilities
- ▸ Handling exceptions globally
- ▸ Documenting and exposing an API with Swagger

Introduction

In this chapter, quite a few changes will be implemented. In fact, this chapter really sets our application development on an acceleration ramp.

Before diving into the code, we need to brush up on a few concepts about REST.

A definition of REST

REST is an architecture style. Its name is an abbreviation for Representational State Transfer. The term was invented by Roy Fielding, one of the principal authors of the HTTP specification. A REST architecture is designed around a few markers:

- ▶ **Identifiable resources**: Resources define the domain. A resource must be identifiable by a URI. This URI must be as self-explanatory as possible using resource categories and hierarchies. Our resources will be indices snapshots, stock snapshots, historical index data, historical stock data, users, and so on.

- ▶ **HTTP as a communication protocol**: We interact with resources using a limited number of HTTP methods (GET, POST, PUT, DELETE, HEAD, and OPTIONS).

- ▶ **Resource representation**: A resource is visualized under a specific representation. A representation usually corresponds to a media type (application/json, application/xml, text/html) and/or a file extension (*.json, *.xml, *.html).

- ▶ **Stateless conversations**: The server must not keep traces of a conversation. The use of HTTP sessions must be forbidden and replaced by navigating through the links provided with resources (hypermedia). The client authentication is repeated on every single request.

- ▶ **Scalability**: Stateless design implies easy scalability. One request can be dispatched to one or another server. This is the role of the load balancers.

- ▶ **Hypermedia**: As we just mentioned, with resources come links, and those links drive conversation transitions.

RESTful CloudStreetMarket

From this chapter on, all of the implemented data retrievals are now handled with REST using AngularJS. We use Angular routing to complete single-page application design (loaded once from the server).There are also a couple of new services that support three new screens about stocks and indices.

The REST implementation is still partial though. We have only implemented data retrievals (GET); we haven't got an effective authentication yet, and hypermedia will also be introduced later on.

Binding requests and marshalling responses

This recipe explains how to configure Spring MVC for REST handlers to be as integrated as possible with their business domain. We focus on designing self-explanatory method handlers, externalized type conversions, and abstracted response marshalling (serialization to specific formats such as json, xml, csv, and so on).

Getting ready

We are going to review the configuration changes applied to the `cloudstreetmarket-api` webapp in order to set up a Type conversion from either a request parameter or a URI template variable.

We will see how to configure automatic marshalling (for responses) into `json`. We will focus on two very simple method handlers created for this chapter.

How to do it...

The following steps describe the codebase changes that relate to the request binding and the response marshalling configuration:

1. From the **Git Perspective** in Eclipse, check out the latest version of the branch `v4.x.x`. Then run a `maven clean install` command on the `cloudstreetmarket-parent` module. To do this, right-click on the module, select **Run as... | Maven Clean**, then select **Run as... | Maven Install** again. After this, select **Maven Update Project** to synchronize Eclipse with the Maven configuration. To do so, right-click on the module and then select **Maven | Update Project...**.

2. The main configuration changes are in the `dispatcher-context.xml` file (in the **cloudstreetmarket-api** module). The `RequestMappingHandlerAdapter` bean has been defined the three `webBindingInitializer`, `messageConverters` and `customArgumentResolvers` properties:

```
<bean class="org.sfw.web. .
  method.annotation.RequestMappingHandlerAdapter">
  <property name="webBindingInitializer">
    <bean class="org.sfw. .
     support.ConfigurableWebBindingInitializer">
      <property name="conversionService"
        ref="conversionService"/>
    </bean>
    </property>
  <property name="messageConverters">
    <list>
        <ref bean="jsonConverter"/>
    </list>
  </property>
  <property name="customArgumentResolvers">
    <list>
      <bean class="net.kaczmarzyk.spring.data.jpa.web.
      SpecificationArgumentResolver"/>
      <bean  class="org.sfw.data.web.
        PageableHandlerMethodArgumentResolver">
        <property name="pageParameterName" value="pn"/>
```

```
                <property name="sizeParameterName" value="ps"/>
                </bean>
            </list>
        </property>
        <property name="requireSession" value="false"/>
    </bean>

    <bean id="jsonConverter" class="org.sfw...
        converter.json.MappingJackson2HttpMessageConverter">
        <property name="supportedMediaTypes"
          value="application/json"/>
      <property name="objectMapper">
        <bean class="com.fasterxml.jackson.
          databind.ObjectMapper">
          <property name="dateFormat">
         <bean class="java.text.SimpleDateFormat">
           <constructor-arg type="java.lang.String"
             value="yyyy-MM-dd HH:mm"/>
           </bean>
          </property>
        </bean>
        </property>
    </bean>
    <bean id="conversionService" class="org.sfw.format.
      support.FormattingConversionServiceFactoryBean">
      <property name="converters">
        <list>
          <bean class="edu.zc.csm.core.
            converters.StringToStockProduct"/>
        </list>
      </property>
    </bean>
```

3. The following Maven dependencies have been added to the parent project (and indirectly to the core and API projects):

```
        <dependency>
            <groupId>com.fasterxml.jackson.core</groupId>
                <artifactId>jackson-annotations</artifactId>
                <version>2.5.1</version>
          </dependency>
            <dependency>
                <groupId>com.fasterxml.jackson.core</groupId>
                <artifactId>jackson-databind</artifactId>
                <version>2.5.1</version>
            </dependency>
```

```xml
<dependency>
    <groupId>commons-collections</groupId>
    <artifactId>commons-collections</artifactId>
    <version>3.2</version>
</dependency>
<dependency>
    <groupId>net.kaczmarzyk</groupId>
    <artifactId>specification-arg-
        resolver</artifactId>
    <version>0.4.1</version>
</dependency>
```

4. In our controllers' superclass `CloudstreetApiWCI`, the `allowDateBinding` method has been created with an `@InitBinder` annotation:

```java
private DateFormat df = new SimpleDateFormat("yyyy-MM-
dd");


@InitBinder
public void allowDateBinding ( WebDataBinder binder ){
  binder.registerCustomEditor( Date.class, new
    CustomDateEditor( df, true ));
}
```

5. All this configuration allows us to define self-explanatory and logic-less method handlers such as the `getHistoIndex()` method in `IndexController`:

```java
@RequestMapping(value="/market}/{index}/histo",
  method=GET)
public HistoProductDTO getHistoIndex(
  @PathVariable("market" MarketCode market,
  @PathVariable("index") String indexCode,
  @RequestParam(value="fd",defaultValue="") Date
    fromDate,
  @RequestParam(value="td",defaultValue="") Date
    toDate,
  @RequestParam(value="i",defaultValue="MINUTE_30")
    QuotesInterval interval){
  return marketService.getHistoIndex(indexCode,
    market, fromDate, toDate, interval);
}
```

6. Now deploy the `cloudstreetmarket-api` module and restart the server. To do so, start by right-clicking on the Tomcat server in the **Servers** tab:

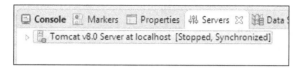

7. Then select **Add and Remove...**from the right-click menu. In the Add and Remove... window, make sure you have the following configuration set up, and start the server.

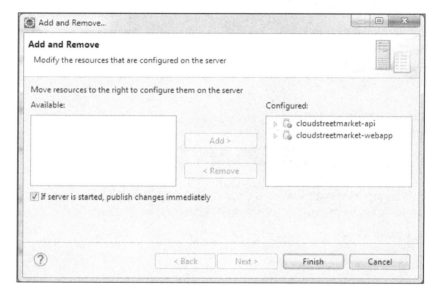

8. Try to call the URL `http://localhost:8080/api/indices/EUROPE/^GDAXI/histo.json`.

9. This URL targets the presented `getHistoIndex` method handler and produces the following `json` output:

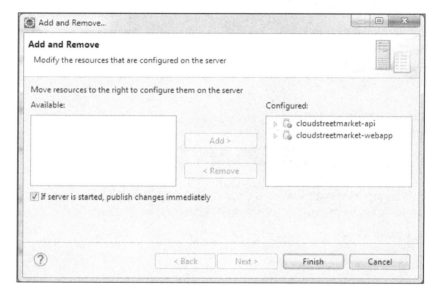

10. Now let's have a look at `StockProductController`. It hosts the following method handler:

```
@RequestMapping(value="/{code}", method=GET)
@ResponseStatus(HttpStatus.OK)
public StockProductOverviewDTO getByCode(
@PathVariable(value="code") StockProduct stock){
  return StockProductOverviewDTO.build(stock);
}
```

 There are no explicit calls to any service layer here. Also, the return. Type of the method handler, which is `StockProductOverviewDTO`, is a simple POJO. The marshalling of the response body is done transparently.

11. In the **cloudstreetmarket-core** module, the `StringToStockProduct` converter must be presented because it was required to achieve the previous step:

```
@Component
public class StringToStockProduct implements Converter<String,
StockProduct> {

@Autowired
private ProductRepository<StockProduct> productRepository;

@Override
public StockProduct convert(String code) {
  StockProduct stock = productRepository.findOne(code);
  if(stock == null){
    throw new NoResultException("No result has been
      found for the value "+ code +" !");
  }
  return stock;
}
}
```

 This converter was registered earlier (*step 2*) in `conversionService`.

12. Try to call the URL `http://localhost:8080/api/products/stocks/NXT.L.json`. This should target the presented `getByCode` handler and produce the following `json` response:

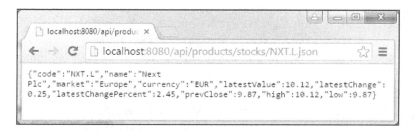

How it works...

To understand how the preceding elements work together, we must introduce the key role of `RequestMappingHandlerAdapter`.

A super RequestMappingHandlerAdapter bean

We briefly introduced `RequestMappingHandlerAdapter` in *Chapter 2, Designing a Microservice Architecture with Spring MVC*. This bean implements the high-level `HandlerAdapter` interface, which allows custom MVC core-workflow implementations. `RequestMappingHandlerAdapter` is the native implementation that comes with the framework.

We mentioned that `RequestMappingHandlerAdapter` and `RequestMappingHandlerMapping` respectively are two replacement classes for the now deprecated `AnnotationMethodHandlerAdapter` and `DefaultAnnotationHandlerMapping`.

In fact, `RequestMappingHandlerAdapter` provides better centralization for all the method handlers. Also, some new capabilities have been opened for `HandlerInterceptors` and `HandlerExceptionResolver`.

Practically, the handler argument that can be found in the `preHandle`, `postHandle`, and `afterCompletion` methods' signature (`WebContentInterceptors`) can be casted into `HandlerMethod` objects. The `HandlerMethod` Type offers interesting examination methods such as `getReturnType`, `getMethodAnnotation`, `getMethodParameters`.

Also, in regard to `RequestMappingHandlerAdapter` and `RequestMappingHandlerMapping`, the Spring documentation specifies that:

> *"The new support classes are enabled by default by the MVC namespace and the MVC Java config but must be configured explicitly if using neither."*

> *JavaDoc*

In both our web apps, we make use of the MVC namespace specifically with the `<mvc:annotation-driven/>` element.

This element is enjoyable from the configuration-by-default feature it activates on a couple of web features. However, in a lot of situations, different behaviors might still be expected.

In most cases, custom definitions are made either on the namespace itself or on with `RequestMappingHandlerAdapter`.

Broad support for @RequestMapping annotations

The main role of `RequestMappingHandlerAdapter` is to provide support and customization for handlers of the Type `HandlerMethod`. These handlers are bound to `@RequestMapping` annotations.

> *"A HandlerMethod object encapsulates information about a handler method consisting of a method and a bean. Provides convenient access to method parameters, the method return value, method annotations."*

> *JavaDoc*

The `RequestMappingHandlerAdapter` gets most of its support methods from the historical `DefaultAnnotationHandlerMapping`. Let's take a closer look at the methods that particularly interest us.

setMessageConverters

The `messageConverters` template can be registered through the `setMessageConverters` setter as `List<HttpMessageConverter>`. Spring will perform the unmarshalling of an HTTP request's body for us into Java object(s) and the marshalling of a Java resource into an HTTP response's body.

It is important to remember that the framework provides converter implementations for the main media types. These are registered by default with `RequestMappingHandlerAdapter` and `RestTemplate` (on the client side).

The following table summarizes the native converters we can make use of:

Provided implementations	Supported media types by default	(Default) behavior
`StringHttpMessageConverter`	`text/*`	Writes with a `text/plain` content type.
`FormHttpMessageConverter`	`application/x-www-form-urlencoded`	Form data is read from and written into `MultiValueMap<String, String>`.
`ByteArrayHttpMessageConverter`	`*/*`	Writes with an `application/octet-stream` content type (can be overridden).
`MarshallingHttpMessage Converter`	`text/xml` and `application/xml`	Requires `org.springframework.oxm` and a `Marshaller`/`Unmarshaller`.
`MappingJackson2HttpMessage Converter`	`application/json`	JSON mapping can be customized with Jackson annotations. If specific types need to be mapped, a custom `ObjectMapper` property has to be injected.
`MappingJackson2XmlHttpMessage Converter`	`application/xml`	XML mapping can be customized with JAXB or Jackson annotations. If specific types need to be mapped, a custom `XmlMapper` property has to be injected into the `ObjectMapper` property.
`SourceHttpMessageConverter`	`text/xml` and `application/xml`	Can read and write `javax.xml.transform.Source` from the HTTP request and response. Only `DOMSource`, `SAXSource`, and `StreamSource` are supported.
`BufferedImageHttpMessage Converter`		Can read and write `java.awt.image.BufferedImage` from the HTTP request and response.

Have a look at the following address to get information on remoting and web services using Spring: `http://docs.spring.io/spring/docs/current/spring-framework-reference/html/remoting.html`.

In our application, we have overridden the definition of the two native `MappingJackson2Http MessageConverter` and `MarshallingHttpMessageConverter` classes.

setCustomArgumentResolvers

The `setCustomArgumentResolvers` setter provides to `RequestMappingHandlerAdapter` a support for custom arguments. If you remember back in *Chapter 2, Using Spring MVC to Support Responsive Designs*, the very first recipe talks about supported annotations for arguments. At the time, we saw `@PathVariable`, `@MatrixVariable`, `@RequestBody`, `@RequestParam`, and so on.

All these annotations are built-in `ArgumentResolver`. They are mapped to registered implementations to externally prepopulate arguments from different sources.

We have the possibility to define our own annotations and prepopulate our method arguments following the required business logic. These resolvers must implement the `HandlerMethodArgumentResolver` interface.

The development of our application didn't specifically require the development of `customArgumentResolver`. However, we have registered two of them:

- `net.kaczmarzyk.spring.data.jpa.web.SpecificationArgumentResolver`: This resolver is a third-party library that we are going to explain in the 3rd recipe of this chapter
- `org.springframework.data.web.PageableHandlerMethodArgumentResolver`: This will allow the automatic resolution of pagination parameters in order to use the native Spring Data pagination support

setWebBindingInitializer

A `WebBindingInitializer` interface is a callback interface to globally initialize `WebDataBinder` and perform data binding in the context of web requests.

Before going forward, we must stop and revisit the 4th step of the recipe that defined the following method:

```
@InitBinder
public void allowDateBinding(WebDataBinder binder) {
  binder.registerCustomEditor(Date.class, new CustomDateEditor(
    df, true ));
}
```

We define this method in a controller to register an abstracted Date conversion binding using a `PropertyEditor`.

Now let's focus on the `WebDataBinder` argument. In this section, we are talking about the initialized part. The `WebDataBinder` interface provides a couple of interesting methods. These methods are mostly validation-related (`validate`, `setRequiredFields`, `isAllowed`, `getErrors`, and so on) and conversion-related (`getTypeConverter`, `registerCustomEditor`, `setBindingErrorProcessor`, `getBindingResult`, and so on).

A `WebDataBinder` argument can also be set as a `ConversionService` object. Rather than doing this locally in our `allowDateBinding` method (with the `WebDataBinder.setConversion` setter), we are going to use a global and declarative initialization.

The `WebBindingInitializer` implementation we have chosen is the Spring `ConfigurableWebBindingInitializer` bean. It is indeed a convenient class for declarative configurations in a Spring application context. It enables the reusability of preconfigured initializers over multiple controllers/handlers.

In our case, the `WebBindingInitializer` will be useful to globally initialize registered Type converters such as `StringToStockProduct`, but also to achieve the global exception handling we are aiming for.

The ConversionService API

The 11th step defines a `StringToStockProduct` converter that allows the definition of a lean and clean `getByCode` method handler:

```
@RequestMapping(value="/{code}", method=GET)
@ResponseStatus(HttpStatus.OK)
public StockProductOverviewDTO getByCode(
@PathVariable(value="code") StockProduct stock){
  return StockProductOverviewDTO.build(stock);
}
```

These converters can be used broadly among the Spring application for any conversion without being restricted to a request scope. Their use of Generics can be very beneficial. They are bound to a `conversionService` bean and there is no specific way to avoid their individual declaration.

Choosing between PropertyEditors or converters

The `PropertyEditors` and the converters from `ConversionService` might appear as an alternative to each other in their String-to-type use.

Spring heavily uses the concept of `PropertyEditors` to set properties for beans. In Spring MVC, they are meant to parse HTTP requests. Their declaration in Spring MVC is bound to the request scope.

Even if they can be initialized globally, you must see `PropertyEditors` as initially restricted scope elements. Seeing them this way legitimates their attachment to `@InitBinder` methods and `WebBinderData`. They are less generic than converters.

When using `PropertyEditors` for enums, Spring offers a naming convention that can avoid the individual declaration of enums. We will make use of this handy convention later on.

There's more...

We are going to look at other `RequestMappingHandlerAdapter` properties in the next recipes. For now, there is more to discuss about `PropertyEditors` and especially the built-in ones.

Built-in PropertyEditor implementations

The following `PropertyEditors` implementations come natively with Spring. They can be applied manually in all controllers for the purpose of binding. You will probably recognize `CustomDateEditor`, which has been registered in `CloudstreetApiWCI`.

Provided implementations	Default behavior
ByteArrayPropertyEditor	This is the editor for byte arrays. Strings will simply be converted to their corresponding byte representations. It is registered by default by BeanWrapperImpl.
ClassEditor	Parses strings represent classes to actual classes and the other way around. When a class is not found, an IllegalArgumentException exception is thrown. It is registered by default by BeanWrapperImpl.
CustomBooleanEditor	This is a customizable property editor for Boolean properties. It is registered by default by BeanWrapperImpl, but it can be overridden by registering a custom instance of it as a custom editor.
CustomCollectionEditor	This is the property editor for collections, converting any source collection to a given target collection type.
CustomDateEditor	This is a customizable property editor for java.util.Date, and supports a custom DateFormat. It is not registered by default. The user must register it as required in the appropriate format.
CustomNumberEditor	This is a customizable property editor for any number subclass such as Integer, Long, Float, or Double. It is registered by default by BeanWrapperImpl, but it can be overridden by registering a custom instance of it as a custom editor.
FileEditor	This editor is capable of resolving strings to java.io.File objects. It is registered by default by BeanWrapperImpl.
InputStreamEditor	This is a one-way property editor capable of taking a text string and producing InputStream (via an intermediate ResourceEditor and Resource). The InputStream properties may be directly set as strings. The default usage will not close the InputStream property. It is registered by default by BeanWrapperImpl.

The Spring IO reference document

Find more details about Type conversion and PropertyEditors in the Spring IO Reference document, check out: http://docs.spring.io/spring/docs/3.0.x/spring-framework-reference/html/validation.html.

Configuring content-negotiation (JSON, XML, and so on)

In this recipe, we will see how to configure the way we want the system to decide which format to render depending upon the client expectations.

Getting ready

We are mostly going to review the XML configuration here. Then, we will test the API with different requests to ensure support is provided to the XML format.

How to do it...

1. The `RequestMappingHandlerAdapter` configuration has been altered in `dispatcher-context.xml`. A `contentNegotiationManager` property has been added, as well as an `xmlConverter` bean:

```
<bean class="org.sfw.web...
  method.annotation.RequestMappingHandlerAdapter">
  <property name="messageConverters">
    <list>
      <ref bean="xmlConverter"/>
      <ref bean="jsonConverter"/>
    </list>
  </property>
  <property name="customArgumentResolvers">
    <list>
      <bean class="net.kaczmarzyk.spring.data.jpa.
      web.SpecificationArgumentResolver"/>
      <bean class="org.sfw.data.web.
      PageableHandlerMethodArgumentResolver">
        <property name="pageParameterName" value="pn"/>
        <property name="sizeParameterName" value="ps"/>
      </bean>
    </list>
  </property>
  <property name="requireSession" value="false"/>
  <property name="contentNegotiationManager"
  ref="contentNegotiationManager"/>
</bean>

<bean id="contentNegotiationManager"
  class="org.sfw.web.accept.
  ContentNegotiationManagerFactoryBean">
```

```xml
        <property name="favorPathExtension" value="true" />
        <property name="favorParameter" value="false" />
        <property name="ignoreAcceptHeader" value="false"/>
        <property name="parameterName" value="format" />
        <property name="useJaf" value="false"/>
        <property name="defaultContentType"
          value="application/json" />
        <property name="mediaTypes">
          <map>
            <entry key="json" value="application/json" />
            <entry key="xml" value="application/xml" />
        </map>
      </property>
    </bean>
    <bean id="xmlConverter"
    class="org.sfw.http...xml.MarshallingHttpMessageConverter">
      <property name="marshaller">
        <ref bean="xStreamMarshaller"/>
      </property>
      <property name="unmarshaller">
        <ref bean="xStreamMarshaller"/>
      </property>
    </bean>
    <bean id="xStreamMarshaller"
    class="org.springframework.oxm.xstream.XStreamMarshaller">
      <property name="autodetectAnnotations" value="true"/>
    </bean>
```

2. A Maven dependency has been added to XStream as follows:

```xml
    <dependency>
      <groupId>com.thoughtworks.xstream</groupId>
       <artifactId>xstream</artifactId>
      <version>1.4.3</version>
    </dependency>
```

3. Calling the URL: `http://localhost:8080/api/indices/EUROPE/^GDAXI/ histo.json` should target the `getHistoIndex()` handler the same way as before and you should receive the same `json` response:

4. Also, calling the URL `http://localhost:8080/api/indices/ EUROPE/^GDAXI/histo.xml` should now generate the following XML formatted response:

How it works...

We have added support for XML using the `MarshallingHttpMessageConverter` bean, defined a default media type (`application/json`), and defined a global content negotiation strategy.

Support for XML marshalling

As we said in the previous recipe, `MarshallingHttpMessageConverter` comes with the framework, but it requires the `spring-oxm` dependency, as well as a definition for a marshaller and unmarshaller. `spring-oxm` is the Maven artefact to reference here:

```
<dependency>
  <groupId>org.springframework</groupId>
  <artifactId>spring-oxm</artifactId>
  <version>${spring.version}</version>
</dependency>
```

The XStream marshaller

We chose `XStreamMarshaller` as the provider for the XML marshalling operations:

```
<bean class="org.springframework.oxm.xstream.XStreamMarshaller">
  <property name="autodetectAnnotations" value="true"/>
</bean>
```

The `XStream` marshaller is part of the `spring-oxm` project. Even if it is *not recommended* for external source parsing (which is *not* what we intend to do), it is very good and requires very few configuration by default (no specific class registration or initial mapping strategy required).

Types and fields can be annotated to customize the default behavior. You can find some examples here from their documentation:

- ▶ `@XStreamAlias`: Used on the type, field, or attribute
- ▶ `@XStreamImplicit`: Used in collections or arrays
- ▶ `@XStreamAsAttribute`: Used to mark a field as an attribute
- ▶ `@XStreamConverter`: Targets a specific converter for the field

In our case, we have applied a minimal marshalling customization in DTOs.

You can find more information about `XStream` on their official website: `http://xstream.codehaus.org`.

Negotiation strategies with ContentNegotiationManager

Here, we are talking about the way we configure the system to choose one media type over another, for responses. The client shows expectations in its request and the server tries to satisfy them at best from the available resolutions.

There are three ways for the client to specify its media type expectations. We discuss them in the following sections.

The Accept header

The client request specifies a mime type or a list of mime types (`application/json`, `application/xml`, and so on) as a value of the `Accept` header. It is the default choice for Spring MVC.

Web browsers can send various `Accept` headers though, and it would be risky to rely entirely on these headers. Therefore, it is good to support at least one alternative.

These headers can even be completely ignored with the `ignoreAcceptHeader` Boolean property in `ContentNegotiationManager`.

The file extension suffix in the URL path

Allowing the specification of a file extension suffix in the URL path is one alternative. It is the discriminator option in our configuration.

The `favorPathExtension` Boolean property in `ContentNegotiationManager` has been set to true for this purpose and our AngularJS factories actually request `.json` paths.

The request parameter

You can define a specific query parameter if you dislike the path extension option. The default name of this parameter is `format`. It is customizable with the `parameterName` property, and the potential expected values are the registered format suffixes (`xml`, `html`, `json`, `csv`, and so on).

This option can be set as the discriminator option with the `favorParameter` Boolean property.

Java Activation Framework

Setting the `useJaf` Boolean property to true configures to rely on the Java Activation Framework, rather than Spring MVC itself, for the suffix to-media type mappings (`json` to correspond to `application/json`, `xml` to correspond to `application/xml`, and so on).

@RequestMapping annotations as ultimate filters

Finally, the controller with the `@RequestMapping` annotations and especially the `produces` attribute should have the final word on which format will be rendered.

There's more...

Now we will look at the implementation of JAXB2 as an XML parser and the `ContentNegotiationManagerFactoryBean` configuration.

Using a JAXB2 implementation as an XML parser

JAXB2 is the current Java specification for XML bindings. Our example with XStream was just an example and another XML marshaller can of course be used. Spring supports JAXB2. It even provides a default JAXB2 implementation in the spring-oxm package: `org.springframework.oxm.jaxb.Jaxb2Marshaller`.

Using JAXB2 annotations in DTOs is probably a better choice for portability. Visit the `Jaxb2Marshaller` JavaDoc for more details about its configuration: `http://docs.spring.io/autorepo/docs/spring/4.0.4.RELEASE/javadoc-api/org/springframework/oxm/jaxb/Jaxb2Marshaller.html`.

The ContentNegotiationManagerFactoryBean JavaDoc

The full possible configuration for `ContentNegotiationManagerFactoryBean` is accessible again in its JavaDoc:

`http://docs.spring.io/spring/docs/current/javadoc-api/org/springframework/web/accept/ContentNegotiationManagerFactoryBean.html`

Adding pagination, filters, and sorting capabilities

Now we have introduced the basis for a REST configuration of Spring MVC, we will improve our REST services by adding pagination, filtering, and sorting capabilities.

Getting ready

Pagination is a concept developed in the Spring Data project. To add pagination, we will introduce the `Pageable` interface for wrapper implementations populated from the request. These are further on recognized and handled by Spring Data.

The `Page` interface and specifically the `PageImpl` instances can be produced by Spring Data to format its results. We will use them, as they are perfectly suited to REST rendering.

Finally, we will detail two data-binding tools used here to abstract filtering and pagination from our controllers' logic.

How to do it...

1. To the method handlers, we have added the parameters we want them to support. The following handler in `IndexController` now offers pagination and sorting:

```java
import org.springframework.data.domain.PageRequest;

    @RequestMapping(value="/{market}", method=GET)
    public Page<IndexOverviewDTO> getIndicesPerMarket(
      @PathVariable MarketCode market,
      @PageableDefault(size=10, page=0,
        sort={"dailyLatestValue"},
        direction=Direction.DESC)
      Pageable pageable){
      return marketService.
        getLastDayIndicesOverview(market, pageable);
}
```

2. In the corresponding service layer implementation, the `pageable` instance is passed to the Spring Data JPA abstracted implementation:

```java
@Override
public Page<IndexOverviewDTO>
  getLastDayIndicesOverview(Pageable pageable) {
    Page<Index> indices =
      indexProductRepository.findAll(pageable);
    List<IndexOverviewDTO> result = new LinkedList<>();
    for (Index index : indices) {
      result.add(IndexOverviewDTO.build(index));
    }
    return new PageImpl<>(result, pageable,   indices.
      getTotalElements());
}
```

That's pretty much all about the pagination and sorting pattern! All the boilerplate code is transparent. It allows us to magically retrieve a resource wrapped in a page element that carries the tools that the front end may need for pagination. For our specific method handler, calling the URL:

http://localhost:8080/api/indices/US.json?size=2&page=0&sort=da
ilyLatestValue,asc results in the following JSON response:

```json
{
  "content": [
    {
      "code": "^OEX",
      "name": "S&P 100 INDEX",
      "market": "US",
      "latestValue": 921.34,
      "latestChange": -1.83,
      "latestChangePercent": -0.2,
      "prevClose": 923.17,
      "high": 923.41,
      "low": 918.45
    },
    {
      "code": "^NDX",
      "name": "NASDAQ-100",
      "market": "US",
      "latestValue": 4411.86,
      "latestChange": 20.95,
      "latestChangePercent": 0.48,
      "prevClose": 4390.91,
      "high": 4415.79,
      "low": 4388.44
    }
  ],
  "size": 2,
  "number": 0,
  "sort": [
    {
      "direction": "ASC",
      "property": "dailyLatestValue",
      "ignoreCase": false,
      "ascending": true
    }
  ],
  "numberOfElements": 2,
  "firstPage": true,
  "lastPage": false,
  "totalPages": 2,
  "totalElements": 3
}
```

3. We have also applied this pattern to dynamically retrieve indices with pagination even though it is almost the same method handler definition.

4. We also applied the same pattern again to retrieve user activities (in CommunityController):

```java
@RequestMapping(value="/activity", method=GET)
@ResponseStatus(HttpStatus.OK)
public Page<UserActivityDTO> getPublicActivities(
  @PageableDefault(size=10, page=0, sort={"quote.date"},
  direction=Direction.DESC) Pageable pageable){
  return communityService.getPublicActivity(pageable);
}
```

5. Now we have adapted the AngularJS layer (detailed in the *See also...* section of this recipe), we have been able to entirely rewire our welcome page to use REST services with also an infinite scrolling for user activities:

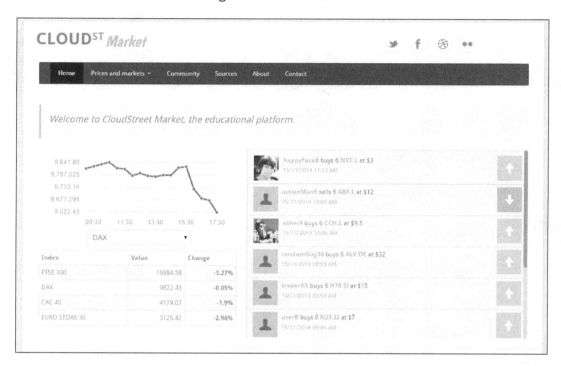

6. To fully use the REST service's capabilities, there is now a new screen called *INDICES BY MARKET* accessible from the **Prices and markets** menu:

The table presented here is entirely autonomous since it features the fully angularized (AngularJS) and asynchronous pagination/sorting capabilities.

7. The `StockProductController` object, in its `search()` method handler, has implemented the pagination and sorting pattern, but also a filtering feature that allows the user to operate `LIKE` SQL operators combined with `AND` restrictions:

```
@RequestMapping(method=GET)
@ResponseStatus(HttpStatus.OK)
public Page<ProductOverviewDTO> search(
@And(value = { @Spec(params = "mkt", path="market.code",spec =
EqualEnum.class)},
    and = { @Or({
@Spec(params="cn", path="code", spec=LikeIgnoreCase.class),
@Spec(params="cn", path="name", spec=LikeIgnoreCase.class)})}
  ) Specification<StockProduct> spec,
@RequestParam(value="mkt", required=false) MarketCodeParam
  market,
```

```
@RequestParam(value="sw", defaultValue="") String
  startWith,
@RequestParam(value="cn", defaultValue="") String contain,
@PageableDefault(size=10, page=0,
  sort={"dailyLatestValue"}, direction=Direction.DESC)
  Pageable pageable){
  return productService.getProductsOverview(startWith,
  spec, pageable);
}
```

8. The `productService` implementation, in its `getProductsOverview` method (as shown), refers to a created `nameStartsWith` method:

```
@Override
public Page<ProductOverviewDTO> getProductsOverview(String
  startWith, Specification<T> spec, Pageable pageable) {
  if(StringUtils.isNotBlank(startWith)){
    spec = Specifications.where(spec).and(new
    ProductSpecifications<T>().nameStartsWith(startWith);
  }
  Page<T> products = productRepository.findAll(spec,
  pageable);
  List<ProductOverviewDTO> result = new LinkedList<>();
  for (T product : products) {
    result.add(ProductOverviewDTO.build(product));
  }
  return new PageImpl<>(result, pageable,
  products.getTotalElements());
}
```

9. The `nameStartsWith` method is a specification factory located in the core module inside the `ProductSpecifications` class:

```
public class ProductSpecifications<T extends Product> {
public Specification<T> nameStartsWith(final String
  searchTerm) {
  return new Specification<T>() {
  private String startWithPattern(final String searchTerm) {
    StringBuilder pattern = new StringBuilder();
    pattern.append(searchTerm.toLowerCase());
    pattern.append("%");
    return pattern.toString();
  }
    @Override
      public Predicate toPredicate(Root<T> root,
        CriteriaQuery<?> query, CriteriaBuilder cb) {
```

```
                return
        cb.like(cb.lower(root.<String>get("name")),
            startWithPattern(searchTerm));
}
        };
    }
}
```

10. Overall, the `search()` REST service is extensively used over three new screens related to stocks retrieval. These screens are accessible through the **Prices and markets** menu. Here is the new **ALL PRICES SEARCH** form:

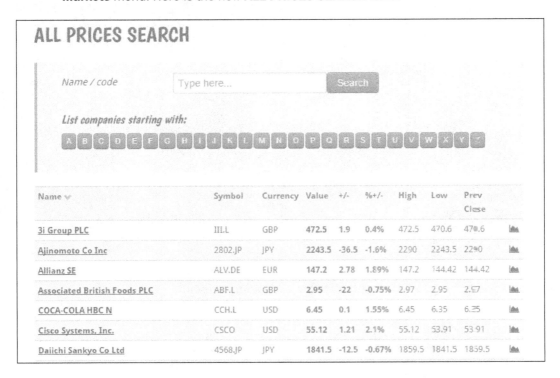

11. The following screenshot corresponds to the **SEARCH BY MARKET** form:

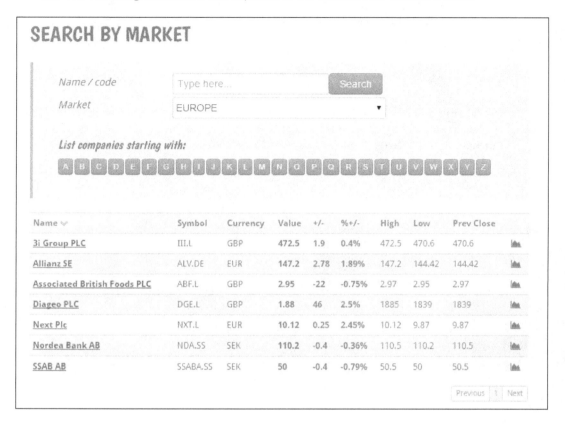

12. Finally, find the following new **Risers and Fallers** screen:

TOP 10 RISERS

Name	Symbol	Currency	Value	+/-	%+/-	High	Low	Prev Close	
Noble Group Limited	N21.SI	SGD	1.05	0.04	3.42%	1.05	1.01	1.01	📊
Diageo PLC	DGE.L	GBP	1.88	46	2.5%	1885	1839	1839	📊
Next Plc	NXT.L	EUR	10.12	0.25	2.45%	10.12	9.87	9.87	📊
Hongkong Land Holdings Limited	H78.SI	USD	7.81	0.18	2.34%	7.81	7.62	7.62	📊
Visa Inc.	V	USD	98.14	2.25	2.3%	100.39	98.14	98.14	📊
Cisco Systems, Inc.	CSCO	USD	55.12	1.21	2.1%	55.12	53.91	53.91	📊
Allianz SE	ALV.DE	EUR	147.2	2.78	1.89%	147.2	144.42	144.42	📊
COCA-COLA HBC N	CCH.L	USD	6.45	0.1	1.55%	6.45	6.35	6.35	📊
SIA	C6L.SI	SGD	3.25	0.04	1.23%	3.25	3.21	3.21	📊
3i Group PLC	III.L	GBP	472.5	1.9	0.4%	472.5	470.6	470.6	📊

TOP 10 FALLERS

Name	Symbol	Currency	Value	+/-	%+/-	High	Low	Prev Close	
McDonald's Corp.	MCD	USD	32.68	-2.25	-6.68%	34.93	32.68	34.93	📊
Fuyao Glass Industry Group Co Ltd	600660.CH	CNY	45.89	-1.25	-2.7%	47.14	45.39	45.89	📊
Hunan TV & Broadcast Intermediary Co Ltd	000917.CH	CNY	12.09	-0.3	-2.45%	12.39	12.09	12.39	📊
Ajinomoto Co Inc	2802.JP	JPY	2243.5	-36.5	-1.6%	2290	2243.5	2290	📊
Wipro Ltd	WPRO.IN	INR	650.55	-8.95	-1.36%	659.5	650.55	659.5	📊
SSAB AB	SSABA.SE	SEK	50	-0.4	-0.79%	50.5	50	50.5	📊

How it works...

Again, this recipe is mostly about Spring Data and how to make Spring MVC support Spring Data for us.

Spring Data pagination support (you will love it!)

We already looked at some of the benefits of the Spring Data repository abstraction in the previous chapter.

In this section, we will see how Spring Data supports the pagination concepts in its abstracted repositories. A very beneficial extension of that, is offered to Spring MVC with a specific argument-resolver to prevent any custom adaption logic.

Pagination and sorting in repositories

You can notice the use of Pageable arguments in the methods of our repository interfaces. For example below is the `IndexRepositoryJpa` repository:

```
public interface IndexRepositoryJpa extends JpaRepository<Index,
    String>{
    List<Index> findByMarket(Market market);
    Page<Index> findByMarket(Market market, Pageable pageable);
    List<Index> findAll();
    Page<Index> findAll(Pageable pageable);
    Index findByCode(MarketCode code);
}
```

Spring Data recognizes the `org.springframework.data.domain.Pageable` Type as the method argument. It also recognizes the `org.springframework.data.domain.Sort` Type when a full `Pageable` instance is not necessary. It applies pagination and sorting to our queries dynamically.

You can see more examples here (taken from the Spring reference document):

```
Page<User> findByLastname(String lastname, Pageable pageable);
Slice<User> findByLastname(String lastname, Pageable pageable);
List<User> findByLastname(String lastname, Sort sort);
List<User> findByLastname(String lastname, Pageable pageable);
```

 Bear in mind that sorting options are also handled through `Pageable`. Incidentally, this is the way we sort in the application.

From these extra examples, you can see that Spring Data can return a `Page` (org.springframework.data.domain.Page), a `Slice` (org.springframework.data.domain.Slice) or simply a `List`.

But here is the amazing part: a `Page` object contains everything we need to build powerful pagination tools at the front end! Earlier, we saw the `json` response provided with one `Page` of elements.

With With the following request: `http://localhost:8080/api/indices/US.json?size=2&page=0&sort=dailyLatestValue,asc`, we have asked for the first page and received a `Page` object telling us whether or not this page is the first or the last one (`firstPage: true/false, lastPage: true/false`), the number of elements within the page (`numberOfElements: 2`), the total number of pages, and the total number of elements (`totalPages: 2, totalElements: 3`).

This means that Spring Data first executed the query we wanted it to execute, and then executed transparently a count query without the pagination filters.

A `Slice` object is a super interface of `Page`, which does not carry the counts for `numberOfElements` and `totalElements`.

PagingAndSortingRepository<T,ID>

If a repository does not already extend `JpaRepository<T, ID>`, we can make it extend `PagingAndSortingRepository<T, ID>`, which is an extension of `CrudRepository<T, ID>`. It will provide extra methods to retrieve Entities using the pagination and sorting abstraction. These methods are:

```
Iterable<T> findAll(Sort sort);
Page<T> findAll(Pageable pageable);
```

The web part – PageableHandlerMethodArgumentResolver

As introduced earlier, we have added the `org.springframework.data.web.PageableHandlerMethodArgumentResolver` bean to our `RequestMappingHandlerAdapter` as a `customArgumentResolver`. Doing so has allowed us to rely on the Spring data binding to transparently prepopulate a `Pageable` instance available as a method handler argument (highlighted in bold in the 1st step of this recipe).

Here is some more information about the request parameters we can use for the binding:

Parameter name	Purpose / usage	Default values
page	The page we want to retrieve	0
size	The size of the page we want to retrieve.	10
sort	The properties that should be sorted in the format `property,property(,ASC|DESC)`. We should use multiple `sort` parameters if we want to switch directions, for example: `?sort=firstname&sort=lastname,asc`.	The default sort direction is ascending.

As implemented in our first step, default values can be customized in cases where specific parameters are missing. This is achieved with the `@PageableDefault` annotation:

```
@PageableDefault(
size=10, page=0, sort={"dailyLatestValue"}, direction=Direction.DESC
)
```

The page, size, and sort parameter names can be overridden by setting the appropriate `PageableHandlerMethodArgumentResolver` properties in the Spring configuration.

If for some reason we don't make use of `PageableHandlerMethodArgumentResolver`, we can still catch our own request parameters (for pagination) and build a `PageRequest` instance from them (for example, `org.springframework.data.domain.PageRequest` is a `Pageable` implementation).

A useful specification argument resolver

Before introducing this useful specification argument resolver, we must introduce the concept of specification.

The JPA2 criteria API and Spring Data JPA specifications

The Spring Data reference document tells us that JPA 2 has introduced a criteria API that can be used to build queries programmatically. When writing `criteria`, we actually define the where clause of a query for a domain class.

The Spring Data JPA takes the concept of specification from Eric Evans's book *Domain Driven Design*, following the same semantics and providing an API to define such specifications using the JPA criteria API.

To support specifications, we can extend our repository interface with the `JpaSpecificationExecutor` interface, as we did in our `ProductRepository` interface:

```
@Repository
public interface ProductRepository<T extends Product> extends
   JpaRepository<T, String>, JpaSpecificationExecutor<T> {
   Page<T> findByMarket(Market marketEntity, Pageable pageable);
   Page<T> findByNameStartingWith(String param, Pageable
     pageable);
   Page<T> findByNameStartingWith(String param, Specification<T>
     spec, Pageable pageable);
}
```

In our example, the `findByNameStartingWith` method retrieves all the products of a specific Type (`StockProduct`) that have a name starting with the `param` argument and that match the `spec` specification.

SpecificationArgumentResolver

As we said earlier, this `CustomArgumentResolver` is not bound to an official Spring project (yet). Its use can fit some use cases such as local search engines to complement Spring Data dynamic queries, pagination, and sorting features.

In the same way we build a `Pageable` instance from specific parameters, this argument resolver also allows us to transparently build a `Specification` instance from specific parameters.

It uses `@Spec` annotations to define `where` clauses such as `like`, `equal`, `likeIgnoreCase`, `in`, and so on. These `@Spec` annotations can then be combined with each other to form groups of `AND` and `OR` clauses with the help of `@And` and `@Or` annotations. A perfect use case is to develop our search features as a complement to the pagination and sorting function.

You should read the following article which is an introduction to the project. This article is entitled *"an alternative API for filtering data with Spring MVC & Spring Data JPA"*:

```
http://blog.kaczmarzyk.net/2014/03/23/alternative-api-for-filtering-
data-with-spring-mvc-and-spring-data
```

Also, find with the following address the project's repository and its documentation:

```
https://github.com/tkaczmarzyk/specification-arg-resolver
```

> As useful as it can be, to bear in mind that the number of users of this library is still much lower than the Spring community.

There's more...

We have been focusing on Spring MVC so far. However with the presented new screens, there are also changes at the front end (AngularJS).

Spring Data

To find out more about Spring Data capabilities, check out the official reference document:

```
http://docs.spring.io/spring-data/jpa/docs/1.8.0.M1/reference/html
```

Angular routes

If you navigate between the **Home** and **Prices and Market** menus, you will see that the whole page is never entirely refreshed. All the content is loaded asynchronously.

To achieve this, we used the AngularJS routing. The `global_routes.js` file has been created for this purpose:

```
cloudStreetMarketApp.config(function($locationProvider,
  $routeProvider) {
  $locationProvider.html5Mode(true);
  $routeProvider
    .when('/portal/index', {
      templateUrl: '/portal/html/home.html',
      controller: 'homeMainController'
```

```
        })
    .when('/portal/indices-:name', {
      templateUrl: '/portal/html/indices-by-market.html',
      controller: 'indicesByMarketTableController'
    })
      .when('/portal/stock-search', {
        templateUrl: '/portal/html/stock-search.html',
        controller:  'stockSearchMainController'
      })
      .when('/portal/stock-search-by-market', {
        templateUrl: '/portal/html/stock-search-by-market.html',
        controller:  'stockSearchByMarketMainController'
      })
      .when('/portal/stocks-risers-fallers', {
        templateUrl: '/portal/html/stocks-risers-fallers.html',
        controller:  'stocksRisersFallersMainController'
      })
      .otherwise({ redirectTo: '/' });
});
```

Here, we defined a mapping table between routes (URL paths that the application queries, as part of the navigation through the `href` tags) and HTML templates (which are available on the server as public static resources). We have created an `html` directory for these templates.

Then, AngularJS asynchronously loads a template each time we request a specific URL path. As often, AngularJS operates transclusions do to this (it basically drops and replace entire DOM sections). Since templates are just templates, they need to be bound to controllers, which operate other AJAX requests through our factories, pull data from our REST API, and render the expected content.

In the previous example:

- `/portal/index` is a route, that is, a requested path
- `/portal/html/home.html` is the mapped template
- `homeMainController` is the target controller

See also

You can read more about AngularJS routing at

`https://docs.angularjs.org/tutorial/step_07`

Bootstrap pagination with the Angular UI

We have used the pagination component of the UI Bootstrap project (http://angular-ui.github.io/bootstrap) from the AngularUI team (http://angular-ui.github.io). This project provides a Boostrap component operated with and for AngularJS.

In the case of pagination, we obtain a Bootstrap component (perfectly integrated with the Bootstrap stylesheet) driven by specific AngularJS directives.

One of our pagination components can be found in the stock-search.html template:

```
<pagination page="paginationCurrentPage"
  ng-model="paginationCurrentPage"
  items-per-page="pageSize"
  total-items="paginationTotalItems"
  ng-change="setPage(paginationCurrentPage)">
</pagination>
```

The page, ng-model, items-per-page, total-items, and ng-change directives use variables (paginationCurrentPage, pageSize and paginationTotalItems), which are attached to the stockSearchController scope.

> To find out more about this project, visit its documentation at
> http://angular-ui.github.io/bootstrap

Handling exceptions globally

This recipe presents a technique for handling exception globally in a web application.

Getting ready

There are different ways to handle exceptions in Spring MVC. We can choose to define controller-specific @ExceptionHandler or we can choose to register @ExceptionHandler globally in the @ControllerAdvice classes.

We developed the second option in our REST API, even if our CloudstreetApiWCI super-class could have shared @ExceptionHandler among its controllers.

Now we will see how to automatically map custom and generic exception types to HTTP status codes, and how to wrap the right error messages in a generic response object that can be used by any client.

How to do it...

1. We need a wrapper object to be sent back to the client when an error occurs:

```java
public class ErrorInfo {
    public final String error;
    public int status;
    public final String date;

    private static final DateFormat dateFormat = new
        SimpleDateFormat("yyyy-MM-dd HH:mm:ss.SSS");
    public ErrorInfo(Throwable throwable, HttpStatus status){
        this.error = ExceptionUtil.getRootMessage(throwable);
        this.date = dateFormat.format(new Date());
        this.status = status.value();
    }
    public ErrorInfo(String message, HttpStatus status) {
        this.error = message;
        this.date = dateFormat.format(new Date());
        this.status = status.value();
    }
    @Override
    public String toString() {
      return "ErrorInfo [status="+status+", error="+error+
        ", date=" + date + "]";
    }
}
```

2. We create a `RestExceptionHandler` class annotated with
   `@ControllerAdvice`. This `RestExceptionHandler` class also inherits the
   `ResponseEntityExceptionHandler` support class, which gives us access
   to a default mapping exception/response status ready to be overridden:

```java
@ControllerAdvice
public class RestExceptionHandler extends
  ResponseEntityExceptionHandler {

    @Override
protected ResponseEntity<Object> handleExceptionInternal(Exception
ex, Object body,
    HttpHeaders headers, HttpStatus status, WebRequest
    request) {
if(body instanceof String){
return new ResponseEntity<Object>(new ErrorInfo((String)
    body, status), headers, status);
    }
    return new ResponseEntity<Object>(new ErrorInfo(ex,
    status), headers, status);
```

```java
}

    // 400
    @Override
protected ResponseEntity<Object>
  handleHttpMessageNotReadable(final
  HttpMessageNotReadableException ex, final HttpHeaders
  headers, final HttpStatus status, final WebRequest
  request) {
return handleExceptionInternal(ex, "The provided request
  body is not readable!", headers, HttpStatus.BAD_REQUEST,
  request);
}


@Override
protected ResponseEntity<Object>
  handleTypeMismatch(TypeMismatchException ex, HttpHeaders
  headers, HttpStatus status, WebRequest request) {
  return handleExceptionInternal(ex, "The request parameters
  were not valid!", headers, HttpStatus.BAD_REQUEST,
  request);
  }
(...)


@ExceptionHandler({
  InvalidDataAccessApiUsageException.class,
  DataAccessException.class ,
  IllegalArgumentException.class })
protected ResponseEntity<Object> handleConflict(final
  RuntimeException ex, final WebRequest request) {
    return handleExceptionInternal(ex, "The request
      parameters were not valid!", new HttpHeaders(),
      HttpStatus.BAD_REQUEST, request);
}
(...)

// 500
@ExceptionHandler({ NullPointerException.class,
  IllegalStateException.class })
public ResponseEntity<Object> handleInternal(final
  RuntimeException ex, final WebRequest request) {
return handleExceptionInternal(ex,  "An internal      error
  happened during the request! Please try      again or
  contact an administrator.", new HttpHeaders(),
  HttpStatus.INTERNAL_SERVER_ERROR, request);
}
}
```

Both the `ErrorInfo` wrapper and this `RestExceptionHandler` will support internationalization. It will be demonstrated in *Chapter 7, Developing CRUD Operations and Validations*.

3. We have created the two following property editors for the MarketCode and QuotesInterval Enums:

```
public class MarketCodeEditor extends
  PropertyEditorSupport{
public void setAsText(String text) {
    try{
      setValue(MarketCode.valueOf(text));
    } catch (IllegalArgumentException e) {
      throw new IllegalArgumentException("The provided
        value for the market code variable is invalid!");
    }
  }
}
public class QuotesIntervalEditor extends
  PropertyEditorSupport {
    public void setAsText(String text) {
    try{
       setValue(QuotesInterval.valueOf(text));
    } catch (IllegalArgumentException e) {
      throw new IllegalArgumentException("The provided
        value for the quote-interval variable is
          invalid!");
    }
  }
}
```

 These two property editors are automatically registered because they are satisfying a naming and location convention. Since `MarketCode` and `QuotesInterval` are enum values, Spring looks for `MarketCodeEditor` (Editor suffix) and `QuotesIntervalEditor` in the Enums' packages.

4. That's it! You can test it by providing an incorrect market code in the `getHistoIndex` method of the AngularJS factory (in the `home_financial_graph.js` file). Change the call from `$http.get("/api/indices/"+market+"wrong/"+index+"/histo.json")` to `$http.get("/api/indices/"+market+"/"+index+"/histo.json")`.

5. After restarting the whole application (**cloudstreetmarket-webapp** and **cloudstreetmarket-api**), the call to `http://localhost:8080/portal/index` will induce the **Ajax GET** request for the index loading to result in a **400** status code:

6. More details about this failed request will show up in the json response:

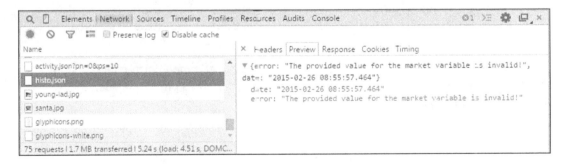

    The received error message—**The provided value for the market variable is invalid!** is acceptable for now.

7. You can reset the `home_financial_graph.js` file after getting this result.

How it works...

Here, we are focusing on the way we handle exceptions in a REST environment. The expectations are slightly different than in a pure web app because the direct user may not necessarily be a human. For this reason, a REST API has to maintain standard, consistent, and self-explanatory communication even if a process has generated an error or has been unsuccessful.

This consistency is achieved by always returning an appropriate HTTP status code feedback to the client from the server about the request treatment, and by always returning a response body in a format that is expected by the client (a format that matches one of the mime types listed in the **Accept** header of the HTTP request).

Global exception handling with @ControllerAdvice

Spring 3.2 has brought a solution that is much more suitable to REST environments than the previous exception handling mechanisms. With this solution, classes annotated with @ControllerAdvice can be registered in a different locations of the API. These annotations are looked-up by classpath scanning and are auto-registered in a common repository to support all of the controllers (by default) or subsets of controllers (using the annotation options).

In our case, we defined one single @ControllerAdvice to monitor this entire API. The idea is to define, in the @ControllerAdvice annotated class(es), the relevant methods that can match match specific exception Type(s) to specific ResponseEntity(ies). A ReponseEntity carries a body and a response status code.

These methods to define are annotated with @ExceptionHandler. The options of this annotation allow you to target specific exception Types. A common pattern when defining a @ControllerAdvice is to make it extend the support class ResponseEntityExceptionHandler.

The support ResponseEntityExceptionHandler class

The support ResponseEntityExceptionHandler class provides a predefined mapping between native exceptions (such as NoSuchRequestHandlingMethodException, ConversionNotSupportedException, TypeMismatchException, and so on) and HTTP status codes.

The ResponseEntityExceptionHandler implements a common pattern for response rendering. It invokes case-specific rendering methods declared as protected, such the following handleNoSuchRequestHandlingMethod

```
protected ResponseEntity<Object> handleNoSuchRequestHandlingMethod(NoS
uchRequestHandlingMethod
  Exception ex, HttpHeaders headers, HttpStatus status,
  WebRequest request) {
    pageNotFoundLogger.warn(ex.getMessage());
  return handleExceptionInternal(ex, null, headers, status,
    request);
}
```

These methods are obviously fully overridable in the `@ControllerAdvice` annotated class(es). The important thing is to return the `handleExceptionInternal` method.

This `handleExceptionInternal` method is also defined as protected and then overridable. This is what we have done—returned a uniform `ErrorInfo` instance:

```
@Override
protected ResponseEntity<Object> handleExceptionInternal
  (Exception ex, Object body, HttpHeaders headers, HttpStatus
  status, WebRequest request) {
  return new ResponseEntity<Object>(new ErrorInfo(ex,
  (body!=null)? body.toString() : null, status), headers, status);
}
```

A uniform error response object

There are no specific standard practices about the fields that the uniform error response object should expose. We decided to offer the following structure for the `ErrorInfo` object:

```
{
  error: "Global categorization error message",
  message: "Specific and explicit error message",
  status: 400,
  date: "yyyy-MM-dd HH:mm:ss.SSS"
}
```

Using two different levels of messages (the global error message coming from the exception Type and the case-specific message) allows the client side to choose the more appropriate one (or even both!) to be rendered in the application for each situation.

As we already said, this `ErrorInfo` object doesn't support internationalization yet. We will improve it later in the *Chapter 7, Developing CRUD Operations and Validations*.

There's more...

We provide here a collection of resources related to exception handling in a web environment:

HTTP Status Codes

The **World Wide Web Consortium** specifies explicit response status codes for HTTP/1.1. More important than the error messages themselves, it is critical for a REST API to implement them. You can read more about this at:

`http://www.w3.org/Protocols/rfc2616/rfc2616-sec10.html`

The official article about exception handling in Spring MVC

An article from in the spring.io blog is a very interesting resource. It is not limited to the REST use case. It can be accessed from this address: `http://spring.io/blog/2013/11/01/exception-handling-in-spring-mvc`.

JavaDocs

Here we provide for configuration or simply usage, the URL for two JavaDoc resources:

ExceptionHandlerExceptionResolver:

```
http://docs.spring.io/spring/docs/current/javadoc-api/
org/springframework/web/servlet/mvc/method/annotation/
ExceptionHandlerExceptionResolver.html
```

ResponseEntityExceptionHandler:

```
http://docs.spring.io/spring/docs/current/javadoc-api/
org/springframework/web/servlet/mvc/method/annotation/
ResponseEntityExceptionHandler.html
```

See also

> ▶ Check out the official demo website, which exposes how the different Types of Spring MVC exceptions can be rendered: `http://mvc-exceptions-v2.cfapps.io`

Documenting and exposing an API with Swagger

This section details how to provide and expose metadata about the REST API using Swagger.

Getting ready

We are often required to document APIs for users and customers. When documenting an API, depending on the tools we use, we often get a few extras such as the ability to generate client code from the API metadata or even the generation of integrated test harnesses for the API.

There isn't yet a recognized and universal standard for the format of the API metadata. This lack of standards leads to a quite a few different solutions on the market for the REST documentation.

We have chosen Swagger here because it has the largest and the most active community. It has existed since 2011, and it offers a very nice UI/test harness and great configuration by default.

How to do it...

This section details what can be done and also what we have done in the code base of the checked-out v4.x.x branch.

1. We have added a Maven dependency for the `swagger-springmvc` project (version 0.9.5) to **cloudstreetmarket-core** and **cloudstreetmarket-parent**:

```
<dependency>
  <groupId>com.mangofactory</groupId>
  <artifactId>swagger-springmvc</artifactId>
  <version>${swagger-springmvc.version}</version>
</dependency>
```

2. The following swagger `configuration` class has been created:

```
@Configuration
@EnableSwagger //Loads the beans required by the framework
public class SwaggerConfig {

    private SpringSwaggerConfig springSwaggerConfig;
    @Autowired
      public void setSpringSwaggerConfig(SpringSwaggerConfig
      springSwaggerConfig) {
      this.springSwaggerConfig = springSwaggerConfig;
      }
    @Bean
    public SwaggerSpringMvcPlugin customImplementation(){
        return new SwaggerSpringMvcPlugin(
          this.springSwaggerConfig)
            .includePatterns ".*")
            .apiInfo(new ApiInfo(
            "Cloudstreet Market / Swagger UI",
            "The Rest API developed with Spring MVC
              Cookbook [PACKT]",
            "",
            "alex.bretet@gmail.com",
            "LGPL",
            "http://www.gnu.org/licenses/gpl-3.0.en.html"
        ));
    }
}
```

3. The following configuration has been added to the `dispatch-context.xml`:

```
<bean class="com.mangofactory.swagger.
  configuration.SpringSwaggerConfig"/>

<bean class="edu.zc.csm.api.swagger.SwaggerConfig"/>
<context:property-placeholder location="classpath*:/META-
  INF/properties/swagger.properties" />
```

4. As per the previous configuration, a swagger.properties file has been added at the path `src/main/resources/META-INF/properties` with the content:

```
documentation.services.version=1.0
documentation.services.basePath=http://localhost:8080/api
```

5. Our three controllers have been added a basic documentation. See the following documentation annotations added to `IndexController`:

```
@Api(value = "indices", description = "Financial indices")
@RestController
@RequestMapping(value="/indices",
  produces={"application/xml", "application/json"})
public class IndexController extends CloudstreetApiWCI {

@RequestMapping(method=GET)
@ApiOperation(value = "Get overviews of indices", notes =
  "Return a page of index-overviews")
public Page<IndexOverviewDTO> getIndices(
@ApiIgnore @PageableDefault(size=10, page=0,
  sort={"dailyLatestValue"}, direction=Direction.DESC)
  Pageable pageable){
    return
    marketService.getLastDayIndicesOverview(pageable);
}


@RequestMapping(value="/{market}", method=GET)
@ApiOperation(value = "Get overviews of indices filtered by
  market", notes = "Return a page of index-overviews")
public Page<IndexOverviewDTO> getIndicesPerMarket(
  @PathVariable MarketCode market,
  @ApiIgnore
@PageableDefault(size=10, page=0,
  sort={"dailyLatestValue"}, direction=Direction.DESC)
  Pageable pageable){
    return
    marketService.getLastDayIndicesOverview(market, pageable);
}


@RequestMapping(value="/{market}/{index}/histo",
  method=GET)
@ApiOperation(value = "Get historical-data for one index",
  notes = "Return a set of historical-data from one index")
public HistoProductDTO getHistoIndex(
  @PathVariable("market") MarketCode market,
  @ApiParam(value="Index code: ^OEX")
  @PathVariable("index") String
```

```
indexCode,@ApiParam(value="Start date: 2014-01-01")
@RequestParam(value="fd",defaultValue="") Date
  fromDate,
@ApiParam(value="End date: 2020-12-12")
@RequestParam(value="td",defaultValue="") Date
  toDate,
@ApiParam(value="Period between snapshots")
@RequestParam(value="i",defaultValue="MINUTE_30")
QuotesInterval interval){
    return marketService.getHistoIndex(indexCode, market,
      fromDate, toDate, interval);
  }
}
```

6. We have downloaded the swagger UI project from `https://github.com/swagger-api/swagger-ui`.This is a collection of static files (JS, CSS, HTML, and pictures). It has been pasted in the webapp directory of our **cloudstreetmarket-api** project.

7. Finally, the following mvc namespace configuration has been added to `dispatch-context.xml` again in order for the Spring MVC to open access to static files in the project:

```
<!-- Serve static content-->
<mvc:default-servlet-handler/>
```

8. When we have this configuration, accessing the following URL on the server `http://localhost:8080/api/index.html` brings up the Swagger UI documentation portal:

More than just a REST documentation repository, it is also a handy test harness:

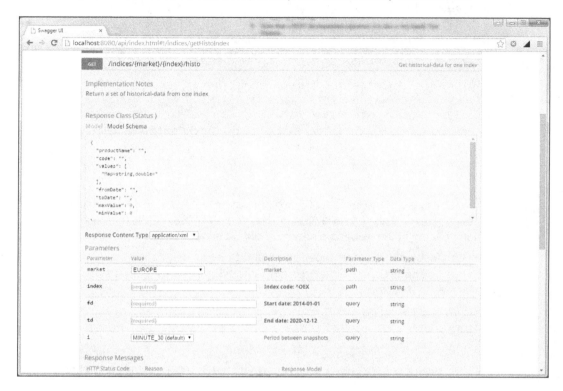

Swagger has its own controller that publishes the metadata of our API. The Swagger UI targets this metadata, parses it, and represents it as a usable interface.

An exposed metadata

On the server side, with the `com.mangofactory/swagger-springmvc` dependency added to the `swagger-springmvc` project and with the presented `SwaggerConfig` class, the library creates a controller on the root path: `/api-docs` and publishes the entire metadata there for the REST API.

If you visit `http://localhost:8080/api/api-docs`, you will reach the root of our REST API documentation:

This content is the exposed metadata that implements the Swagger specification. The metadata is a navigable structure. Links to other parts of the metadata can be found in the `<path>` nodes of the XML content.

The Swagger UI

The Swagger UI is only made of static files (CSS, HTML, JavaScript, and so on). The JavaScript logic implements the Swagger specification and recursively parses the entire exposed metadata. It then dynamically builds the API documentation website and test harness that we have presented, digging out every single endpoint and its metadata.

There's more...

In this section, we suggest you to look further into Swagger and its Spring MVC project implementation.

The Swagger.io

Visit the framework's website and its specification: `http://swagger.io`.

The swagger-springmvc documentation

The swagger-springmvc project is changing as it is becoming part of a bigger project named SpringFox. SpringFox now also supports the second version of the Swagger specification. We recommend you to visit their current reference document:

`http://springfox.github.io/springfox/docs/current`

They also provide a migration guide to move from the swagger specification 1.2 (that we have implemented here) to the swagger specification 2.0:

`https://github.com/springfox/springfox/blob/master/docs/transitioning-to-v2.md`

See also

This section guides you toward alternative tools and specification to Swagger:

Different tools, different standards

We have mentioned that there isn't a common standard yet that would clearly legitimize one tool over another. Thus, it is probably good to acknowledge tools other than Swagger because things are moving quite fast in this domain. Here, you can find two great comparison articles:

- `http://www.mikestowe.com/2014/07/raml-vs-swagger-vs-api-blueprint.php`
- `http://apiux.com/2013/04/09/rest-metadata-formats`

5

Authenticating with Spring MVC

This chapter covers the following recipes:

- ▶ Configuring Apache HTTP to proxy your Tomcat(s)
- ▶ Adapting users and roles to fit Spring Security
- ▶ Authenticating over a BASIC scheme
- ▶ Storing credentials in a REST environment
- ▶ Authenticating with a third-party OAuth2 scheme
- ▶ Authorizing on services and controllers

Introduction

In this chapter, developing the `CloudStreetMarket` application, we cover two ways of authenticating in a Spring environment.

We believe that only providing Security annotations to restrict controllers and services wouldn't be sufficient to give a big picture of Spring Authentication. It's clearly not possible to feel confident about the Security tools that can be used with Spring MVC, without a few key concepts such as the role of the `Authentication` object, the Spring Security filter-chain, the `SecurityInterceptor` workflow, and so on. As it is necessary for configuring OAuth, we will also show you how to set up an Apache HTTP proxy and a host alias on your machine to emulate the `cloudstreetmarket.com` domain locally.

Configuring Apache HTTP to proxy your Tomcat(s)

We are going to access the application using a local alias `cloudstreetmarket.com` (on the port 80) rather than the former `localhost:8080`. Implementing the configuration for that is sometimes a mandatory step, when developing third-party integrations. In our case, the third-party will be *Yahoo!* and its *OAuth2* authentication servers.

Getting ready

It will mostly be about configuration. We will install an Apache HTTP server and stick to the Apache Tomcat How-To. This will drive us to update our Tomcat connector and to create a virtual host in the Apache configuration file.

You will discover how this configuration can allow a great flexibility and simply serve web content to the customers with an advanced and scalable architecture.

How to do it...

1. On MS Windows, download and install Apache HTTP Server.

    ❑   The easiest way is probably to download directly the binaries from an official distributor. Select and download the appropriated latest Zip archive from one of the following URLs:

    `http://www.apachelounge.com/download`

    `http://www.apachehaus.com/cgi-bin/download.plx`

    ❑   Create a directory `C:\apache24` and unzip the downloaded archive into this location.

     You should be able to reach the bin directory through this form: `C:\apache24\bin`.

2. On Linux / Mac OS, download and install Apache HTTP Server.

    1. Download the latest sources (compressed in a `tar.gz` archive) from the apache website:

    `http://httpd.apache.org/download.cgi#apache24`

    2. From the downloaded archive, extract the sources:

    ```
    $ tar -xvzf httpd-NN.tar.gz
    $ cd httpd-NN
    ```

The NN command being the current version of Apache HTTP.

   3. Autoconfigure the arborescence:

```
$ ./configure
```

   4. Compile the package:

```
$ make
```

   5. Install the arborescence:

```
$ make install
```

3. On MS Windows, add a new alias in the hosts file.

   1. Edit with Notepad the file that can be found at the following path:

```
%SystemRoot%\system32\drivers\etc\hosts
```

 This file has no extension, Notepad 'doesn't complain about that when you want to save the file.

   2. Add the following entry at the end of the file:

```
127.0.0.1 cloudstreetmarket.com
```

   3. Save the modification.

4. On Linux/Mac OS, add a new alias in the hosts file.

   1. Edit the file that can be found at the following path: /etc/hosts

   2. Add the following entry at the end of the file:

```
127.0.0.1 cloudstreetmarket.com
```

   3. Save the modification.

5. For all Operation Systems, edit the httpd.conf Apache configuration file.

   1. This file can either be found at C:\apache24\conf (on Windows) or at /usr/local/apache2/conf (on Linux or Mac).

   2. Uncomment the following two lines:

```
LoadModule proxy_module modules/mod_proxy.so
LoadModule proxy_http_module modules/mod_proxy_http.so
```

   3. Add the following block at the very bottom of the file:

```
<VirtualHost cloudstreetmarket.com:80>
    ProxyPass        /portal http://localhost:8080/portal
```

```
ProxyPassReverse /portal http://localhost:8080/portal
ProxyPass        /api   http://localhost:8080/api
ProxyPassReverse /api   http://localhost:8080/api
RedirectMatch ^/$ /portal/index
</VirtualHost>
```

A sample of a modified `httpd.conf` file (for Apache HTTP 2.4.18) can be found in the `chapter_5/source_code/app/apache` directory.

6. Edit the `server.xml` Tomcat configuration file.

    1. This file can either be found at `C:\tomcat8\conf` (on Windows) or at `/home/usr/{system.username}/tomcat8/conf` (on Linux or Mac).

    2. Find the `<Connector port"="8080"" protocol"="HTTP/1.1""`...`>` definition and edit it as follows:

    ```
    <Connector port"="8080"" protocol"="HTTP/1.1""
    connectionTimeout"="20000"
    redirectPort"="8443""
    proxyName"="cloudstreetmarket.com"" proxyPort"="80""/>
    ```

A sample of a modified `server.xml` file (for Apache Tomcat 8.0.30) can be found in the `chapter_5/source_code/app/tomcat` directory.

7. On MS Windows, start the Apache HTTP server.

    1. Open a command prompt window.

    ❑   Enter the following command:

    ```
    $ cd C:/apache24/bin
    ```

    2. Install an Apache service:

    ```
    $ httpd.exe -k install
    ```

    ❑   Start the server:

    ```
    $ httpd.exe -k start
    ```

8. On Linux/Mac OS, start the Apache HTTP server::

    ❑   Start the server:

    ```
    $ sudo apachectl start
    ```

Now start the Tomcat server and open your favorite web browser. Go to `http://cloudstreetmarket.com`, you should obtain the following landing-page:

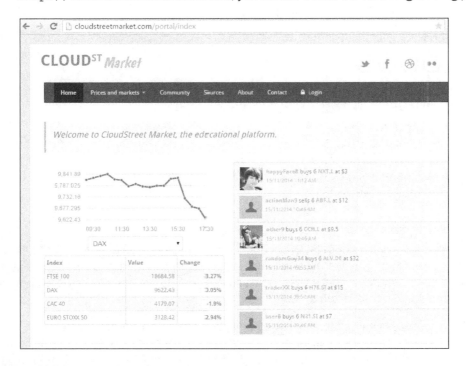

How it works...

The Apache HTTP configuration we made here is somehow a standard nowadays. It supplies an infinite level of customization on a network. It also allows us to initiate the scalability.

DNS configuration or host aliasing

Let's revisit how web browsers work. When we target a URL in the web browser, the final server is accessed from its IP, to establish a TCP connection on a specific port. The browser needs to resolve this IP for the specified name.

To do so, it queries a chain of Domain Name Servers (on the Internet, the chain often starts with the user's **Internet Service Provider** (**ISP**). Each DNS basically works this way:

 ▸ It tries to resolve the IP by itself, looking-up in its database or its cache

 ▸ If unsuccessful, it asks another DNS and waits for the response to cache the result and sends it back to the caller

A DNS managing one specific domain is called a **Start Of Authority** (**SOA**). Such DNS are usually provided by registrars, and we usually use their services to configure records (and our server IP) for a domain zone.

Around the web, each DNS tries to resolve the ultimate SOA. The top hierarchy of DNS servers is called **root name servers**. There are hundreds of them bound to one specific **Top-Level Domain** (**TLD** such as .com, `.net`, `.org`...).

When the browser gets the IP, it tries to establish a TCP connection on the specified port (it defaults to 80). The remote server accepts the connection and the HTTP request is sent over the network.

In production – editing DNS records

As soon as we approach the production stage, we need the real domain name to be configured for DNS records, online, with a domain-name provider. There are different types of records to edit. Each one serves a specific purpose or resource type: host, canonical names, mail-exchanger, name server, and others. Specific guidance can usually be found on the domain name provider website.

An alias for the host

Before contacting any kind of DNS, the operating system may be able to resolve the IP by itself. For this purpose, the host file is a plain-text `registry`. Adding aliases to this registry defines proxies to whatever final server. Doing so is a common technique for development environments but isn't restricted to them.

Each line represents an IP address followed by one or more host names. Each field is separated by white space or tabs. Comments can be specified at the very beginning of a line with a #character. Blank lines are ignored and IPs can be defined in *IPv4* or *IPv6*.

This file is only for hosts aliasing, we don't deal with ports at this stage!

Alias definition for OAuth developments

In this chapter, we will authenticate with an OAuth2 protocol. In OAuth, there is an **Authentication Server (AS)** and a **Service Provider** (**SP**). In our case, the authentication server will be a third-party system (Yahoo!) and the service provider will be our application (`cloudstreetmarket.com`).

The OAuth2 authentication and authorization happen on the third-party side. As soon as these steps are completed, the authentication Server redirects the HTTP request to the service provider using a call-back URL passed as a parameter or stored as a variable.

Third-parties sometimes block call-back URLs that are pointing to `localhost:8080`. Testing and developing OAuth2 conversations locally remains a necessity.

Configuring a proxy for the hostname (in the hosts file) and a virtual host in an HTTP server to manage ports, URL rewriting, and redirections is a good solution for the local environment but also for a production infrastructure.

Apache HTTP configuration

The Apache HTTP server uses the TCP/IP protocol and provides an implementation of HTTP. TCP/IP allows computers to talk with each other throughout a network.

Each computer using TCP/IP on a network (Local Network Area or Wide Network Area) has an IP address. When a request arrives on an interface (an Ethernet connection for example), it is attempted to be mapped to a service on the machine (DNS, SMTP, HTTP, and so on) using the targeted port number. Apache usually uses the port 80 to listen to. This is a situation when Apache HTTP takes care of one site.

Virtual-hosting

This feature allows us to run and maintain more than one website from a single instance of Apache. We usually group in a `<VirtualHost...>` section, a set of Apache directives for a dedicated site. Each group is identified by a **site ID**.

Different sites can be defined as follows:

1. By name:

    ```
    NameVirtualHost 192.168.0.1
    <VirtualHost portal.cloudstreetmarket.com>…</VirtualHost>
    <VirtualHost api.cloudstreetmarket.com>…</VirtualHost>
    ```

2. By IP (you will still have to define a `ServerName` inside the block):

    ```
    <VirtualHost 192.168.0.1>…</VirtualHost>
    <VirtualHost 192.168.0.2>…</VirtualHost>
    ```

3. By port:

    ```
    Listen 80
    Listen 8080
    <VirtualHost 192.168.0.1:80>…</VirtualHost>
    <VirtualHost 192.168.0.2:8080>…</VirtualHost>
    ```

Our current configuration with one machine and one Tomcat server is not the ideal scenario to demonstrate all the benefits of virtual hosting. However, we have delimited one site with its configuration. It's a first step towards scalability and load-balancing.

The mod_proxy module

This Apache module offers proxy/gateway capabilities to Apache HTTP server. It's a central feature as it can turn an Apache instance into a unique interface able to manage a complex set of applications balanced across multiple machines on the network.

It pushes Apache beyond its initial purpose: exposing a directory on the filesystem via HTTP. It depends on five specific sub-modules: `mod_proxy_http`, `mod_proxy_ftp`, `mod_proxy_ajp`, `mod_proxy_balancer`, and `mod_proxy_connect`. Each of them, when needed, requires the main `mod_proxy` dependency. Proxies can be defined as forward (`ProxyPass`) and/or as reverse (`ProxyPassReverse`). They are often used to provide internet-access to servers located behind firewalls.

The `ProxyPass` can be replaced with `ProxyPassMatch` to offer regex-matching capabilities.

ProxyPassReverse

Reverse-proxies handle responses and redirections exactly as if they were webservers on their own. To be activated, they are usually bound to a `ProxyPass` definition as in our use case here:

```
ProxyPass          /api  http://localhost:8080/api
ProxyPassReverse   /api  http://localhost:8080/api
```

Workers

Proxies manage the configuration of underlying servers and also the communication parameters between them with objects called **workers** (see them as a set of parameters). When used for a reverse-proxy, these workers are configured using `ProxyPass` or `ProxyPassMatch`:

```
ProxyPass /api http://localhost:8080/api connectiontimeout=5
    timeout=30
```

Some examples of worker-parameters are: `connectiontimeout` (in seconds), `keepalive` (On/Off), `loadfactor` (from 1 to 100), `route` (bound to `sessionid` when used inside a load balancer), `ping` (it sends CPING requests to ajp13 connections to ensure Tomcat is not busy), `min`/`max` (number of connection pool entries to the underlying server), `ttl` (expiry time for connections to underlying server)..

The mod_alias module

This module provides URL aliasing and client-request redirecting. We have used this module for redirecting (by default) the requests to `cloudstreetmarket.com` to the index page of the portal web application (`cloudstreetmarket.com/portal/index`).

Note that, in the same way `ProxyPassMatch` improves `ProxyPass`, `RedirectMatch` improves `Redirect` with regex-matching capability.

Tomcat connectors

A **connector** represents a process unit that: listens to a specific port to receive requests, forwards these requests to a specific engine, receives the dynamic content generated by the engine and finally sends back the generated content to the port. Several connectors can be defined in a `Service` component, sharing one single *engine*. One or more *service(s)* can be defined for one Tomcat instance (`Server`). There are two types of connectors in Tomcat..

HTTP connectors

This connector is setup by default in Tomcat on the 8080 port. It supports the HTTP1/1 protocol and allows Catalina to work as a standalone webserver. HTTP connectors can be used behind a proxy. Tomcat supports `mod_proxy` as a load balancer. This is our intended configuration. When implemented behind a proxy, the attributes `proxyName` and `proxyPort` can be set so the servlets bind the specified values to the request attributes `request.getServerPort()` and `request.getServerName()`.

"This connector features the lowest latency and best overall performance."

The Tomcat documentation also states the following about HTTP proxying:

"It should be noted that the performance of HTTP proxying is usually lower than the performance of AJP."

However, configuring an AJP clustering adds an extra layer on the architecture. The necessity for this extra-layer is arguable for a stateless architecture.

AJP connectors

AJP connectors behave as HTTP connectors except that they support the AJP protocol instead of HTTP. **Apache JServ Protocol (AJP)** is an optimized binary version of HTTP connector.

It allows Apache HTTP to balance effectively requests among different Tomcats. It also allows Apache HTTP to serve the static content of web applications while Tomcat focuses on the dynamic content.

On the Apache HTTP side, this connector requires `mod_proxy_ajp`. Our configuration would probably have been:

```
ProxyPass / ajp://localhost:8009/api
ProxyPassReverse / http://cloudstreetmarket.com/api/
```

There is more...

In this section, we will provide a few links for a deeper understanding on the topics:

- DNS and the distributed system:

  `http://computer.howstuffworks.com/dns.htm`

  `https://en.wikipedia.org/wiki/Root_name_server`

- How the domain name system works:

  `http://wiki.bravenet.com/How_the_domain_name_system_works`

- Apache HTTP:

  `http://httpd.apache.org/docs/trunk/getting-started.html`

- ▸ The modules we have used:

  `http://httpd.apache.org/docs/2.2/mod/mod_alias.html`

  `http://httpd.apache.org/docs/2.2/en/mod/mod_proxy.html`

- ▸ Tomcat connectors:

  `http://tomcat.apache.org/tomcat-8.0-doc/connectors.html`

  `http://wiki.apache.org/tomcat/FAQ/Connectors`

  `https://www.mulesoft.com/tcat/tomcat-connectors`

- ▸ In proxy mode:

  `http://tomcat.apache.org/tomcat-8.0-doc/proxy-howto.html#Apache_2.0_Proxy_Support`

See also

- ▸ When using an AJP connector, the ProxyPassReverse definition is slightly different from an HTTP connector:

  `http://www.apachetutor.org/admin/reverseproxies`

  `http://www.humboldt.co.uk/the-mystery-of-proxypassreverse`

- ▸ If you wish to implement an AJP Cluster, go through the following URL:

  `http://www.richardnichols.net/2010/08/5-minute-guide-clustering-apache-tomcat/`

Alternatives to Apache HTTP

The use of Apache HTTP can be argued on very high traffic, especially because the default configuration can lead the program to create a new process for every single connection.

If we only look for a proxy and load-balancer, we should also consider HAProxy. HAProxy is a high-availability load-balancer and proxy server. It is a free and open source (GPL v2) product used in references such as GitHub, StackOverflow, Reddit, Twitter, and others (`http://haproxy.org`).

Nginx is probably (and currently) the most adopted alternative to Apache HTTP. Being focused on high concurrency and low memory usage, its license is a 2-clause BSD license (`http://nginx.org`).

Adapting users and roles to Spring Security

We have thought interesting to split apart this section, since users and roles are usually borderline between the application and Spring Security.

Getting ready

In this recipe, we will install the Spring Security dependencies and update the `User` Entity. We will also create an `Authority` entity that is based on a custom `Role` enum that we created. Finally, we update the `init.sql` script to add a set of existing users.

How to do it...

1. From the **Git Perspective** in Eclipse, checkout the latest version of the branch `v5.x.x`. Then, run a `maven clean install` command on the `cloudstreetmarket-parent` module (right-click on the module, go to **Run as...** | **Maven Clean**, and then navigate to **Run as...** | **Maven Install**). Execute a `Maven Update Project` to synchronize Eclipse with the maven configuration (right-click on the module and then navigate to **Maven | Update Project...**).

    You will notice a few changes both in the frontend and backend of the code.

2. Spring Security comes with the following dependencies, added in `cloudstreetmarket-parent`, `cloudstreetmarket-core` and `cloudstreetmarket-api`::

   ```xml
   <!-- Spring Security -->
   <dependency>
       <groupId>org.springframework.security</groupId>
       <artifactId>spring-security-web</artifactId>
       <version>4.0.0.RELEASE</version>
   </dependency>
   <dependency>
       <groupId>org.springframework.security</groupId>
       <artifactId>spring-security-config</artifactId>
       <version>4.0.0.RELEASE</version>
   </dependency>
   ```

3. The `User` entity has been updated. It now reflects the `users` table (instead of the previous `user` table). It also implements the `UserDetails` interface:

   ```
   @Entity
   @Table(name="users")
   ```

```java
public class User implements UserDetails{
private static final long serialVersionUID =
    1990856213905768044L;

@Id
@Column(name = "user_name", nullable = false)
private String username;

@Column(name = "full_name")
private String fullName;

private String email;
private String password;
private boolean enabled = true;
private String profileImg;

@Column(name="not_expired")
private boolean accountNonExpired;

@Column(name="not_locked")
private boolean accountNonLocked;

@Enumerated(EnumType.STRING)
private SupportedCurrency currency;

@OneToMany(mappedBy= "user", cascade = CascadeType.ALL,
    fetch = FetchType.LAZY)
@OrderBy("id desc")
private Set<Action> actions = new LinkedHashSet<Action>();

@OneToMany(mappedBy="user", cascade = CascadeType.ALL,
    fetch = FetchType.EAGER)
private Set<Authority> authorities = new
    LinkedHashSet<Authority>();

@OneToMany(cascade=CascadeType.ALL, fetch = FetchType.LAZY)
private Set<SocialUser> socialUsers = new
    LinkedHashSet<SocialUser>();

//getters and setters as per the UserDetails interface
...
}
```

This `User` Entity has a relationship with `SocialUser`. `SocialUser` comes into play with the OAuth2 authentication, and we will develop this part later.

4. An Authority Entity has been created and maps a `authorities` table. This Entity also implements the `GrantedAuthority` interface. The class is the following:

```
@Entity
@Table(name"="authorities"",
  uniqueConstraints={@UniqueConstraint(columnNames =
  "{"username""","authority""})})
public class Authority implements GrantedAuthority{
  private static final long serialVersionUID =
    1990856213905768044L;
  public Authority() {}
  public Authority(User user, Role authority) {
    this.user = user;
    this.authority = authority;
  }
  @Id
  @GeneratedValue
  private Long  id;
  @OneToOne(fetch = FetchType.LAZY)
  @JoinColumn(name = ""username"", nullable=false)
  private User user;
  @Column(nullable = false)
  @Enumerated(EnumType.STRING)
  private Role authority;
  //getters and setters as per the GrantedAuthority
  //interface
  ...
}
```

5. For a more readable code, we have created a `Role` Enum in the `cloudstreetmarket-core` module, for the different roles:

```
public enum Role {
  ROLE_ANONYMOUS,
  ROLE_BASIC,
  ROLE_OAUTH2,
  ROLE_ADMIN,
  ROLE_SYSTEM,
  IS_AUTHENTICATED_REMEMBERED; //Transitory role
}
```

6. Also, we have made a few changes in the `init.sql` file. The existing pre-initialization scripts related to users, have been adapted to suit the new schema:

```
insert into users(username, fullname, email, password,
  profileImg, enabled, not_expired, not_locked) values
  ('userC', '', 'fake12@fake.com', '123456', '', true,
  true, true);
insert into authorities(username, authority) values
  ('userC', 'ROLE_'BASIC');
```

7. Start the application. (No exceptions should be observed).

8. Click on the **login** button (on the right-hand side of the main menu). You will see the following popup that allows entering a username and a password to log in:

9. You also have the option to create a new user. In the previous popup, click on the **Create new account** link that can be found at the bottom right. This will load the following pop-up content:

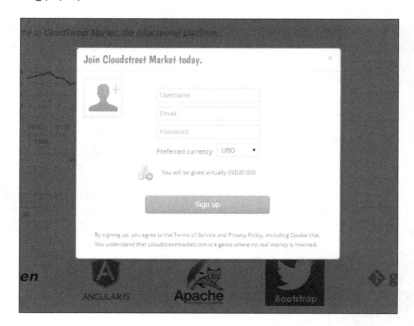

10. Let's create a new user with the following values:

```
username: <marcus>
email: <marcus@chapter5.com>
password: <123456>
preferred currency: <USD>
```

 For the profile picture, you must create on your file system, the directory structure corresponding to the property `pictures.user.path` in `cloudstreetmarket-api/src/main/resources/application.properties`.

Then, click on the user icon in order to upload a profile picture.

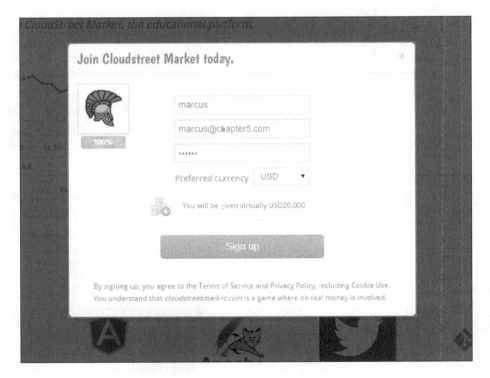

Finally, hit the **Sign up** button and the popup should disappear.

11. Now, call the following URI: `http://cloudstreetmarket.com/api/users/marcus`. The application should fetch the following persisted data for the *Marcus* user:

How it works...

The recipe at this stage preconfigures our entities so they comply with Spring Security. A couple of concepts about Spring Security are mentioned in this part and developed in the following sections.

Introduction to Spring Security

Spring Security is built around three core components: the `SecurityContextHolder` object, the `SecurityContext`, and the `Authentication` object.

The `SecurityContextHolder` object allows us to define and carry for one JVM a `SecurityContextHolderStrategy` implementation (focused on storing and retrieving a `SecurityContext`).

> The `SecurityContextHolder` has the following `static` field:
> ```
> private static SecurityContextHolderStrategy
>     strategy;
> ```

By default, and in most of the designs, the selected-strategy uses `Threadlocals` (`ThreadLocalSecurityContextHolderStrategy`).

ThreadLocal context holders

A Tomcat instance manages a Spring MVC servlet (like any other servlet) with multiple threads as the multiple HTTP requests come in. The code is as follows:

```
final class ThreadLocalSecurityContextHolderStrategy implements
    SecurityContextHolderStrategy {
  private static final ThreadLocal<SecurityContext>
    contextHolder = new ThreadLocal<SecurityContext>();
  ...
}
```

Each thread allocated to a request on Spring MVC has access to a copy of the `SecurityContext` carrying an `Authentication` object for one user (or one other identifiable thing).

Once a copy of the `SecurityContext` is no longer referred, it gets garbage-collected.

Noticeable Spring Security interfaces

There is a bunch of noticeable interfaces in Spring Security. We will particularly visit `Authentication`, `UserDetails`, `UserDetailsManager`, and `GrantedAuthority`.

The Authentication interface

The Spring `Authentication` object can be retrieved from the `SecurityContext`. This object is usually managed by Spring Security but applications still often need to access it for their business.

Here is the interface for the `Authentication` object:

```
public interface Authentication extends Principal, Serializable {
  Collection<? extends GrantedAuthority> getAuthorities();
  Object getCredentials();
  Object getDetails();
  Object getPrincipal();
  boolean isAuthenticated();
  void setAuthenticated(boolean isAuthenticated) throws
    IllegalArgumentException;
}
```

It provides access to the `Principal` (representing the identified user, entity, company or customer), its credentials, its authorities and to some extra-details that may be needed. Now let's see how, from the `SecurityContextHolder`, a user can be retrieved:

```
Object principal = SecurityContextHolder.getContext()
  .getAuthentication()
  .getPrincipal();
if (principal instanceof UserDetails) {
```

```
        String username = ((UserDetails) principal).getUsername();
    } else {
      String username = principal.toString();
    }
```

The `Principal` class can be cast into the Spring `UserDetails` Type, which is exposed by the core framework. This interface is used as a standard bridge in several extension-modules (*Spring Social, Connect, Spring Security SAML, Spring Security LDAP,* and so on.).

The UserDetails interface

The `UserDetails` implementations represent a Principal in an extensible and application-specific way.

You must be aware of the one-method `UserDetailsService` interface that provides the key-method `loadUserByUsername` for account-retrieval within the core framework:

```
public interface UserDetailsService {
  UserDetails loadUserByUsername(String username) throws
    UsernameNotFoundException;
}
```

Spring Security offers two implementations for this interface: `CachingUserDetailsService` and `JdbcDaoImpl`, whether we want to benefit from an in-memory `UserDetailsService` or from a JDBC-based `UserDetailsService` implementation. More globally, what usually matters is where and how users and roles are persisted so Spring Security can access this data on itself and process authentications.

Authentication providers

The way Spring Security accesses the user and role data is configured with the selection or the reference of an authentication-provider in the Spring Security configuration file with the security namespace.

Here are two examples of configuration when using the native `UserDetailsService` implementations:

```
<security:authentication-manager alias="authenticationManager">
  <security:authentication-provider>
    <security:jdbc-user-service data-source-ref="dataSource" />
  </security:authentication-provider>
</security:authentication-manager>
```

This first example specifies a JDBC-based `UserDetailsService`. The next example specifies an in-memory `UserDetailsService`.

```
<security:authentication-manager alias="authenticationManager">
  <security:authentication-provider>
    <security:user-service id="inMemoryUserDetailService"/>
```

```
    </security:authentication-provider>
  </security:authentication-manager>
```

In our case, we have registered our own `UserDetailsService` implementation (`communityServiceImpl`) as follows:

```
<security:authentication-manager alias="authenticationManager">
  <security:authentication-provider user-service-
    ref='communityServiceImpl'>
    <security:password-encoder ref="passwordEncoder"/>
  </security:authentication-provider>
</security:authentication-manager>
```

We thought more appropriate to continue accessing the database layer through the JPA abstraction.

The UserDetailsManager interface

Spring Security provides a `UserDetails` implementation `org.sfw.security.core.userdetails.User`, which can be used directly or extended. The User class is defined as follows:

```
public class User implements UserDetails, CredentialsContainer {
    private String password;
    private final String username;
    private final Set<GrantedAuthority> authorities;
    private final boolean accountNonExpired;
    private final boolean accountNonLocked;
    private final boolean credentialsNonExpired;
    private final boolean enabled;
    ...
}
```

 Managing users (create, update, and so on) can be a shared responsibility for Spring Security. It is usually mainly performed by the application though.

Guiding us towards a structure for `UserDetails`, Spring Security also provides a `UserDetailsManager` interface for managing users:

```
public interface UserDetailsManager extends UserDetailsService {
    void createUser(UserDetails user);
    void updateUser(UserDetails user);
    void deleteUser(String username);
    void changePassword(String oldPassword, String newPassword);
    boolean userExists(String username);
}
```

Spring Security has two native implementations for non-persistent (`InMemoryUserDetailsManager`) and JDBC-based (`JdbcUserDetailsManager`) user-managements.

When deciding not to use a built-in authentication-provider, it is a good practice to implement the presented interfaces, especially for guaranteeing backward compatibility on the coming versions of Spring Security.

The GrantedAuthority interface

Within Spring Security, `GrantedAuthorities` reflects the application-wide permissions granted to a `Principal`. Spring Security guides us towards a role-based authentication. This kind of authentication imposes the creation of groups of users able to perform operations.

 Unless there is a strong business meaning for a feature, do prefer for example ROLE_ADMIN or ROLE_GUEST to ROLE_DASHBOARD or ROLE_PAYMENT...

Roles can be pulled out of the `Authentication` object from `getAuthorities()`, as an array of `GrantedAuthority` implementations.

The `GrantedAuthority` interface is quite simple:

```
public interface GrantedAuthority extends Serializable {
    String getAuthority();
}
```

The `GrantedAuthority` implementations are wrappers carrying a textual representation for a role. These textual representations are potentially matched against the configuration attributes of secure objects (we will detail this concept in the *Authorizing on services and controllers* recipe).

The `Role` embedded in a `GrantedAuthority`, which is accessed from the `getAuthority()` getter, is more important to Spring Security than the wrapper itself.

We have created our own implementation: the `Authority` that entity that has an association to `User`. The framework also provides the `SimpleGrantedAuthority` implementation.

In the last recipe, we will talk about the Spring Security authorization process. We will see that Spring Security provides an `AccessDecisionManager` interface and several `AccessDecisionManager` implementations. These implementations are based on voting and use `AccessDecisionVoter` implementations. The most commonly used of these implementations is the `RoleVoter` class.

The `RoleVoter` implementation votes positively for the user authorization when a configuration attribute (the textual representation of an Authority) starts with a predefined prefix. By default, this prefix is set to `ROLE_`.

There is more...

The Spring Security authentication and authorization process will be covered in depth in the Authorizing on services and controllers recipe. This section introduces more details from the Spring Security reference document.

Spring Security reference

The Spring Securitysecurity reference is an amazing source of theoretical and practical information.

Technical overview

The technical overview is a great introduction to the Spring Security Framework:

```
http://docs.spring.io/spring-security/site/docs/3.0.x/reference/
technical-overview.html
```

Sample applications

The Spring Security reference provides many Spring Security examples on different authentications types (*LDAP, OPENID, JAFS*, and so on.). Other role-based examples can also be found at:

```
http://docs.spring.io/spring-security/site/docs/3.1.5.RELEASE/
reference/sample-apps.html
```

Core services

Find out more about the built-in `UserDetailsService` implementations (in-memory or JDBC) at:

```
http://docs.spring.io/spring-security/site/docs/3.1.5.RELEASE/
reference/core-services.html
```

Authenticating over a BASIC scheme

Authenticating through a BASIC scheme is a popular solution for stateless applications like ours. Credentials are sent over with HTTP requests.

Getting ready

In this recipe, we complete the Spring Security configuration. We make it support the BASIC authentication scheme required for the application.

We slightly customize the generated response-headers, so they don't trigger the browser to show-up a native BASIC authentication form (which is not an optimal experience for our users).

How to do it...

1. In order to use the Spring security namespace, we add the following filter to the `cloudstreetmarket-api` `web.xml`:

```
<filter>
  <filter-name>springSecurityFilterChain</filter-name>
  <filter-class> org.sfw.web.filter.DelegatingFilterProxy
  </filter-  class>
</filter>
<filter-mapping>
  <filter-name>springSecurityFilterChain</filter-name>
  <url-pattern>/*</url-pattern>
</filter-mapping>
```

2. A Spring configuration file has been created specifically for Spring Security in the `cloudstreetmarket-api` module. This file hosts the following bean definitions:

```
<bean id="authenticationEntryPoint"
  class="edu.zc.csm.api.authentication.CustomBasicAuthenti
    cationEntryPoint">
  <property name="realmName" value="cloudstreetmarket.com" />
</bean>
<security:http create-session="stateless" authentication-
  manager-ref="authenticationManager" entry-point-
  ref="authenticationEntryPoint">
    <security:custom-filter ref="basicAuthenticationFilter"
      after="BASIC_AUTH_FILTER" />
   <security:csrf disabled="true"/>
</security:http>

<bean id="basicAuthenticationFilter"
  class="org.sfw.security.web.authentication.www.
  BasicAuthenticationFilter">
```

```xml
    <constructor-arg name="authenticationManager"
      ref="authenticationManager" />
    <constructor-arg name="authenticationEntryPoint"

      ref="authenticationEntryPoint" />
  </bean>
  <security:authentication-manager
    alias="authenticationManager">
      <security:authentication-provider user-service-
      ref='communityServiceImpl'>
        <security:password-encoder ref="passwordEncoder'/>
      </security:authentication-provider>
  </security:authentication-manager>

  <security:global-method-security secured-
    annotations="enabled" pre-post-annotations="enabled"
    authentication-manager-ref="authenticationManager"/>
```

3. This new configuration refers to the `CustomBasicAuthenticationEntryPoint` class. This class has the following content:

```java
public class CustomBasicAuthenticationEntryPoint extends
  BasicAuthenticationEntryPoint {
  @Override
  public void commence(HttpServletRequest request,
  HttpServletResponse response, AuthenticationException
  authException) throws IOException, ServletException {
    response.setHeader("WWW-Authenticate", "CSM_Basic
      realm=\ + getRealmName() + \");
    response.sendError(HttpServletResponse.SC_UNAUTHORIZED,
      authException.getMessage()
    );
  }
}
```

4. A new `@ExceptionHandler` has been added to catch authentication Exceptions:

```java
@ExceptionHandler({BadCredentialsException.class,
  AuthenticationException.class,
  AccessDeniedException.class})
protected ResponseEntity<Object> handleBadCredentials(final
  RuntimeException ex, final WebRequest request) {
  return handleExceptionInternal(ex, "The attempted
    operation has been denied!", new HttpHeaders(),   FORBIDDEN,
    request);
}
...
```

That's pretty much it! We have made our backend support a BASIC authentication. However, we haven't restricted our services (as secure objects) yet. We will do that now.

5. For the example purpose, please do update the `IMarketService` interface in `cloudstreetmarket-core`. Add the `@Secured("ROLE_BASIC")` annotation to the `Type` as follows:

```
@Secured ("ROLE_BASIC")
public interface IMarketService {
  Page<IndexOverviewDTO> getLastDayIndicesOverview(
    MarketCode market, Pageable pageable);
  Page<IndexOverviewDTO> getLastDayIndicesOverview(
    Pageable pageable);
  HistoProductDTO getHistoIndex(String code, MarketCode
    market, Date fromDate, Date toDate, QuotesInterval
    interval);
}
```

6. Now restart the Tomcat server (doing this will drop your previous user creation).

7. In your favorite web browser, open the developer-tab and observe the AJAX queries when you refresh the home page. You should notice that two AJAX queries have returned a `403` status code (`FORBIDDEN`).

These queries have also returned the JSON response:

```
{"error":"Access is denied","message":"The attempted
  operation has been denied!","status":403,"date":"2015-
  05-05 18:01:14.917"}
```

8. Now, using the login feature/popup, do log in with one of the previously created users that have a BASIC role:

```
Username: <userC>
Password: <123456>
```

9. Refresh the page and observe the same two AJAX queries. Amongst the request headers, you can see that our frontend has sent a special **Authorization** header:

```
▼ Request Headers      view source
    Accept: application/json, text/plain, */*
    Accept-Encoding: gzip, deflate, sdch
    Accept-Language: fr-FR,fr;q=0.8,en-US;q=0.6,en;q=0.4,sv;q=0.2
    Authorization: Basic dXNlckM6MTIzNDU2
```

10. This Authorization header carries the value: `Basic dXNlckM6MTIzNDU2`. The encoded `dXNlckM6MTIzNDU2` is the base64-encoded value for `userC:123456`.

11. Let's have a look at the response to these queries:

```
▼ General
    Remote Address: 127.0.0.1:80
    Request URL: http://cloudstreetmarket.com/api/indices/EUROPE.json?ps=6
    Request Method: GET
    Status Code: ● 200 OK
▼ Response Headers      view source
    Cache-Control: no-store
    Cache-Control: no-cache
    Connection: Keep-Alive
    Content-Type: application/json
    Date: Tue, 05 May 2015 17:10:45 GMT
    Expires: Thu, 01 Jan 1970 00:00:00 GMT
    Keep-Alive: timeout=5, max=88
    Pragma: no-cache
    Server: Apache-Coyote/1.1
    Transfer-Encoding: chunked
    WWW-Authenticate: CSM_Basic realm="cloudstreetmarket.com"
```

The status is now `200 (OK)` and you should also have received the right JSON result:

```
Headers  Preview  Response  Cookies  Timing
{"content":[{"code":"^FTSE","name":"FTSE 100","market":"EUROPE","latestValue":18684.58,"latestChange":-610.00,"
```

12. The Server sent back a `WWW-Authenticate` header in the response to the value: **CSM_Basic realm"="cloudstreetmarket.com"**

13. Finally, do revert the change you made in `IMarketService` (in the 5th step).

How it works...

We are going to explore the concepts behind a BASIC authentication with Spring Security:

The Spring Security namespace

As always, a Spring configuration namespace brings a specific syntax that suits the needs and uses for a module. It lightens the overall Spring configuration with a better readability. Namespaces often come with configuration by default or auto configuration tools.

The Spring Security namespace comes with the spring-security-config dependency and can be defined as follows in a Spring configuration file:

```
<beans xmlns="http://www.springframework.org/schema/beans"
  xmlns:security="http://www.springframework.org/schema/security"
  xmlns:xsi=http://www.w3.org/2001/XMLSchema-instance
  xsi:schemaLocation"="http://www.springframework.org/schema/beans
  http://www.springframework.org/schema/beans/spring-beans.xsd
  http://www.springframework.org/schema/security
  http://www.springframework.org/schema/security/spring-security-
  4.0.0.xsd">

    ...
</beans>
```

The namespace stages three top-level components: `<http>` (about web and HTTP security), `<authentication-manager>`, and `<global-method-security>` (service or controller restriction).

Then, other concepts are referenced by those top-level components as attribute or as child element: `<authentication-provider>`, `<access-decision-manager>` (provides access decisions for web and security methods), and `<user-service>` (as `UserDetailsService` implementations).

The <http> component

The `<http>` component of the namespace provides an `auto-config` attribute that we didn't use here. The `<http auto-config"="true">` definition would have been a shortcut for the following definition:

```
<http>
  <form-login />
  <http-basic />
  <logout />
</http>
```

It isn't worth it for our REST API because we didn't plan to implement a server-side generated view for a form login. Also, the `<logout>` component would have been useless for us since our API doesn't manage sessions.

Finally, the `<http-basic>` element creates underlying `BasicAuthenticationFilter` and `BasicAuthenticationEntryPoint` to the configuration.

We have made use of our own `BasicAuthenticationFilter` in order to customize the `WWW-Authenticate` response's header value from `Basic base64token` to `CSM_Basic base64token`. This because the AJAX HTTP responses (from our API) containing a `WWW-Authenticate` header with a value starting with a **Basic** keyword automatically trigger the web-browser to open a native Basic-form popup. It was not the type of user experience we wanted to set up.

The Spring Security filter-chain

In the very first step of the recipe, we have declared a filter named `springSecurityFilterChain` in `web.xml`:

```
<filter>
  <filter-name>springSecurityFilterChain</filter-name>
  <filter-class>org.sfw.web.
  filter.DelegatingFilterProxy</filter-class>
</filter>
<filter-mapping>
  <filter-name>springSecurityFilterChain</filter-name>
  <url-pattern>/*</url-pattern>
</filter-mapping>
```

Here, `springSecurityFilterChain` is also a Spring bean that is created internally by the Spring Security namespace (specifically the `http` component). A `DelegatingFilterProxy` is a Spring infrastructure that looks for a specific bean in the application context and invokes it. The targeted bean has to implement the `Filter` interface.

The whole Spring Security machinery is hooked-up in this way through finally one single bean.

The configuration of the `<http>` element plays a central-role in the definition of what the filter-chain is made of. It is directly the elements it defines, that create the related filters.

> *"Some core filters are always created in a filter chain and others will be added to the stack depending on the attributes and child elements which are present."*
>
> *Spring Security reference*

It is important to distinguish between the configuration-dependant filters and the core filters that cannot be removed. As core filters, we can count `SecurityContextPersistenceFilter`, `ExceptionTranslationFilter`, and `FilterSecurityInterceptor`. These three filters are natively bound to the `<http>` element and can be found in the next table..

This table comes from the Spring Security reference document and it contains all the core filters (coming with the framework) that can be activated using specific elements or attributes. They are listed here in the order of their position in the chain.

Alias	Filter Class	Namespace Element or Attribute
CHANNEL_FILTER	ChannelProcessingFilter	http/intercept-url@ requires-channel
SECURITY_CONTEXT_ FILTER	SecurityContextPersistenceFilter	http
CONCURRENT_SESSION_ FILTER	ConcurrentSessionFilter	session-management/ concurrency-control
HEADERS_FILTER	HeaderWriterFilter	http/headers
CSRF_FILTER	CsrfFilter	http/csrf
LOGOUT_FILTER	LogoutFilter	http/logout
X509_FILTER	X509AuthenticationFilter	http/x509
PRE_AUTH_FILTER	AbstractPreAuthenticatedProcessingFilter Subclasses	N/A
CAS_FILTER	CasAuthenticationFilter	N/A
FORM_LOGIN_FILTER	UsernamePasswordAuthenticationFilter	http/form-login
BASIC_AUTH_FILTER	BasicAuthenticationFilter	http/http-basic
SERVLET_API_ SUPPORT_FILTER	SecurityContextHolderAwareRequestFilter	http/@servlet-api-provision
JAAS_API_SUPPORT_ FILTER	JaasApiIntegrationFilter	http/@jaas-api-provision
REMEMBER_ME_FILTER	RememberMeAuthenticationFilter	http/remember-me
ANONYMOUS_FILTER	AnonymousAuthenticationFilter	http/anonymous
SESSION_MANAGEMENT_ FILTER	SessionManagementFilter	session-management
EXCEPTION_ TRANSLATION_FILTER	ExceptionTranslationFilter	http
FILTER_SECURITY_ INTERCEPTOR	FilterSecurityInterceptor	http
SWITCH_USER_FILTER	SwitchUserFilter	N/A

Remember that custom filters can be positioned relatively, or can replace any of these filters using the `custom-filter` element:

```
<security:custom-filter ref="myFilter" after="BASIC_AUTH_FILTER"/>
```

Our <http> configuration

We have defined the following configuration for the <http> 'namespace's component:

```
<security:http create-session="stateless" entry-point-
  ref="authenticationEntryPoint" authentication-manager-
  ref="authenticationManager">
  <security:custom-filter ref="basicAuthenticationFilter"
  after="BASIC_AUTH_FILTER" />
  <security:csrf disabled="true"/>
</security:http>
<bean id="basicAuthenticationFilter" class="org.sfw.security.web.
authentication.www.BasicAuthenticationFilter">
  <constructor-arg name="authenticationManager"
  ref="authenticationManager" />
  <constructor-arg name="authenticationEntryPoint"
  ref="authenticationEntryPoint" />
</bean>
<bean id="authenticationEntryPoint" class="edu.zc.csm.api.
authentication.CustomBasicAuthenticationEntryPoint">
  <property name="realmName" value="${realm.name}" />
</bean>
```

Here, we tell Spring not to create sessions and to ignore incoming sessions using create-session=="stateless". We have done this to pursue the stateless and scalable Microservices design.

We have also disabled the **Cross-Site Request Forgery (csrf)** support for now, for the same reason. This feature has been enabled by default by the framework since the Version 3.2.

It has been necessary to define an entry-point-ref because we didn't implement any authentication strategy preconfigured by the namespace (http-basic or login-form).

We have defined a custom filter BasicAuthenticationFilter to be executed after the theoretical position of the core BASIC_AUTH_FILTER.

We are now going to see which roles play the three references made to: authenticationEntryPoint, authenticationManager, and basicAuthenticationFilter.

The AuthenticationManager interface

First of all, `AuthenticationManager` is a single-method interface:

```
public interface AuthenticationManager {
  Authentication authenticate(Authentication authentication)
    throws AuthenticationException;
}
```

Spring Security provides one implementation: `ProviderManager`. This implementation allows us to plug in several `AuthenticationProviders`. The `ProviderManager` tries all the `AuthenticationProviders` in order, calling their `authenticate` method. The code is as follows:

```
public interface AuthenticationProvider {
  Authentication authenticate(Authentication authentication)
    throws AuthenticationException;
  boolean supports(Class<?> authentication);
}
```

The `ProviderManager` stops its iteration when it finds a non-null `Authentication` object. Alternatively, it fails the `Authentication` when an `AuthenticationException` is thrown.

Using the namespace, a specific `AuthenticationProviders` can be targeted using the `ref` element as shown here:

```
<security:authentication-manager >
  <security:authentication-provider
    ref='myAuthenticationProvider'/>
</security:authentication-manager>
```

Now, here is our configuration:

```
<security:authentication-manager alias"="authenticationManager"">
  <security:authentication-provider user-service-
   ref='communityServiceImpl'>
    <security:password-encoder ref="passwordEncoder"/>
  </security:authentication-provider>
</security:authentication-manager>
```

There is no `ref` element in our configuration. The namespace will by default instantiate a `DaoAuthenticationProvider`. It will also inject our `UserDetailsService` implementation: `communityServiceImpl`, because we have specified it with `user-service-ref`.

This `DaoAuthenticationProvider` throws an `AuthenticationException` when the password submitted in a `UsernamePasswordAuthenticationToken` doesn't match the one which is loaded by `UserDetailsService` (making use of the `loadUserByUsername` method).

It exists a few other `AuthenticationProviders` that could be used in our projects, for example,, `RememberMeAuthenticationProvider`, `LdapAuthenticationProvider`, `CasAuthenticationProvider`, or `JaasAuthenticationProvider`.

Basic authentication

As we have said using a BASIC scheme is a great technique for REST applications. However when using it, it is critical to use an encrypted communication protocol (HTTPS) as the passwords are sent in plain text.

As demonstrated in the *How to do it* section. the principle is very simple. The HTTP requests are the same as usual with an extra header `Authentication`. This header has the value made of the keyword `Basic` followed by a space, followed by a String encoded in base 64.

We can find online a bunch of free services to quickly encode/decode in base 64 a String. The String to be encoded in base 64 has to be in the following form: `<username>:<password>`.

BasicAuthenticationFilter

To implement our Basic authentication, we have added `BasicAuthenticationFilter` to our filter chain. This `BasicAuthenticationFilter` (`org.sfw.security. web.authentication.www.BasicAuthenticationFilter`) requires an `authenticationManager` and optionally an `authenticationEntryPoint`.

The optional configuration of an `authenticationEntryPoint` drives the filter towards two different behaviours presented next.

Both starts the same way: the filter is triggered from its position in the chain. It looks for the authentication header in the request and delegates to the `authenticationManager`, which then relies on the `UserDetailsService` implementation to compare it with the user credentials from the database.

With an authenticationEntryPoint

This is our configuration, which behaves in the following way:

- When the authentication succeeds, the filter-chain stops, and an `Authentication` object is returned.
- When the authentication fails, the `authenticationEntryPoint` method is invoked in an interruption of the filter-chain. Our authentication entry-point sets a custom `WWW-Authenticate` response header and a `401` status-code (FORBIDDEN).

This type of configuration provides a preauthentication where the `Authentication Header` in the HTTP Request is checked to see whether or not the business services require an authorization (Secure Object).

This configuration allows a quick feedback with a potential native BASIC form prompted by the web browser. We have chosen this configuration for now in our application.

Without an authenticationEntryPoint

Without an authenticationEntryPoint, the filter behaves as follows:

> ▸ When the authentication succeeds, the filter-chain stops, and an `Authentication` object is returned..

> ▸ When the authentication fails, the filter chain continues. After that, if another authentication succeeds in the chain, the user is authenticated accordingly. But, if no other authentication succeeds in the chain, then the user is authenticated with an anonymous role and this may or may not suit the services access levels.

There is more...

In the Spring Security reference

This section has been largely inspired from the Spring rsecurity reference, which is again a great resource:

```
http://docs.spring.io/spring-security/site/docs/current/reference/
htmlsingle
```

An appendix provides a very complete guide to the Spring Security namespace:

```
http://docs.spring.io/spring-security/site/docs/current/reference/
html/appendix-namespace.html
```

The remember-me cookie/feature

We passed over the `RememberMeAuthenticationFilter` that provides different ways for the server to remember the identity of a Principal between sessions. The Spring Security reference provides extensive information on this topic.

Authenticating with a third-party OAuth2 scheme

This recipe uses the Spring social project in order to use the OAuth2 protocol from a client perspective.

Getting ready

We won't create an OAuth2 **Authentication Server** (**AS**) here. We will establish connections to third-party Authentication servers (Yahoo!) to authenticate on our application. Our application will be acting as a **Service Provider** (**SP**).

We will use Spring social whose first role is to manage social connections transparently and to provide a facade to invoke the provider APIs (Yahoo! Finance) using Java objects.

How to do it...

1. Two Maven dependencies have been added for Spring social:

```
<!- Spring Social Core ->
  <dependency>
    <groupId>org.springframework.social</groupId>
    <artifactId>spring-social-core</artifactId>
    <version>1.1.0.RELEASE</version>
</dependency>
<!- Spring Social Web (login/signup controllers) ->
<dependency>
  <groupId>org.springframework.social</groupId>
  <artifactId>spring-social-web</artifactId>
  <version>1.1.0.RELEASE</version>
</dependency>
```

2. If we want to handle an OAuth2 connection to Twitter or Facebook, we would have to add the following dependencies as well:

```
<!- Spring Social Twitter ->
<dependency>
  <groupId>org.springframework.social</groupId>
  <artifactId>spring-social-twitter</artifactId>
  <version>1.1.0.RELEASE</version>
</dependency>
<!- Spring Social Facebook ->
<dependency>
  <groupId>org.springframework.social</groupId>
  <artifactId>spring-social-facebook</artifactId>
  <version>1.1.0.RELEASE</version>
</dependency>
```

3. After the BASIC authentication section, the Spring Security configuration file hasn't changed much. A few interceptors can be noticed in the `http` bean:

```
<security:http create-session="stateless" entry-point-
  ref="authenticationEntryPoint" authentication-manager-
  ref="authenticationManager">
  <security:custom-filter ref="basicAuthenticationFilter"
    after="BASIC_AUTH_FILTER" />
  <security:csrf disabled="true"/>
  <security:intercept-url pattern="/signup"
    access="permitAll"/>

  ...
```

```
    <security:intercept-url pattern
     ="/**"
     access="permitAll"/>
</security:http>
```

With the following `SocialUserConnectionRepositoryImpl`, we have created our own implementation of `org.sfw.social.connect.ConnectionRepository`, which is a `Spring Social` core interface with methods to manage the social-users connections. The code is as follows:

```
@Transactional(propagation = Propagation.REQUIRED)
@SuppressWarnings("unchecked")
public class SocialUserConnectionRepositoryImpl implements
  ConnectionRepository {
@Autowired
private SocialUserRepository socialUserRepository;
private final String userId;
private final ConnectionFactoryLocator
  connectionFactoryLocator;
private final TextEncryptor textEncryptor;
public SocialUserConnectionRepositoryImpl(String userId,
  SocialUserRepository socialUserRepository,
  ConnectionFactoryLocator connectionFactoryLocator,
  TextEncryptor textEncryptor){
    this.socialUserRepository = socialUserRepository;
    this.userId = userId;
    this.connectionFactoryLocator =
      connectionFactoryLocator;
    this.textEncryptor = textEncryptor;
}
  ...
public void addConnection(Connection<?> connection) {
try {
   ConnectionData data = connection.createData();
  int rank = socialUserRepository.getRank(userId,
      data.getProviderId()) ;
  socialUserRepository.create(userId,
      data.getProviderId(),
      data.getProviderUserId(),
      rank, data.getDisplayName(),
      data.getProfileUrl(),
      data.getImageUrl(),
      encrypt(data.getAccessToken()),
      encrypt(data.getSecret()),
      encrypt(data.getRefreshToken()),
      data.getExpireTime()     );
    } catch (DuplicateKeyException e) {
```

```
      throw new    DuplicateConnectionException(connection.getKey());
    }
  }
  ...
  public void removeConnections(String providerId) {
    socialUserRepository.delete(userId,providerId);
  }
    ...
  }
```

 In reality, this custom implementation extends and adapts the work from `https://github.com/mschipperheyn/` `spring-social-jpa` published under a GNU GPL license.

4. As you can see, `SocialUserConnectionRepositoryImpl` makes use of a custom Spring Data JPA `SocialUserRepository` interface whose definition is as follows:

```
public interface SocialUserRepository {
  List<SocialUser> findUsersConnectedTo(String
  providerId);

    ...
  List<String> findUserIdsByProviderIdAndProviderUserIds(
   String providerId, Set<String> providerUserIds);
  ...
  List<SocialUser> getPrimary(String userId, String
    providerId);
    ...
  SocialUser findFirstByUserIdAndProviderId(String userId,
    String providerId);
  }
```

5. This Spring Data JPA repository supports a `SocialUser` entity (social connections) that we have created. This Entity is the direct model of the `UserConnection` SQL table that `JdbcUsersConnectionRepository` would expect to find if we would use this implementation rather than ours. The `SocialUser` definition is the following code:

```
@Entity
@Table(name="userconnection", uniqueConstraints =
  {@UniqueConstraint(columnNames = { ""userId", "providerId",
"providerUserId" }),
@UniqueConstraint(columnNames = { "userId", "providerId"
   ,
   "rank" })})
public class SocialUser {
  @Id
```

```
    @GeneratedValue
    private Integer id;

    @Column(name = "userId")
    private String userId;

    @Column(nullable = false)
    private String providerId;
    private String providerUserId;

    @Column(nullable = false)
    private int rank;
    private String displayName;
    private String profileUrl;
    private String imageUrl;

    @Lob
    @Column(nullable = false)
    private String accessToken;
    private String secret;
    private String refreshToken;
    private Long expireTime;
    private Date createDate = new Date();
    //+ getters / setters
    ...
}
```

6. The SocialUserConnectionRepositoryImpl is instantiated in a higher-level
   service layer: SocialUserServiceImpl, which is an implementation of the Spring
   UsersConnectionRepository interface. This implementation is created as follows:

```
@Transactional(readOnly = true)
public class SocialUserServiceImpl implements
   SocialUserService {
    @Autowired
    private SocialUserRepository socialUserRepository;
    @Autowired
    private ConnectionFactoryLocator
       connectionFactoryLocator;
    @Autowired
    private UserRepository userRepository;
    private TextEncryptor textEncryptor =
       Encryptors.noOpText();
public List<String> findUserIdsWithConnection(
       Connection<?> connection) {
    ConnectionKey key = connection.getKey();
```

```
    return socialUserRepository.
      findUserIdsByProviderIdAndProviderUserId(
      key.getProviderId(), key.getProviderUserId());
}
public Set<String> findUserIdsConnectedTo(String
  providerId, Set<String> providerUserIds) {
    return Sets.newHashSet(
      socialUserRepository.findUserIdsByPro
    viderIdAndProviderUserIds(providerId,
    providerUserIds));
}
public ConnectionRepository createConnectionRepository(
  String userId) {
  if (userId == null) {
    throw new IllegalArgumentException("userId cannot
      be null"");
  }
  return new SocialUserConnectionRepositoryImpl(
      userId,
      socialUserRepository,
      connectionFactoryLocator,
      textEncryptor);
}
    . . .
}
```

7. This higher level `SocialUserServiceImpl` is registered in the `cloudstreetmarket-api` Spring configuration file (`dispatcher-context.xml`) as a factory-bean that has the capability to produce `SocialUserConnectionRepositoryImpl` under a request-scope (for a specific social-user profile). The code is as follows:

```
<bean id="usersConnectionRepository"
  class="edu.zc.csm.core.services.SocialUserServiceImpl"/>
<bean id="connectionRepository" factory-
  method="createConnectionRepository" factory-
  bean="usersConnectionRepository" scope="request">
  <constructor-arg value="#{request.userPrincipal.name}"/>
  <aop:scoped-proxy proxy-target-class="false" />
</bean>
```

8. Three other beans are defined in this `dispatcher-context.xml` file:

```
<bean id="signInAdapter"
  class="edu.zc.csm.api.signin.SignInAdapterImpl"/>
<bean id="connectionFactoryLocator"
  class="org.sfw.social.connect.support.
  ConnectionFactoryRegistry">
```

```xml
          <property name="connectionFactories">
            <list>
            <bean class"="org.sfw.social.yahoo.connect.
              YahooOAuth2ConnectionFactory"">
              <constructor-arg value="${yahoo.client.token}"/>
              <constructor-arg value="${yahoo.client.secret}" />
              <constructor-arg value="${yahoo.signin.url}" />
            </bean>
            </list>
          </property>
        </bean>
        <bean class="org.sfw.social.connect.web.
          ProviderSignInController">
          <constructor-arg ref="connectionFactoryLocator"/>
          <constructor-arg ref="usersConnectionRepository"/>
          <constructor-arg ref="signInAdapter"/>
          <property name="signUpUrl" value="/signup"/>
          <property name="postSignInUrl"
              value="${frontend.home.page.url}"/>
        </bean>
```

9. The The `SignInAdapterImpl` signs in a user in our application after the OAuth2 authentication. It performs what we want it to perform at this step from the application business point of view. The code is as follows:

```java
@Transactional(propagation = Propagation.REQUIRED)
@PropertySource("classpath:application.properties")
public class SignInAdapterImpl implements SignInAdapter{
  @Autowired
  private UserRepository userRepository;
  @Autowired
  private CommunityService communityService;
  @Autowired
  private SocialUserRepository socialUserRepository;
  @Value("${oauth.success.view}")
  private String successView;
  public String signIn(String userId, Connection<?>
    connection, NativeWebRequest request) {
      User user = userRepository.findOne(userId);
      String view = null;
      if(user == null){
        //temporary user for Spring Security
        //won't be persisted
```

```
        user = new User(userId,
        communityService.generatePassword(), null,
        true, true, true, true,
        communityService.createAuthorities(new
      Role[]{Role.ROLE_BASIC, Role.ROLE_OAUTH2}));
    }
    else{
        //We have a successful previous oAuth
        //authentication
        //The user is already registered
        //Only the guid is sent back
        List<SocialUser> socialUsers =
        socialUserRepository.
          findByProviderUserIdOrUserId(userId, userId);
        if(CollectionUtils.isNotEmpty(socialUsers)){
          //For now we only deal with Yahoo!
          view = successView.concat(
            "?spi=" + socialUsers.get(0)
            .getProviderUserId());
    }
    }
    communityService.signInUser(user);
    return view;
  }
}
```

10. The `connectionFactoryLocator` can also refer to more than one connection factories. In our case, we have only one: `YahooOAuth2ConnectionFactory`. These classes are the entry points of social providers APIs (written for Java). We can normally find them on the web (from official sources or not) for the OAuth protocol we target (OAuth1, OAuth1.0a, and OAuth2).

> There are few existing OAuth2 adaptors right now for Yahoo! We've had to do it ourselves. That's why these classes are available as sources and not as jar dependencies (in the Zipcloud project).

11. When it comes to controllers' declarations, the `dispatcher-context.xml` configures a `ProviderSignInController`, which is completely abstracted in `Spring Social Core`. However, to register a OAuth2 user in our application (the first time the user visits the site), we have created a custom `SignUpController`:

```
@Controller
@RequestMapping("/signup")
@PropertySource("classpath:application.properties")
public class SignUpController extends CloudstreetApiWCI{
  @Autowired
```

```
private CommunityService communityService;
@Autowired
private SignInAdapter signInAdapter;
@Autowired
private ConnectionRepository connectionRepository;
@Value("${oauth.signup.success.view}")
private String successView;
@RequestMapping(method = RequestMethod.GET)
public String getForm(NativeWebRequest request,
  @ModelAttribute User user) {
  String view = successView;
  // check if this is a new user signing in via
  //Spring Social
  Connection<?> connection =
    ProviderSignInUtils.getConnection(request);
    if (connection != null) {
      // populate new User from social connection
      //user profile
      UserProfile userProfile =
        connection.fetchUserProfile();
      user.setUsername(userProfile.getUsername());
      // finish social signup/login
      ProviderSignInUtils.
        handlePostSignUp(user.getUsername(),
        request);
      // sign the user in and send them to the user
      //home page
      signInAdapter.signIn(user.getUsername(),
       connection, request);
    view += ?spi=+ user.getUsername();
  }
  return view;
  }
 }
```

12. It's time to try it now. To proceed, we suggest you to create a Yahoo! account. We are not actually sponsored by Yahoo! It is only for the strategy of our great Zipcloud company which is oriented on financial services. It is not only for Marissa Mayer's blue eyes! (`https://login.yahoo.com`).

13. Start your Tomcat server and click on the login button (at the far right of the main menu). Then hit the **Sign-in with Yahoo!** button

14. You should be redirected to the Yahoo! servers in order for you to authenticate on their side (if you are not logged-in already):

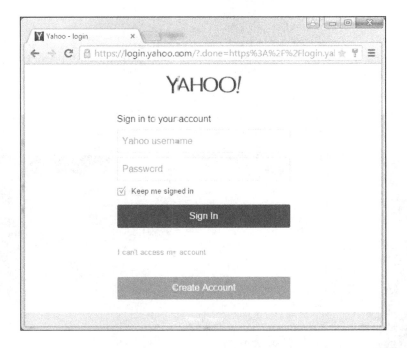

15. Once logged-in, agree that Cloudstreet Market will be able to access your profile and your contacts. We won't make use of contacts; however, we have the Java adaptors to access them. If it's too scary, just create an empty new Yahoo! account:

16. Click on the **Agree** button.

17. Yahoo! should now redirect to the local `cloudstreetmarket.com` server and specifically to the `/api/signin/yahoo` handler with an authorization code as URL parameter.

18. The application detects when in the `Cloudstreet Market` database there isn't any `User` registered for the `SocialUser`. This triggers the following popup and it should come back to the user until the account actually gets created:

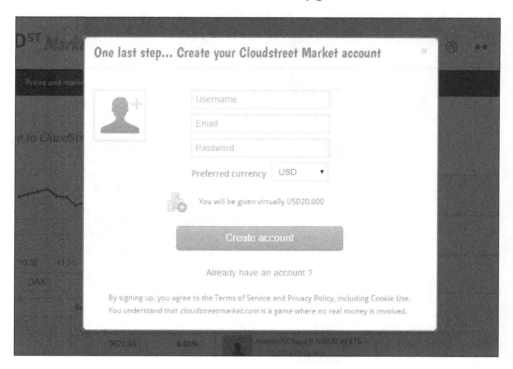

19. Fill the form with the following data:

```
username: <marcus>
email: <marcus@chapter5.com>
password: <123456>
preferred currency: <USD>
```

Also, click on the user icon in order to upload a profile picture (if you wish). While doing so, make sure the property `pictures.user.path` in `cloudstreetmarket-api/src/main/resources/application.properties` is pointing to a created path on the filesystem.

20. Once this step is done, the new public activity **Marcus registers a new account** should appear on the welcome page.

21. Also, bound to each REST response from the API, the extra-headers **Authenticated** and **WWW-Authenticate** must be present. This is proof that we are authenticated with OAuth2 capability in the application.

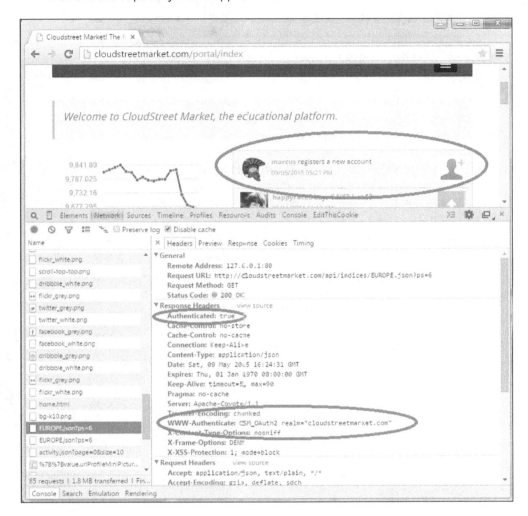

How it works...

We perform in this recipe a social integration within our application. An OAuth2 authentication involves a service provider (cloudstreetmarket.com) and an identity provider (Yahoo!).

This can only happen if a user owns (or is ready to own) an account on both parties. It is a very popular authentication protocol nowadays. As most of Internet users have at least one account in one of the main Social SaaS providers (*Facebook, Twitter, LinkedIn, Yahoo!,* and so on), this technique dramatically drops the registration time and login time spent on web service providers.

From the application point of view

When the sign in with Yahoo! button is clicked by the user, a HTTP POST request is made to one of our API handler `/api/signin/yahoo`. This handler corresponds to `ProviderSignInController`, which is abstracted by `Spring Social`..

> ▸ This handler redirects the user to the Yahoo! servers where he can authenticate and give the right for the application to use his social identity and access some of his *Yahoo!* data.

> ▸ Yahoo! sends an authorization-code to the application as a parameter of the redirection to the callback URL it performs..

> ▸ The application processes the callback with the authorization code as parameter. This callback targets a different method-handler in the abstracted `ProviderSignInController`. This handler completes the connection recalling Yahoo! in order to exchange the authorization code against a **refresh token** and an **access token**. This operation is done transparently in the `Spring Social` background..

> ▸ The same handler looks-up in database for an existing persisted social connection for that user:
>
>> ❑ If one connection is found, the user is authenticated with it in `Spring Security` and redirected to the home page of the portal with the Yahoo! user-ID as request parameter (parameter named `spi`).
>
>> ❑ If no connection is found, the user is redirected to the `SignupController` where his connection is created and persisted. He is then authenticated in Spring Security and redirected to the portal's home page with the Yahoo! user ID as request parameter (named `spi`).

> ▸ When the portal home page is loaded, the Yahoo! user ID request parameter is detected and this identifier is stored in the HTML5 `sessionStorage` (we have done all this).

> ▸ From now on, in every single AJAX request the user makes to the API, the `spi` identifier will be passed as a request header, until the user actually logs out or closes his browser.

From the Yahoo! point of view

The Yahoo! APIs provide two ways of authenticating with OAuth2. This induces two different flows: the Explicit OAuth2 flow, suited for a server-side (web) application and the Implicit OAuth2 flow that particularly benefits to frontend web clients. We will focus on the implemented explicit flow here.

OAuth2 explicit grant flow

Here's a summary picture of the communication protocol between our application and Yahoo!. This is more or less a standard OAuth2 conversation:

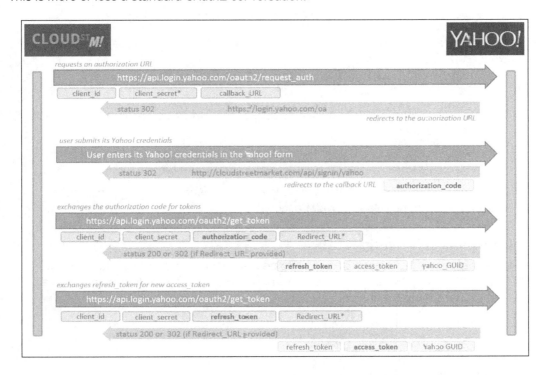

The parameters marked with the * symbol are optional in the communication. This flow is also detailed on the OAuth2 Yahoo! guide:

```
https://developer.yahoo.com/oauth2/guide/flows_authcode
```

Refresh-token and access-token

The difference between these two tokens must be understood. An access-token is used to identify the user (Yahoo! user) when performing operations on the Yahoo! API. As an example, below is a GET request that can be performed to retrieve the Yahoo! profile of a user identified by the Yahoo! ID abcdef123:

```
GET https://social.yahooapis.com/v1/user/abcdef123/profile
Authorization: Bearer aXJUKyrsTUXLVY
```

To provide identification to this call, the **access-token** must be passed in as the value of the `Authorization` request header with the `Bearer` keyword. In general, access-tokens have a very limited life (for Yahoo!, it is an hour).

A refresh-token is used to request new access-tokens. Refresh-tokens have much longer lives (for Yahoo!, they actually never expire, but they can be revoked).

Spring social – role and key features

The role of Spring social is to establish connections with **Software-as-a-Service** (**SaaS**) providers such as *Facebook, Twitter, or Yahoo!* Spring social is also responsible for invoking APIs on the application (*Cloudstreet Market*) server side on behalf of the users.

These two duties are both served in the spring-social-core dependency using the Connect Framework and the OAuth client support, respectively.

In short, Spring social is:

- A `Connect Framework` handling the core authorization and connection flow with service providers
- A `Connect Controller` that handles the OAuth exchange between a service provider, consumer, and user in a web application environment
- A `Sign-in Controller` that allows users to authenticate in our application, signing in with their Saas provider account

Social connection persistence

The Spring social core provides classes able to persist social connections in database using JDBC (especially with `JdbcUsersConnectionRepository`). The module even embeds a SQL script for the schema definition:

```
create table UserConnection (userId varchar(255) not null,
    providerId varchar(255) not null,
    providerUserId varchar(255),
    rank int not null,
    displayName varchar(255),
    profileUrl varchar(512),
    imageUrl varchar(512),
    accessToken varchar(255) not null,
    secret varchar(255),
    refreshToken varchar(255),
    expireTime bigint,
    primary key (userId, providerId, providerUserId));
create unique index UserConnectionRank on UserConnection(userId,
    providerId, rank);
```

When an application (like ours) uses JPA, an Entity can be created to represent this table in the persistence context. We have created the `SocialUser` Entity for this purpose in the *sixth step* of the recipe.

In this table Entity, you can see the following fields:

- ▶ userId: This field matches the @Id (username) of the User when the user is registered. If the user is not yet registered, userId is the GUID (Yahoo! user ID, also called spi on the web side)

- ▶ providerId: This field is the lowercase name of the provider: Yahoo, Facebook or Twitter.

- ▶ providerUserId: This field is the GUID, the unique identifier in the provider's system (Yahoo! user ID or **spi**.).

- ▶ accessToken, secret, refreshToken, and expireTime: These are the OAuth2 tokens (credentials) for the connection and their related information..

Two interfaces come with the framework:

- ▶ ConnectionRepository: This manages the persistence of one user connection. Implementations are request-scoped for the identified user.

- ▶ UsersConnectionRepository: This provides access to the global store of connections across all users.

If you remember, we created our own UsersConnectionRepository implementation (SocialUserServiceImpl). Registered in the dispatcher-servlet.xml file, this implementation acts as a factory to produce request-scope connectionRepository implementations (SocialUserConnectionRepositoryImpl):

```
<bean id="connectionRepository" factory-
  method="createConnectionRepository" factory-
  bean="usersConnectionRepository" scop="request">
  <constructor-arg value="#{request.userPrincipal.name}" />
  <aop:scoped-proxy proxy-target-class="false" />
</bean>
<bean id="usersConnectionRepository"
  class="edu.zc.csm.core.services.SocialUserServiceImpl"/>
```

Those two custom implementations both use the Spring Data JPA SocialUserRepository that we have created for finding, updating, persisting, and removing connections.

In the SocialUserServiceImpl implementation of the UsersConnectionRepository interface, a ConnectionFactoryLocator property is autowired and a TextEncryptor property is initialized with a default NoOpTextEncryptor instance.

> The default TextEncryptor instance can be replaced with a proper encryption for the SocialUser data maintained in the database. Take a look at the spring-security-crypto module:
>
> http://docs.spring.io/spring-security/site/
> docs/3.1.x/reference/crypto.html

Provider-specific configuration

The provider-specific configuration (Facebook, Twitter, Yahoo!) starts with definitions of the connectionFactoryLocator bean.

One entry-point – connectionFactoryLocator

The connectionFactoryLocator bean that we have defined in the dispatcher-servlet.xml plays a central role in Spring Social. Its registration is as follows:

```
<bean id="connectionFactoryLocator" class="org.sfw.social.connect.
support.ConnectionFactoryRegistry">
  <property name="connectionFactories">
    <list>
    <bean class"="org.sfw.social.yahoo.connect.
      YahooOAuth2ConnectionFactory"">
        <constructor-arg value="${yahoo.client.token}" />
        <constructor-arg value="${yahoo.client.secret}" />
        <constructor-arg value="${yahoo.signin.url}" />
      </bean>
    </list>
  </property>
</bean>
```

With this bean, Spring social implements a ServiceLocator pattern that allows us to easily plug-in/plug-out new social connectors. Most importantly, it allows the system to resolve at runtime a provider-specific connector (a connectionFactory).

The specified Type for our connectionFactoryLocator is ConnectionFactoryRegistry, which is a provided implementation of the ConnectionFactoryLocator interface:

```
public interface ConnectionFactoryLocator {
    ConnectionFactory<?> getConnectionFactory(String providerId);
    <A> ConnectionFactory<A> getConnectionFactory(Class<A>
      apiType);
    Set<String> registeredProviderIds();
}
```

We have an example of the connectionFactory lookup in the ProviderSignInController.signin method:

```
ConnectionFactory<?> connectionFactory =
  connectionFactoryLocator.getConnectionFactory(providerId);
```

Here, the providerId argument is a simple String (yahoo in our case).

Provider-specific ConnectionFactories

The `ConnectionFactory` such as `YahooOAuth2ConnectionFactory` are registered in `ConnectionFactoryRegistry` with the OAuth2 consumer key and consumer secret, which identify (with authorization) our application on the provider's side.

We have developed the `YahooOAuth2ConnectionFactory` class, but you should be able to find your `ProviderSpecificConnectionFactory` either from official `Spring Social` subprojects (`spring-social-facebook`, `spring-social-twitter`, and so on) or from open sources projects.

Signing in with provider accounts

In order to perform the OAuth2 authentication steps, Spring social provides an abstracted Spring MVC Controller: `ProviderSignInController`.

This controller performs the OAuth flows and establishes connections with the provider. It tries to find a previously established connection and uses the connected account to authenticate the user in the application.

If no previous connection matches, the flow is sent to the created `SignUpController` matching the specific request mapping/`signup`. The user is not automatically registered as a *CloudStreetMarket* `User` at this point. We force the user to create his account manually via a `Must-Register` response header when an API call appears OAuth2 authenticated without a bound local user. This `Must-Register` response header triggers the **create an account now** popup on the client side (see in `home_community_activity.js`, the `loadMore` function).

It is during this registration that the connection (the `SocialUser` Entity) is synchronized with the created `User` Entity (see the `CommunityController.createUser` method).

The `ProviderSignInController` works closely with a `SignInAdapter` implementation (that we had to build as well) which actually authenticates the user into *CloudStreetMarket* with Spring Security. The authentication is triggered with the call to `communityService.signInUser(user)`.

Here are the details of the method that creates the `Authentication` object and stores it into the `SecurityContext`:

```
@Override
public Authentication signInUser(User user) {
  Authentication authentication = new
    UsernamePasswordAuthenticationToken(user,
      user.getPassword(), user.getAuthorities());
  SecurityContextHolder.getContext().setAuthentication
    (authentication);
  return authentication;
}
```

We register and initialize a Spring bean for `ProviderSigninController` with the following configuration:

```
<bean class"="org.sfw.social.connect.web.ProviderSignInController"">
  <constructor-arg ref="connectionFactoryLocator"/>
  <constructor-arg ref="usersConnectionRepository"/>
  <constructor-arg ref="signInAdapter"/>
  <property name="signUpUrl"" value"="/signup"/>
  <property name="postSignInUrl"
    value="${frontend.home.page.url}"/>
</bean>
```

As you can see, we have specified the `signUpUrl` request mapping to redirect to our custom `SignupController` when no previous connection is found in database.

Alternatively, the specified `postSignInUrl` allows the user to be redirected to the home page of the portal when the `ProviderSignInController` resolves an existing connection to reuse.

There is more...

Let's have a look at other features of Spring social.

Performing authenticated API calls

In this recipe, we focused on presenting the OAuth2-client authentication process. In the next chapter, we will see how to use Spring social to perform requests to Yahoo! APIs on behalf of the users. We will see how can be used existing libraries in this purpose and how they work. In our case, we had to develop API connectors to Yahoo! financial APIs.

The Spring social ConnectController

Spring social web provides another abstracted controller which allows social users to directly interact with their social connections to connect, disconnect, and obtain their connection status. The `ConnectController` can also be used to build an interactive monitoring screen for managing connections to all the providers a site could possibly handle. Check out the Spring social reference for more details:

http://docs.spring.io/spring-social/docs/current/reference/
htmlsingle/#connecting

See also

SocialAuthenticationFilter

This is a filter to be added to Spring Security so that a social authentication can be performed from the Spring Security filter-chain (and not externally as we did).

```
http://docs.spring.io/spring-social/docs/current/
reference/htmlsingle/#enabling-provider-sign-in-with-code-
socialauthenticationfilter-code
```

The list of Spring social connectors

You will find a list of implemented connectors to Saas-providers from the main page of the project: `http://projects.spring.io/spring-social`

Implementing an OAuth2 authentication server

You can use the Spring Security OAuth project:

```
http://projects.spring.io/spring-security-oauth
```

The harmonic development blog

The articles about Spring social have inspired this recipe. Feel free to visit this blog:

```
http://harmonicdevelopment.tumblr.com/post/13613051804/adding-spring-
social-to-a-spring-mvc-and-spring
```

Storing credentials in a REST environment

This recipe presents a solution for storing credentials in RESTful applications.

Getting ready

The solution is a compromise between temporary client-side storage and permanent server-side storage.

On the client side, we are using HTML5 session storage to store temporarily the usernames and passwords encoded in base 64. On the server side, only hashes are stored for passwords. Those hashes are created with `passwordEncoder`. This `passwordEncoder` is registered in Spring Security, autowired, and used in the `UserDetailsService` implementation.

How to do it...

Client side (AngularJS)

1. We have made use of the HTML5 `sessionStorage` attribute. The main change has been the creation of a `httpAuth` factory. Presented in the `http_authorized.js` file, this factory is a wrapper around `$http` to take care transparently of client-side storage and authentication headers. The code for this factory is as follows:

```
cloudStreetMarketApp.factory("httpAuth", function ($http) {
  return {
    clearSession: function () {
      var authBasicItem =
        sessionStorage.getItem('basicHeaderCSM');
      var oAuthSpiItem =
        sessionStorage.getItem('oAuthSpiCSM');
    if(authBasicItem || oAuthSpiItem){
      sessionStorage.removeItem('basicHeaderCSM');
      sessionStorage.removeItem('oAuthSpiCSM');
      sessionStorage.removeItem('authenticatedCSM');
      $http.defaults.headers.common.Authorization =
        undefined;
      $http.defaults.headers.common.Spi = undefined;
      $http.defaults.headers.common.OAuthProvider =
        undefined;
    }
    },
    refresh: function(){
      var authBasicItem =
        sessionStorage.getItem('basicHeaderCSM');
      var oAuthSpiItem =
        sessionStorage.getItem('oAuthSpiCSM');
      if(authBasicItem){
        $http.defaults.headers.common.Authorization =
        $.parseJSON(authBasicItem).Authorization;
        }
        if(oAuthSpiItem){
          $http.defaults.headers.common.Spi =
            oAuthSpiItem;
          $http.defaults.headers.common.OAuthProvider =
          "yahoo";
      }
      },
      setCredentials: function (login, password) {
      //Encodes in base 64
      var encodedData = window.btoa(login+":"+password);
```

```
      var basicAuthToken = 'Basic '+encodedData;
      var header = {Authorization: basicAuthToken};
      sessionStorage.setItem('basicHeaderCSM',
      JSON.stringify(header));
      $http.defaults.headers.common.Authorization =
        basicAuthToken;
    },
    setSession: function(attributeName, attributeValue) {
      sessionStorage.setItem(attributeName,
        attributeValue);
    },
    getSession: function (attributeName) {
      return sessionStorage.getItem(attributeName);
    },
    post: function (url, body) {
      this.refresh();
    return $http.post(url, body);
    },
    post: function (url, body, headers, data) {
      this.refresh();
      return $http.post(url, body, headers, data);
    },
    get: function (url) {
      this.refresh();
      return $http.get(url);
    },
    isUserAuthenticated: function () {
      var authBasicItem =
      sessionStorage.getItem('authenticatedCSM');
    if(authBasicItem){
      return true;
      }
    return false;
    }
}});
```

2. This factory is invoked everywhere (or almost) in the former place of `$http` to pass and handle transparently the credentials or identification headers required for AJAX requests.

3. We have avoided dealing directly with the `sessionStorage` attribute from the different controllers, in order to prevent being tightly coupled with this storage solution.

4. The `account_management.js` file regroups different controllers (`LoginByUsernameAndPasswordController`, `createNewAccountController`, and `OAuth2Controller`) that store credentials and provider IDs in `sessionStorage` through `httpAuth`.

5. A couple of factories have also been modified to pull and push data through the `httpAuth` factory. For example, the `indiceTableFactory` (from `home_financial_table.js`) requests the indices of a market with credentials handled transparently:

```
cloudStreetMarketApp.factory("indicesTableFactory",
  function (httpAuth) {
    return {
        get: function (market) {
        return httpAuth.get("/api/indices/" + market +
          ".json?ps=6");
        }
    }
});
```

Server side

1. We have declared a `passwordEncoder` bean in `security-config.xml` (in the `cloudstreetmarket-core` module):

```
<bean id="passwordEncoder"
  class="org.sfw.security.crypto.bcrypt.BCryptPasswordEnco  der"/>
```

2. In `security-config.xml`, a reference to the password-encoder is made, as follows, in our `authenticationProvider` to.

```
<security:authentication-manager
  alias"="authenticationManager">
  <security:authentication-provider user-service-
    ref='communityServiceImpl'>
    <security:password-encoder ref="passwordEncoder"/>
  </security:authentication-provider>
</security:authentication-manager>
```

3. The `passwordEncoder` bean is autowired in `CommunityServiceImpl` (our `UserDetailsService` implementation). Passwords are hashed here with `passwordEncoder` when accounts are registered. The stored hash is then compared to the user-submitted password when the user attempts to log in. The `CommunityServiceImpl` code is as follows:

```
@Service(value="communityServiceImpl")
@Transactional(propagation = Propagation.REQUIRED)
public class CommunityServiceImpl implements
  CommunityService {
  @Autowired
  private ActionRepository actionRepository;
  ...
  @Autowired
  private PasswordEncoder passwordEncoder;
```

```
...
@Override
public User createUser(User user, Role role) {
  if(findByUserName(user.getUsername()) != null){
    throw new ConstraintViolationException("The
    provided user name already exists!", null, null);
    }
  user.addAuthority(new Authority(user, role));
  user.addAction(new AccountActivity(user,
UserActivityType.REGISTER new Date()));
  user.setPassword(passwordEncoder.
    encode(user.getPassword()));
  return userRepository.save(user);
}
@Override
public User identifyUser(User user) {
  Preconditions.checkArgument(user.getPassword() !=
    null, "The provided password cannot be null!");
 Preconditions.checkArgument(
    StringUtils.isNotBlank(user.getPassword()), "The
    provided password cannot be empty!");
  User retreivedUser =
    userRepository.findByUsername(user.getUsername());
  if(!passwordEncoder.matches(user.getPassword(),
    retreivedUser.getPassword())){
    throw new BadCredentialsException"("No match has
      been found with the provided credentials!");
  }
return retreivedUser;
}
...
}
```

4. Our `ConnectionFactory` implementation
   `SocialUserConnectionRepositoryImpl` is instantiated in
   `SocialUserServiceImpl` with an instance of the Spring `TextEncryptor`.
   This gives the possibility to encrypt the stored connection-data for OAuth2 (most
   importantly, the access-tokens and refresh-tokens). At the moment, this data is not
   encrypted in our code.

How it works...

In this chapter, wetried to maintain the statelessness of our RESTful API for the benefits it provides (scalability, easy deployment, fault tolerance, and so on).

Authenticating for Microservices

Staying stateless matches a key concept of Microservices: the self-sufficiency of our modules. We won't be using sticky sessions for scalability. When a state is maintained, it is only by the client, keeping for a limited time the user's identifier and/or his credentials.

Another key concept of Microservices is the concept of limited and identified responsibilities (horizontal scalability). Our design supports this principle even if the size of the application doesn't require domain segmentation. We can fully imagine splitting our API by domains (community, indices and stocks, monitoring, and so on). Spring Security, which is located in the core-module, would be embedded in every API war without any problem.

Let's focus on how a state is maintained on the client side. We offer to our users two ways of signing-in: using a BASIC scheme or using OAuth2.

> ▶ A user can register his account for a BASIC authentication and then later decide to sign-in using OAuth2 (to do so, he has to bind his social account to his existing account).

> ▶ Alternatively, a user can register his account with OAuth2 and later sign in with a BASIC form. His OAuth2 credentials will naturally be bound to his authentication.

Using the BASIC authentication

When a user registers an account, he defines a username and a password. These credentials are stored using the `httpAuth` factory and the `setCredentials` method.

In the `account_management.js` file and especially in the `createNewAccountController` (invoked through the `create_account_modal.html` modal), the `setCredentials` call can be found in the success handler of the `createAccount` method:

```
httpAuth.setCredentials($scope.form.username,
  $scope.form.password);
```

Right now, this method uses HTML5 `sessionStorage` as storage device:

```
setCredentials: function (login, password) {
  var encodedData = window.btoa(login"+":"+password);
  var basicAuthToken = 'Basic '+encodedData;
  var header = {Authorization: basicAuthToken};
```

```
    sessionStorage.setItem('basicHeaderCSM',
      JSON.stringify(header));
    $http.defaults.headers.common.Authorization = basicAuthToken;
  }
```

The `window.btoa(...)` function encodes in base 64 the provided String. The `$httpProvider.defaults.headers` configuration object is also added a new header which will potentially be used by the next AJAX request.

When a user signs in using the BASIC form (see also the `account_management.js` and especially the `LoginByUsernameAndPasswordController` that is invoked from the `auth_modal.html` modal), the username and password are stored using the same method:

```
    httpAuth.setCredentials($scope.form.username,
      $scope.form.password);
```

Now with the `httpAuth` abstraction layer the angular `$http` service, we make sure that the **Authorization** header is set in each call to the API that is made using `$http`..

```
▼ Request Headers      view source
    Accept: application/json, text/plain, */*
    Accept-Encoding: gzip, deflate, sdch
    Accept-Language: fr-FR,fr;q=0.8,en-US;q=0.6,en;q=0.4,sv;q=0.2
    Authorization: Basic bWFyY3VzOjEyMzQ1Ng==
    Connection: keep-alive
    Cookie: JSESSIONID=F047CL4810B490F7CEF826DE599DEDF6
    Host: cloudstreetmarket.com
    Referer: http://cloudstreetmarket.com/portal/index
```

Using OAuth2

Initiated from `auth_modal.html`, signing in using OAuth2 creates a POST HTTP request to the API handler `/api/signin/yahoo` (this handler is located in the abstracted `ProviderSignInController`).

The sign in request is redirected to the Yahoo! authentication screens. The whole page goes to Yahoo! until completion. When the API ultimately redirects the request to the home page of the portal, a `spi` request parameter is added: `http://cloudstreetmarket.com/portal/index?spi=F2YY6VNSXIU7CTAUB2A6U6KD7E`

This `spi` parameter is the Yahoo! user ID (GUID). It is caught by the `DefaultController` (cloudstreetmarket-webapp) and injected into the model:

```
    @RequestMapping(value="/*", method={RequestMethod.GET, RequestMethod.
    HEAD})
    public String fallback(Model model, @RequestParam(value="spi",
      required=false) String spi) {
      if(StringUtils.isNotBlank(spi)){
```

```
        model.addAttribute("spi", spi);
    }
    return "index";
}
```

The `index.jsp` file renders the value directly in the top menu's DOM:

```
<div id="spi" class="hide">${spi}</div>
```

When the `menuController` (bound to the top menu) initializes itself, this value is read and stored in `sessionStorage`:

```
$scope.init = function () {
  if($('#spi').text()){
    httpAuth.setSession('oAuthSpiCSM', $('#spi').text());
  }
}
```

In our `httpAuth` factory (`http_authorized.js`), the `refresh()` method that is invoked before every single call to the API checks if this value is present and add two extra headers: `Spi` with the GUID value and the **OAuthProvider** (yahoo in our case). The code is as follows:

```
refresh: function(){
  var authBasicItem = sessionStorage.getItem('basicHeaderCSM');
  var oAuthSpiItem = sessionStorage.getItem('oAuthSpiCSM');
  if(authBasicItem){
    $http.defaults.headers.common.Authorization =
      $.parseJSON(authBasicItem).Authorization;
  }
  if(oAuthSpiItem){
    $http.defaults.headers.common.Spi = oAuthSpiItem;
    $http.defaults.headers.common.OAuthProvider = "yahoo";
  }
}
```

The screenshot here shows those two headers for one of our an AJAX requests:

```
▼Request Headers      view source
    Accept: application/json, text/plain, */*
    Accept-Encoding: gzip, deflate, sdch
    Accept-Language: fr-FR,fr;q=0.8,en-US;q=0.6,en;q=0.4,sv;q=0.2
    Cache-Control: max-age=0
    Connection: keep-alive
    Cookie: JSESSIONID=FB477DA810B490F7CEF826DE599DEDF6
    Host: cloudstreetmarket.com
    OAuthProvider: yahoo
    Referer: http://cloudstreetmarket.com/portal/index?spi=F2YY6VNSXIU7CTAUB2A6U6KD7E
    Spi: F2YY6VNSXIU7CTAUB2A6U6KD7E
    User-Agent: Mozilla/5.0 (Windows NT 6.1; WOW64) AppleWebKit/537.36 (KHTML, like Geck
```

HTML5 SessionStorage

We used the SessionStorage as storage solution on the client side for user credentials and social identifiers (GUIDs).

In HTML5, web pages have the capability to store data locally in the browser using the Web Storage technology. Data in stored Web Storage can be accessed from the page scripts' and values can be relatively large (up to 5MB) with no impact on client-side performance.

Web Storage is per origin (the combination of protocol, hostname, and port number). All pages from one origin can store and access the same data. There are two types of objects that can be used for storing data locally:

- ▶ `window.localStorage`: This stores data with no expiration date.
- ▶ `window.sessionStorage`: This stores data for one session (data is lost when the tab is closed).

These two objects can be accessed directly from the window object and they both come with the self-explanatory methods:

```
setItem(key,value);
getItem(key);
removeItem(key);
clear();
```

As indicated by `http://www.w3schools.com/`, localStorage is almost supported by all browsers nowadays (between 94% and 98% depending upon your market). The following table shows the first versions that fully support it

API					
Web Storage	4.0	8.0	3.5	4.0	11.5

We should implement a fallback option with cookies for noncompliant web browsers, or at least a warning message when the browsers seem outdated.

SSL/TLS

An encrypted communication protocol must be setup when using a BASIC authentication. We have seen that the credentials username:password and the Yahoo! GUID are sent as request headers. Even though those credentials are encoded in base 64, this doesn't represent a sufficient protection.

BCryptPasswordEncoder

On the server side, we don't store the User passwords in plain text. We only store an encoded description of them (a hash). Therefore, a hashing function is supposedly not reversible.

"A hash function is any function that can be used to map digital data of arbitrary size to digital data of fixed size".

Wikipedia

Let's have a look at the following mapping:

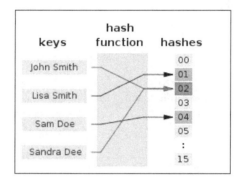

This diagram shows a hash function that maps names to integers from 0 to 15.

We used a PasswordEncoder implementation invoked manually while persisting and updating Users. Also PasswordEncoder is an Interface of Spring Security core:

```
public interface PasswordEncoder {
    String encode(CharSequence rawPassword);
    boolean matches(CharSequence rawPassword, String
        encodedPassword);
}
```

Spring Security provides three implementations: StandardPasswordEncoder, NoOpPasswordEncoder, and BCryptPasswordEncoder.

We used BCryptPasswordEncoder as it is recommended on new projects. Instead of implementing a MD5 or SHA hashing algorithm, BCryptPasswordEncoder uses a stronger hashing algorithm with randomly generated salt.

This allows the storage of different HASH values for the same password. Here's an example of different BCrypt hashes for the 123456 value:

```
$2a$10$Qz5slUkuV7RXfaH/otDY9udROisOwf6XXAOLt4PHWnYgOhG59teC6
$2a$10$GYCkBzp2NlpGS/qjp5f6NOWHeF56ENAlHNuSssSJpE1MMYJevHBWO
$2a$10$5uKS72xK2ArGDgb2CwjYnOzQcOmB7CPxK6fz2MGcDBM9vJ4rUql36
```

There is more...

Setting HTTP headers with AngularJS

As we have set Headers, check out the following page for more information about headers management with AngularJS:

```
https://docs.angularjs.org/api/ng/service/$http
```

Browser support for localStorage

Get an insight about the overall support per bbrowser version:

```
http://caniuse.com/#search=localstorage
```

About SSL and TLS

We have installed a SSL certificate on our production server. To buy and get issued a SSL certificate, we have had to provide our web server type (Apache 2) and a **Certificate Signing Request** (**CSR**) generated from the keytool program (embedded in the JDK).

- `http://arstechnica.com/information-technology/2012/11/securing-your-web-server-with-ssltls/`
- `http://en.wikipedia.org/wiki/Certificate_signing_request`
- `https://www.namecheap.com/support/knowledgebase/article.aspx/9422/0/tomcat-using-keytool`

Authorizing on services and controllers

In this recipe, we restrict the access to services and controllers depending upon the authorities that are granted to users.

Getting ready

We are going to install interceptors on specific URL paths and method-invocations, which will trigger a predefined authorization workflow: the `AbstractSecurityInterceptor` workflow.

In order for us to test these services' restrictions, we also slightly customized the Swagger UI to use it over a BASIC authentication.

How to do it...

1. We updated our `CustomBasicAuthenticationEntryPoint` class for this new
    version that allows the browser native BASIC-form to be prompted when the call is
    made from Swagger UI:

```java
public class CustomBasicAuthenticationEntryPoint extends
  BasicAuthenticationEntryPoint {
  @Override
  public void commence(HttpServletRequest request,
    HttpServletResponse response, AuthenticationException
    authException) throws IOException, ServletException {
    String referer = (String)
      request.getHeader("referer");
    if(referer != null &&
      referer.contains(SWAGGER_UI_PATH)){
      super.commence(request, response, authException);
      return;
    }
    response.setHeader("WWW-Authenticate", "CSM_Basic
      realm=\" + getRealmName() + \");
    response.sendError(
      HttpServletResponse.SC_UNAUTHORIZED,
      authException.getMessage());
  }
}
```

2. We created a `MonitoringController` (a `RestController`) that offers the
    possibility to manage users for an administration purpose.

3. The GET method returns `User` objects directly (and not the `UserDTO`), which provides
    all the data about the users. Also, a `delete` method shows up at this location. The
    `MonitoringController` code is as follows:

```java
@RestController
@RequestMapping(value="/monitoring",        produces={"application/
xml", "application/json"})
@PreAuthorize("hasRole('ADMIN')")
public class MonitoringController extends
  CloudstreetApiWCI{
  @Autowired
  private CommunityService communityService;
  @Autowired
  private SocialUserService socialUserService;
  @RequestMapping(value="/users/{username}", method=GET)
  @ResponseStatus(HttpStatus.OK)
  @ApiOperation(value = "Details one account", notes = )
```

```
public User getUserDetails(@PathVariable String
  username){
  return communityService.findOne(username);
}
@RequestMapping(value="/users/{username}",
  method=DELETE)
@ResponseStatus(HttpStatus.OK)
@ApiOperation(value = "Delete user account", notes =)
public void deleteUser(@PathVariable String username){
  communityService.delete(username);
}
@RequestMapping(value="/users", method=GET)
@ResponseStatus(HttpStatus.OK)
@ApiOperation(value = "List user accounts", notes =)
public Page<User> getUsers(@ApiIgnore
  @PageableDefault(size=1), page=0) Pageable pageable){
  return communityService.findAll(pageable);
}
}
```

4. In the `communityService` implementation, the two used methods (`findAll`, `delete`) have been secured:

```
@Override
@Secured({"ROLE_ADMIN", "ROLE_SYSTEM"})
public void delete(String userName) {
  userRepository.delete(userName);
}
@Override
@Secured("ROLE_ADMIN")
public Page<User> findAll(Pageable pageable) {
  return userRepository.findAll(pageable);
}
```

5. As a reminder, we have set a global method-security in `security-config.xml`:

```
<security:global-method-security secured-
  annotations"="enabled"" pre-post-annotations"="enabled""
  authentication-manager-ref"="authenticationManager""/>
```

6. Let's try it now. Restart your Tomcat and open a new window in your favorite browser. Open **Swagger UI** (`http://cloudstreetmarket.com/api/index.html`) as shown here:

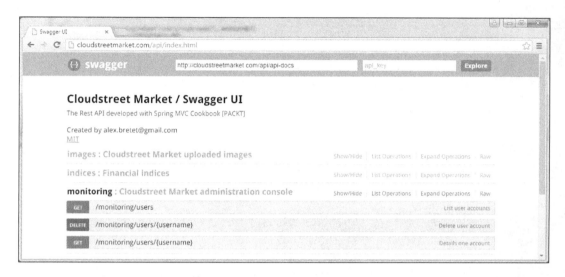

7. Open the **monitoring** tab. Try to call the **GET /monitoring/users** method in order to list user accounts.

8. Your web browser should prompt a BASIC authentication form as follows:

9. If you cancel this form, you should receive a **401 (Unauthorized)** response code.

10. For test purpose, there is a `delete` method in `communityController` that is not secured by any annotation. Also, remember that there is no specific URL interceptor defined for the `communityController` path:

```
@RequestMapping(value"="/{username}", method=DELETE)
@ResponseStatus(HttpStatus.OK
@ApiOperation(value = "Delete a user account", notes =)
public void deleteUser(@PathVariable String username){
    communityService.delete(username);
}
```

11. Without sign in, try to call this handler from Swagger UI. As shown in the following screenshot, try to delete the user named **other10**.

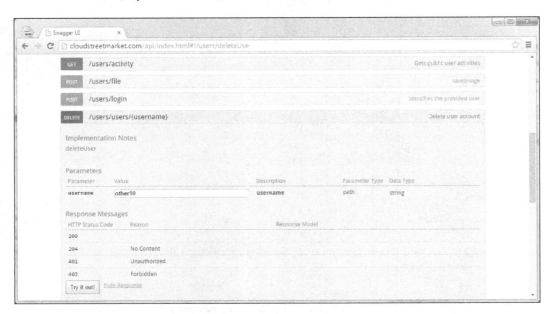

12. You should receive a **403 (Forbidden)** response status because the underlying service-method is secured!

13. You will see that you haven't been prompted a BASIC login form. Also, take a look at the response headers. You shouldn't see any **WWW-Authenticate** header, which could have triggered this popup.

> An `AuthenticationEntryPoint` is called if the user is not authenticated and if the requested HTTP resource appears to be secured. Securing the service alone is not sufficient for Spring Security to consider the Controller method-handler as secured.

14. Try to GET the users again in the **monitoring** tab. You should see again the BASIC authentication form. Fill it with the following details:

    <User Name> admin
    <Password> admin

    You should now receive the following response with a **200 status code**:

Request URL

http://cloudstreetmarket.com:80/api/monitoring/users

Response Body

can't parse JSON. Raw result:

{"content":[{"username":"actionMan10","fullname":"","email":"fake8@fake.com","password":"$2a$10$Qz5slUkuV7RXfaH/otDY9udROisOwf6XX

Response Code

200

Response Headers

```
{
  "pragma": "no-cache",
  "date": "Sun, 10 May 2015 13:50:46 GMT",
  "www-authenticate": "CSM_Basic realm=\"cloudstreetmarket.com\"",
  "server": "Apache-Coyote/1.1",
  "x-frame-options": "DENY",
  "authenticated": "true",
  "content-type": "application/json",
  "cache-control": "no-cache, no-store",
  "transfer-encoding": "chunked",
  "x-content-type-options": "nosniff",
  "connection": "Keep-Alive",
  "keep-alive": "timeout=5, max=100",
  "x-xss-protection": "1; mode=block",
  "expires": "Thu, 01 Jan 1970 00:00:00 GMT"
}
```

15. Swagger UI cannot beautify the body when we request a JSON response but everything is there.

 Notice the response code: **WWW-Authenticate: CSM_Basic realm"="cloudstreetmarket.com"**.

How it works...

We will see how the Spring Security authorization process works and how to configure it.

Spring Security authorities

An AuthenticationManager implementation stores GrantedAuthorities into an Authentication object in the SecurityContext. These GrantedAuthorities are read by the AccessDecisionManager in an attempt to match them against accesses' requirements.

The `AccessDecisionManager` implementations can be native or external and this explains why the infrastructure forces the authorities to be rendered as Strings.

If a `getAuthority()` method is not able to represent the `GrantedAuthority` as a String, then it should return `null`, indicating to the `AuthenticationManager` that it has to support this type of `Authority`.

This mechanism constraints the different `getAuthority()` implementations into limited responsibilities.

Configuration attributes

We have mentioned the Configuration attributes when we were introducing the `GrantedAuthority` objects (*Authenticating over a BASIC scheme* recipe).

Configuration attributes play a key role in `SecurityInterceptor` and indirectly in `AccessDecisionManager` implementations, since `SecurityInterceptor` delegates to `AccessDecisionManager`. Configuration attributes implement the one-method `ConfigAttribute` interface:

```
public interface ConfigAttribute extends Serializable {
    String getAttribute();
}
```

 Configuration attributes are specified as annotations on secured methods or as access attributes on secured URLs (intercept-urls).

We have defined the following instruction in our `security-config.xml` file as a way to tell Spring Security to expect the configuration attributes `ROLE_BASIC` on web requests matching the `/basic.html` pattern:

```
<security:intercept-url pattern="/basic.html"
    access="hasRole('BASIC')"/>
```

With the default `AccessDecisionManager` implementation, any user having a matching `GrantedAuthority` will be granted the access.

For a voter-based `AccessDecisionManager` implementation, a configuration attribute beginning with `ROLE_` the prefix will be considered as a role and should be examined by a `RoleVoter`. We will see more about `AccessDecisionManager` in the next sections.

SecurityInterceptor protecting Secure objects are objects or actions that require a security examination. There are two types of secure objects that are handled by the Framework:

- ▶ Web resources such as `ServletRequest` or `ServletResponse`. Those are checked by **FilterSecurityInterceptor**: a core Filter positioned almost at the end of the filter chain.

> ▶ Method invocations, which are implementations of `org.aopalliance.intercept.MethodInvocation`. Those are checked by **MethodSecurityInterceptor**.

A security interceptor (method or HTTP request) intercepts asynchronously (event-based) every single secure object invocations before they actually reach the resource. Spring Security always applies a simple pattern when handling those invocations. This pattern comes from the use of `AbstractSecurityInterceptor` subclasses.

The `AbstractSecurityInterceptor` examinations impose a consistent workflow to Secure Objects:

> ▶ Looking up the **configuration attributes** associated with the .secure object.

> ▶ Submitting the secure object, current authentication object, and configuration attributes to the `AccessDecisionManager` interface for an authorization decision.

> ▶ Optionally changing the `Authentication` object under which the invocation takes place.

> ▶ Allowing the secure object invocation to proceed (assuming access was granted).

> ▶ Calling the `AfterInvocationManager` interface if configured, once the invocation has returned. If the invocation raised an exception, the `AfterInvocationManager` will not be invoked.

This workflow can be summarized with the following diagram:

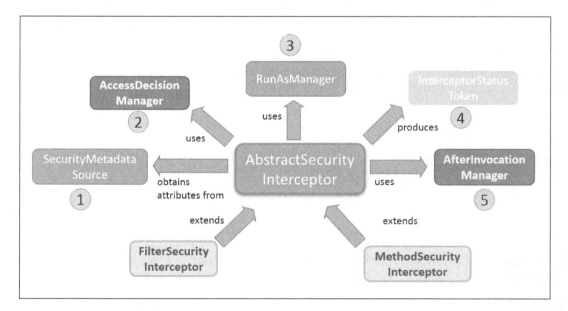

The original graph for this picture comes from the Spring Security reference. It is interesting because it highlights the different elements that `SecurityInterceptor` can use when examining a secure object.

> The main idea is the delegation to an `AccessDecisionManager` interface and then optionally to an `AfterInvocationManager` interface, using the pulled attributes from `SecurityMetadaSource` and eventually the `AuthenticationManager` capability to authenticate.

A `RunAsManager` dependency can optionally be added to `SecurityInterceptor` on rare occasions where the `SecurityContext Authentication` object may need to be altered (*step 3* of the workflow). The interface is defined as follows:

```
public interface RunAsManager {
  Authentication buildRunAs(Authentication authentication,
      Object object, Collection<ConfigAttribute> attributes);
  boolean supports(ConfigAttribute attribute);
  boolean supports(Class<?> clazz);
}
```

If no dependency is set for `RunAsManager`, the `SecurityInterceptor` will run a `NullRunAsManager` implementation. An `AfterInvocationManager` interface may optionally be configured and used to alter the `statusToken` object returned by the invocation (*step 5* of the workflow).

Pre-invocation handling

An `AccessDecisionManager` decides whether an access must be allowed or not.

AccessDecisionManager

The `AccessDecisionManager` interface is called by the `SecurityInterceptor` (in *step 2* of its workflow) and is responsible for making the final access control decision.

The interface is made of the following three methods:

```
public interface AccessDecisionManager {
  void decide(Authentication authentication, Object object,
    Collection<ConfigAttribute> configAttributes) throws
      AccessDeniedException, InsufficientAuthenticationException;
  boolean supports(ConfigAttribute attribute);
  boolean supports(Class<?> clazz);
}
```

As you can see, the method names are pretty explicit:

- ▸ The `decide` method resolves an access control decision for the provided arguments. The `Authentication` object represents the caller invoking the method, the object is the Secured Object to be examined, the `configAttributes` are the configuration attributes associated with the secured object. Also, it throws an `AccessDeniedException` when access is denied.

- ▸ The `supports(ConfigAttribute attribute)` method is called at an early stage of the examination to determine whether the `AccessDecisionManager` can process a specific `ConfigAttribute..`

- ▸ The `supports(Class<?> clazz)` method is called prior the invocation to ensure the configured `AccessDecisionManager` supports the type of Secure Object that will be presented.

 When using a namespace configuration, Spring Security automatically registers a default instance of `AccessDecisionManager` for assessing method invocations and web accesses, based on the access attributes which are specified in the intercept-url and protect-pointcut declarations (and in annotations if using annotations to secure methods).

A specific or custom `AccessDecisionManager` can be specified in the following cases:

- ▸ On the **http** Namespace when handling web resources:

    ```
    <security:http ... access-decision-manager-ref"="xxx"">
    </security:http>
    ```

- ▸ On the **global-method-security** Namespace when handling method invocations:

    ```
    <security:global-method-security access-decision-manager-
      ref""=""... />
    ```

Spring Security includes three `AccessDecisionManager` implementations (`AffirmativeBased`, `ConsensusBased`, and `UnanimousBased`) that are based on voting. Voters are eligible `AccessDecisionVoter` implementations. The interface is defined as follows:

```
public interface AccessDecisionVoter<S> {
  boolean supports(ConfigAttribute attribute);
  boolean supports(Class<?> clazz);
  int vote(Authentication authentication, S object,
  Collection<ConfigAttribute> attributes);
}
```

A few `AccessDecisionVoter` implementations come along with the Framework (`AuthenticatedVoter`, `Jsr250Voter`, `PreInvocationAuthorizationAdviceVoter`, `WebExpressionVoter`, `RoleVoter`, and so on). During the examination, eligible `AccessDecisionVoters` are polled on the authorization decision. Voters' eligibility depends on the voters' registration in the `AccessDecisionManager.decisionVoters` property. It also depends on the voters' supports methods.

The `AccessDecisionManager` decides whether or not it should be thrown an `AccessDeniedException` based on its assessment of the votes. Each `AccessDecisionVoter` assesses the Secure Object against different criteria.

> *"The most commonly used AccessDecisionVoter provided with Spring Security is the simple RoleVoter, which treats configuration attributes as simple role names and votes to grant access if the user has been assigned that role"."*
>
> *Spring Security reference*

After invocation handling

There is only one `AfterInvocationManager` implementation in Spring Security: `AfterInvocationProviderManager`. This class aligns all the eligible `AfterInvocationProvider` implementations to give them the opportunity to alter the `SecurityInterceptor` result.

Similar to the `AccessDecisionManager` interface, the `AfterInvocationProvider` interface looks like this:

```
public interface AfterInvocationProvider {
  Object decide(Authentication authentication, Object object
    Collection<ConfigAttribute> attributes, Object
    returnedObject) throws AccessDeniedException;
  boolean supports(ConfigAttribute attribute);
  boolean supports(Class<?> clazz);
}
```

Expression-based access control

Since Spring Security 3, it is now possible to use Spring **Expression Language** (**EL**) in order to define the Web security and methods security.

> *"Expressions are evaluated with a root object as part of the evaluation context. Spring Security uses specific classes for web and method security as the root object, in order to provide built-in expressions and access to values such as the current principal."*
>
> *Spring Security reference*

The base class for expression root objects is `SecurityExpressionRoot`. This abstract class gives access to the following methods and properties which represent the common built-in expressions:

Expression	Description
`hasRole([role])`	Returns `true` if the current principal has the specified role. By default if the supplied role does not start with `ROLE_` it will be added. This can be customized by modifying the `defaultRolePrefix` on `DefaultWebSecurityExpressionHandler`.
`hasAnyRole([role1,role2])`	Returns `true` if the current principal has any of the supplied roles (given as a comma-separated list of strings). By default, if the supplied role does not start with `ROLE_` it will be added. This can be customized by modifying the `defaultRolePrefix` on `DefaultWebSecurityExpressionHandler`.
`hasAuthority([authority])`	Returns `true` if the current principal has the specified authority.
`hasAnyAuthority([authority1,authority2])`	Returns `true` if the current principal has any of the supplied roles (given as a comma-separated list of strings).
`principal`	Allows direct access to the principal object representing the current user.
`authentication`	Allows direct access to the current `Authentication` object obtained from the `SecurityContext`.
`permitAll`	Always evaluates to `true`.
`denyAll`	Always evaluates to `false`.
`isAnonymous()`	Returns `true` if the current principal is an anonymous user.
`isRememberMe()`	Returns `true` if the current principal is a remember-me user.
`isAuthenticated()`	Returns `true` if the user is not anonymous.
`isFullyAuthenticated()`	Returns `true` if the user is not an anonymous or a remember-me user.
`hasPermission(Object target, Object permission)`	Returns `true` if the user has access to the provided target for the given permission. For example, `hasPermission(domainObject, 'read')`.
`hasPermission(Object targetId, String targetType, Object permission)`	Returns `true` if the user has access to the provided target for the given permission. For example, `hasPermission(1,'com.example.domain.Message', 'read')`.

Web Security expressions

Using the Spring Security namespace, the `<http>` block has a `use-expression` attribute that defaults to true. This property makes the access attributes in the `intercept-url` elements expecting expressions as values.

For Web security, the base class for expression root objects is `WebSecurityExpressionRoot`, which inherits the methods of `SecurityExpressionRoot` and provides one extra method: `hasIpAddress(...)`.

Also, `WebSecurityExpressionRoot` exposes in the evaluation context the `HttpServletRequest` object accessible under the name `request`.

If expressions are being used, a `WebExpressionVoter` will be added to the `AccessDecisionManager`.

Method security expressions

Expressions for methods security have been introduced with Spring Security 3.0. Four security annotations support the use of expressions: `@PreAuthorize`, `@PostAuthorize`, `@PreFilter`, and `@PostFilter`.

Access control using @PreAuthorize and @PostAuthorize

The use of these annotations has to be activated in the global security bean:

```
<security:global-method-security pre-post-annctations"="enabled"">
```

`@PreAuthorize` is commonly used to allow or disallow methods' invocations.

We have implemented this annotation on the `MonitoringController` class:

```
@PreAuthorize("hasRole('ADMIN')")
public class MonitoringController extends CloudstreetApiWCI{
    ...
}
```

The specified Expression `hasRole('ADMIN')` meant that the accesses to the controller will only be allowed to users within the role `ROLE_ADMIN`.

> You can note the automatic prefixing of `ROLE_` that avoids a word repetition. This nice feature can be used in Expressions, both in web security (intercept-url: access attribute) and methods security

Let's also consider this example from the Spring security reference documents:

```
@PreAuthorize("hasPermission #contact, 'admin')")
public void deletePermission Contact contact, Sid recipient,
    Permission permission);
```

Here, a method argument is passed into the expression to decide whether the current user has the `admin` permission for the given contact.

The `@PostAuthorize` is less commonly used but can perform an access-control check after the method has been invoked. To access the `AccessDecisionManager` return value in the Expression, use the built-in name `returnObject`.

Filtering collections using @PreFilter and @PostFilter

It is now possible to rely on Spring Security to filter collections (using expressions) that may be returned from a method invocation.

Consider this example from the reference document:

```
@PreAuthorize("hasRole('USER')")
@PostFilter("hasPermission(filterObject, 'read') or
    hasPermission(filterObject, 'admin')")
public List<Contact> getAll();
```

Spring Security iterates through the returned collection and removes any elements for which the supplied expression is false. The name filter object refers to the current object in the collection. You can also filter before the method call, using `@PreFilter`, though this is a less common requirement.

Actually, in order to use `hasPermission()` in expressions, it is necessary to explicitly configure a `PermissionEvaluator` in the application context. The following code is a example:

```
<security:global-method-security...>
  <security:expression-handler ref="expressionHandler"/>
</security:global-method-security>
<bean id="expressionHandler"
  class="org.sfw.security.access.expression.method.DefaultMethod
  SecurityExpressionHandler">
  <property name="permissionEvaluator"
    ref="myPermissionEvaluator"/>
</bean>
```

With `myPermissionEvaluator` being a `PermissionEvaluator` implementation:

```
public interface PermissionEvaluator extends AopInfrastructureBean {
  boolean hasPermission(Authentication authentication, Object
    targetDomainObject, Object permission);
  boolean hasPermission(Authentication authentication,
    Serializable targetId, String targetType, Object
   permission);
}
```

JSR-250 and legacy method security

JSR-250 is a Java specification request that has been released in 2006. It specifies a set of annotations to address common semantic patterns. Among these annotations, some relate to security:

Annotation name	Description
RolesAllowed	Specifies the security roles permitted to access method(s) in an application
PermitAll	Specifies that all security roles are permitted to access the annotated method, or all methods in the annotated class
DenyAll	Specifies that no security roles are allowed to invoke the specified method(s)
DeclareRoles	Used to specify the security roles by the application

Spring Security supports these annotations but this support has to be activated:

```
<security:global-method-security jsr250-annotations"="enabled""…/>
```

Spring Security also supports its legacy @Secured annotations, if enabled:

```
<security:global-method-security secured-annotations"="enabled""…/>
```

There is more...

Domain Object Security (ACLs)

Some more complex applications may require authorization decisions to be taken, depending upon the actual domain object that is subject to method invocation:

```
http://docs.spring.io/spring-security/site/docs/current/reference/
htmlsingle/#domain-acls
```

Spring EL

You might need to find extra information about the Spring EL:

```
http://docs.spring.io/spring/docs/current/spring-framework-reference/
html/expressions.html
```

The Spring Security reference

The Spring and Security reference and the Spring JavaDoc have been the main source of information for this recipe. We hope you have enjoyed our information selection, analysis, and point of view.

```
http://docs.spring.io/spring-security/site/docs/current/apidocs/
```

```
http://docs.spring.io/spring-security/site/docs/current/reference/
htmlsingle
```

See also

> ▸ Hierarchical Roles and role nesting appear to be recurring requirements:
>
> ```
> http://docs.spring.io/spring-security/site/docs/current/
> reference/htmlsingle/#authz-hierarchical-roles
> ```

6
Implementing HATEOAS

This chapter contains the following recipes:

- ▶ Turning DTOs into Spring HATEOAS resources
- ▶ Building links for a Hypermedia-driven API
- ▶ Choosing a strategy to expose JPA entities
- ▶ Retrieving data from a third-party API with OAuth

Introduction

What is HATEOAS? If you have never seen this word before, it can appear to be difficult to pronounce. Some pronounce it hate-ee-os; others say hate O-A-S. The important point is to remember that this abbreviation stands for **Hypermedia as the Engine of Application State** (**HATEOAS**). At the very least, you should remember Hypermedia. Hypermedia as a resource's capability to embed nodes that target external resources. Being connected to other resources, a hypermedia resource is also constrained to its domain, as it can't technically develop (as part of itself) other resources' domains.

Think of it as **Wikipedia**. If we create a page whose sections are not self contained in the page title (domain), and if one of these sections is already covered in an external page, there are few chances that this situation will be raised by an administrator.

HATEOAS is a constraint applicable to a REST architecture. It imposes on its resources a domain consistency, and at the same time, it imposes an explicit self documentation that the owner has to maintained for the sake of the whole cohesion.

The Richardson Maturity Model

The Richardson Maturity Model (by Leonard Richardson) provides a way to grade and qualify a REST API by its level of REST constraints:

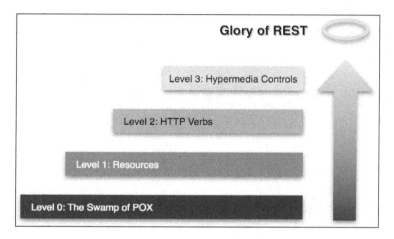

The more REST-compliant an API is, the higher its grade.

The initial state in this model is **Level 0: The Swamp of POX**. Here, the protocol (usually HTTP) is only used for its transport capabilities (not for its state description features). Also, there are no resource-specific URIs here, just one endpoint is used for one method (normally, POST in HTTP).

Level 1: Resources is characterized by the implementation of resource-specific URIs. The resource identifiers can be found in URIs. However, still, only one method of the protocol is used (POST for HTTP again).

Level 2: HTTP Verbs reflects an improved use of the protocol properties. For HTTP, this actually means that the API is making use of the HTTP methods for their purpose (GET to read, POST to create, PUT to edit, DELETE to delete, and so on). Also, the API provides response codes that reliably inform the user about the operation state.

Level 3: Hypermedia Controls is the highest level in this model. It indicates the use of HATEOAS, which provides API-discovery features to the client.

You can read more on the Richardson Maturity Model on Martin Fowler's blog at

```
http://martinfowler.com/articles/richardsonMaturityModel.html
```

Turning DTOs into Spring HATEOAS resources

This recipe presents how to create Spring HATEOAS resources. Even if the emphasis here is on one specific resource—`IndexResource` (in place of the former `IndexOverviewDTO`), feel free to browse **cloudstreetmarket-api** and **cloudstreetmarket-core** to discover more changes.

The HATEOAS principle has been applied at this stage to all the resources that make the core of our business, which strongly reflects the financial data structure of Yahoo! (indices, quotes, products, historical data, graphs, and so on.

How to do it...

1. From the **Git Perspective** in Eclipse, checkout the latest version of the v6.x.x branch. Then, run a `maven clean install` command on the **cloudstreetmarket-parent** module (right-click on the **Maven Clean** menu under **Run as...** and then again on **Maven Install** under **Run as...**) followed by a click on **Maven Update Project** menu to synchronize Eclipse with the Maven configuration (right-click on the module and then navigate to **Maven | Update Project....**)

> This branch includes SQL scripts that prepopulate the database with real financial data coming from Yahoo!.

2. Among the pulled changes, a new `/app` configuration directory shows up at the same level as `cloudstreetmarket-parent` and `zipcloud-parent`. This `/app` directory has to be copied to your system's home directory:

   ❑ Copy it to `C:\Users\{system.username}\app` if you are on Windows

   ❑ Copy it to `/home/usr/{system.username}/app` if you are on Linux

   ❑ If you are on Mac OS X, copy it at `/Users/{system.username}/app`

3. Spring HATEOAS comes with the following dependency. This dependency has been added to **cloudstreetmarket-parent**, **cloudstreetmarket-core**, and **cloudstreetmarket-api**:

```
<dependency>
  <groupId>org.springframework.hateoas</groupId>
  <artifactId>spring-hateoas</artifactId>
  <version>0.17.0.RELEASE</version>
</dependency>
```

4. As the recipe title suggests, the goal is to get rid of the existing DTOs that were exposed with the REST API. We have, for now, removed IndexOverviewDTO, MarketOverviewDTO, ProductOverviewDTO, and StockProductOverviewDTO.

5. Those DTOs have been replaced by these classes: IndexResource, StockProductResource, ChartResource, ExchangeResource, IndustryResource, and MarketResource.

6. As shown with IndexResource, which is presented as follows, all these new classes inherit the Spring HATEOAS Resource class:

```
@XStreamAlias("resource")
public class IndexResource extends Resource<Index> {
  public static final String INDEX = "index";
  public static final String INDICES = "indices";
  public static final String INDICES_PATH = "/indices";

  public IndexResource(Index content, Link... links) {
    super(content, links);
  }
}
```

7. As you can see, with IndexResource, resources are created from JPA entities (here, Index.java). These entities are stored in the Resource supertype under the content property name.

8. We have transformed the JPA entities, abstracting their @Id in an implementation of the Identifiable interface:

```
@Entity
@Table(name="index_value")
@XStreamAlias("index")
public class Index extends ProvidedId<String> {

  private String name;

  @Column(name="daily_latest_value")
  private BigDecimal dailyLatestValue;

  @Column(name="daily_latest_change")
  private BigDecimal dailyLatestChange;

  @Column(name="daily_latest_change_pc")
  private BigDecimal dailyLatestChangePercent;

  @Column(name = "previous_close")
  private BigDecimal previousClose;

  private BigDecimal open;
```

```java
    private BigDecimal high;

    private BigDecimal low;

    @ManyToOne(fetch = FetchType.EAGER)
    @JsonSerialize(using=IdentifiableSerializer.class)
    @JsonProperty("exchangeId")
    @XStreamConverter(value=IdentifiableToIdConverter.class,
    strings={"id"})
    @XStreamAlias("exchangeId")
     private Exchange exchange;

    @JsonIgnore
    @XStreamOmitField
    @ManyToMany(fetch = FetchType.LAZY)
    @JoinTable(name = "stock_indices", joinColumns =
    {@JoinColumn(name = "index_code") },
    inverseJoinColumns = {@JoinColumn(name =
      "stock_code")})
    private Set<StockProduct> components = new
    LinkedHashSet<>();

    @Column(name="last_update", insertable=false,
      columnDefinition="TIMESTAMP DEFAULT CURRENT_TIMESTAMP")

    @Temporal(TemporalType.TIMESTAMP)
    private Date lastUpdate;

    public Index(){}

    public Index(String indexId) {
      setId(indexId);
    }

    //getters & setters

      @Override
      public String toString() {
      return "Index [name=" + name + ", dailyLatestValue=" +
       dailyLatestValue + "  dailyLatestChange=" +
       dailyLatestChange + ", dailyLatestChangePercent=" +
       dailyLatestChangePercent + ", previousClose=" +
       previousClose + ", open=" + open + ", high=" + high + ",
       low=" + low + ", exchange=" + exchange + ", lastUpdate="
       + lastUpdate + ", id=" + id + "]";
      }
    }
```

9. Here are the details of the ProvidedId class, which is one of our Identifiable implementations:

```java
@MappedSuperclass
public class ProvidedId<ID extends Serializable> implements
  Identifiable<ID> {
  @Id
  protected ID id;
  @Override
  public ID getId() {
    return id;
  }
  public void setId(ID id) {
    this.id = id;
  }
  @Override
  public String toString() {
    return id;
  }
  @Override
  public int hashCode() {
    return Objects.hash(id);
  }
  @Override
  public boolean equals(Object obj) {
    if (this == obj)
      return true;
    if (obj == null)
      return false;
    if (getClass() != obj.getClass())
      return false;
    ProvidedId <?> other = (ProvidedId <?>) obj;
    return Objects.equals(this.id, other.id);
  }
}
```

How it works...

One new Spring dependency, a few new resource objects (Resource subclasses), and finally some modifications to our Entities so that they implement the Identifiable interface. Let's debrief all this in detail.

Spring HATEOAS resources

As introduced at the beginning of this chapter, HATEOAS is about links. It is fair to say that we can expect, as part of the Framework, an existing Type that supports and standardizes the representation of links.

This is the role of the `ResourceSupport` class (part of Spring HATEOAS): to support the collection and management of links attached to a resource.

Alternatively, a REST resource is also a content. The Framework also offers a `Resource` class that already inherits `ResourceSupport`.

To summarize, using Spring HATEOAS, we can decide to model our resource objects (`IndexResource`, `StockProductResource`, and so on) in two different ways:

- ▶ We can model them either by making them inherit `ResourceSupport` directly. By doing so, we have to manage the resource-content as part of the wrapper object by ourselves. The content here is out of control for the Framework.

- ▶ We can also model them by making them inherit the generic `Resource<T>` class whose Type `T` corresponds to the Type of the `POJO` content for the resource. This is the strategy we have chosen. The Framework offers goodies for our resource-object (`Inde3xResource`) on content binding, link creation, and even at the controller's level. We will see all this soon.

The ResourceSupport class

The `ResourceSupport` class is an object that implements `Identifiable<Link>`:

```
public class ResourceSupport extends Object implements
    Identifiable<Link>
```

The following is a sample from the `ResourceSupport` JavaDoc, which will provide you with an insight on its constructors and methods:

Constructors	Description
ResourceSupport ()	This creates a new ResourceSupport class

Methods	Description
Void add(Iterable<Link> links)	This adds all the given links to the resource
Void add(Link... links)	This adds all the given links to the resource
Void add(Link link)	This adds the given link to the resource
Link getId()	This returns the link with rel of Link.REL_SELF

Methods	Description
`Link    getLink(String rel)`	This returns the link with the given `rel`
`List<Link>    getLinks()`	This returns all the links contained in this resource
`boolean    hasLink(String rel)`	This returns whether the resource contains a link with the given `rel`
`boolean    hasLinks()`	This returns whether the resource contains links at all
`boolean    removeLinks()`	This removes all the links added to the resource so far
`Boolean equals(Object obj)`	
`int hashCode()`	
`String toString()`	

As introduced earlier, this class is all about links! We will see that Spring HATEOAS provides a small machinery around links.

The Resource class

The `Resource` class is a wrapper for a `POJO`. The `POJO` is stored in a `content` property of this class. A `Resource` class natively extends `ResourceSupport`:

```
public class Resource<T> extends ResourceSupport
```

Here is a sample from the `Resource` JavaDoc that provides an insight into its constructors and methods:

Constructors	Description
`Resource(T content, Iterable<Link> links)`	This creates a new resource with the given content and links
`Resource(T content, Link... links)`	This creates a new resource with the given content and links (optional)

Methods	Description
TgetContent()	This returns the underlying entity
void add(Iterable<Link> links)	This adds all the given links to the resource
void add(Link... links)	This adds all the given links to the resource
void add(Link link)	This adds the given link to the resource
Link getId()	This returns the link with a rel of Link.REL_SELF
Link getLink(String rel)	This returns the link with the given rel
List<Link> getLinks()	This returns all the links contained in this resource
boolean hasLink(String rel)	This returns whether the resource contains a link with the given rel
boolean hasLinks()	This returns whether the resource contains links at all
boolean removeLinks()	This removes all the links added to the resource so far
Boolean equals(Object obj)	
int hashCode()	
String toString()	

Two handy constructors, one getter for the content, and all the link-related helpers, this is what the Resource class is made of.

The Identifiable interface

The Identifiable interface plays a central role in Spring HATEOAS, since the key classes Resource, ResourceSupport, Resources, and PagedResources classes, which we'll present later on, are all Identifiable implementations. We will present later on, all these key classes.

The Identifiable interface is a Spring HATEOAS one-method interface (a generic interface) that is used to define an Id in an object:

```
public interface Identifiable<ID extends Serializable> {
  ID getId();
}
```

Consequently, the Framework uses this method to retrieve the ID with very few requirements about the nature of the passed-in object. With the capability of a class to implement several interfaces, it is costless to add such a qualifier to an object. Also, the contract of this interface is minimal.

The most important use of this interface (and method) by the framework is to build links out of a `Resource` object. Have a look at the `slash` method of `LinkBuilderSupport`. You will note that, if `ID` is not an instance of `Identifiable` (this is what it usually ends up with), the `Link` is appended with the `toString()` representation of the `ID` type.

> Bear this behavior in mind if you are thinking of implementing custom ID types.

Abstracting the Entities' @Id

If you plan to stick with Spring HATEOAS without extending it to Spring Data REST, it is probably not an absolute necessity to decouple the base entities from their `@Id`. At least not in the way we did it.

Here, this practice comes from Oliver Gierke, in his `Spring RestBucks` application. Spring RestBucks is a showcase application for several modern Spring REST features.

> Oliver Gierke is the Spring Data lead developer at Pivotal Software, Inc.. He has also been involved in Spring HATEOAS. Spring Data is an amazing project and product. We can trust Oliver Gierke for his vision and decisions.

In his `AsbtractId` implementation, O. Gierke defines the `Id` property as private and annotates it as `@JsonIgnore`. He drives us toward the nonexposure of the `Id` attribute as part of the resource-content. In REST, the ID of a resource should be its URI.

If you have the chance to take a look at Spring Data REST, this approach fully makes sense as part of the Framework, which strongly correlates REST resources to Spring Data repositories.

We have made the choice of not covering Spring Data REST as part of this book. However, not exposing entity IDs is not critical for our application. For these reasons, and also because we wish to maintain conventionality on this point in regard to the *Chapter 7, Developing CRUD Operations and Validations*, IDs will be exposed as resource-attributes.

There's more...

If our HATEOAS introduction wasn't clear enough to give you an idea of the principle, do read this presentation from Pivotal (`Spring.io`) at:

`https://spring.io/understanding/HATEOAS`

See also

- We recommend that you visit O. Gierke's Spring REST showcase application, which presents both Spring HATEOAS in practice coupled or not to Spring Data REST, at `https://github.com/olivergierke/spring-restbucks`.

- You can find a few discussions about ID exposure at `https://github.com/spring-projects/spring-hateoas/issues/66`.

- We advise you to read more about Spring Data REST since we have only introduced a little bit of it. Spring Data REST builds REST resources on top of Spring Data repositories and automatically publishes their CRUD services. You can learn more about it at `http://docs.spring.io/spring-data/rest/docs/current/reference/html`.

Building links for a hypermedia-driven API

In this recipe, we will focus on how to create links with Spring HATEOAS and how to bind them to resources.

We will detail the resource assemblers, which are reusable transition components used to pass from entities (such as `Index`) to their resources (`IndexResource`). These components also provide support for link creation.

How to do it...

1. The created resources (IndexResource, ChartResource, ExchangeResource, IndustryResource, MarketResource, and so on) are created from their associated Entity (Index, ChartIndex, ChartStock, Exchange, Industry, Market, and so on) using resource assemblers registered as @Component:

```
import static
  org.sfw.hateoas.mvc.ControllerLinkBuilder.linkTo;
import static
  org.sfw.hateoas.mvc.ControllerLinkBuilder.methodOn;
import org.sfw.hateoas.mvc.ResourceAssemblerSupport;
import org.sfw.hateoas.EntityLinks;
import static edu.zc.csm.api.resources.ChartResource.CHART;
import static
  edu.zc.csm.api.resources.ExchangeResource.EXCHANGE;
import static
  edu.zc.csm.api.resources.StockProductResource.COMPONENTS;

@Component
public class IndexResourceAssembler extends
  ResourceAssemblerSupport<Index, IndexResource> {
  @Autowired
```

```java
private EntityLinks entityLinks;
public IndexResourceAssembler() {
  super(IndexController.class, IndexResource.class);
}
@Override
public IndexResource toResource(Index index) {
  IndexResource resource =
    createResourceWithId(index.getId(), index);
  resource.add(
    entityLinks.linkToSingleResource(index.getExchange
      ()).withRel(EXCHANGE)
);
  resource.add(
  linkTo(methodOn(ChartIndexController.class).get(in
    dex.getId(), ".png", null, null, null, null, null,        null,
    null)).withRel(CHART)
);
  resource.add(
    linkTo(methodOn(StockProductController.class).getS
    everal(null, null, index.getId(), null, null,       null,
    null)).withRel(COMPONENTS)
);
return resource;
  }
  @Override
  protected IndexResource instantiateResource(Index
    entity) {
    return new IndexResource(entity);
  }
}
```

 We've used these assemblers to generate the links that come with a resource. They use static methods from `ControllerLinkBuilder` (`linkTo` and `methodOn`) and explicit labels defined as constants in the resources themselves (`EXCHANGE`, `CHART`, and `COMPONENTS`).

2. We have altered our previous SwaggerConfig class so that this class can be used for annotation-based configuration in other domains that Swagger. This class has been renamed to AnnotationConfig.

3. We have also added to this AnnotationConfig class the following two annotations:

```java
@EnableHypermediaSupport(type = { HypermediaType.HAL })
```

```java
@EnableEntityLinks
```

(Because these two annotations don't have an XML equivalent yet).

4. All the targeted controllers in these converters have been annotated with the @ExposesResourceFor annotation (on the class level).

5. These controllers now also return the created resources or pages of resources:

```
@RestController
@ExposesResourceFor(Index.class)
@RequestMapping(value=INDICES_PATH,
  produces={"application/xml", "application/json"})
public class IndexController extends
  CloudstreetApiWCI<Index> {
  @Autowired
  private IndexService indexService;
  @Autowired
  private IndexResourceAssembler assembler;
  @RequestMapping(method=GET)
  public PagedResources<IndexResource> getSeveral(
    @RequestParam(value="exchange", required=false) String
    exchangeId,@RequestParam(value="market", required=false)
    MarketId marketId, @PageableDefault(size=10, page=0,
    sort={"previousClose"}, direction=Direction.DESC)
    Pageable pageable){
      return pagedAssembler.toResource(
        indexService.gather(exchangeId,marketId,
        pageable), assembler);
  }
  @RequestMapping(value="/{index:[a-zA-Z0-9^.-]+}{extension:\\.[a-
  z]+}", method=GET)
  public IndexResource get(
    @PathVariable(value="index") String indexId,
    @PathVariable(value="extension") String extension){
    return assembler.toResource(
      indexService.gather(indexId));
}
}
```

6. Here, we have made CloudstreetApiWCI generic. In this way, CloudstreetApiWCI can have a generic PagedResourcesAssembler @Autowired:

```
@Component
@PropertySource("classpath:application.properties")
public class CloudstreetApiWCI<T extends Identifiable<?>>
  extends WebContentInterceptor {
...
    @Autowired
    protected PagedResourcesAssembler<T> pagedAssembler;
...
}
```

Since it is not the legacy purpose of a `WebCommonInterceptor` class to be used as a super controller sharing properties and utility methods, we will create an intermediate component between controllers and `WebCommonInterceptor`.

7. In order to @Autowire the PagedResourcesAssemblers, as we did, we have registered a PagedResourcesAssembler bean in dispatcher-servlet.xml:

```xml
<bean class="org.sfw.data.web.PagedResourcesAssembler">
  <constructor-arg><null/></constructor-arg>
  <constructor-arg><null/></constructor-arg>
</bean>
```

8. As a result, now calling the API for a ^GDAXI index code (http://cloudstreetmarket.com/api/indices/%5EGDAXI.xml) produces the following output:

```
cloudstreetmarket.com/api/indices/%5EGDAXI.xml

This XML file does not appear to have any style information associated with it. The document tree is shown below.

▼<resource>
 ▼<links>
  ▼<link>
     <rel>self</rel>
     <href>http://cloudstreetmarket.com/api/indices/%5EGDAXI</href>
   </link>
  ▼<link>
     <rel>exchange</rel>
     <href>http://cloudstreetmarket.com/api/exchanges/GER</href>
   </link>
  ▼<link>
     <rel>chart</rel>
     <href>http://cloudstreetmarket.com/api/charts/%5EGDAXI</href>
   </link>
  ▼<link>
     <rel>components</rel>
    ▼<href>
       http://cloudstreetmarket.com/api/products/stocks?index=%5EGDAXI
     </href>
   </link>
 </links>
 ▼<content class="index">
    <id class="string">^GDAXI</id>
    <name>DAX</name>
    <dailyLatestValue>11040.10</dailyLatestValue>
    <dailyLatestChange>-60.20</dailyLatestChange>
    <dailyLatestChangePercent>-0.54</dailyLatestChangePercent>
    <previousClose>11100.30</previousClose>
    <open>11121.30</open>
    <high>11246.27</high>
    <low>10997.90</low>
    <exchangeId>GER</exchangeId>
    <lastUpdate class="sql-timestamp">2015-06-21 15:30:25.712</lastUpdate>
 </content>
</resource>
```

As links, we have expressed endpoints and URI paths. From those links we can retrieve other Entities in relationship with an index (if we want to expose them obviously).

How it works...

This section specifically details the links creation.

Resource assemblers

This kind of specialized converters (Resource assemblers) are thought for reusability. Their main functions are as follows:

- Instantiating the resource and hydrating it with content
- Creating the resource's links from the Entity state or from the static global design

The Framework provides a `ResourceAssemblerSupport` super-class whose role is to reduce boilerplate code in the assemblers' duties.

The `ResourceAssemblerSupport` class s an abstract generic class. It enriches an assembler by providing a couple of extra methods. With `T` being a controller's class or super. Type, its signature is the following:

```
public abstract class ResourceAssemblerSupport<T, D extends
ResourceSupport> implements ResourceAssembler<T, D>
```

The table here provides a glimpse of the `ResourceAssemblerSupport` JavaDoc:

Methods	Description
`List<D> toResources(Iterable<? extends T> entities)`	This converts all the given entities into resources
`protected D createResourceWithId(Object id, T entity)`	This creates a new resource with a self link to the given ID
`D createResourceWithId(Object id, T entity, Object... parameters)`	-
`protected D instantiateResource(T entity)`	This instantiates the resource object. The default implementation will assume a `no-arg` constructor and use a reflection. However it can be overridden to manually set up the object instance initially (for example, to improve performance if this becomes an issue

The `ResourceAssemblerSupport` class also implements `ResourceAssembler`, which is the one-method interface presented here that forces the assembler to provide a `toResource(T entity)` method:

```
public interface ResourceAssembler<T, D extends ResourceSupport> {
  D toResource(T entity);
}
```

It can be noticed that we have overridden the `instantiateResource` method in our assemblers. As specified in the JavaDoc, not overriding it causes the Framework to instantiate the resource by reflection, looking for a `no-arg` constructor in the resource.

We have preferred here to avoid such constructors in our resources, as they can be a bit of an overhead.

PagedResourcesAssembler

This amazing, generic super assembler is used to build link-based pages of resources for the client. With an incredibly small amount of configuration, Spring HATEOAS builds for us a complete and out-of-the-box, fully populated page of typed-resources.

Based on our presented configuration, you can try calling the following URL:

```
http://cloudstreetmarket.com/api/indices.xml
```

Doing this, you should obtain the following output:

Can you see the **next rel** link and how it has been built by reflection from our method-handler annotations and their default and used values? Try to follow the **next** link to see how the navigation gets updated and incremented smoothly.

In the `IndexController.getSeveral()` method-handler (shown in the following snippet), we make sure that every single resource is built properly (content and links) by making the `PagedResourcesAssembler` using our custom `IndexResourceAssembler`:

```
@RequestMapping(method=GET)
public PagedResources<IndexResource> getSeveral(
@RequestParam(value="exchange", required=false) String exchangeId,
@RequestParam(value="market", required=false) MarketId marketId,
@PageableDefault(size=10, page=0, sort={"previousClose"},
  direction=Direction.DESC) Pageable pageable){
  return pagedAssembler.toResource(
  indexService.gather(exchangeId, marketId, pageable),
  assembler);
}
```

Building links

Let's have a look at the way we build resource links in assemblers. The presented `toResource()` method in `IndexResourceAssembler` uses two different techniques.

The first technique through **EntityLinks** uses JPA Entities; the second one, through the `ControllerLinkBuilder` static methods, uses `Controllers` directly.

EntityLinks

By declaring the `@EnableEntityLinks` annotation in a configuration class, an `EntityLinks` implementation gets registered: `ControllerEntityLinks`. All the Spring MVC controllers of **ApplicationContext** are looked up to search for the ones carrying a `@ExposesResourceFor(xxx.class)` annotation.

The `@ExposesResourceFor` annotation on a Spring MVC controller exposes the model Type that the controller manages. This registration enables the required mapping between the controller and a JPA entity.

It must also be noted that the registered `ControllerEntityLinks` implementation assumes a certain `@RequestMapping` configuration on controllers. The `@RequestMapping` configuration is made as follows:

- For a collection of resources, a class-level `@RequestMapping` annotation is expected. The controller then has to expose a method-handler mapped to an empty path, for example, `@RequestMapping(method = RequestMethod.GET)`.
- For individual resources, those are exposed with the `id` of the managed JPA Entity, for example, `@RequestMapping("/{id}")`.

Acknowledging these points, the `EntityLinks` implementation
(`ControllerEntityLinks`) is used from `@Autowiring` to generate `Links` using the
collection of methods it provides:

```
public interface EntityLinks extends Plugin<Class<?>>{
  LinkBuilder linkFor(Class<?> type);
  LinkBuilder linkFor(Class<?> type, Object... parameters);
  LinkBuilder linkForSingleResource(Class<?> type, Object id);
  LinkBuilder linkForSingleResource(Identifiable<?> entity);
  Link linkToCollectionResource(Class<?> type);
  Link linkToSingleResource(Class<?> type, Object id);
  Link linkToSingleResource(Identifiable<?> entity);
}
```

ControllerLinkBuilder

As introduced, Spring HATEOAS provides the `ControllerLinkBuilder` utility, which allows
the creation of links by pointing to controller classes:

```
resource.add(
  linkTo(
  methodOn(StockProductController.class)
  .getSeveral(null, null, index.getId(), null, null, null, null)
  )
  .withRel(COMPONENTS)
);
```

As specified in the Spring HATEOAS reference, `ControllerLinkBuilder` uses Spring's
`ServletUriComponentsBuilder` under the hood to obtain the basic URI information from
the current request.

If our application runs at `http://cloudstreetmarket/api`, then the Framework builds
`Links` on top of this root URI, appending it with the root controller mapping (`/indices`) and
then with the subsequent method-handler specific path.

There's more...

The use of regular expressions in @RequestMapping

In `IndexController`, `StockProductController`, `ChartStockController`, and
`ChartIndexController`, the `GET` method-handlers to retrieve single resources have a
special `@RequestMapping` definition.

Here is the IndexController's `get()` method:

```
@RequestMapping(value="/{index:[a-zA-Z0-9^.-]+}{extension:\\.
    [a-z]+}", method=GET)
public IndexResource get(
    @PathVariable(value="index") String indexId,
    @PathVariable(value="extension") String extension){
    return assembler.toResource(indexService.gather(indexId));
}
```

We ended up with this option because the Yahoo! Index codes appeared a bit more complex than simple strings. Especially considering the fact that these codes can carry one or more dots.

This situation caused Spring MVC not to be able to distinguish correctly the `@PathVariable` index from `extension` (stripping them out half the way).

Luckily, Spring MVC allows us to define URI template patterns with regular expressions. The syntax is `{varName:regex}`, where the first part defines the variable name and the second defines the regular expression.

You will note the regular expression we defined for our indices:

The `[a-zA-Z0-9^.-]` + expression, which specifically allows the `^` and `.` characters, is commonly used in the index code by Yahoo!

See also

- ▸ To know more about Spring HATEOAS, refer to `http://docs.spring.io/spring-hateoas/docs/current/reference/html/`.
- ▸ The introduced HATEOAS representation implements the **Hypertext Application Language** (**HAL**). HAL is supported by Spring HATEOAS as the default rendering. Learn more about the HAL specification at `https://tools.ietf.org/html/draft-kelly-json-hal-06` and `http://stateless.co/hal_specification.html`.

Choosing a strategy to expose JPA Entities

The `content` object(s) exposed in resources are JPA Entities. The interesting point about wrapping a JPA Entity in a resource comes with the low-level nature of an Entity itself, which supposedly represents a restricted identifiable domain area. This definition should ideally be entirely translated to the exposed REST resources.

So, how do we represent an Entity in REST HATEOAS? How do we safely and uniformly represent the JPA associations?

This recipe presents a simple and conservative method to answer these questions.

How to do it...

1. We have presented one entity used as a resource (Index.java). Here is another entity that is used: Exchange.java. This entity presents a similar strategy to expose its JPA associations:

```java
import edu.zc.csm.core.converters.IdentifiableSerializer;
import edu.zc.csm.core.converters.
  IdentifiableToIdConverter;


@Entity
public class Exchange extends ProvidedId<String> {
  private String name;

  @ManyToOne(fetch = FetchType.EAGER)
  @JoinColumn(name = "market_id", nullable=true)
  @JsonSerialize(using=IdentifiableSerializer.class)
  @JsonProperty("marketId")
  @XStreamConverter(value=IdentifiableToIdConverter.class,
    strings={"id"})
  @XStreamAlias("marketId")
  private Market market;

  @OneToMany(mappedBy = "exchange", cascade =
    CascadeType.ALL, fetch=FetchType.LAZY)
  @JsonIgnore
  @XStreamOmitField
  private Set<Index> indices = new LinkedHashSet<>();

  @OneToMany(mappedBy = "exchange", cascade =
    CascadeType.ALL, fetch=FetchType.LAZY)
  @JsonIgnore
  @XStreamOmitField
  private Set<StockProduct> stocks = new
    LinkedHashSet<>();

  public Exchange(){}
  public Exchange(String exchange) {
    setId(exchange);
  }

  //getters & setters

  @Override
```

```
public String toString() {
    return "Exchange [name=" + name + ", market=" +
        market + ", id=" + id+ "]";
}
```
}

2. The `Exchange.java` Entity references two custom utility classes that are used to transform the way external Entities are fetched as part of the main entity rendering (JSON or XML). Those utility classes are the following `IdentifiableSerializer` and the `IdentifiableToIdConverter`:

  ❑ The `IdentifiableSerializer` class is used for JSON marshalling:

```
import org.springframework.hateoas.Identifiable;
import com.fasterxml.jackson.core.JsonGenerator;
import com.fasterxml.jackson.core.JsonProcessingException;
import com.fasterxml.jackson.databind.JsonSerializer;
import com.fasterxml.jackson.databind.SerializerProvider;
public class IdentifiableSerializer extends
    JsonSerializer<Identifiable<?>> {
    @Override
    public void serialize(Identifiable<?> value, JsonGenerator
    jgen, SerializerProvider provider) throws IOException,
    JsonProcessingException {
    provider.defaultSerializeValue(value.getId(), jgen);
    }
}
```

  ❑ The `IdentifiableToIdConverter` class is used for XML marshlling and is built with XStream dependencies:

```
import com.thoughtworks.xstream.converters.Converter;
public class IdentifiableToIdConverter implements Converter
    {
    private final Class <Identifiable<?>> type;
    public IdentifiableToIdConverter(final Class
        <Identifiable<?>> type, final Mapper mapper, final
        ReflectionProvider reflectionProvider, final
        ConverterLookup lookup, final String valueFieldName) {
        this(type, mapper, reflectionProvider, lookup,
        valueFieldName, null);
    }
    public IdentifiableToIdConverter(final
        Class<Identifiable<?>> type, final Mapper mapper, final
        ReflectionProvider reflectionProvider, final
        ConverterLookup lookup, final String valueFieldName,
        Class valueDefinedIn) {
        this.type = type;
        Field field = null;
        try {
```

```
      field = (valueDefinedIn != null? valueDefinedIn :
        type.getSuperclass()).getDeclaredField("id");
      if (!field.isAccessible()) {
      field.setAccessible(true);
      }
        } catch (NoSuchFieldException e) {
          throw new IllegalArgumentException(
            e.getMessage()+": "+valueFieldName);
            }
        }
        public boolean canConvert(final Class type) {
          return type.isAssignableFrom(this.type);
      }
      public void marshal(final Object source, final
        HierarchicalStreamWriter writer,final
          MarshallingContext context) {
            if(source instanceof Identifiable){
              writer.setValue(
                ((Identifiable<?>)source).getId()
              .toString()
            );
          }
        }
      public Object unmarshal(final
        HierarchicalStreamReader reader, final
        UnmarshallingContext context) {
        return null;
      }
    }
  }
```

How it works...

Let's understand how this strategy works.

The REST CRUD principle

One REST architectural constraint is to present a uniform interface. A uniform interface is achieved by exposing resources from endpoints that can all be targeted from different HTTP methods (if applicable).

Resources can also be exposed under several representations (json, xml, and so on), and information or error messages must be self-descriptive. The implementation of HATEOAS provides a great bonus for the self-explanatory character of an API.

In REST, the more intuitive and inferable things are, the better. From this perspective, as a web/UI developer, I should be able to assume the following:

▶ The structure of the object I receive from the `GET` call on an endpoint will be the expected structure that I have to send back with a `PUT` call (the edition of the object)

▶ Similarly, the same structure should be used for the creation of a new object (the `POST` method)

This consistency of payload structures among different HTTP methods is a *SOLID* and conservative argument that is used when it is time to defend the API interests. *It's pretty much always the time to defend the API interests.*

Exposing the minimum

Exposing the minimum amount of information has been the core idea during the refactoring for this chapter. It's usually a great way to ensure that one endpoint won't be used to expose information data that would be external to the initial controller.

A JPA Entity can have associations to other Entities (`@OneToOne`, `@OneToMany`, `@ManyToOne`, or `@ManyToMany`).

Some of these associations have been annotated with `@JsonIgnore` (and `@XStreamOmitField`), and some other associations have been annotated with `@JsonSerialize` and `@JsonProperty` (and `@XStreamConverter` and `@XStreamAlias`).

If the Entity doesn't own the relationship

In this situation, the database table of the Entity doesn't have a foreign key to the table of the targeted second Entity.

The strategy here is to completely ignore the relationship in REST to reflect the database state.

The `ignore` instructions depend on the supported representations and the chosen implementations.

For `json`, we are using `Jackson`, the solution has been: `@JsonIgnore`.

For `xml`, we are using `XStream`, the solution has been: `@XstreamOmitField`.

If the Entity owns the relationship

Here, the database table of the Entity has a foreign key the table of the targeted second Entity.

If we plan to update an entity of this table, which depends on an entity of the other table, we will have to provide this foreign key for the entity.

The idea then is to expose this foreign key as a dedicated field just as all the other columns of the database table. Again, the solution to implement this depends on the supported representations and the configured marshallers.

For json and Jackson, we have done it with the following code snippet:

```
@JsonSerialize(using=IdentifiableSerializer.class)
@JsonProperty("marketId")
```

As you can see, we rename the attribute to suggest that we are presenting (and expecting) an ID. We have created the IdentifiableSerializer class that extracts the ID from the entity (from the Identifiable interface) and places only this ID into the value of the attribute.

For xml and XStream, it has been:

```
@XStreamConverter(value=IdentifiableToIdConverter.class,
    strings={"id"})
@XStreamAlias("marketId")
```

In the same way, we rename the attribute to suggest that we are presenting an ID, and we target the custom converter IdentifiableToIdConverter that also chooses only the **ID** of the Entity as a value for the attribute.

Here is an example of the xml representation example of the ^AMBAPT index:

```
  ▼<href>
      http://cloudstreetmarket.com/api/products/stocks?index=%5EAMBAPT
    </href>
   </link>
 </links>
▼<content class="index">
   <id class="string">^AMBAPT</id>
   <name>A.M. Best's Asian/Pacific Insur</name>
   <dailyLatestValue>1379.17</dailyLatestValue>
   <dailyLatestChange>-1.65</dailyLatestChange>
   <dailyLatestChangePercent>-0.12</dailyLatestChangePercent>
   <previousClose>1380.82</previousClose>
   <open>1379.17</open>
   <high>1379.17</high>
   <low>1379.17</low>
   <exchangeId>SNP</exchangeId>
   <lastUpdate class="sql-timestamp">2015-06-25 01:33:24.231</lastUpdate>
 </content>
</resource>
```

Separation of resources

This strategy promotes a clear separation between resources. The displayed fields for each resource match the database schema entirely. This is a standard practice in web developments to keep the HTTP request payload unchanged for the different HTTP methods.

When HATEOAS is adopted, we should then fully encourage the use of links to access related entities instead of nested views.

The previous recipe *Building links for a Hypermedia-Driven API* features examples to access (using links) the Entities that are associated with @...ToOne and @...ToMany. Below is an example of these links in an exposed Entity as it is achieved in the previous recipe:

```
←  →  C  ⌂ cloudstreetmarket.com/api/indices/%5EGDAXI.xml

This XML file does not appear to have any style information associated with it. The document tree is shown below.

▼<resource>
  ▼<links>
    ▼<link>
        <rel>self</rel>
        <href>http://cloudstreetmarket.com/api/indices/%5EGDAXI</href>
      </link>
    ▼<link>
        <rel>exchange</rel>
        <href>http://cloudstreetmarket.com/api/exchanges/GER</href>
      </link>
    ▼<link>
        <rel>chart</rel>
        ▼<href>
          http://cloudstreetmarket.com/api/charts/indices/%5EGDAXI.png
          </href>
      </link>
    ▼<link>
        <rel>components</rel>
        ▼<href>
          http://cloudstreetmarket.com/api/products/stocks?index=%5EGDAXI
          </href>
      </link>
    </links>
  ▼<content class="index">
      <id class="string">^GDAXI</id>
      <name>DAX</name>
      <dailyLatestValue>0.00</dailyLatestValue>
      <dailyLatestChange>0.00</dailyLatestChange>
      <dailyLatestChangePercent>0.00</dailyLatestChangePercent>
      <previousClose>0.00</previousClose>
      <high>0.00</high>
      <low>0.00</low>
      <exchangeId>GER</exchangeId>
      <lastUpdate class="sql-timestamp">2016-01-01 07:52:19.795</lastUpdate>
    </content>
</resource>
```

There's more...

We detail here official sources of information for the implemented marshallers.

Jackson custom serializers

You can find the official wiki page guide for these serializers at

http://wiki.fasterxml.com/JacksonHowToCustomSerializers

XStream converters

XStream has been migrated from codehaus.org to **Github**. To follow an official tutorial about XStream converters, go to:

http://x-stream.github.io/converter-tutorial.html

Retrieving data from a third-party API with OAuth

After having authenticated a user with OAuth 2, it is useful to know how to call a remote third-party API with the user's OAuth2 account.

How to do it...

1. You may have noticed that `IndexController`, `StockProductController`, `ChartIndexController`, and `ChartStockController` invoke underlying service methods named `gather(...)`. This concept suggests that lookups to third-party providers (Yahoo!) are proceeded.

2. In `IndexServiceImpl`, for example, you can find the `gather(String indexId)` method:

```
@Override
public Index gather(String indexId) {
    Index index = indexRepository.findOne(indexId);
    if(AuthenticationUtil.userHasRole(Role.ROLE_OAUTH2)){
        updateIndexAndQuotesFromYahoo(index != null ?
          Sets.newHashSet(index) : Sets.newHashSet(new
              Index(indexId)));
        return indexRepository.findOne(indexId);
    }
    return index;
}
```

3. It is really the `updateIndexAndQuotesFromYahoo(...)` method that bridges the service layer to the third-party API:

```
@Autowired
private SocialUserService usersConnectionRepository;

@Autowired
private ConnectionRepository connectionRepository;

private void updateIndexAndQuotesFromYahoo(Set<Index>
  askedContent) {
    Set<Index> recentlyUpdated = askedContent.stream()
    .filter(t -> t.getLastUpdate() != null &&
      DateUtil.isRecent(t.getLastUpdate(), 1))
      .collect(Collectors.toSet());

    if(askedContent.size() != recentlyUpdated.size()){
      String guid =
      AuthenticationUtil.getPrincipal().getUsername();
```

```
String token = usersConnectionRepository
  .getRegisteredSocialUser(guid) .getAccessToken();
Connection<Yahoo2> connection = connectionRepository
  .getPrimaryConnection(Yahoo2.class);
if (connection != null) {
  askedContent.removeAll(recentlyUpdated);
    List<String> updatableTickers =
    askedContent.stream()
      .map(Index::getId)
      .collect(Collectors.toList());
  List<YahooQuote> yahooQuotes = connection.getApi()
   .financialOperations().
     getYahooQuotes(updatableTickers, token);

  Set<Index> upToDateIndex = yahooQuotes.stream()
    .map(t -> yahooIndexConverter.convert(t))
    .collect(Collectors.toSet());

   final Map<String, Index> persistedStocks =
     indexRepository.save(upToDateIndex)    .stream()
     .collect(Collectors.toMap(Index::getId,
     Function.identity()));

  yahooQuotes.stream()
    .map(sq -> new IndexQuote(sq,
      persistedStocks.get(sq.getId())))
     .collect(Collectors.toSet());
   indexQuoteRepository.save(updatableQuotes);
  }
 }
}
```

4. In the case of Facebook, Twitter, or LinkedIn, you should be able to find a complete API adaptor to execute calls to their APIs without having to alter it. In our case, we had to develop the needed adaptor so that financial data can be retrieved and exploited from Yahoo!

5. We added two methods to a `FinancialOperations` interface as shown in this code snippet:

```
public interface FinancialOperations {
  List<YahooQuote> getYahooQuotes(List<String> tickers,
    String accessToken) ;
  byte[] getYahooChart(String indexId, ChartType type,
    ChartHistoSize histoSize, ChartHistoMovingAverage
    histoAverage, ChartHistoTimeSpan histoPeriod, Integer
    intradayWidth, Integer intradayHeight, String token);
}
```

6. This interface has a `FinancialTemplate` implementation as follows:

```
public class FinancialTemplate extends
  AbstractYahooOperations implements FinancialOperations {
    private RestTemplate restTemplate;
  public FinancialTemplate RestTemplate restTemplate,
    boolean isAuthorized, String guid) {
    super(isAuthorized, guid);
    this.restTemplate = restTemplate;
    this.restTemplate.getMessageConverters()
      add( new YahooQuoteMessageConverter(
        MediaType.APPLICATION_OCTET_STREAM));
    }
  @Override
  public List<YahooQuote> getYahooQuotes(List<String>
    tickers, String token)  {
      requiresAuthorization();
      final StringBuilder sbTickers = new StringBuilder();
      String url = "quotes.csv?s=";
      String strTickers = "";
      if(tickers.size() > 0){
        tickers.forEach(t ->
          strTickers = sbTickers.toString();
          strTickers = strTickers.substring(0,
            strTickers.length()-1);
      }
       HttpHeaders headers = new HttpHeaders();
       headers.set("Authorization", "Bearer "+token);
       HttpEntity<?> entity = new HttpEntity<>(headers);
       return restTemplate.exchange(buildUri(FINANCIAL,
        url.concat(strTickers).concat("&f=snopl1c1p2hgbavx  c4")),
        HttpMethod.GET, entity ,
      QuoteWrapper.class).getBody();
  }
  ...
}
```

7. The `FinancialTemplate` class is initialized as part of the global `Yahoo2Template` that is returned with the `connection.getApi()` calls of `IndexServiceImpl`.

8. Using this technique to pull (as needed) not only indices and stock quotes from Yahoo! but also graphs, we are now able to display real-time data from more than 25,000 stocks and 30,000 indices.

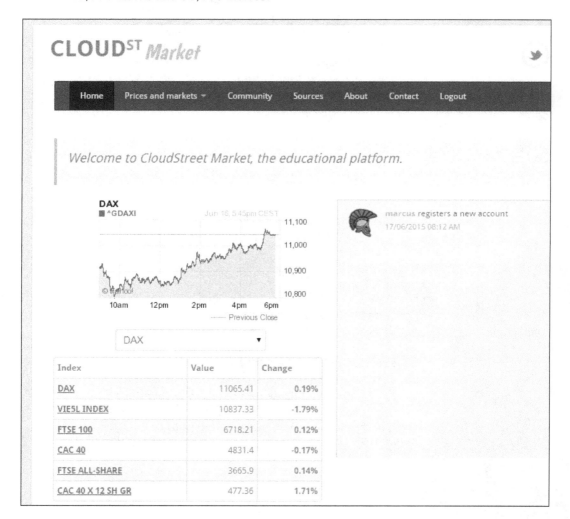

9. The client side is capable of using the provided HATEOAS links that come along with each result element. It uses these links to render detail views such as **Index detail** or **Stock detail** (new screens).

How it works...

Let's understand the theory behind this recipe.

Introduction to the financial data of Yahoo!

In the context of our application, there is still one refactoring that needs to be explained. It is about historical data and graphs.

The Yahoo! financial API provides historical data. This data can be used to build graphs, and it was initially planned to do it this way. Now, Yahoo! also generates graphs (for both historical and intraday data) and these graphs are quite customizable (time period, average lines, chart or stock's display option, and so on).

We have decided to drop the historical part, which technically is very similar to quote retrieval (data snapshots), to exclusively use graphs generated by Yahoo!

Graph generation/display

Our implementation provides an interesting example of image serving in REST. Have a look at `ChartIndexController` (or `ChartStockController`) and see how images are returned as byte arrays.

Also have a look at the `home_financial_graph.js` file, how the received content is set into an HTML `<img...>` markup.

How is the financial data pulled/refreshed?

The idea here is to rely on OAuth authenticated users. Yahoo! provides different rates and limits for authenticated and non-authenticated users. Non-authenticated calls are identified on the Yahoo! side by the calling IP, which will be (more or less) the entire `CloudstreetMarket` application IP in our case. If Yahoo! considers that there are too many calls coming from our IP, that will be an issue. However, if there are too many calls coming from one specific user, Yahoo! will restrict that user without affecting the rest of the application (and this situation can further be recovered by the application).

As you can see, the method-handlers that potentially deal with the financial data of Yahoo! call the appropriated underlying service through methods named `gather()`.

In these `gather()` methods, the Yahoo! third-party API interferes between our database and our controllers.

If the user is authenticated with OAuth2, the underlying service checks whether the data exists or not in the database and whether it has been updated recently enough to match a predefined buffer period for the data type (one minute for `indices` and `stocks`):

- ▸ If the answer is yes, this data is returned to the client
- ▸ If the answer is no, the expected data is requested from Yahoo!, transformed, stored in the database, and returned to the client

There is nothing planned at the moment for users who are not authenticated with OAuth, but we can imagine easily making them using a common Yahoo! OAuth account.

Calling third-party services

For the presented recipe, this part is done in the `updateIndexAndQuotesFromYahoo` method. Our Spring configuration defines a `connectionRepository` bean created with a `request` scope for each user. The `connectionRepository` instance is created from the `createConnectionRepository` factory method of our `SocialUserServiceImpl`.

Based on this, we `@Autowire` these two beans in our service layer:

```
@Autowired
```

```
private SocialUserService usersConnectionRepository;
@Autowired
private ConnectionRepository connectionRepository;
```

Then, the `updateIndexAndQuotesFromYahoo` method obtains the logged-in `userId` (`guid`) from the Spring Security:

```
String guid = AuthenticationUtil.getPrincipal().getUsername();
```

The access token is extracted from the `SocialUser` Entity (coming from the database):

```
String token = usersConnectionRepository
  .getRegisteredSocialUser(guid).getAccessToken();
```

The Yahoo! connection is retrieved from the database:

```
Connection<Yahoo2> connection =
connectionRepository.getPrimaryConnection(Yahoo2.class);
```

If the connection is not null, the third-party API is called from the connection object:

```
List<YahooQuote> yahooQuotes = connection.getApi()
  .financialOperations().getYahooQuotes(updatableTickers, token);
```

Once again, we had to develop the actual `FinancialTemplate` (the Java representation of the Yahoo! financial API), but you should be able to find such existing implementations for your third-party provider.

There's more...

This section provides a list of many existing open-source Spring Social adaptors that we can use in our projects

Spring Social — existing API providers

The following address provides an up-to-date aggregation of Spring social extensions for connection-support and API-binding to many popular service providers:

```
https://github.com/spring-projects/spring-social/wiki/Api-Providers
```

See also

- ▶ **Yahoo! financial stock tickers**: We have prefilled our database with a set of financial references to Yahoo! (stock references and index references), which allows us to point and search for resources that can, for the second time, be updated with real-time data through the Yahoo! APIs. This set of references comes from the great work published by **Samir Khan** on his blog accessible at `http://investexcel.net/all-yahoo-finance-stock-tickers`. This XLS data has then been transformed into SQL by us, using a basic text editor and macros.

7

Developing CRUD
Operations and
Validations

Until now, we have seen how to build the read-only HTTP methods of an API. These methods in Spring MVC Controllers required you to master, or at least understand the presentation of a few techniques. Developing non-readonly HTTP methods raises a new set of underlying topics. Each of these topics has a direct impact on the customer experience and therefore each of them is important. We introduce the following four recipes as a frame to cover the subject:

- Extending REST handlers to all HTTP methods
- Validating resources using bean validation support
- Internationalizing messages and contents for REST
- Validating client-side forms with HTML5 and AngularJS

Introduction

Developing CRUD operations and validations at this stage turns out to be one of the topics with the widest spectrum.

Our application will be transformed in many ways, from the transaction management standardisation to the internationalization of errors (and content), passing through the REST handlers, HTTP compliance.

In line with the previous chapters and with the global strategy of this book, we are focusing on how Spring MVC plays a key role in today's and tomorrow's best practices in regards to scalability and Microservices communications. It is a hard choice to decide skipping bits, but the Framework keeps adapting itself to new designs and challenges. This book tries to present a consistent integration of Spring MVC in a modern, sustainable, and scalable application.

Four recipes are presented here. The first one transforms two controllers to support the CRUD operations for their respective resources. Doing so requires a review of the database transactions and a review of the HTTP specification.

This chapter presents two validation strategies supported by Spring MVC. Since validation errors are often meant to be rendered in more than one language, we have made sure that our application supports internationalization. We briefly see how AngularJS can be used in this perspective and how it can be used to process frontend validations that are always necessary to constrain the customer experience into the reality of the business-specific data management.

Extending REST handlers to all HTTP methods

This is the core recipe of the chapter. We will detail how to use the Spring MVC method-handlers for HTTP methods that we haven't covered yet: the non-readonly ones.

Getting ready

We will see the returned status codes and the HTTP standards driving the use of the PUT, POST, and DELETE methods. This will get us to configure HTTP-compliant Spring MVC controllers.

We will also review how request-payload mapping annotations such as @RequestBody work under the hood and how to use them efficiently.

Finally, we open a window on Spring transactions, as it is a broad and important topic in itself.

How to do it...

Following the next steps will present the changes applied to two controllers, a service and a repository:

1. From the **Git Perspective** in Eclipse, checkout the latest version of the branch v7.x.x. Then, run a maven clean install on the cloudstreetmarket-parent module (right-click on the module and go to **Run as... | Maven Clean** and then again go to **Run as... | Maven Install**) followed by a Maven Update project to synchronize Eclipse with the maven configuration (right-click on the module and then go to **Maven | Update Project...**).

2. Run the `Maven clean` and `Maven install` commands on `zipcloud-parent` and then on `cloudstreetmarket-parent`. Then, go to **Maven | Update Project**.

3. In this chapter, we are focused on two REST controllers: the `UsersController` and a newly created `TransactionController`.

 The `TransactionController` allows users to process financial transactions (and thus to buy or sell products).

4. A simplified version of `UserController` is given here:

```
@RestController
@RequestMapping(value=USERS_PATH,
  produces={"application/xml", "application/json"})
public class UsersController extends CloudstreetApiWCI{
  @RequestMapping(method=POST)
  @ResponseStatus(HttpStatus.CREATED)
  public void create(@RequestBody User user,
  @RequestHeader(value="Spi", required=false) String guid, @Reques
tHeader(value="OAuthProvider", required=false)
  String provider,
  HttpServletResponse response) throws
  IllegalAccessException{
  ...
  response.setHeader(LOCATION_HEADER, USERS_PATH +
  user.getId());
  }
  @RequestMapping(method=PUT)
  @ResponseStatus(HttpStatus.OK)
  public void update(@RequestBody User user,
    BindingResult result).
    ...
  }
  @RequestMapping(method=GET)
  @ResponseStatus(HttpStatus.OK)
  public Page<UserDTO> getAll(@PageableDefault(size=10,
    page=0) Pageable pageable){
  return communityService.getAll(pageable);
  }
  @RequestMapping(value="/{username}", method=GET)
  @ResponseStatus(HttpStatus.OK)
  public UserDTO get(@PathVariable String username){
    return communityService.getUser(username);
  }
  @RequestMapping(value="/{username}", method=DELETE)
```

```
    @ResponseStatus(HttpStatus.NO_CONTENT)
    public void delete(@PathVariable String username){
      communityService.delete(username);
    }
  }
```

5. The **TransactionController** is represented here in a simplified version:

```
@RestController
@ExposesResourceFor(Transaction.class)
@RequestMapping(value=ACTIONS_PATH + TRANSACTIONS_PATH,
produces={"application/xml", "application/json"})
public class TransactionController extends
  CloudstreetApiWCI<Transaction> {
```

(The GET method-handlers given here come from previous recipes.)

```
    @RequestMapping(method=GET)
    @ResponseStatus(HttpStatus.OK)
    public PagedResources<TransactionResource> search(
      @RequestParam(value="user", required=false) String
        userName,
      @RequestParam(value="quote:[\\d]+", required=false) Long
        quoteId,
      @RequestParam(value="ticker:[a-zA-Z0-9-:]+",
        required=false) String ticker,
      @PageableDefault(size=10, page=0, sort={"lastUpdate"},
        direction=Direction.DESC) Pageable pageable){
      Page<Transaction> page =
        transactionService.findBy(pageable, userName, quoteId,
        ticker);
        return pagedAssembler.toResource(page, assembler);
    }
    @RequestMapping(value="/{id}", method=GET)
    @ResponseStatus(HttpStatus.OK)
  public TransactionResource get(@PathVariable(value="id")
    Long transactionId){
    return assembler.toResource(
      transactionService.get(transactionId));
    }
```

(The PUT and DELETE method-handlers introduced here are non-readonly methods.)

```
    @RequestMapping(method=POST)
    @ResponseStatus(HttpStatus.CREATED)
  public TransactionResource post(@RequestBody Transaction
    transaction) {
      transactionService.hydrate(transaction);
      ...
```

```
TransactionResource resource =
  assembler.toResource(transaction);
response.setHeader(LOCATION_HEADER,
  resource.getLink("self").getHref());
  return resource;
}
@PreAuthorize("hasRole('ADMIN')")
@RequestMapping(value="/{id}", method=DELETE)
@ResponseStatus(HttpStatus.NO_CONTENT)
public void delete(@PathVariable(value="id") Long
  transactionId){
    transactionService.delete(transactionId);
  }
}
```

6. The call to the `hydrate` method in the `post` method prepares the Entity for underlying service uses. It populates its relationships from IDs received in the request payload.

 This technique will be applied to all the REST resources used for CRUD.

7. Here are the details of the `hydrate` method in `transactionServiceImpl`:

```
@Override
public Transaction hydrate(final Transaction transaction) {

    if(transaction.getQuote().getId() != null){
      transaction.setQuote(
        stockQuoteRepository.findOne(
          transaction.getQuote().getId()));
    }
    if(transaction.getUser() getId() != null){
     transaction.setUser(userRepository.findOne(transaction.
       getUser().getId()));
    }
    if(transaction.getDate() == null){
      transaction.setDate(new Date());
    }
    return transaction;
  }
```

 Nothing amazing here; it is mainly about building our Entity to suit our needs. An interface can be created to standardize the practice.

8. All the service layers have been reviewed to drive uniform database transactions.

9. The service implementations are now annotated by default with
`@Transactional(readOnly = true)`. Check the following
`TransactionServiceImpl` example:

```
@Service
@Transactional(readOnly = true)
public class TransactionServiceImpl implements
  TransactionService{
  ...
}
```

10. The non-readonly methods of these service implementations override the class
definition with the `@Transactional` annotation:

```
@Override
@Transactional
public Transaction create(Transaction transaction) {
if(!transactionRepository.findByUserAndQuote(transaction.
  getUser(), transaction.getQuote()).isEmpty()){
    throw new DataIntegrityViolationException("A transaction
      for the quote and the user already exists!");
  }
  return transactionRepository.save(transaction);
}
```

11. This principle has also been applied to custom repository implementations (such as
`IndexRepositoryImpl`):

```
@Repository
@Transactional(readOnly = true)
public class IndexRepositoryImpl implements
  IndexRepository{
  @PersistenceContext
  private EntityManager em;

  @Autowired
  private IndexRepositoryJpa repo;
  ...
  @Override
  @Transactional
  public Index save(Index index) {
    return repo.save(index);
  }
  ...
}
```

How it works...

First, let's quickly review the different CRUD services presented in the controllers of this recipe. The following table summarizes them:

URI	Method	Purpose	Normal response codes
`/actions/transactions`	GET	Search transactions	200 OK
`/actions/transactions/{id}`	GET	Get a transaction	200 OK
`/actions/transactions`	POST	Create a transaction	201 Created
`/actions/transactions/{id}`	DELETE	Delete a transaction	204 No Content
`/users/login`	POST	Logs in a user	200 OK
`/users`	GET	Get all	200 OK
`/users/{username}`	GET	Get a user	200 OK
`/users`	POST	Create a user	201 Created
`/users/{username}`	PUT	Update a user	200 OK
`/users/{username}`	DELETE	Delete a user	204 No Content

HTTP/1.1 specifications – RFC 7231 semantics and content

To understand the few decisions that have been taken in this recipe (and to legitimate them), we must shed some light on a few points of the HTTP specification.

Before starting, feel free to visit Internet standards track document (RFC 7231) for **HTTP 1/1** related to Semantics and Content:

`https://tools.ietf.org/html/rfc7231`

Basic requirements

In the HTTP specification document, the request methods overview (section 4.1) states that it is a requirement for a server to support the GET and HEAD methods. All other request methods are optional.

The same section also specifies that a request made with a recognized method name (GET, POST, PUT, DELETE, and so on) but that doesn't match any method-handler should be responded with a `405 Not supported` status code. Similarly, a request made with an unrecognized method name (nonstandard) should be responded with a `501 Not implemented` status code. These two statements are natively supported and auto-configured by Spring MVC.

Safe and Idempotent methods

The document introduces introduces the Safe and Idempotent qualifiers that can be used to describe a request method. Safe methods are basically readonly methods. A client using such a method does not explicitly requests a state change and cannot expect a state change as a result of the request.

As the Safe word suggests, such methods can be trusted to not cause any harm to the system.

An important element is that we are considering the client's point of view. The concept of Safe methods don't prohibit the system from implementing "potentially" harmful operations or processes that are not effectively read only. Whatever happens, the client cannot be held responsible for it. Among all the HTTP methods, only the GET, HEAD, OPTIONS, and TRACE methods are defined as safe.

The specification makes use of the idempotent qualifier to identify HTTP requests that, when identically repeated, always produce the same consequences as the very first one. The client's point of view must be considered here.

The idempotent HTTP methods are GET, HEAD, OPTIONS, TRACE (the Safe methods) as well as PUT and DELETE.

A method's idempotence guarantees a client for example that sending a **PUT** request can be repeated even if a connection problem has occurred before any response is received.

 The client knows that repeating the request will have the same intended effect, even if the original request succeeded, though the response might differ.

Other method-specific constraints

The POST methods are usually associated with the creation of resources on a server. Therefore, this method should return the 201 (Created) status code with a location header that provides an identifier for the created resource.

However, if there hasn't been creation of resource, a POST method can (in practice) potentially return all types of status codes except 206 (Partial Content), 304 (Not Modified), and 416 (Range Not Satisfiable).

The result of a POST can sometimes be the representation of an existing resource. In that case, for example, the client can be redirected to that resource with a 303 status code and a Location header field. As an alternative to POST methods, PUT methods are usually chosen to update or alter the state of an existing resource, sending a 200 (OK) or a 204 (No Content) to the client.

Edge cases with inconsistent matches raise errors with 409 (Conflict) or 415 (Unsupported Media Type).

Edge cases of no match found for an update should induce the creation of the resource with a 201 (Created) status code.

Another set of constraints applies on the DELETE requests that are successfully received. Those should return a 204 (No Content) status code or a 200 (OK) if the deletion has been processed. If not, the status code should be 202 (Accepted).

Mapping request payloads with @RequestBody

In *Chapter 4, Building a REST API for a Stateless Architecture*, we have presented the RequestMappingHandlerAdapter. We have seen that Spring MVC delegates to this bean to provide an extended support to @RequestMapping annotations.

In this perspective, RequestMappingHandlerAdapter is the central piece to access and override HttpMessageConverters through getMessageConverters() and setMessageConverters(List<HttpMessageConverter<?>> messageConverters).

The role of @RequestBody annotations is tightly coupled to HttpMessageConverters. We will introduce the HttpMessageConverters now.

HttpMessageConverters

HttpMessageConverters, custom or native, are bound to specific mime types. They are used in the following instances:

- To convert Java objects into HTTP response payloads. Selected from Accept request header mime types, they serve the @ResponseBody annotation's purposes (and indirectly @RestController annotations that abstract the @ResponseBody annotations).

- To convert HTTP request payloads into Java objects. Selected from the Content-Type request header mime types, these converters are called when the @RequestBody annotation are present on a method handler argument.

More generally, HttpMessageConverters match the following HttpMessageConverter interface:

```
public interface HttpMessageConverter<T> {
  boolean canRead(Class<?> clazz, MediaType mediaType);
  boolean canWrite(Class<?> clazz, MediaType mediaType);
  List<MediaType> getSupportedMediaTypes();
  T read(Class<? extends T> clazz, HttpInputMessage inputMessage)
    throws IOException, HttpMessageNotReadableException;
  void write(T t, MediaType contentType, HttpOutputMessage
    outputMessage) throws IOException,
    HttpMessageNotWritableException;
}
```

The `getSupportedMediaTypes()` method returns the list of `mediaTypes` (mime types) that a specific converter supports. This method is mainly used for reporting purposes and for the `canRead` and `canWrite` implementations. These `canRead` and `canWrite` eligibility methods are used by the framework to pick up at runtime the first `HttpMessageConverter` that either:

▸ Matches the client-provided `Content-Type` request header for the given Java class targeted by `@RequestBody`

▸ Matches the client-provided `Accept` request header for the Java class that the HTTP response-payload will correspond to (the Type targeted by `@ResponseBody`)

Provided HttpMessageConverters

With the latest versions of Spring MVC (4+), a few extra `HttpMessageConverters` come natively with the framework. We have thought that summarizing them would be helpful. The following table represents all the native `HttpMessageConverters`, the mime types, and the Java Types they can be associated with. Short descriptions, mostly coming from the JavaDoc, give more insight about each of them.

URI	Supported MediaTypes (by default)	Convert to/from
`FormHttpMessage Converter`	Can READ/WRITE application/x-www-form-urlencoded, Can READ multipart/form-data.	`MultiValueMap<String, ?>`
	For part conversions, it also embeds (by default) `ByteArrayHttpMessageConverter`, `StringHttpMessageConverter` and `ResourceHttpMessageConverter`.	
`AllEncompassing FormHttpMessage Converter`	Can READ/WRITE application/x-www-form-urlencoded, Can READ multipart/form-data.	`MultiValueMap<String, ?>`
	This converter extends `FormHttpMessageConverter` embedding extra `HttpMessageConverters` JAXB or Jackson if they are found in the classpath for XML/JSON-based parts.	
`XmlAwareFormHttp MessageConverter`	Can READ/WRITE application/x-www-form-urlencoded, Can READ multipart/form-data.	`MultiValueMap<String, ?>`
	This converter extends `FormHttpMessageConverter`, adding support for XML-based parts through a `SourceHttpMessageConverter`.	

URI	Supported MediaTypes (by default)	Convert to/from
BufferedImageHttp MessageConverter	Can READ all media types that are supported by the registered image readers. Can WRITE the media type of the first available registered image writer.	java.awt.image. BufferedImage
ByteArrayHttp MessageConverter	Can READ */*, WRITE with application/octet-stream.	byte[]
GsonHttpMessage Converter	CAN READ/WRITE application/json, application/*+json.	java.lang.Object
	Uses the Google Gson library's Gson class. This converter can be used to bind with typed beans or untyped HashMaps.	
Jaxb2Collection HttpMessage Converter	Can READ XML collections.	T extends java.util. Collection
	This converter can read collections that contain classes annotated with XmlRootElement and XmlType. Note that this converter does not support writing. (JAXB2 must be present on the classpath.)	
Jaxb2RootElement HttpMessage Converter	Can READ/WRITE XML	java.lang.Object
	This converter can read classes annotated with XmlRootElement and XmlType, and write classes annotated with XmlRootElement or subclasses thereof. (JAXB2 must be present on the classpath.)	
MappingJackson2 HttpMessage Converter	Can READ/WRITE application/json, application/*+json.	java.lang.Object
	Uses Jackson 2.x ObjectMapper. This converter can be used to bind with typed beans or untyped HashMap instances. (Jackson 2 must present on the classpath.)	
MappingJackson2 XmlHttpMessage Converter	Can READ/WRITE application/xml, text/xml, application/*+xml.	java.lang.Object
	This uses the Jackson 2.x extension component for reading and writing XML encoded data (https://github.com/FasterXML/jackson-dataformat-xml). (Jackson 2 must be present on the classpath.)	
MarshallingHttp MessageConverter	Can READ/WRITE text/xml application/xml.	java.lang.Object
	This uses Spring's Marshaller and Unmarshaller abstractions (OXM).	
ObjectToStringHttp MessageConverter	Can READ/WRITE text/plain.	java.lang.Object
	This uses StringHttpMessageConverter for reading and writing content and a ConversionService for converting the String content to and from the target object type. (It must be configured)	

URI	Supported MediaTypes (by default)	Convert to/from
`ProtobufHttp MessageConverter`	Can READ application/json, application/xml, text/plain and application/x-protobuf. Can WRITE application/json, application/xml, text/plain and application/x-protobuf, text/html.	`javax.mail.Message`
	This uses Google protocol buffers (`https://developers.google.com/protocol-buffers`) to generate message Java classes you need to install the `protoc` binary.	
`ResourceHttp MessageConverter`	Can READ/WRITE */*.	`org.springframework.core.io.Resource`
	The **Java Activation Framework** (**JAF**), if available, is used to determine the content-type of written resources. If JAF is not available, application/octet-stream is used.	
`RssChannelHttp MessageConverter`	Can READ/WRITE application/rss+xml.	`com.rometools.rome.feed.rss.Channel`
	This converter can handle Channel objects from the ROME project (`https://github.com/rometools`). (ROME must be present on the classpath.)	
`AtomFeedHttp MessageConverter`	Can READ/WRITE application/atom+xml.	`com.rometools.rome.feed.atom.Feed`
	This can handle Atom feeds from the ROME project (`https://github.com/rometools`). (ROME must be present on the classpath.)	
`SourceHttpMessage Converter`	Can READ/WRITE text/xml, application/xml, application/*-xml.	`javax.xml.transform.Source`
`StringHttpMessage Converter`	Can READ/WRITE */*.	`java.lang.String`

Using MappingJackson2HttpMessageConverter

In this recipe, the `MappingJackson2HttpMessageConverter` is used extensively. We used this converter for both the financial transaction creation/update side and the User-Preferences update side.

Alternatively, we used AngularJS to map an HTML form to a built json object whose properties match our Entities. Proceeding this way, we POST/PUT the `json` object as the `application/json` mime type.

This method has been preferred to posting an `application/x-www-form-urlencoded` form content, because we can actually map the object to an Entity. In our case, the form matches exactly a backend resource. This is a beneficial result (and constraint) of a REST design.

Using @RequestPart to upload an image

The @RequestPart annotation can be used to associate part of a multipart/form-data request with a method argument. It can be used with argument Types such as org.springframework.web.multipart.MultipartFile and javax.servlet.http.Part.

For any other argument Types, the content of the part is passed through an HttpMessageConverter just like @RequestBody.

The @RequestBody annotation has been implemented to handle the user-profile picture. Here's our sample implementation from the UserImageController:

```java
@RequestMapping(method=POST, produces={"application/json"})
@ResponseStatus(HttpStatus.CREATED)
public String save( @RequestPart("file") MultipartFile file,
  HttpServletResponse response){
String extension =
  ImageUtil.getExtension(file.getOriginalFilename());
String name =
  UUID.randomUUID().toString().concat(".").concat(extension);
if (!file.isEmpty()) {
   try {
            byte[] bytes = file.getBytes();
            Path newPath =
              Paths.get(pathToUserPictures);
            Files.write(newPath, bytes,
              StandardOpenOption.CREATE);
      ...
  ...
response.addHeader(LOCATION_HEADER,
  env.getProperty("pictures.user.endpoint").concat(name));
return "Success";
  ...
}
```

The file part of the request is injected as an argument. A new file is created on the server filesystem from the content of the request file. A new Location header is added to the Response with a link to the created image.

On the client side, this header is read and injected as background-image CSS property for our div (see user-account.html).

Transaction management

The recipe highlights the basic principles we applied to handle transactions across the different layers of our REST architecture. Transaction management is a whole chapter in itself and we are constrained here to present just an overview.

The simplistic approach

To build our transaction management, we kept in mind that Spring MVC Controllers are not transactional. Under this light, we cannot expect a transaction management over two different service calls in the same method handler of a Controller. Each service call starts a new transaction, and this transaction is expected to terminate when the result is returned.

We defined our services as `@Transactional(readonly="true")` at the Type level, then methods the that need Write access override this definition with an extra `@Transactional` annotation at the method level. The *tenth step* of our recipe presents the Transactional changes on the `TransactionServiceImpl` service. With the default propagation, transactions are maintained and reused between Transactional services, repositories, or methods.

By default, abstracted Spring Data JPA repositories are transactional. We only had to specify transactional behaviors to our custom repositories, as we did for our services.

The *eleventh step* of our recipe shows the Transactional changes made on the custom repository `IndexRepositoryImpl`.

There's more...

As mentioned earlier, we configured a consistent transaction management over the different layers of our application.

Transaction management

Our coverage is limited and we advise you to find external information about the following topics if you are not familiar with them.

ACID properties

Four properties/concepts are frequently used to assess the transaction's reliability. It is therefore useful and important to keep them in mind when designing transactions. Those properties are Atomicity, Consistency, Isolation and Durability. Read more about ACID transactions on the Wikipedia page:

```
https://en.wikipedia.org/wiki/ACID
```

Global versus local transactions

We only defined local transactions in the application. Local transactions are managed at the application level and cannot be propagated across multiple Tomcat servers. Also, local transactions cannot ensure consistency when more than one transactional resource type is involved. For example, in a use case of database operations associated with messaging, when we rollback a message that couldn't have been delivered, we might need to also rollback the related database operations that have happened beforehand. Only global transactions implementing 2-step commits can take on this kind of responsibility. Global transactions are handled by JTA transaction manager implementations.

Read more about the difference in this Spring reference document:

`http://docs.spring.io/spring/docs/2.0.8/reference/transaction.html`

Historically, JTA transaction managers were exclusively provided by J2EE/JEE containers. With application-level JTA transaction manager implementations, we now have other alternatives such as Atomikos (`http://www.atomikos.com`), Bitronix (`https://github.com/bitronix/btm`), or JOTM (`http://jotm.ow2.org/xwiki/bin/view/Main/WebHome`) to assure global transactions in J2SE environments.

Tomcat (7+) can also work along with application-level JTA transaction manager implementations to reflect the transaction management in the container using the `TransactionSynchronizationRegistry` and JNDI datasources.

`https://codepitbull.wordpress.com/2011/07/08/tomcat-7-with-full-jta`

See also

Performance and useful metadata benefits can be obtained from these three headers that are not detailed in the recipe.

> ▸ **Cache-Control, ETag, and Last-Modified**: Spring MVC supports these headers and as an entry point, we suggest you check out the Spring reference: `http://docs.spring.io/spring-framework/docs/current/spring-framework-reference/html/mvc.html#mvc-caching-etag-lastmodified`

Validating resources using bean validation support

After introducing the request-payload data binding process, we must talk about validation.

Getting ready

The goal of this recipe is to show how to get Spring MVC to reject request body payloads that are not satisfying a bean validation (JSR-303) or not satisfying the constraints of a defined Spring validator implementation.

After the Maven and Spring configuration we will see how to bind a validator to an incoming request, how to define the validator to perform custom rules, how to set up a JSR-303 validation, and how to handle the validation results.

How to do it...

1. We added a Maven dependency to the hibernate validator:

```
<dependency>
  <groupId>org.hibernate</groupId>
  <artifactId>hibernate-validator</artifactId>
  <version>4.3.1.Final</version>
</dependency>
```

2. A `LocalValidatorFactoryBean` has been registered in our `dispatcher-servlet.xml` (cloudstreetmarket-api):

```
<bean id="validator"
class="org.sfw.validation.beanvalidation.
LocalValidatorFactoryBean"/>
```

3. The `UsersController` and `TransactionController` have seen their POST and PUT method signature altered with the addition of a `@Valid` annotation on the `@RequestBody` arguments:

```
@RequestMapping(method=PUT)
@ResponseStatus(HttpStatus.OK)
public void update(@Valid @RequestBody User user,
BindingResult result){
  ValidatorUtil.raiseFirstError(result);
  user = communityService.updateUser(user);
}
```

> Note here the `BindingResult` object injected as method argument.
> Also we will present the `ValidatorUtil` class in about a minute.

4. Our two CRUD controllers now have a new `@InitBinder` annotated method:

```
@InitBinder
  protected void initBinder(WebDataBinder binder) {
      binder.setValidator(new UserValidator());
  }
```

5. This method binds an instance of a created Validator implementation to the requests. Check out the created `UserValidator` which is `Validator` implementation:

```
package edu.zipcloud.cloudstreetmarket.core.validators;
import java.util.Map;
import javax.validation.groups.Default;
import org.springframework.validation.Errors;
import org.springframework.validation.Validator;
import edu.zc.csm.core.entities.User;
```

```
import edu.zc.csm.core.util.ValidatorUtil;
public class UserValidator implements Validator {
  @Override
  public boolean supports(Class<?> clazz) {
    return User.class.isAssignableFrom(clazz);
  }
  @Override
  public void validate(Object target, Errors err) {
    Map<String, String> fieldValidation =
      ValidatorUtil.validate((User)target, Default.class);
    fieldValidation.forEach(
      (k, v) -> err.rejectValue(k, v)
    );
  }
}
```

6. In the User entity, a couple of special annotations have been added:

```
@Entity
@Table(name="users")
public class User extends ProvidedId<String> implements
  UserDetails{
  ...
  private String fullName;
  @NotNull
  @Size(min=4, max=30)
  private String email;
  @NotNull
  private String password;
  private boolean enabled = true;
  @NotNull
  @Enumerated(EnumType.STRING)
  private SupportedLanguage language;
  private String profileImg;

  @Column(name="not_expired")
  private boolean accountNonExpired;
  @Column(name="not_locked")
  private boolean accountNonLocked;

  @NotNull
  @Enumerated(EnumType.STRING)
  private SupportedCurrency currency;

  private BigDecimal balance;
  ...
}
```

7. We have created the `ValidatorUtil` class to make those validations easier and to reduce the amount of boilerplate code:

```
package edu.zipcloud.cloudstreetmarket.core.util;
import java.util.Arrays;
import java.util.HashMap;
import java.util.Map;
import java.util.Set;
import javax.validation.ConstraintViolation;
import javax.validation.Validation;
import javax.validation.Validator;
import javax.validation.ValidatorFactory;
import javax.validation.groups.Default;
import org.springframework.validation.BindingResult;

public class ValidatorUtil {
    private static Validator validator;
    static {
      ValidatorFactory factory =
        Validation.buildDefaultValidatorFactory();
      validator = factory.getValidator();
    }
```

The following `validate` method allows us to call for a JSR validation from whichever location that may require it:

```
public static <T> Map<String, String> validate(T object,
  Class<?>... groups) {
  Class<?>[] args = Arrays.copyOf(groups, groups.length + 1);
  args[groups.length] = Default.class;
  return extractViolations(validator.validate(object, args));
}
private static <T> Map<String, String> extractViolations(Set<Const
  raintViolation<T>> violations) {
  Map<String, String> errors = new HashMap<>();
  for (ConstraintViolation<T> v: violations) {
    errors.put(v.getPropertyPath().toString(),
  "["+v.getPropertyPath().toString()+"] " +
  StringUtils.capitalize(v.getMessage()));
  }
  return errors;
  }
```

The following `raiseFirstError` method is not of a specific standard, it is our way of rendering to the client the server side errors:

```
public static void raiseFirstError(BindingResult result)
{
  if (result.hasErrors()) {
    throw new
    IllegalArgumentException(result.getAllErrors().
    get(0).getCode());
  }
else if (result.hasGlobalErrors()) {
throw new
  IllegalArgumentException(result.getGlobalError().
  getDefaultMessage());
    }
}
}
```

8. As per *Chapter 4, Building a REST API for a Stateless Architecture*, the cloudstreetmarket-api's `RestExceptionHandler` is still configured to handle `IllegalArgumentExceptions`, rendering them with `ErrorInfo` formatted responses:

```
@ControllerAdvice
public class RestExceptionHandler extends
  ResponseEntityExceptionHandler {
  @Autowired
  private ResourceBundleService bundle;
  @Override
  protected ResponseEntity<Object>
    handleExceptionInternal(Exception ex, Object body,
    HttpHeaders headers, HttpStatus status, WebRequest
      request) {
    ErrorInfo errorInfo = null;
    if(body!=null &&
      bundle.containsKey(body.toString())){
        String key = body.toString();
        String localizedMessage = bundle.get(key);
        errorInfo = new ErrorInfo(ex, localizedMessage,
          key, status);
    }
    else{
      errorInfo = new ErrorInfo(ex, (body!=null)?
      body.toString() : null, null, status);
    }
```

```
  return new ResponseEntity<Object>(errorInfo, headers,
    status);
}
  @ExceptionHandler({
    InvalidDataAccessApiUsageException.class,
    DataAccessException.class,
    IllegalArgumentException.class })
  protected ResponseEntity<Object> handleConflict(final
    RuntimeException ex, final WebRequest request) {
      return handleExceptionInternal(ex,
        I18N_API_GENERIC_REQUEST_PARAMS_NOT_VALID, new
        HttpHeaders(), BAD_REQUEST, request);
    }
}
```

9. Navigating through the UI improvements, you will notice a new form for updating the user's **Preferences**. This form is accessible via the **Login** menu, as shown in the following screenshots:

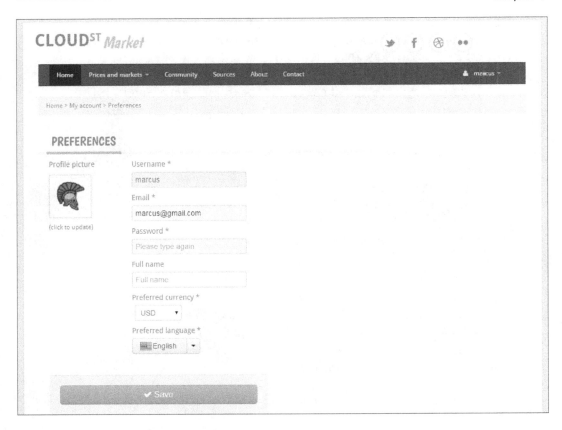

10. In this user **Preferences** form, when the frontend validations are deactivated (frontend validations will be developed in the last recipe of this chapter), not filling the e-mail field results in the following (customizable) `ErrorInfo` object in the HTTP response:

```
{"error":"[email] Size must be between 4 and 30",
"message":"The request parameters were not valid!",
"i18nKey":"error.api.generic.provided.request.parameters.no
  t.valid",
"status":400,
"date":"2016-01-05 05:59:26.584"}
```

11. On the frontend side, in order to handle this error, the `accountController` (in `account_management.js`) is instantiated with a dependency to a custom `errorHandler` factory. The code is as follows:

```
cloudStreetMarketApp.controller('accountController',
    function ($scope, $translate, $location, errorHandler,
    accountManagementFactory, httpAuth, genericAPIFactory){
        $scope.form = {
        id: "",
    email: "",
    fullName: "",
    password: "",
    language: "EN",
    currency: "",
    profileImg: "img/anon.png"
        };
    ...
}
```

12. The `accountController` has an `update` method that invokes the `errorHandler.renderOnForm` method:

```
$scope.update = function () {
    $scope.formSubmitted = true;

    if(!$scope.updateAccount.$valid) {
        return;
    }
    httpAuth.put('/api/users',
        JSON.stringify($scope.form)).success(
        function(data, status, headers, config) {
            httpAuth.setCredentials($scope.form.id,
                $scope.form.password);
        $scope.updateSuccess = true;
        }
    ).error(function(data, status, headers, config) {
        $scope.updateFail = true;
        $scope.updateSuccess = false;
        $scope.serverErrorMessage =
        errorHandler.renderOnForms(data);
        }
    );
};
```

13. The `errorHandler` is defined as follows in `main_menu.js`. It has the capability to pull translations messages from `i18n` codes:

```
cloudStreetMarketApp.factory("errorHandler", ['$translate',
function ($translate) {
    return {
        render: function (data) {
        if(data.message && data.message.length > 0){
          return data.message;
        }
        else if(!data.message && data.i18nKey &&
          data.i18nKey.length > 0){
          return $translate(data.i18nKey);
          }
        return $translate('error.api.generic.internal");
        },
        renderOnForms: function (data) {
        if(data.error && data.error.length > 0){
          return data.error;
        }
        else if(data.message && data.message.length > 0){
          return data.message;
        }
        else if(!data.message && data.i18nKey &&
          data.i18nKey.length > 0){
          return $translate(data.i18nKey);
        }
        return $translate("error.api.generic.internal");
        }
    }
}]);
```

The **Preferences** form is as shown here:

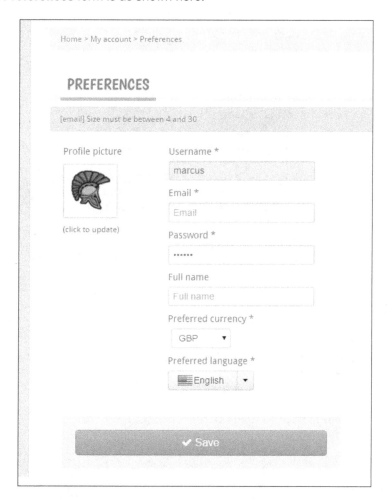

> As we said, to simulate this error, frontend validations need to be deactivated. This can be done adding a `novalidate` attribute to the `<form name="updateAccount" … novalidate>` markup in `user-account.html`.

14. Back in the server side, we have also created a custom validator for the financial Transaction Entity. This validator makes use of the Spring `ValidationUtils`:

```
@Component
public class TransactionValidator implements Validator {
  @Override
  public boolean supports(Class<?> clazz) {
    return Transaction.class.isAssignableFrom(clazz);
```

```
    }
    @Override
    public void validate(Object target, Errors errors) {
      ValidationUtils.rejectIfEmpty(errors, "quote", "
        transaction.quote.empty");
      ValidationUtils.rejectIfEmpty(errors, "user", "
        transaction.user.empty");
      ValidationUtils.rejectIfEmpty(errors, "type", "
        transaction.type.empty");
    }
  }
```

How it works...

Using Spring validator

Spring offers a `Validator` interface (`org.sfw.validation.Validator`) for creating components to be injected or instantiated in the layer we want. Therefore, Spring validation components can be used in Spring MVC Controllers. The `Validator` interface is the following:

```
public interface Validator {
  boolean supports(Class<?> clazz);
  void validate(Object target, Errors errors);
}
```

The `supports(Class<?> clazz)` method is used to assess the domain of a `Validator` implementation, and also to restrict its use to a specific Type or super-Type.

The `validate(Object target, Errors errors)` method imposes its standard so that the validation logic of the validator lives in this place. The passed `target` object is assessed, and the result of the validation is stored in an instance of the `org.springframework. validation.Errors` interface. A partial preview of the `Errors` interface is shown here:

```
public interface Errors {
  ...
  void reject(String errorCode);

  void reject(String errorCode, String defaultMessage);

void reject(String errorCode, Object[] errorArgs, String
  defaultMessage);
void rejectValue(String field, String errorCode);
  void rejectValue(String field, String errorCode, String
  defaultMessage);
void rejectValue(String field, String errorCode, Object[]
  errorArgs, String defaultMessage);
```

```
      void addAllErrors(Errors errors);
      boolean hasErrors();
      int getErrorCount();
      List<ObjectError> getAllErrors();
      ...
}
```

Using Spring MVC, we have the possibility to bind and trigger a `Validator` to a specific method-handler. The framework looks for a validator instance bound to the incoming request. We have configured such a binding in our recipe at the *fourth step*:

```
@InitBinder
  protected void initBinder(WebDataBinder binder) {
      binder.setValidator(new UserValidator());
  }
```

 We have already used the `@InitBinder` annotation to attach other objects (formatters) to incoming requests (see the *Binding requests, marshalling responses* recipe of the Chapter 4, *Building a REST API for a Stateless Architecture*).

The `Binders` (`org.springframework.validation.DataBinder`) allow setting property values onto a target object. Binders also provide support for validation and binding-results analysis.

The `DataBinder.validate()` method is called after each binding step and this method calls the `validate` of the primary validator attached to the `DataBinder`.

The binding-process populates a result object, which is an instance of the `org.springframework.validation.BindingResult` interface. This result object can be retrieved using the `DataBinder.getBindingResult()` method.

Actually, a `BindingResult` implementation is also an `Errors` implementation (as shown here). We have presented the `Errors` interface earlier. Check out the following code:

```
public interface BindingResult extends Errors {
   Object getTarget();
   Map<String, Object> getModel();
   Object getRawFieldValue(String field);
   PropertyEditor findEditor(String field, Class<?> valueType);
   PropertyEditorRegistry getPropertyEditorRegistry();
   void addError(ObjectError error);
   String[] resolveMessageCodes(String errorCode);
   String[] resolveMessageCodes(String errorCode, String field);
   void recordSuppressedField(String field);
   String[] getSuppressedFields();
}
```

The whole design can be summarized as follows:

We create a validator implementation. When an incoming request comes in for a specific Controller method handler, the request payload is converted into the class that is targeted by the @RequestBody annotation (an Entity in our case). An instance of our validator implementation is bound to the injected @RequestBody object. If the injected @RequestBody object is defined with a @Valid annotation, the framework asks DataBinder to validate the object on each binding step and to store errors in the BindingResultobject of DataBinder.

Finally, this BindingResult object is injected as argument of the method handler, so we can decide what to do with its errors (if any). During the binding process, missing fields and property access exceptions are converted into FieldErrors. These FieldErrors are also stored into the Errors instance. The following error codes are used for FieldErrors:

```
Missing field error: "required"
Type mismatch error: "typeMismatch"
Method invocation error: "methodInvocation"
```

When it is necessary to return nicer error messages for the user, a MessageSource helps us to process a lookup and retrieve the right localized message from a MessageSourceResolvable implementation with the following method:

```
MessageSource.getMessage(org.sfw.context.MessageSourceResolvable,
    java.util.Locale).
```

The FieldError extends ObjectError and ObjectError extends DefaultMessageSourceResolvable, which is a MessageSourceResolvable implementation.

ValidationUtils

The ValidationUtils utility class (org.sfw.validation.ValidationUtils) provides a couple of convenient static methods for invoking validators and rejecting empty fields. These utility methods allow one-line assertions that also handle at the same time, the population of the Errors objects. In this recipe, the 14th step details our TransactionValidator that makes use of ValidationUtils.

I18n validation errors

The next recipe will focus on internationalization of errors and content. However, let's see how we catch our errors from the controllers and how we display them. The update method of UserController has this custom method call on its first line:

```
ValidatorUtil.raiseFirstError(result);
```

We created the `ValidatorUtil` support class for our needs; the idea was to throw an `IllegalArgumentException` for any type of error that can be detected by our validator. The `ValidatorUtil.raiseFirstError(result)` method call can also be found in the `TransactionController.update(...)` method-handler. This method-handler relies on the `TransactionValidator` presented in the *14th step.*

If you remember this `TransactionValidator`, it creates an error with a `transaction.quote.empty` message code when a quote object is not present in the financial Transaction object. An `IllegalArgumentException` is then thrown with the `transaction.quote.empty` message detail.

In the next recipe, we will revisit how a proper internationalized JSON response is built and sent back to the client from an `IllegalArgumentException`.

Using JSR-303/JSR-349 Bean Validation

Spring Framework version 4 and above supports bean validation 1.0 (JSR-303) and bean validation 1.1 (JSR-349). It also adapts this bean validation to work with the `Validator` interface, and it allows the creation of class-level validators using annotations.

The two specifications, JSR-303 and JSR-349, define a set of constraints applicable to beans, as annotations from the `javax.validation.constraints` package.

Generally, a big advantage of using the code from specifications instead of the code from implementations is that we don't have to know which implementation is used. Also, the implementation can always potentially be replaced with another one.

Bean validation was originally designed for persistent beans. Even if the specification has a relatively low coupling to JPA, the reference implementation stays Hibernate validator. Having a persistence provider that supports those validation specifications is definitely an advantage. Now with JPA2, the persistent provider automatically calls for JSR-303 validation before persisting. Ensuring such validations from two different layers (controller and model) raises our confidence level.

On-field constraint annotations

We defined the `@NotNull` and `@Size` JSR-303 annotations on the presented `User` entity. There are obviously more than two annotations to be found in the specification.

Here's a table summarizing the package of annotations (`javax.validation.constraints`) in JEE7:

Annotation Type	Description
`AssertFalse`	The annotated element must be false.
`AssertFalse.List`	Defines several `AssertFalse` annotations on the same element.
`AssertTrue`	The annotated element must be true.

Annotation Type	Description
AssertTrue.List	Defines several AssertTrue annotations on the same element.
DecimalMax	The annotated element must be a number whose value must be lower or equal to the specified maximum.
DecimalMax.List	Defines several DecimalMax annotations on the same element.
DecimalMin	The annotated element must be a number whose value must be higher or equal to the specified minimum.
DecimalMin.List	Defines several DecimalMin annotations on the same element.
Digits	The annotated element must be a number within the accepted range. Supported types are: BigDecimal, BigInteger, CharSequence, byte, short, int, long, and their respective wrapper types. However, null elements are considered valid.
Digits.List	Defines several Digits annotations on the same element.
Future	The annotated element must be a date in the future.
Future.List	Defines several Future annotations on the same element.
Max	The annotated element must be a number whose value must be lower than or equal to the specified maximum.
Max.List	Defines several Max annotations on the same element.
Min	The annotated element must be a number whose value must be higher than or equal to the specified minimum.
Min.List	Defines several Min annotations on the same element.
NotNull	The annotated element must not be null.
NotNull.List	Defines several NotNull annotations on the same element.
Past	The annotated element must be a date in the past.
Past.List	Defines several Past annotations on the same element.
Pattern	The annotated CharSequence must match the specified regular expression.
Pattern.List	Defines several Pattern annotations on the same element.
Size	The annotated element size must be between the specified boundaries (included).
Size.List	Defines several Size annotations on the same element.

Implementation-specific constraints

Bean validation implementations can also go beyond the specification and offer their set of extra validation annotations. Hibernate Validator has a few interesting ones such as @NotBlank, @SafeHtml, @ScriptAssert, @CreditCardNumber, @Email, and so on. These are all listed from the hibernate documentation accessible at the following URL

```
http://docs.jboss.org/hibernate/validator/4.3/reference/en-US/html_
single/#table-custom-constraints
```

LocalValidator (reusable)

We have defined the following validator bean in our Spring context:

```
<bean id="validator" class="org.sfw.validation.beanvalidation.
LocalValidatorFactoryBean"/>
```

This bean produces validator instances that implement JSR-303 and JSR-349. You can configure a specific provider class here. By default, Spring looks in the classpath for the Hibernate Validator JAR. Once this bean is defined, it can be injected wherever it is needed.

We have injected such validator instances in our `UserValidator` and this makes it compliant with JSR-303 and JSR-349.

For internationalization, the validator produces its set of default message codes. These default message codes and values look like the following ones:

```
javax.validation.constraints.Max.message=must be less than or
    equal to {value}
javax.validation.constraints.Min.message=must be greater than or
    equal to {value}
javax.validation.constraints.Pattern.message=must match "{regexp}"
javax.validation.constraints.Size.message=size must be between
    {min} and {max}
```

Feel free to override them in your own resource files!

There's more...

In this section we highlight a few validation concepts and components that we didn't explain.

ValidationUtils

The `ValidationUtils` Spring utility class provides convenient static methods for invoking a `Validator` and rejecting empty fields populating the error object in one line:

```
http://docs.spring.io/spring/docs/3.1.x/javadoc-api/org/
springframework/validation/ValidationUtils.html
```

Grouping constraints

We can couple constraints across more than one field to define a set of more advanced constraints:

```
http://beanvalidation.org/1.1/spec/#constraintdeclarationvalidationpr
ocess-groupsequence
```

```
http://docs.jboss.org/hibernate/stable/validator/reference/en-US/
html_single/#chapter-groups
```

Creating a custom validator

It can sometimes be useful to create a specific validator that has its own annotation. Check link, it should get us to:

```
http://howtodoinjava.com/2015/02/12/spring-mvc-custom-validator-
example/
```

The Spring reference on validation

The best source of information remains the Spring reference on `Validation`. Check link, it should get us to:

```
http://docs.spring.io/spring/docs/current/spring-framework-reference/
html/validation.html
```

See also

> ▸ The whole bean validation specification (JSR-303 and JSR-349) has its own website:
> `http://beanvalidation.org/1.1/spec`.

Internationalizing messages and contents for REST

It was necessary to talk about validation before talking about internationalizing content and messages. With global and cloud-based services, supporting content in only one language is often not sufficient.

In this recipe, we provide an implementation that suits our design and therefore continue to meet our scalability standards for not relying on HTTP Sessions.

We will see how to define the `MessageSource` beans in charge of fetching the most suited message for a given location. We will see how to serialize resource properties to make them available to the frontend. We will implement a dynamic translation of content on this frontend with AngularJS and angular-translate.

How to do it...

There is both backend and a frontend work in this recipe.

Backend

1. The following bean has been registered in the core context (`csm-core-config.xml`):

```
<bean id="messageBundle"
  class="edu.zc.csm.core.i18n.
SerializableResourceBundleMessageSource">
```

```
<property name="basenames" value="classpath:/META-
  INF/i18n/messages,classpath:/META-INF/i18n/errors"/>
  <property name="fileEncodings" value="UTF-8" />
  <property name="defaultEncoding" value="UTF-8" />
</bean>
```

2. This bean references a created `SerializableResourceBundleMessageSource` that gathers the resource files and extracts properties:

```
/**
 * @author rvillars
 * {@link https://github.com/rvillars/bookapp-rest}
 */
public class SerializableResourceBundleMessageSource
  extends ReloadableResourceBundleMessageSource {
    public Properties getAllProperties(Locale locale) {
        clearCacheIncludingAncestors();
        PropertiesHolder propertiesHolder =
          getMergedProperties(locale);
        Properties properties = propertiesHolder.getProperties();
      return properties;
    }
}
```

3. This bean bundle is accessed from two places:

   A newly created `PropertiesController` exposes publicly (serializing) all the messages and errors for a specific location (here, just a language):

```
@RestController
@ExposesResourceFor(Transaction.class)
@RequestMapping(value="/properties")
public class PropertiesController{
  @Autowired
  protected SerializableResourceBundleMessageSource
    messageBundle;
  @RequestMapping(method = RequestMethod.GET,
    produces={"application/json; charset=UTF-8"})
  @ResponseBody
  public Properties list(@RequestParam String lang) {
    return messageBundle.getAllProperties(new
      Locale(lang));
  }
}
```

   A specific service layer has been built to easily serve messages and errors across controllers and services:

```
@Service
@Transactional(readOnly = true)
public class ResourceBundleServiceImpl implements
  ResourceBundleService {
```

```
    @Autowired
  protected SerializableResourceBundleMessageSource
    messageBundle;
    private static final Map<Locale, Properties>
      localizedMap = new HashMap<>();
    @Override
    public Properties getAll() {
      return getBundleForUser();
    }
    @Override
    public String get(String key) {
      return getBundleForUser().getProperty(key);
    }
    @Override
    public String getFormatted(String key, String...
      arguments) {
      return MessageFormat.format(
        getBundleForUser().getProperty(key), arguments
      );
    }
    @Override
    public boolean containsKey(String key) {
      return getAll().containsKey(key);
    }
    private Properties getBundleForUser(){
      Locale locale =
        AuthenticationUtil.getUserPrincipal().getLocale();
      if(!localizedMap.containsKey(locale)){
        localizedMap.put(locale,
          messageBundle.getAllProperties(locale));
      }
      return localizedMap.get(locale);
    }
  }
}
```

 The `ResourceBundleServiceImpl` uses the same `SerializableResourceBundleMessageSource` for now. It also extracts the locale from the logged-in user (Spring Security) with a fallback to English.

4. This `ResourceBundleServiceImpl` service is injected in our `WebContentInterceptor CloudstreetApiWCI`:

```
    @Autowired
    protected ResourceBundleService bundle;
```

5. In the `TransactionController`, for example, the bundle is targeted to extract error messages:

```
if(!transaction.getUser().getUsername()
    .equals(getPrincipal().getUsername())){
  throw new AccessDeniedException(
    bundle.get(I18nKeys.I18N_TRANSACTIONS_USER_FORBIDDEN)
);
}
```

6. `I18nKeys` is just a class that hosts resource keys as constants:

```
public class I18nKeys {
  //Messages
public static final String I18N_ACTION_REGISTERS =
  "webapp.action.feeds.action.registers";
public static final String I18N_ACTION_BUYS =
  "webapp.action.feeds.action.buys";
public static final String I18N_ACTION_SELLS =
  "webapp.action.feeds.action.sells";
  ...
}
```

7. The resource files are located in the core module:

Frontend

1. Two dependencies for angular-translate have been added in the `index.jsp`:

```
<script src="js/angular/angular-translate.min.js"></script>
<script src="js/angular/angular-translate-loader-url.min.js"></script>
```

2. The translate module is configured as follows in the `index.jsp`:

```
cloudStreetMarketApp.config(function ($translateProvider) {
        $translateProvider.useUrlLoader('/api/properties.json');
    $translateProvider.useStorage('UrlLanguageStorage');
    $translateProvider.preferredLanguage('en');
    $translateProvider.fallbackLanguage('en');
});
```

You can see that it targets our API endpoint that only serves messages and errors.

3. The user language is set from the main menu (`main_menu.js`). The user is loaded and the language is extracted from user object (defaulted to EN):

```
cloudStreetMarketApp.controller('menuController', function
  ($scope, $translate, $location, modalService, httpAuth,
  genericAPIFactory) {
    $scope.init = function () {
    ...
  genericAPIFactory.get("/api/users/"+httpAuth.getLoggedInUse
    r()+".json")
  .success(function(data, status, headers, config) {
      $translate.use(data.language);
      $location.search('lang', data.language);
  });
  }
  ...
  }
```

4. In the DOM, the i18n content is directly referenced to be translated through a translate directive. Check out in the `stock-detail.html` file for example:

```
<span translate="screen.stock.detail.will.remain">Will remain</
span>
```

Another example from the `index-detail.html` file is the following:

```
<td translate>screen.index.detail.table.prev.close</td>
```

In `home.html`, you can find scope variables whose values are translated as follows:

```
{{value.userAction.presentTense | translate}}
```

5. In the application, update your personal preferences and set your language to **French** for example. Try to access, for example, a **stock-detail** page that can be reached from the **stock-search** results:

6. From a **stock-detail** page, you can process a transaction (in French!):

How it works...

Let's have a look at the backend changes. What you first need to understand is the autowired `SerializableResourceBundleMessageSource` bean from which internationalized messages are extracted using a message key.

This bean extends a specific `MessageSource` implementation. Several types of `MessageSource` exist and it is important to understand the differences between them. We will revisit the way we extract a Locale from our users and we will see how it is possible to use a `LocaleResolver` to read or guess the user language based on different readability paths (Sessions, Cookies, Accept header, and so on).

MessageSource beans

First of all, a `MessageSource` is a Spring interface (`org.sfw.context.MessageSource`). The `MessageSource` objects are responsible for resolving messages from different arguments.

The most interesting arguments being the key of the message we want and the Locale (language/country combination) that will drive the right language selection. If no Locale is provided or if the MessageSource fails to resolve a matching language/country file or message entry, it falls back to a more generic file and tries again until it reaches a successful resolution.

As shown here, MessageSource implementations expose only getMessage (...) methods:

```
public interface MessageSource {
   String getMessage(String code, Object[] args, String
      defaultMessage, Locale locale);
   String getMessage(String code, Object[] args, Locale locale)
      throws NoSuchMessageException;
   String getMessage(MessageSourceResolvable resolvable, Locale
      locale) throws NoSuchMessageException;
}
```

This lightweight interface is implemented by several objects in Spring (especially in context components). However, we are looking specifically for MessageSource implementations and three of them in Spring 4+ particularly deserve to be mentioned.

ResourceBundleMessageSource

This MessageSource implementation accesses the resource bundles using specified basenames. It relies on the underlying JDK's ResourceBundle implementation, in combination with the JDK's standard message-parsing provided by MessageFormat (java. text.MessageFormat).

Both the accessed ResourceBundle instances and the generated MessageFormat are cached for each message. The caching provided by ResourceBundleMessageSource is significantly faster than the built-in caching of the java.util.ResourceBundle class.

With java.util.ResourceBundle, it's not possible to reload a bundle when the JVM is running. Because ResourceBundleMessageSource relies on ResourceBundle, it faces the same limitation.

ReloadableResourceBundleMessageSource

In contrast to ResourceBundleMessageSource, this class uses Properties instances as custom data structure for messages. It loads them via a PropertiesPersister strategy using Spring Resource objects.

This strategy is not only capable of reloading files based on timestamp changes, but also loads properties files with a specific character encoding.

ReloadableResourceBundleMessageSource supports reloading of properties files using the cacheSeconds setting and also supports the programmatic clearing of the properties cache.

The base names for identifying resource files are defined with the `basenames` property (in the ReloadableResourceBundleMessageSource configuration). The defined base names follow the basic `ResourceBundle` convention that consists in not specifying the file extension nor the language code. We can refer to any Spring resource location. With a `classpath:` prefix, resources can still be loaded from the classpath, but `cacheSeconds` values other than `-1` (caching forever) will not work in this case.

StaticMessageSource

The `StaticMessageSource` is a simple implementation that allows messages to be registered programmatically. It is intended for testing rather than for a use in production.

Our MessageSource bean definition

We have implemented a specific controller that serializes and exposes the whole aggregation of our resource bundle properties-files (errors and message) for a given language passed in as a query parameter.

To achieve this, we have created a custom `SerializableResourceBundleMessageSource` object, borrowed from Roger Villars, and its *bookapp-rest* application (`https://github.com/rvillars/bookapp-rest`).

This custom `MessageSource` object extends `ReloadableResourceBundleMessageSource`. We have made a Spring bean of it with the following definition:

```
<bean id="messageBundle" class="edu.zc.csm.core.i18n.
SerializableResourceBundleMessageSource">
<property name="basenames" value="classpath:/META-
  INF/i18n/messages,classpath:/META-INF/i18n/errors"/>
  <property name="fileEncodings" value="UTF-8" />
  <property name="defaultEncoding" value="UTF-8" />
</bean>
```

We have specifically specified the paths to our resource files in the classpath. This can be avoided with a global resource bean in our context:

```
<resources location="/, classpath:/META-INF/i18n" mapping="/
  resources/**"/>
```

Note that Spring MVC, by default, expects the i18n resource files to be located in a `/WEB-INF/i18n` folder.

Using a LocaleResolver

In our application, in order to switch the `Locale` to another language/country, we pass through the user preferences screen. This means that we somehow persist this information in the database. This makes easy the `LocaleResolution` that is actually operated on the client side, reading the user data and calling the internationalized messages for the language preference asynchronously.

However, some other applications might want to operate `LocaleResolution` on the server side. To do so, a `LocaleResolver` bean must be registered.

`LocaleResolver` is a Spring Interface (`org.springframework.web.servlet.LocaleResolver`):

```
public interface LocaleResolver {
  Locale resolveLocale(HttpServletRequest request);
  void setLocale(HttpServletRequest request, HttpServletResponse
  response, Locale locale);
}
```

There are four concrete implementations in Spring MVC (version four and above):

AcceptHeaderLocaleResolver

The AcceptHeaderLocaleResolver makes use of the `Accept-Language` header of the HTTP request. It extracts the first Locale that the value contains. This value is usually set by the client's web browser that reads it from OS configuration.

FixedLocaleResolver

This resolver always returns a fixed default Locale with optionally a time zone. The default Locale is the current JVM's default Locale

SessionLocaleResolver

This resolver is the most appropriate when the application actually uses user sessions. It reads and sets a session attribute whose name is only intended for internal use:

```
public static final String LOCALE_SESSION_ATTRIBUTE_NAME =
  SessionLocaleResolver.class.getName() + ".LOCALE";
```

By default, it sets the value from the default `Locale` or from the `Accept-Language` header. The session may also optionally contain an associated time zone attribute. Alternatively, we may specify a default time zone.

The practice in these cases is to create an extra and specific web filter.

CookieLocaleResolver

`CookieLocaleResolver` is a resolver that is well suited to stateless applications like ours. The cookie name can be customized with the `cookieName` property. If the `Locale` is not found in an internally defined request parameter, it tries to read the cookie value and falls back to the `Accept-Language` header.

The cookie may optionally contain an associated time zone value as well. We can still specify a default time zone as well.

There's more...

Translating client-side with angular-translate.js

We used `angular-translate.js` to handle translations and to switch the user Locale from the client side. `angular-translate.js` library is very complete and well documented. As a dependency, it turns out to be extremely useful.

The main points of this product are to provide:

- Components (filters/directives) to translate contents
- Asynchronous loading of i18n data
- Pluralization support using `MessageFormat.js`
- Expandability through easy to use interfaces

A quick overview of **angular-translate** is shown in this figure:

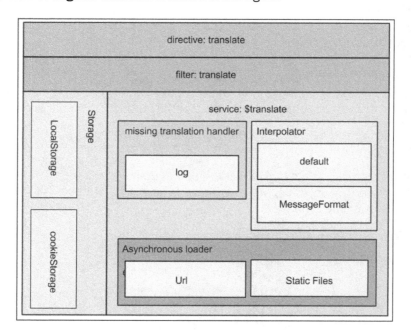

International resources are pulled down either dynamically from an API endpoint (as we did), either from static resource files published on the web application path. These resources for their specific Locale are stored on the client-side using `LocalStorage` or using `ccokies`.

The stored data corresponds to a variable (`UrlLanguageStorage` in our case) that is accessible and injectable in whatever modu e that may require translation capabilities.

As shown in the following examples, the `translate` directive can be used to actually render translated messages:

```
<span translate>i18n.key.message</span> or
<span translate=" i18n.key.message" >fallBack translation in
English (better for Google indexes) </span>
```

Alternatively, we can use a predefined translate filter to translate our translation keys in the DOM, without letting any controller or service know of them:

```
{{data.type.type == 'BUY' ?
  'screen.stock.detail.transaction.bought' :
    'screen.stock.detail.transaction.sold' | translate}}
```

You can read more about angular-translate on their very well done documentation:

```
https://angular-translate.github.io
```

Validating client-side forms with HTML5 AngularJS

It is a good practice to validate submitted cata both on the frontend and the backend. It is also good, talking about validation, to distinguish the user experience, from the data integrity conservation from the data integrity conservation. Both are two different responsibilities, potentially for different teams.

We believe the *frontend* validation has replaced the form-validations that was previously managed by the *backend*. In a scalable env ronment where API is decoupled from web content, the validation experiences are now the responsibility of client interfaces that can be multiples (even implemented by third parties) such as websites, mobile websites, mobile apps, and so on.

In this recipe, we will focus on form validaton and more specifically on AngularJS form validation.

How to do it...

1. Let's consider the **User Preferences** form again. Here is the HTML definition (user-account.html):

```
<form name="updateAccount" action="#" ng-
  class="formSubmitted ? 'submitted':''">
  <fieldset>
    <div class="clearfix span">
      <label for="id" translate>
        screen.preference.field.username</label>
        <div class="input">
<input type="text" name="id" placeholder="Username" ng-
  model="form.id" ng-minlength="4" ng-maxlength="15"
  readonly required/>
<span class="text-error" ng-show="formSubmitted &&
  updateAccount.id.$error.required" translate>
  error.webapp.user.account.username.required</span>
        </div>
<label for="email" translate>
  screen.preference.field.email</label>
      <div class="input">
<input type="email" name="email" placeholder="Email" ng-
  model="form.email"/>
<span class="text-error" ng-show="formSubmitted &&
  updateAccount.email.$error" translate>error.webapp.user.account.
email</span>
        </div>
<label for="password" translate>
  screen.preference.field.password</label>
        <div class="input">
<input type="password" name="password" ng-minlength="5"
  placeholder="Please type again" ng-model="form.password"
  required/>
<span class="text-error" ng-show="formSubmitted &&
  updateAccount.password.$error.required" translate>
  error.webapp.user.account.password.type.again</span>
<span class="text-error" ng-show="formSubmitted &&
  updateAccount.password.$error.minlength" translate>
  error.webapp.user.account.password.too.short</span>
</div>
<label for="fullname" translate>
  screen.preference.field.full.name</label>
        <div class="input" >
<input type="text" name="fullname" placeholder="Full name"
  ng-model="form.fullname"/>
        </div>
```

```
<label for="currencySelectcr" translate>
  screen.preference.field.preferred.currency</label>
        <div class="input">
<select class="input-small" id="currencySelectcr" ng-
  model="form.currency" ng-init="form.currency='USD'" ng-
  selected="USD" ng-change="updateCredit()">
          <option>USD</option><option>GBP</option>
          <option>EUR</option><option>INR</option>
          <option>SGD</option><option>CNY</option>
          </select>
          </div>
<label for="currencySelector" translate>
  screen.preference.field.preferred.language</label>
          <div class="input">
        <div class="btn-group">
<button onclick="return false;" class="btn" tabindex="-
  1"><span class="lang-sm lang-lbl" lang="{{form.language |
  lowercase}}"></button>
<button class="btn dropdown-toggle" data-toggle="dropdown"
  tabindex="-1">
          <span class="caret"></span>
          </button>
          <ul class="dropdown-menu">
<li><a href="#" ng-click="setLanguage('EN')"><span
  class="lang-sm lang-lbl-full" lang="en"></span></a></li>
<li><a href="#" ng-click="setLanguage('FR')"> <span
  class="lang-sm lang-lbl-full" lang="fr"></span></a></li>
          </ul>
          </div>
          </div>
        </div>
      </fieldset>
</form>
```

2. The JavaScript side of things in the controller of `account_management.js` includes two referenced functions and four variables to control form validation and its style:

```
$scope.update = function () {
    $scope.formSubmitted = true;
    if(!$scope.updateAccount.$valid) {
    return;
}
httpAuth.put('/api/users'
  JSON.stringify($scope.form)).success(
    function(data, status. headers, config) {
      httpAuth.setCredentials(
```

```
                    $scope.form.id, $scope.form.password);
                    $scope.updateSuccess = true;
                    }).error(function(data,status,headers,config) {
                      $scope.updateFail = true;
                      $scope.updateSuccess = false;
        $scope.serverErrorMessage =
          errorHandler.renderOnForms(data);
             });
        };
           $scope.setLanguage = function(language) {
           $translate.use(language);
           $scope.form.language = language;
           }


           //Variables initialization
           $scope.formSubmitted = false;
           $scope.serverErrorMessage ="";
           $scope.updateSuccess = false;
           $scope.updateFail = false;
```

Two CSS classes have been created to render properly errors on fields:

```
.submitted  input.ng-invalid{
  border: 2px solid #b94a48;
  background-color: #EBD3D5;!important;
}
.submitted .input .text-error {
  font-weight:bold;
  padding-left:10px;
}
```

3. If you try to enter a wrong e-mail or f you try to submit the form without entering your password, you should observe the following validation control:

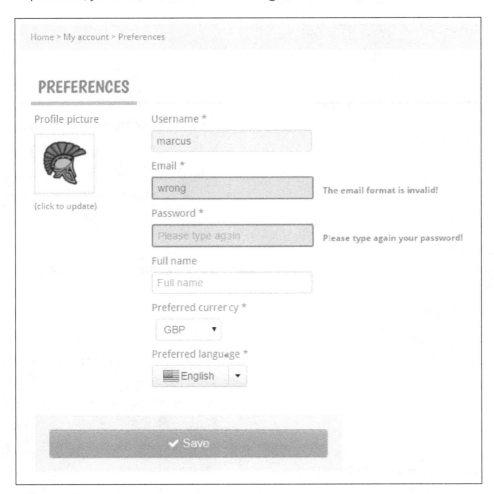

How it works...

AngularJS provides tools to set up a client-side form validation. As usual with AngularJS, these tools integrate well with modern HTML5 techniques and standards.

HTML5 forms provide a native validation that can be defined using tags and attributes on the different form elements (input, select...) to set up a basic field validation (max-length, required...)

AngularJS completes and extends fluently these standard definitions to make them interactive and responsive from the beginning and with no overhead.

Validation-constraints

Let's have a closer look at the available validation-options that can be placed on form controls.

Required

An `input` field can be tagged as `required` (HTML5 tag):

```
<input type="text" required />
```

Minimum/maximum length

The `ng-minlength` directive can be used to assert that the number of entered characters matches a given threshold:

```
<input type="text" ng-minlength="3" />
```

Similarly, `ng-maxlength` drastically limits the number of entered characters to a maximum:

```
<input type="text" ng-maxlength="15" />
```

Regex pattern

The `ng-pattern` directive is often used to make sure that the entered data matches a predefined shape:

```
<input type="text" ng-pattern="[a-zA-Z]" />
```

Number/e-mail/URL

Those HTML5 input types are handled by AngularJS to be constrained within the format they represent:

```
<input type="number" name="quantity" ng-model="form.quantity" />
<input type="email" name="email" ng-model=" form.email" />
<input type="url" name="destination" ng-model=" form.url" />
```

Control variables in forms

AngularJS publishes properties on the containing `$scope` to match the form state in the DOM. This makes the JavaScript form validation very easy to control errors and to render the state.

These properties are accessible from the following structure:

```
formName.inputFieldName.property
```

Modified/Unmodified state

This state can be assessed using the following properties:

```
formName.inputFieldName.$pristine;
formName.inputFieldName.$dirty;
```

Valid/Invalid state

This valid state of a form can be assessed in regards to the defined validation for a field or globally:

```
formName.inputFieldName.$valid;
formName.inputFieldName.$invalid;
formName.$valid;
formName.$invalid;
```

Errors

After the validity assessment that we have defined previously, more information about what went wrong can be extracted from the `$error` property:

```
myForm.username.$error.pattern
myForm.username.$error.required
myForm.username.$error.minlength
```

The `$error` object contains all about the validations of a particular form and reflects whether those validations are satisfactory or not.

Form state transclusions and style

As often with AngularJS, transclusions are proceeded to bind the DOM state with the scope. Thus, the form state and the control state are reflected in real time with CSS classes. These CSS classes can obviously be defined/overridden, so that a global validation style can be defined:

```
input.ng-invalid {
  border: 1px solid red;
}
input.ng-valid {
  border: 1px solid green;
}
```

See also

▸ **AngularJS documentation on forms:** Read more about AngularJS validation capabilities on Forms (we have only introduced them here): `https://docs.angularjs.org/guide/forms`

8

Communicating Through WebSockets and STOMP

Four recipes are covered in this chapter. All of them fully embrace our CloudStreet Market application. Improving, they make it more reactive, more interactive.

These recipes have the following titles:

▶ Streaming social events with STOMP over SockJS

▶ Using RabbitMQ as a multiprotocol message broker

▶ Stacking and consuming tasks in RabbitMQ with AMQP

▶ Securing messages with Spring Session and Redis

Introduction

Let's quickly review what we hope you have learned so far in the previous chapters. Chapter by chapter, you must have found out:

▶ How to initiate a project, and how to rely on standards to keep the code base scalable and adaptive. These standards came from a selection of tools such as Maven or the Java Persistence API. The presented standards also came with a selection of common practices, on the client side for example, with the AngularJS MVC pattern or the Bootstrap Framework UI.

▶ How to make the most of Spring MVC while facing modern challenges. Spring MVC has been demonstrated as a web MVC framework (with its request flow, the content negotiation, the view resolution, the model binding, the exception handling, and so on), but also demonstrated as an integrated Spring component within its Spring environment. An integrated framework able to relay the Spring Security authentication or the Spring Social abstraction. It is also able to serve Spring Data pagination tools as well as a very competitive implementation of the HTTP specification.

▶ How to design a Microservice architecture implementing an advanced stateless and HyperMedia API that promotes the segregation of duties. A segregation of duties between the front end and the back end, but also a segregation of duties in the functional divisibility of components (horizontal scalability) into independent web archives (`.war`).

This chapter focuses on the emerging WebSocket technology and on building a **Messaging-oriented-middleware** (**MOM**) for our application. It is a rare showcase that implements so much about WebSockets in Spring. From the use of the default embedded WebSocket message broker to a full-featured RabbitMQ broker (using STOMP and AMQP protocols). We will see how to broadcast messages to multiple clients and defer the execution of time-consuming tasks, offering significant scalability benefits.

With a new Java project dedicated to WebSockets that required access to the common database Server, and also in the perspective of a production-like environment, we are going to replace HSQLDB with MySQL Server.

We will see how to dynamically create private queues and how to get authenticated clients to post and receive messages from these private queues. We will do all of this, to implement real application features in our application.

To achieve a WebSocket authentication and an authentication of messages, we will turn the API stateful. By stateful, this means that the API will use HTTP sessions to keep users authenticated between their requests. With the support of Spring Session and the use of the highly clusterable Redis Server, the sessions will be shared across multiple webapps.

Streaming social events with STOMP over SockJS

In this recipe, we broadcast user activities (events) with STOMP over SockJS. SockJS provides a custom implementation of WebSocket.

Getting ready

There is some configuration work to be done beforehand, especially on the Apache HTTP proxy. After that, we will see how to initiate a WebSocket with SockJS and with AngularJS on the client side.

Our WebSocket will subscribe to a topic (for broadcasting) published via Spring from the `cloudstreetmarket-api` module.

How to do it...

1. From the **Git Perspective** in Eclipse, checkout the latest version of the branch `v8.1.x`.

2. Run the `Maven clean` and `Maven install` commands on the `zipcloud-parent` project (right-click on the project, select **Run as...** | **Maven Clean**, then select **Run as...** | **Maven Install**). After this, operate a **Maven | Update Project** to synchronize Eclipse with the Maven configuration (right-click on the project and then click **Maven | Update Project...**)..

3. Similarly, run the **Maven clean** and **Maven install** commands on `cloudstreetmarket-parent` followed by a **Maven | Update Project...** (in order to update all `cloudstreetmarket-parent` modules).

Apache HTTP Proxy configuration

1. In the Apache `httpd.conf` file, change the `VirtualHost` definition to:

```
<VirtualHost cloudstreetmarket.com:80>
    ProxyPass          /portal http://localhost:8080/portal
    ProxyPassReverse /portal http://localhost:8080/portal
    ProxyPass          /api    http://localhost:8080/api
    ProxyPassReverse /api     http://localhost:8080/api
    RewriteEngine on
    RewriteCond %{HTTP:UPGRADE} ^WebSocket$ [NC]
    RewriteCond %{HTTP:CONNECTION} ^Upgrade$ [NC]
    RewriteRule .* ws://localhost:8080%{REQUEST_URI} [P]
    RedirectMatch ^/$ /portal/index
</VirtualHost>
```

2. Still in `httpd.conf`, uncomment the line:

```
LoadModule proxy_wstunnel_module
    modules/mod_proxy_wstunnel.so
```

Frontend

1. In the `index.jsp` file (in the `cloudstreetmarket-webapp` module), two extra JavaScript files are imported:

```
<script src="js/util/sockjs-1.0.2.min.js"></script>
<script src="js/util/stomp-2.3.3.js"></script>
```

These two files have been copied locally, but originally, both were found online at:

`https://cdnjs.cloudflare.com/ajax/libs/sockjs-client/1.0.2/sockjs.min.js`

`https://cdnjs.cloudflare.com/ajax/libs/stomp.js/2.3.3/stomp.js`

2. For this recipe, all the changes on the client side, are related to the file `src/main/webapp/js/home/home_community_activity.js` (which drives the feed of **User Activities** on the landing page). This file is associated with the template `/src/main/webapp/html/home.html.`.

3. As part of the `init()` function of `homeCommunityActivityController`, the following section was added:

```
cloudStreetMarketApp.controller('homeCommunityActivityContr
  oller', function ($scope, $rootScope, httpAuth,
  modalService, communityFactory, genericAPIFactory,
  $filter){
var $this = this,
socket = new SockJS('/api/users/feed/add'),
stompClient = Stomp.over(socket);
pageNumber = 0;
$scope.communityActivities = {};
$scope.pageSize=10;
$scope.init = function () {
  $scope.loadMore();
  socket.onclose = function() {
    stompClient.disconnect();
  };
  stompClient.connect({}, function(frame) {
  stompClient.subscribe('/topic/actions',
    function(message){
   var newActivity =
        $this.prepareActivity(
        JSON.parse(message.body)
      );
      $this.addAsyncActivityToFeed(newActivity);
      $scope.$apply();
  });
  });
  ...
  }
  ...
```

4. The `loadMore()` function is still invoked to pull new activities when the bottom of the scroll is reached. However now, because new activities can be inserted asynchronously, the `communityActivities` variable is no longer an array but an object used as a map with activity IDs as keys. Doing so allows us to merge the synchronous results with the asynchronous ones::

```
$scope.loadMore = function () {
  communityFactory.getUsersActivity(pageNumber,
    $scope.pageSize).then function(response) {
    var usersData = response.data,
    status = response.status,
    headers  = response.headers,
    config = response.config;
    $this.handleHeaders(headers);
    if(usersData.content)
      if(usersData.content.length > 0){
        pageNumber++;
      }
      $this.addActivitiesToFeed(usersData.content);
    }
  });
};
```

5. As before (since the *Chapter4, Building a REST API for a Stateless Architecture*), we loop over the community activities to build the activity feed. Now each activity carries a number of **likes** and **comments**. Currently, if a user is authenticated, he has the capability to see the number of **likes**:

6. TheAngularized HTML bound to the thumb-up image is the following:

```
<span ng-if="userAuthenticated() && value.amountOfLikes
  == 0">
<img ng-src="{{image}}" class="like-img"
  ng-init="image='img/icon-
    finder/1441189591_1_like.png'"
  ng-mouseover="image= img/icon-
    finder/1441188631_4_like.png'"
  ng-mouseleave="image='img/icon-
    finder/1441189591_1_like.png'"
  ng-click="like(value.id)"/>
</span>
```

7. In the controller, the `like()` scope function supports this DOM element to create a new `like` activity that targets the original activity:

```
$scope.like = function (targetActionId){
  var likeAction = {
    id: null,
    type: 'LIKE',
    date: null,
    targetActionId: targetActionId,
    userId: httpAuth.getLoggedInUser()
  };
  genericAPIFactory.post("/api/actions/likes",
    likeAction);
}
```

8. The opposite logic can also be found to **unlike** an activity.

Backend

1. The following Maven dependencies have been added to `cloudstreetmarket-api`:

```
<dependency>
    <groupId>org.springframework</groupId>
    <artifactId>spring-websocket</artifactId>
    <version>${spring.version}</version>
</dependency>
<dependency>
    <groupId>org.springframework</groupId>
    <artifactId>spring-messaging</artifactId>
    <version>${spring.version}</version>
</dependency>
```

2. In the `web.xml` file (the one from `cloudstreetmarket-api`), the following attribute must be added to our servlet and to each of its filters:

```
<async-supported>true</async-supported>
```

3. The following dedicated configuration bean has been created:

```
@Configuration
@ComponentScan("edu.zipcloud.cloudstreetmarket.api")
@EnableWebSocketMessageBroker
public class WebSocketConfig extends
  AbstractWebSocketMessageBrokerConfigurer {

    @Override
    public void registerStompEndpoints(final
      StompEndpointRegistry registry) {
        registry.addEndpoint("/users/feed/add")
```

```
        .withSockJS();
    }
    @Override
    public void configureMessageBroker(final
      MessageBrokerRegistry registry) {
        registry.setApplicationDestinationPrefixes("/app");
        registry.enableSimpleBroker("/topic");
    }
}
```

A new controller `ActivityFeedWSController` has been added as follows:

```
@RestController
public class ActivityFeedWSController extends
  CloudstreetApiWCI{
    @MessageMapping("/users/feed/add")
    @SendTo("/topic/actions")
    public UserActivityDTO handle(UserActivityDTO message)
      throws Exception{
        return message;
    }
    @RequestMapping(value='/users/feed/info", method=GET)
    public String infoWS(){
        return "v0";
    }
}
```

4. As Spring configuration, we have added the following bean to the `dispatcher-servlet.xml`:

```
<bean
  class="org.sfw.web.socket.server.support.CriginHandshake
    Interceptor">
    <property name="allowedOrigins">
      <list>
      <value>http://cloudstreetmarket.com</value>
      </list>
    property>
</bean>
```

In `security-config.xml`, the following configuration has been added to the http Spring Security namespace:

```
<security:http create-session="stateless"
    entry-point-ref="authenticationEntryPoint"
    authentication-manager-ref="authenticationManager">
  ...
```

```
          <security:headers>
            <security:frame-options policy="SAMEORIGIN"/>
          </security:headers>
          . . .
          </security:http>
```

Now let's see how events are generated.

1. When a new financial transaction is created, a message is sent to the topic `/topic/actions`. This is done in the `TransactionController`:

```
@RestController
@ExposesResourceFor(Transaction.class)
@RequestMapping(value=ACTIONS_PATH + TRANSACTIONS_PATH,
  produces={"application/xml", "application/json"})
public class TransactionController extends
  CloudstreetApiWCI<Transaction> {
  @Autowired
  private SimpMessagingTemplate messagingTemplate;
  @RequestMapping(method=POST)
  @ResponseStatus(HttpStatus.CREATED)
  public TransactionResource post(@Valid @RequestBody
  Transaction transaction, HttpServletResponse response,
  BindingResult result) {
    . . .
   messagingTemplate.convertAndSend("/topic/actions", new
     UserActivityDTO(transaction));
    . . .
  }
}
```

Similarly, when a `like` activity is created, a message is also sent to the `/topic/actions` topic in `LikeActionController`:

```
 @RequestMapping(method=POST)
@ResponseStatus(HttpStatus.CREATED)
public LikeActionResource post(@RequestBody LikeAction
  likeAction, HttpServletResponse response) {
    . . .
    likeAction = likeActionService.create(likeAction);
   messagingTemplate.convertAndSend("/topic/actions", new
     UserActivityDTO(likeAction));
    . . .
}
```

2. Now start the Tomcat server. Log in to the application using Yahoo! Oauth2 and your personal Yahoo! account (if you don't have one yet, please create one). Register a new user for the `Cloudstreet Market` application.

3. In your web browser, open two different tabs in the application with your logged-in user. Keep one of these tabs on the landing page.

4. With the other tab, navigate to the **Prices and market | All prices search** menu. Search for a ticker, let's say Facebook, and buy three stocks of it.

5. Wait to receive the information message:

Congratulations !
You have bought 3 FB at USD 94.55 See your wallet

Then check the first tab of the browser (the tab you were not using).

marcus buys 3 FB at **$94.55** (USD)
25/09/2015 07:00 AM

marcus registers a new account
25/09/2015 06:56 AM

You will notice that the activity feed has received a new element at the top!

6. Also, in the console you should have the following log trace:

```
<<< MESSAGE                                                    stomp-2.3.3.js:134
destination:/topic/actions
content-type:application/json;charset=UTF-8
subscription:sub-0
message-id:1vjczjlk-2
content-length:396

{"userName":"marcus","urlProfilePicture":"../api/images/users/80a106da-7deb-4ff8-bbfb-
782504737ed2.jpg","date":"25/09/2015 07:00
AM","id":2,"amountOfLikes":0,"amountOfComments":0,"authorOfLikes":{},"authorOfComments":
[],"valueShortId":"FB","amount":3,"price":94.55,"currency":"USD","targetActionId":null,"comment
":null,"userAction":{"presentTense":"webapp.action.feeds.action.buys","type":"BUY"}}

> |

Console  Search  Emulation  Rendering
```

7. Similarly, **like** events are refreshed in real time::

marcus buys 2 FB at **$92.50** (USD)
23/09/2015 07:58 AM (1)

How it works...

Here, we are going to look at a couple of general concepts about WebSockets, STOMP, and SockJS before introducing the Spring-WebSocket support tools.

An introduction to WebSockets

WebSocket is a full-duplex communication protocol based on TCP. A full-duplex communication system allows two parties to *speak* and to be *heard* simultaneously through a bidirectional channel. A conversation by telephone is probably the best example of a full-duplex system.

This technology is particularly useful for applications that need to leverage the overhead induced by new HTTP connections. Since 2011, the WebSocket protocol has been an Internet Standard (`https://tools.ietf.org/html/rfc6455`).

WebSocket Lifecycle

Before the WebSocket connection is established, the client initiates a handshake HTTP to which the server responds. The handshake request also represents a protocol upgrade request (from HTTP to WebSocket), formalized with an `Upgrade` header. The server confirms this protocol upgrade with the same `Upgrade` header (and value) in its response. In addition to the `Upgrade` header, and in a perspective of protection against caching-proxy attacks, the client also sends a base-64 encoded random key. To this, the server sends back a hash of this key in a `Sec-WebSocket-Accept` header.

Here is an example of a handshake occurring in our application:

The protocol lifecycle can be summarized by the following sequence diagram:

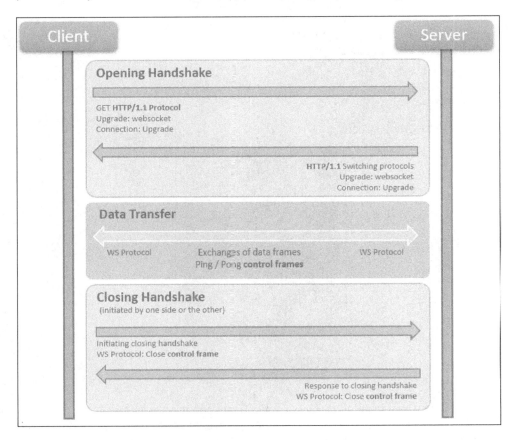

Two dedicated URI schemes

The protocol defines two URI schemes for WebSockets ws:// and wss:// (with wss allowing encrypted connections).

The STOMP protocol

STOMP stands for **Simple Text Oriented Messaging Protocol**. This protocol provides a frame-based interoperable format that allows STOMP clients to communicate with STOMP message brokers.

It is a messaging protocol that requires and trusts an existing 2-way streaming network protocol on a higher level. WebSocket provides a frame-based data-transfer, and the WebSocket frames can indeed be STOMP-formatted frames.

Here is an example of a STOMP frame:

```
CONNECTED
session:session-4F_y4UhJTEjabe0LfFH2kg
heart-beat:10000,10000
server:RabbitMQ/3.2.4
version:1.1
user-name:marcus
```

A frame has the following structure:

The STOMP protocol specification defines a set of client commands (SEND, SUBSCRIBE, UNSUBSCRIBE, BEGIN, COMMIT, ABORT, ACK, NACK, DISCONNECT, CONNECT, and STOMP) and server commands (CONNECTED, MESSAGE, RECEIPT, and ERROR).

Only SEND, MESSAGE, and ERROR frames can have a body. The protocol specification can be found online at: http://stomp.github.io/stomp-specification-1.2.html.

On the client side, we have used the JavaScript library **STOMP Over WebSocket** identified with the file stomp.js. This library maps STOMP formatted frames to WebSocket frames. By default, it looks up the web browser WebSocket class to make the STOMP client create the WebSocket.

The library can also create STOMP clients from custom WebSocket implementations. From the SockJS WebSockets, we create STOMP clients like so:

```
var socket = new SockJS('/app/users/feed/add');
var stompClient = Stomp.over(socket);
    stompClient.connect({}, function(frame) {
...
```

```
    });
    socket.onclose = function() {
    stompClient.disconnect();
};
```

SockJS

WebSockets are supported by almost all browsers nowadays. Still, we don't have control over the versions that our customers are using. In many cases, hiding such a technology from 7 to 15% of the audience is simply not an option.

On the client side, SockJS provides a custom implementation that can be seen as a decorator around the browser-native `WebSocket` implementation. With a simple and handy library, SockJS ensures cross-browser compatibility. With a list of fallback transport options (`xhr-streaming`, `xdr-streaming`, `iframe-eventsource`, `iframe-htmlfile`, `xhr-polling`, and so on), it emulates WebSockets as much as possible.

For server implementations, to match the clients' fallback behaviors, SockJS also defines its own protocol:

`http://sockjs.github.io/sockjs-protocol/sockjs-protocol-0.3.3.html`

Spring WebSocket support

As per the Java WebSocket API specification (JSR-356), Spring 4+ provides a solution that is packaged within the modules `spring-websocket` and `spring-messaging`. But Spring provides more than just an implementation of JSR-356. For example, based upon the facts that:

▶ WebSockets without the use of a message protocol are too low level to be directly used in applications without custom handling frameworks: the Spring team made the choice to provide and support a messaging protocol implementation (STOMP).

▶ WebSockets are not supported by all browsers yet: Spring also provides a WebSocket fallback support with its implementation of the SockJS protocol.

All-in-one configuration

We have enabled the WebSocket engine and configured it for SockJS and STOMP from only one configuration bean—WebSocketConfig::

```
@Configuration
@ComponentScan("edu.zipcloud.cloudstreetmarket.api")
@EnableWebSocketMessageBroker
public class WebSocketConfig extends
AbstractWebSocketMessageBrokerConfigurer {
```

```
@Override
public void registerStompEndpoints(final
    StompEndpointRegistry registry) {
      registry.addEndpoint("/users/feed/add")
      .withSockJS();
}

@Override
public void configureMessageBroker(final
  MessageBrokerRegistry registry) {
      registry.setApplicationDestinationPrefixes("/app");
      registry.enableSimpleBroker("/topic");
}
}
```

The WebSocket endPoint is defined for the context path `/users/feed/add`. It matches on the client side, the defined SockJS client constructor argument:

```
var socket = new SockJS('/api/users/feed/add');
```

From the endpoint (`clientInboundChannel`), the WebSocket engine needs to choose where to route the message to, and we have two options here for this. Depending on the situation and what we want to achieve, we can target an in-app consumer (message handler) or directly the message broker in order to dispatch the message to the subscribed clients.

This split is configured by defining two different destination prefixes. In our case, we decided to use the `/app` prefix to route messages to the corresponding message handlers and the `/topic` prefix to identify messages that are ready to be dispatched to clients.

Let's see now how message handlers can be defined and how they can be used.

Defining message handlers via @MessageMapping

`@MessageMapping` annotations are used in Spring MVC controller methods to mark them available as message handler methods.

From a message in the `clientInboundChannel` to be routed to a message handler, the WebSocket engine narrows down the right `@MessageMapping` method based upon their configured value.

As usual in Spring MVC, this value can be defined in an Ant-style (such as `/targets/**` for example). However, in the same way as the `@RequestParam` and `@PathVariable` annotations, template variables can also be passed through using `@DestinationVariable` annotations on method arguments (destination templates are defined like so: `/targets/{target}`).

Sending a message to dispatch

A message broker must be configured. In the case of this recipe, we are using a `simple` message broker (`simpMessageBroker`) that we have enabled from `MessageBrokerRegistry`. This type of in-memory broker is suited to stack STOMP messages when there is no need for external brokers (RabbitMQ, ActiveMQ, and so on). When there is availability to dispatch messages to WebSocket clients, these messages are sent to `clientOutboundChannel`.

We have seen that when message destinations are prefixed with `/topic` (like in our case), messages are directly sent to the message broker. But what about sending messages for dispatch when we are in a message handler method or elsewhere in the back-end code? We can use for this the `SimpMessagingTemplate` described in the next section.

SimpMessagingTemplate

We auto-wired a `SimpMessagingTemplate` in the CSMReceiver class and we will use it later to forward the payload of AMQP messages to WebSocket clients.

A `SimpMessagingTemplate` serves the same purpose as the Spring `JmsTemplate` (if you are familiar with it), but it suits simple messaging protocols (such as STOMP).

A handy and inherited famous method is the `convertAndSend` method, which tries to identify and use a `MessageConverter` to serialize an object and put it into a new message before sending this message to the specified destination::

```
simpMessagingTemplate.convertAndSend(String destination, Object
message);
```

The idea is to target an identified destination (with a `/topic` prefix in our case) for a message broker.

The @SendTo annotation

This annotation saves us from having to explicitly use the `SimpMessagingTemplate`. The destination is specified as the annotation value. This method will also handle the conversion from payload to message:

```
@RestController
public class ActivityFeedWSController extends CloudstreetApiWCI{

  @MessageMapping("/users/feed/add")
  @SendTo("/topic/actions")
  public UserActivityDTO handle(UserActivityDTO payload) throws
    Exception{
        return payload;
  }
}
```

There's more...

In this section, we provide and extra source of information related to the SockJS fallback options.

As introduced earlier, Spring provides a SockJS protocol implementation. It is easy to configure SockJS in Spring using the `withSockJS()` functional method during the `StompEndPoint` registration. This little piece of configuration alone, tells Spring to activate SockJS fallback options on our endpoint.

The very first call of the SockJS client to the server is an HTTP request to the endpoint path concatenated with `/info` to assess the server configuration. If this HTTP request does not succeed, no other transport is attempted (not even WebSocket).

You can read more in the Spring reference guide if you want to understand how a SockJS client queries the server for a suitable fallback option:

```
http://docs.spring.io/spring/docs/current/spring-framework-reference/
html/websocket.html#websocket-server-handshake
```

See also

> ▸ **JSR-356**: You can find the specification document online to read more about the Java API for WebSocket specification that spring-websocket is complying with: `https://jcp.org/en/jsr/detail?id=356`

Using RabbitMQ as a multiprotocol message broker

Installing and using an external RabbitMQ as a full-featured message broker enables new technological opportunities and the design of a production-like infrastructure.

Getting ready

In this recipe, we will install RabbitMQ as a standalone server and configure it so it supports STOMP messages.

We will also update our WebSocket Spring configuration to rely on this full-featured message broker, instead of the internal simple message broker.

How to do it...

1. From the **Git Perspective** in Eclipse check out the `v8.2.x` branch this time.

2. Two new Java projects have been added, and they must be imported. From Eclipse, select the **File | Import...** menu.

3. The **Import** wizard opens so you can select a type of project within a hierarchy. Open the **Maven** category, select **Existing Maven Projects** option, and click on **Next**.

4. The **Import Maven Project** wizard opens. As the root directory, select (or type) the workspace location (which should be `<home-directory>/workspace`).

5. As shown in the following screenshot, select the following two **pom.xml** files: **cloudstreetmarket-shared/pom.xml** and **cloudstreetmarket-websocket/pom.xml**.

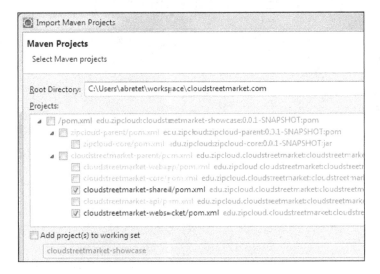

6. The two projects `cloudstreetmarket-shared` and `cloudstreetmarket-websocket` must show up in the project hierarchy.

7. Target a runtime environment on the web module with the following instructions: In Eclipse, right-click on the **cloudmarket-websocket** project, select the **Properties** menu, in the navigation panel, select **Targeted Runtimes**. In the central window, check the tick of the Server **Apache Tomcat v8.0**.

8. In the `/app` directory, the `cloudstreetmarket.properties` file has been updated. Reflect the changes in your file located in `<home-directory>/app/cloudstreetmarket.properties`.

9. Run the `Maven clean` and `Maven install` commands on `zipcloud-parent` and then on `cloudstreetmarket-parent`, followed by a **Maven | Update Project** on all the modules.

10. Running RabbitMQ in the way we want, requires us to download and install the product as a standalone product.

11. Depending upon the configuration of the local machine, different ways of proceeding apply. You will find the appropriate links and installation guides on the RabbitMQ website: `https://www.rabbitmq.com/download.html`

 If you are using Windows OS, please note that it is a prerequisite to download and install Erlang (`http://www.erlang.org/download.html`).

12. Once RabbitMQ is installed and once its service is running, open your favourite web browser in order to check that RabbitMQ is running as a web console at the URL: `http://localhost:15672` (like in the following screenshot).

 We will come back to this later to set up the RabbitMQ configuration. For now, just remember that this console can be used to monitor messages and administrate connections, queues, topics, and exchanges.

13. The RabbitMQ STOMP plugin needs to be activated. This is done from the `rabbitmq_server-x.x.x\sbin` directory, by executing the command line:

```
rabbitmq-plugins enable rabbitmq_stomp
```

14. The following Maven dependencies have been added:

```xml
<dependency>
    <groupId>org.springframework.amqp</groupId>
    <artifactId>spring-rabbit</artifactId>
    <version>1.4.0.RELEASE</version>
</dependency>
<dependency>
    <groupId>io.projectreactor</groupId>
    <artifactId>reactor-core</artifactId>
    <version>2.0.5.RELEASE</version>
</dependency>
<dependency>
    <groupId>io.projectreactor</groupId>
    <artifactId>reactor-net</artifactId>
    <version>2.0.5.RELEASE</version>
</dependency>
<dependency>
    <groupId>io.projectreactor.spring</groupId>
    <artifactId>reactor-spring-context</artifactId>
    <version>2.0.5.RELEASE</version>
</dependency>
<dependency>
    <groupId>io.netty</groupId>
    <artifactId>netty-all</artifactId>
    <version>4.0.31.Final</version>
</dependency>
```

15. In the `dispatcher-servlet.xml` of the `cloudstreetmarket-api` module, the following beans have been added making use of the `rabbit` namespace:

```xml
<beans xmlns="http://www.sfw.org/schema/beans"
    xmlns:xsi="http://www.w3.org/2001/XMLSchema-instance"
    ...
    xmlns:rabbit="http://www.sfw.org/schema/rabbit"
    xsi:schemaLocation="http://www.sfw.org/schema/beans
    ...
    http://www.sfw.org/schema/rabbit
    http://www.sfw.org/schema/rabbit/spring-rabbit-1.5.xsd">
    ...
```

```xml
    <rabbit:connection-factory id="connectionFactory"
      host="localhost" username="guest" password="guest" />
    <rabbit:admin connection-factory="connectionFactory" />
    <rabbit:template id="messagingTemplate" connection-
      factory="connectionFactory"/>
</beans>
```

16. In the `csmcore-config.xml` file (in `cloudstreetmarket-core`), the following beans have been added with the `task` namespace:

```xml
<beans xmlns="http://www.sfw.org/schema/beans"
    xmlns:xsi="http://www.w3.org/2001/XMLSchema-instance"
    ...
    xmlns:task=http://www.sfw.org/schema/task
    http://www.sfw.org/schema/task/spring-task-4.0.xsd">
    ...
    <task:annotation-driven scheduler="wsScheduler"/>
    <task:scheduler id="wsScheduler" pool-size="1000"/>
    <task:executor id="taskExecutor"/>
</beans>
```

17. Still in the Spring configuration side of things, our `AnnotationConfig` bean (the main configuration bean for `cloudstreetmarket-api`) has been added the two annotations:

```java
@EnableRabbit
@EnableAsync
public class AnnotationConfig {

        ...

}
```

18. Finally, the `WebSocketConfig` bean has been updated as well; especially the broker registration. We now make use of a `StompBrokerRelay` instead of a simples broker:

```java
@Configuration
@ComponentScan("edu.zipcloud.cloudstreetmarket.api")
@EnableWebSocketMessageBroker
@EnableScheduling
@EnableAsync
public class WebSocketConfig extends
  AbstractWebSocketMessageBrokerConfigurer {
...
    @Override
    public void configureMessageBroker(final
      MessageBrokerRegistry registry) {
```

```
registry.setApplicationDestinationPrefixes(
  WEBAPP_PREFIX_PATH);
registry.enableStompBrokerRelay(TOPIC_ROOT_PATH);
}
}
```

> That's it! Everything is set to use RabbitMQ as external broker for our system. However, please note that if you try to start the server right now, the code will be expecting MySQL to be installed as well as the Redis Server. These two third-party systems are going to be detailed over the two next recipes.

How it works...

Using a full-featured message broker

In comparison to a simple message broker, using a full-featured message broker such as RabbitMQ provides interesting benefits, which we will discuss now.

Clusterability – RabbitMQ

A RabbitMQ broker is made of one or more Erlang nodes. Each of these nodes represent an instance of RabbitMQ in itself and can be started independently. Nodes can be linked with each other using the command line tool `rabbitmqctl`. For example, `rabbitmqctl join_cluster rabbit@rabbit.cloudstreetmarket.com` would actually connect one node to an existing cluster network. RabbitMQ nodes use cookies to communicate with one another. To be connected on the same cluster, two nodes must have the same cookie.

More STOMP message types

A full-featured message message broker (in comparison with a simple message broker) supports additional STOMP frame commands. For example, `ACK` and `RECEIPT` are not supported by simple message brokers.

StompMessageBrokerRelay

In the previous recipe, we talked about the flow that a message passes through in the Spring WebSocket engine. As shown with the following image, this flow is not affected at all when switching to an external message broker relay.

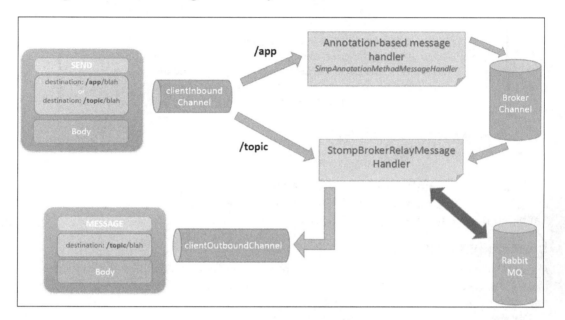

Only the RabbitMQ external message broker shows up as an extra piece. `BrokerMessageHandler` (`StompBrokerRelayMessageHandler`) acts only as a proxy targeting a RabbitMQ node behind the scenes. Only one TCP connection is maintained between the `StompBrokerRelay` and its message broker. The `StompBrokerRelay` maintains the connection by sending heartbeat messages.

See also

> ► **RabbitMQ guide and documentation**: This recipe is just an overview, however the RabbitMQ documentation is well done and very complete. It is a great source of information, and you can find it at:
>
> http://www.rabbitmq.com/documentation.html
>
> http://www.rabbitmq.com/stomp.html

Stacking and consuming tasks with RabbitMQ and AMQP

This recipe will demonstrate how to implement a **Message-oriented-Middleware (MoM)**. This is a very popular technique in scalability based on asynchronous communication between components.

Getting ready

We have already introduced the new `cloudstreetmarket-shared` and `cloudstreetmarket-websocket` Java projects. WebSockets are now split away from `cloudstreetmarket-api`, but `cloudstreetmarket-websocket` and `cloudstreetmarket-api` will still communicate with each other using messaging.

In order to decouple secondary tasks from the request thread (secondary tasks like event producing), you need to learn how to configure and use AMQP message templates and listeners with RabbitMQ.

How to do it...

1. Access the RabbitMQ web console at `http://localhost:15672`.

> If you cannot reach the web console for some reason, please return to the previous recipe where the download and installation guidance can be found.

2. In the **Queue** tab of the web console, create a new queue named `AMQP_USER_ACTIVITY`. Create it with the parameters **Durable** and **Auto-delete: "No"**:

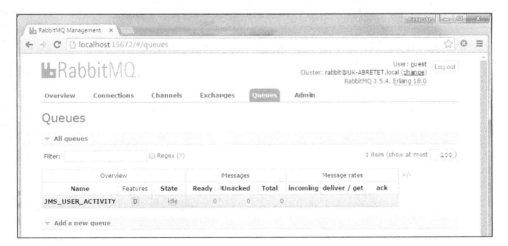

Sender side

When the API is requested to perform operations such as **create a transaction** or **create a like activity**, we produce events.

 With very few adjustments changes, we now use the RabbitTemplate rather than the former SimpMessagingTemplate and we target an intermediate AMQP queue instead of the ultimate STOMP client.

In the `TransactionController`, the POST handler has been updated as follows:

```
import org.springframework.amqp.rabbit.core.RabbitTemplate;
@RestController
public class TransactionController extends
  CloudstreetApiWCI<Transaction> {
  @Autowired
  private RabbitTemplate messagingTemplate;

  @RequestMapping(method=POST)
  @ResponseStatus(HttpStatus.CREATED)
  public TransactionResource post(@Valid @RequestBody Transaction
    transaction, HttpServletResponse response, BindingResult
      result) {
   ...
   messagingTemplate.convertAndSend("AMQP_USER_ACTIVITY", new
     UserActivityDTO(transaction));
   ...
   return resource;
  }
}
```

In the `LikeActionController`, the POST handler has been updated as follows:

```
import org.springframework.amqp.rabbit.core.RabbitTemplate;

@RestController
public class LikeActionController extends
  CloudstreetApiWCI<LikeAction> {
  @Autowired
  private RabbitTemplate messagingTemplate;
  @RequestMapping(method=POST)
  @ResponseStatus(HttpStatus.CREATED)
  public LikeActionResource post(@RequestBody LikeAction
    likeAction, HttpServletResponse response) {
   ...
```

```
messagingTemplate.convertAndSend("AMQP_USER_ACTIVITY", new
   UserActivityDTO(likeAction));
...
return resource;
}
}
```

Consumer side

As explained previously, the `cloudstreetmarket-websocket` module now listens to the `AMQP_USER_ACTIVITY` queue.

1. The necessary configuration is set in the `displatcher-servlet.xml` (`cloudstreetmarket-websocket`). There, we create a `rabbitConnectionFactory` and a `rabbitListenerContainerFactory` bean:

   ```xml
   <rabbit:connection-factory id="rabbitConnectionFactory"
     username="guest" host="localhost" password="guest"/>
   <bean id="rabbitListenerContainerFactory"
     class="org.sfw.amqp.rabbit.config.SimpleRabbitListenerCo
       ntainerFactory">
     <property name="connectionFactory"
       ref="rabbitConnectionFactory"/>
     <property name="concurrentConsumers" value="3"/>
     <property name="maxConcurrentConsumers" value="10"/>
     <property name="prefetchCount" value="12"/>
   </bean>
   ```

2. Finally, the listener bean is created as follows with a `CSMReceiver` class:

   ```java
   @Component
   public class CSMReceiver {
     @Autowired
     private SimpMessagingTemplate simpMessagingTemplate;

     @RabbitListener(queues = "AMQP_USER_ACTIVITY_QUEUE")
     public void handleMessage(UserActivityDTO payload) {
     simpMessagingTemplate.convertAndSend("/topic/actions",
       payload);
     }
   }
   ```

> You can recognize the `SimpMessagingTemplate` used here to forward incoming message payloads to the final STOMP clients.

3. A new `WebSocketConfig` bean has been created in `cloudstreetmarket-websocket`. This one is very similar to the one we had in `cloudstreetmarket-api`.

Client-side

We haven't changed many things on the client side (`cloudstreetmarket-webapp`), as we are still focused on the landing page (`home_community_activity.js`) at this point.

The main difference is that the STOMP endpoint now targets the `/ws` context path. WebSockets are initiated from the `init()` function after a 5-second delay. Also, the `SockJS` socket and the STOMP client are now centralized in global variables (using the `Window` object) to simplify the WebSockets lifecycle during user navigation:

```
var timer = $timeout( function(){
  window.socket = new SockJS('/ws/channels/users/broadcast');
  window.stompClient = Stomp.over(window.socket);
    window.socket.onclose = function() {
        window.stompClient.disconnect();
      };
  window.stompClient.connect({}, function(frame) {
    window.stompClient.subscribe('/topic/actions',
      function(message){
        var newActivity =
          $this.prepareActivity(JSON.parse(message.body));
        $this.addAsyncActivityToFeed(newActivity);
        $scope.$apply();
      });
    });
    $scope.$on(
     "$destroy",
       function( event ) {
         $timeout.cancel( timer );
         window.stompClient.disconnect();
         }
    );
              }, 5000);
```

How it works...

This type of infrastructure couples application components together in a loose but reliable way.

Messaging architecture overview

In this recipe, we have given our application a MoM. The main idea was to decouple processes as much as possible from the client-request lifecycle.

In an effort to keep our REST API focused on resource handling, some business logic clearly appeared secondary, such as:

- ▸ Notifying the community that a new user has registered an account
- ▸ Notifying the community that a user has performed a specific transaction
- ▸ Notifying the community that a user has liked another user's action

We have decided to create a new webapp dedicated to handle WebSockets. Our API now communicates with the `ws` web app by sending messages to it.

The message payloads are community `Action` objects (from the `Action.java` superclass). From the `cloudstreetmarket-api` web app to the `cloudstreetmarket-websocket` webapp, these action objects are serialized and wrapped in AMQP messages. Once sent, they are stacked in one single RabbitMQ queue (`AMQP_USER_ACTIVITY`).

Both the sender and the receiver parts are AMQP implementations (`RabbitTemplate` and `RabbitListener`). This logic will now be processed at the pace that the websocket web app can afford without having an impact on the user experience. When received (on the `cloudstreetmarket-websocket` side), message payloads are sent on the fly to WebSocket clients as STOMP messages.

The benefit in direct performance here is arguable (in this example). We have after all mostly deferred the publishing of secondary events with an extra messaging layer. However, the benefits in design clarity and business components separation are priceless.

A scalable model

We have talked much about the benefits of keeping web apps stateless. This is what we have tried to do so far with the API and we have been proud of it!

Without HTTP sessions, it would be pretty easy for us to react to traffic surges on the `api` web app, or on the `portal` web app. Without too much hassle, we would be able to set up a load balancer on the Apache HTTP proxy with `mod_proxy_balancer` for HTTP connections.

You can read more about this in the Apache HTTP doc: `http://httpd.apache.org/docs/2.2/mod/mod_proxy_balancer.html`

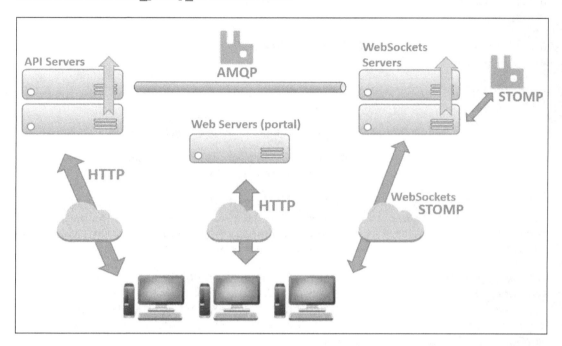

For WebSocket web apps, it would work basically the same in stateless. In the Apache HTTP configuration, a configured `mod_proxy_wstunnel` should handle load balancing over WebSockets and provide an application failover.

AMQP or JMS?

Advanced Message Queuing Protocol (**AMQP**) defines a **wire-level** protocol and guarantees interoperability between senders and consumers. Any party compliant with this protocol can create and interpret messages, and thus interoperate with any other compliant component regardless of the underlying technologies.

In comparison, JMS is part of Java platform **Enterprise Edition (EE)**. Coming with the JSR-914, JMS is a standard for APIs that defines how APIs should create, send, receive, and read messages. JMS does not provide wire-level guidance, and it doesn't guarantee interoperability between parties either.

AMQP controls the format of the messages and the flow these messages go through, while JMS controls the technical implementations of the boundaries (operators). When we look for communication consistency within a potentially complex environment, AMQP appears to be a good choice for MoM protocols.

There's more...

This section provides external resources to extend your knowledge about AMQP and about event publishing methods.

A great introduction to AMQP by pivotal

If you want to get a better understanding of AMQP and its differences with JMS, check out the following article on the `spring.io` website:

```
https://spring.io/understanding/AMQP
```

A better way to publish application events

Right now, we didn't implement a proper pattern to publish events. The article accessible from the link below comes from the `spring.io` blog. It introduces best practices for event publishing with Spring 4.2+:

```
https://spring.io/blog/2015/02/11/better-application-events-in-
spring-framework-4-2
```

See also

▶ **Load balancing WebSockets**: Read more about this topic in the following article by Arun Gupta (at Red Hat at the time:

```
http://blog.arungupta.me/load-balance-websockets-apache-httpd-
techtip48
```

Securing messages with Spring Session and Redis

To summarize, so far we have seen how to broadcast STOMP messages to StockJS clients, how to stack messages in an external multi-protocol broker, and how to interact with this broker (RabbitMQ) in the Spring ecosystem.

Getting ready

This recipe is about implementing dedicated queues, no longer topics (broadcast), so that users can receive real-time updates related to the specific content they are viewing. It is also a demonstration of how SockJS clients can send data to their private queues.

For private queues, we had to secure messages and queue accesses. We have broken down our stateless rule of thumb for the API to make use of Spring Session. This extends the authentication performed by `cloudstreetmarket-api` and reuses the Spring Security context within `cloudstreetmarket-websocket`.

How to do it...

Apache HTTP proxy configuration

Because the `v8.2.x` branch introduced the new `cloudstreetmarket-websocket` web app, the Apache HTTP proxy configuration needs to be updated to fully support our WebSocket implementation. Our `VirtualHost` definition is now:

```
<VirtualHost cloudstreetmarket.com:80>
  ProxyPass          /portal http://localhost:8080/portal
  ProxyPassReverse /portal http://localhost:8080/portal
  ProxyPass          /api     http://localhost:8080/api
  ProxyPassReverse /api     http://localhost:8080/api
  ProxyPass          /ws      http://localhost:8080/ws
  ProxyPassReverse /ws      http://localhost:8080/ws
  RewriteEngine on
  RewriteCond %{HTTP:UPGRADE} ^WebSocket$ [NC]
  RewriteCond %{HTTP:CONNECTION} ^Upgrade$ [NC]
  RewriteRule .* ws://localhost:8080%{REQUEST_URI} [P]
  RedirectMatch ^/$ /portal/index
</VirtualHost>
```

Redis server installation

1. If you are on a Linux-based machine, download the latest stable version (3+) at `http://redis.io/download`. The format of the archive to download is `tar.gz`. Follow the instructions on the page to install it (unpackage it, uncompress it, and build it with the make command).

    Once installed, for a quick start, run Redis with:

    ```
    $ src/redis-server
    ```

2. If you are on a Windows-based machine, we recommend this repository: `https://github.com/ServiceStack/redis-windows`. Follow the instructions on the `README.md` page. Running Microsoft's native port of Redis allows you to run Redis without any other third-party installations.

    To quickly start Redis server, run the following command:

    ```
    $ redis-server.exe redis.windows.conf
    ```

3. When Redis is running, you should be able to see the following welcome screen:

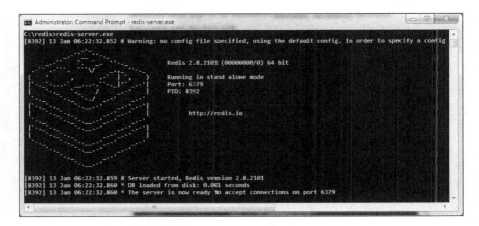

4. Update your Tomcat configuration in Eclipse to use the local Tomcat installation. To do so, double-click on your current server (the **Servers** tab):

5. This should open the configuration panel as follows:

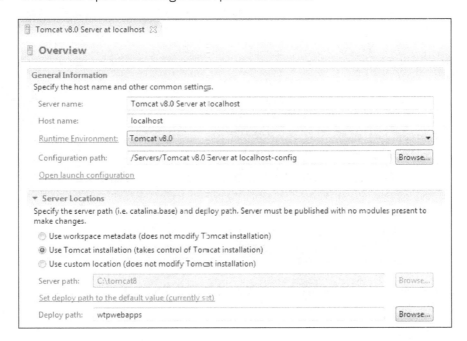

Make sure the **Use Tomcat installation** radio button is checked.

 If the panel is greyed out, right-click on your current server again, then click **Add, Remove**... Remove the three deployed web apps from your server and right click on the server once more, then click **Publish**

6. Now, download the following jars:

   ❑ **jedis-2.5.2.jar**: A small Redis Java client library

   ❑ **commons-pool2-2.2.jar**: The Apache common object pooling library

   You can download them respectively from `http://central.maven.org/maven2/redis/clients/jedis/2.5.2/jedis-2.5.2.jar` and `http://central.maven.org/maven2/org/apache/commons/commons-pool2/2.2/commons-pool2-2.2.jar`

   You can also find these jars in the `chapter_8/libs` directory.

7. In the `chapter_8/libs` directory, you will also find the **tomcat-redis-session-manager-2.0-tomcat-8.jar** archive. Copy the three jars `tomcat-redis-session-manager-2.0-tomcat-8.jar`, `commons-pool2-2.2.jar`, and `jedis-2.5.2.jar` into the `lib` directory of your local Tomcat installation that Eclipse is referring to. This should be `C:\tomcat8\lib` or `/home/usr/{system.username}/tomcat8/lib` if our instructions have been followed in *Chapter 1, Setup Routine for an Enterprise Spring Application*.

8. Now in your workspace, open the **context.xml** file of your **Server** project.

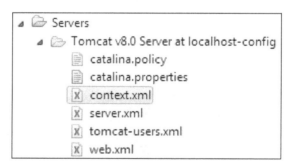

9. Add the following `Valve` configuration:

```
<Valve asyncSupported="true"
className="edu.zipcloud.catalina.session.
RedisSessionHandlerValve"/>
<Manager
className="edu.zipcloud.catalina.session.RedisSessionManager"
        host="localhost"
```

```
port="6379"
database="0"
maxInactiveInterval="60"/>
```

MySQL server installation

While creating the new `cloudstreetmarket-websocket` web app, we have also changed the database engine from HSQLDB to MySQL. Doing so has allowed us to share the database between the `api` and `websocket` modules

1. The first step for this section is to download and install the MySQL community server from `http://dev.mysql.com/downloads/mysql.`. Download the generally available release suited to your system. If you are using MS Windows, we recommend installing the installer.

2. You can follow the installation instructions provided by the MySQL team at `http://dev.mysql.com/doc/refman/5.7/en/installing.html`.

    We are now going to define a common configuration for schema users and a database name.

3. Create a root user with the password of your choice.

4. Create a technical user (with the administrator role) that the application will use. This user needs to be called `csm_tech` and needs to have the password `csmDB1$55`:

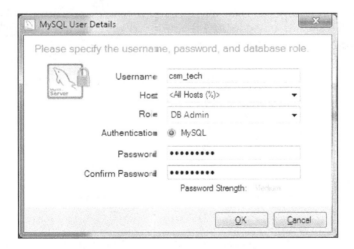

5. Start the MySQL Client (the command line tool), as follows:

    ❏   On MS Windows, start the program `mysql.exe` in the MySQL servers installation directory:`\MySQL Server 5.6\bin\mysql.exe`

    ❏   On Linux or Mac OS, invoke the `mysql` command from the terminal

    On both platforms, the first step is then to provide the root password chosen earlier.

6. Create a `csm` database either with the MySQL workbench or with MySQL client::

```
mysql> CREATE DATABASE csm;
```

7. Select the `csm` database as the current database:

```
mysql> USE csm;
```

8. From Eclipse, start the local Tomcat server. Once it has started, you can shut it down again; this step was only to get Hibernate to generate the schema.

9. We need then to insert the data manually. To do so, execute the following import commands one after the other:

```
mysql> csm < <home-directory>\cloudstreetmarket-parent\
cloudstreetmarket-core\src\main\resources\META-INF\db\currency_
exchange.sql;

mysql> csm < <home-directory>\cloudstreetmarket-parent\
cloudstreetmarket-core\src\main\resources\META-INF\db\init.sql;

mysql> csm < <home-directory>\cloudstreetmarket-parent\
cloudstreetmarket-core\src\main\resources\META-INF\db\stocks.sql;

mysql> csm < <home-directory>\cloudstreetmarket-parent\
cloudstreetmarket-core\src\main\resources\META-INF\db\indices.sql;
```

Application-level changes

1. In `cloudstreetmarket-api` and `cloudstreetmarket-websocket`, the following filter has been added to the `web.xml` files. This filter has to be positioned before the Spring Security chain definition:

```
<filter>
  <filter-name>springSessionRepositoryFilter</filter-name>
  <filter-class>
  org.springframework.web.filter.DelegatingFilterProxy
  </filter-class>
  <async-supported>true</async-supported>
</filter>
<filter-mapping>
  <filter-name>springSessionRepositoryFilter</filter-name>
  <url-pattern>/*</url-pattern>
</filter-mapping>
```

2. A couple of Maven dependencies have also been added to `cloudstreetmarket-api`:

```
<!-- Spring Session -->
<dependency>
  <groupId>org.springframework.session</groupId>
  <artifactId>spring-session</artifactId>
  <version>1.0.2.RELEASE</version>
</dependency>
```

```xml
<dependency>
  <groupId>org.apache.commons</groupId>
  <artifactId>commons-pool2</artifactId>
  <version>2.2</version>
</dependency>
<dependency>
  <groupId>org.springframework.session</groupId>
  <artifactId>spring-session-data-redis</artifactId>
  <version>1.0.2.RELEASE</version>
</dependency>
<!-- Spring Security -->
<dependency>
  <groupId>org.springframework.security</groupId>
  <artifactId>spring-security-messaging</artifactId>
  <version>4.0.2.RELEASE</version>
</dependency>
  <dependency>
    <groupId>commons-io</groupId>
    <artifactId>commons-io</artifactId>
    <version>2.4</version>
  </dependency>
```

3. In `cloudstreetmarket-api` again, `security-config.xml` has been updated to reflect the following changes in the Spring Security filter chain:

```xml
<security:http create-session="ifRequired"
  authentication-manager-ref="authenticationManager"
    entry-point-ref="authenticationEntryPoint">
 <security:custom-filter ref="basicAuthenticationFilter"
   after="BASIC_AUTH_FILTER" />
   <security:csrf disabled="true"/>
 <security:intercept-url pattern="/oauth2/**"
   access="permitAll"/>
 <security:intercept-url pattern="/basic.html"
   access="hasRole('ROLE_BASIC')"/>
   <security:intercept-url pattern="/**"
   access="permitAll"/>
 <security:session-management session-authentication-
   strategy-ref="sas"/>
</security:http>
<bean id="sas"
  class="org.springframework.security.web.authentication.s
    ession.SessionFixationProtectionStrategy" />
```

4. Also, this same `security-config.xml` file, as well as the `security-config.xml` file in `cloudstreetmarket-websocket` now define three extra beans:

```
<bean
  class="org.springframework.data.redis.connection.jedis.J
  edisConnectionFactory" p:port="6379"/>
<bean
  class="org.springframework.session.data.redis.config.ann
  otation.web.http.RedisHttpSessionConfiguration"/>
<bean
class="edu.zipcloud.cloudstreetmarket.core.util.RootPath
CookieHttpSessionStrategy"/>
```

5. Care was taken with `cloudstreetmarket-webapp` not to create sessions. We wanted sessions to be created only in the `cloudstreetmarket-api`. We have achieved this with adding the following configuration to the `web.xml` file in `cloudstreetmarket-webapp`:

```
<session-config>
    <session-timeout>1</session-timeout>
    <cookie-config>
        <max-age>0</max-age>
    </cookie-config>
</session-config>
```

6. Regarding Spring Security, `cloudstreetmarket-websocket` has the following configuration:

```
<bean id="securityContextPersistenceFilter"
  class="org.springframework.security.web.context.
  SecurityContextPersistenceFilter"/>
<security:http create-session="never"
authentication-manager-ref="authenticationManager" entry-
  point-ref="authenticationEntryPoint">
  <security:custom-filter
    ref="securityContextPersistenceFilter"
    before="FORM_LOGIN_FILTER" />
  <security:csrf disabled="true"/>
  <security:intercept-url pattern="/channels/private/**"
    access="hasRole('OAUTH2')"/>
  <security:headers>
      <security:frame-options policy="SAMEORIGIN" />
  </security:headers>
</security:http>
<security:global-method-security secured-
  annotations="enabled" pre-post-annotations="enabled"
  authentication-manager-ref="authenticationManager"/>
```

7. Two configuration-beans in `cloudstreetmarket-websocket` complete the XML configuration:

The WebSocketConfig bean in edu.zipcloud.cloudstreetmarket.ws.config is defined as follows:

```
@EnableScheduling
@EnableAsync
@EnableRabbit
@Configuration
@EnableWebSocketMessageBroker
public class WebSocketConfig extends     AbstractSessionWebSocketMes
sageBrokerConfigurer<Expiring
 Session> {
  @Override
  protected void
  configureStompEndpoints(StompEndpointRegistry registry) {
        registry.addEndpoint("/channels/users/broadcast")
        .setAllowedOrigins(protocol.concat(realmName))
        .withSockJS()
        .setClientLibraryUrl(
        Constants.SOCKJS_CLIENT_LIB);

        registry.addEndpoint("/channels/private")
        .setAllowedOrigins(protocol.concat(realmName))
        .withSockJS()
        .setClientLibraryUrl(
        Constants.SOCKJS_CLIENT_LIB);
  }


  @Override
  public void configureMessageBroker(final
        MessageBrokerRegistry registry) {
        registry.enableStompBrokerRelay("/topic",
                "/queue");
        registry.setApplicationDestinationPrefixes("/app");
  }


  @Override
  public void
  configureClientInboundChannel(ChannelRegistration
  registration) {
        registration.taskExecutor()
          .corePoolSize(Runtime.getRuntime().availableProcessors()
        *4);
  }
```

```
@Override
//Increase number of threads for slow clients
public void configureClientOutboundChannel(
    ChannelRegistration registration) {
        registration.taskExecutor().corePoolSize(
        Runtime.getRuntime().availableProcessors() *4);
}
@Override
public void configureWebSocketTransport(
    WebSocketTransportRegistration registration) {
        registration.setSendTimeLimit(15*1000)
            .setSendBufferSizeLimit(512*1024);
}
}
```

The `WebSocketSecurityConfig` bean in `edu.zipcloud.cloudstreetmarket.ws.config` is defined as follows:

```
@Configuration
public class WebSocketSecurityConfig extends
    AbstractSecurityWebSocketMessageBrokerConfigurer {
        @Override
        protected void configureInbound(
        MessageSecurityMetadataSourceRegistry messages) {
        messages.simpMessageDestMatchers("/topic/actions",
        "/queue/*", "/app/queue/*").permitAll();
        }
        @Override
        protected boolean sameOriginDisabled() {
        return true;
        }
}
```

8. The `ActivityFeedWSController` class has been copied over to `cloudstreetmarket-websocket` to broadcast user activities. It still doesn't require any specific role or authentication:

```
@RestController
public class ActivityFeedWSController extends
    CloudstreetWebSocketWCI{

    @MessageMapping("/channels/users/broadcast")
    @SendTo("/topic/actions")
    public UserActivityDTO handle(UserActivityDTO message)
    throws Exception {
        return message;
    }
```

```
      @RequestMapping(value="/channels/users/broadcast/info",
      produces={"application/json"})
      @ResponseBody
      public String info(HttpServletRequest request) {
        return "v0";
      }
}
```

9. One extra controller sends messages (which are up-to-date stocks values) into private queues:

```
@RestController
public class StockProductWSController extends CloudstreetWebSocket
WCI<StockProduct>{

    @Autowired
    private StockProductServiceOffline stockProductService;

    @MessageMapping("/queue/CSM_QUEUE_{queueId}")
    @SendTo("/queue/CSM_QUEUE_{queueId}")
    @PreAuthorize("hasRole('OAUTH2')")
    public List<StockProduct> sendContent(@Payload
    List<String> tickers, @DestinationVariable("queueId")
    String queueId) throws Exception {
        String username = extractUserFromQueueId(queueId);
        if(!getPrincipal().getUsername().equals(username)){
          throw new
          IllegalAccessError("/queue/CSM_QUEUE_"+queueId);
        }
        return stockProductService.gather(username,
          tickers.toArray(new String[tickers.size()]));
    }

    @RequestMapping(value=PRIVATE_STOCKS_ENDPOINT+"/info",
      produces={"application/xml", "application/json"})
    @ResponseBody
    @PreAuthorize("hasRole('OAUTH2')")
    public String info(HttpServletRequest request) {
        return "v0";
    }

    private static String extractUserFromQueueId(String
    token){
        Pattern p = Pattern.compile("_[0-9]+$");
        Matcher m = p.matcher(token);
```

```
        String sessionNumber = m.find() ? m.group() : "";
        return token.replaceAll(sessionNumber, "");
      }
  }
```

10. On the client side, new WebSockets are initiated from the stock-search screens (stocks result lists). Especially in `stock_search.js` and `stock_search_by_market.js`, the following block has been added in order to regularly request data updates for the set of results that is displayed to the authenticated user:

```javascript
if(httpAuth.isUserAuthenticated()){
  window.socket = new SockJS('/ws/channels/private');
  window.stompClient = Stomp.over($scope.socket);
  var queueId = httpAuth.generatedQueueId();

  window.socket.onclose = function() {
    window.stompClient.disconnect();
  };
  window.stompClient.connect({}, function(frame) {
    var intervalPromise = $interval(function() {
      window.stompClient.send(
      '/app/queue/CSM_QUEUE_'+queueId,
      {}, JSON.stringify($scope.tickers));
      }, 5000);

    $scope.$on(
        "$destroy",
        function( event ) {
          $interval.cancel(intervalPromise);
          window.stompClient.disconnect();
        }
    );

  window.stompClient.subscribe('/queue/CSM_QUEUE_'+queueId,
  function(message){
    var freshStocks = JSON.parse(message.body);
    $scope.stocks.forEach(function(existingStock) {
      //Here we update the currently displayed stocks
    });

    $scope.$apply();
    dynStockSearchService.fadeOutAnim(); //CSS animation
      //(green/red backgrounds...)
      });
    });
  };
```

The `httpAuth.generatedQueueId()` function generates a random queue name based on the authenticated username (see `http_authorized.js` for more details).

RabbitMQ configuration

1. Open the RabbitMQ WebConsole, select the **Admin** tab, then select the **Policy** menu (also accessible from the `http://localhost:15672/#/policies` URL).

2. Add the following policy:

This policy (named PRIVATE) applies to all auto-generated queues matching the pattern `CSM_QUEUE_*`, with an auto-expiration of 24 hours.

The results

1. Let's have a look ... before starting the Tomcat Server, ensure that:

   ❑ MySQL is running with the loaded data

   ❑ The Redis server is running

   ❑ RabbitMQ is running

   ❑ Apache HTTP has been restarted/reloaded

2. When all these signals are green, start the Tomcat servers.

3. Log in to the application with your Yahoo! account, register a new user, and navigate to the screen: **Prices and markets | Search by markets**. If you target a market that is potentially open at your time, you should be able to notice real-time updates on the result list:

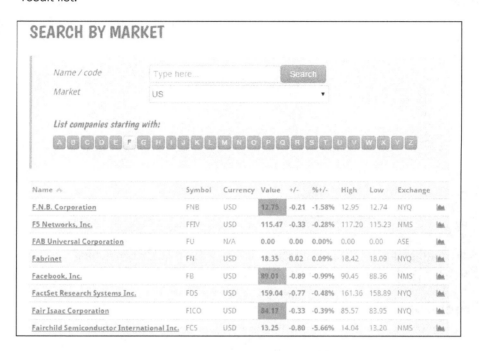

How it works...

The Redis server

Redis is an open source in-memory data-structure store. Day-after-day, it is becoming increasingly popular as a NoSQL database and as a key-value store.

Its ability to store keys with optional expiration times and with very high availability (over its remarkable cluster) makes it a very solid underlying technology for session manager implementations. This is precisely the use we make of it through Spring Session.

Spring session

Spring Session is a relatively new Spring project, but it is meant to grow up and take a substantial space in the Spring ecosystem, especially with the recent Microservices and IoT trends. The project is managed by Rob Winch at Pivotal inc. As introduced previously, Spring Session provides an API to manage users' sessions from different Spring components.

The most interesting and notable feature of Spring Session is its ability to integrate with the container (Apache Tomcat) to supply a custom implementation of `HttpSession`.

SessionRepositoryFilter

To make use of a custom `HttpSession` implementation, Spring Session completely replaces the `HttpServletRequest` with a custom wrapper (`SessionRepositoryRequestWrapper`). This operation is performed inside `SessionRepositoryFilter`, which is the servlet filter that needs to be configured in the `web.xml` to intercept the request flow (before Spring MVC).

To do its job, the `SessionRepositoryFilter` must have an `HttpSession` implementation. At some point, we registered the `RedisHttpSessionConfiguration` bean. This bean defines a couple of other beans, and among them is a `sessionRepository`, which is a `RedisOperationsSessionRepository`.

See how the `SessionRepositoryFilter` is important for bridging across the application all the performed session operations to the actual engine implementation that will execute those operations.

RedisConnectionFactory

A `RedisConnectionFactory` implementation is necessary in order to produce a suitable connection to Redis. Selecting a `RedisConnectionFactory` implementation, we have been following the Spring team's choice which appeared to be the `JedisConnectionFactory`. This `RedisConnectionFactory` relies on Jedis (a lightweight Redis Java client). `https://github.com/xetorthio/jedis`.

CookieHttpSessionStrategy

We have registered an `HttpSessionStrategy` implementation: `RootPathCookieHttpSessionStrategy`. This class is a customized version (in our codebase) of the Spring `CookieHttpSessionStrategy`.

Because we wanted to pass the cookie from `cloudstreetmarket-api` to `cloudstreetmarket-websocket`, the cookie path (which is a property of a cookie) needed to be set to the root path (and not the servlet context path). Spring Session 1.1+ should offer a configurable path feature.

`https://github.com/spring-projects/spring-session/issues/155`

For now, our `RootPathCookieHttpSessionStrategy` (basically `CookieHttpSessionStrategy`) produces and expects cookies with a **SESSION** name::

Currently, only `cloudstreetmarket-api` produces such cookies (the two other web apps have been restricted in their cookie generation capabilities so they don't mess up our sessions).

Spring Data Redis and Spring Session Data Redis

Do you remember our good friend Spring Data JPA? Well now, Spring Data Redis follows a similar purpose but for the Redis NoSQL key-value store:

> *"The Spring Data Redis (framework makes it easy to write Spring applications that use the Redis key value store by eliminating the redundant tasks and boiler plate code required for interacting with the store through Spring's excellent infrastructure support."*

> *Spring Data Redis reference*

Spring Session Data Redis is the Spring module that specifically implements Spring Data Redis for the purpose of Spring Session management.

The Redis Session manager for Tomcat

Apache Tomcat natively provides clustering and session-replication features. However, these features rely on load balancers sticky sessions. Sticky sessions have pros and cons for scalability. As cons, we can remember that sessions can be lost when servers go down. Also the stickiness of sessions can induce a slow loading time when we actually need to respond to a surge of traffic.

We have also been using an open source project from James Coleman that allows a Tomcat servers to store non-sticky sessions in Redis immediately on session creation for potential uses by other Tomcat instances. This open source project can be reached at the following address:

`https://github.com/jcoleman/tomcat-redis-session-manager`

However, this project doesn't officially support Tomcat 8. Thus, another fork went further in the Tomcat Release process and is closer from the Tomcat 8 requirements:

```
https://github.com/rmohr/tomcat-redis-session-manager
```

We forked this repository and provided an adaptation for Tomcat 8 in https://github.com/alex-bretet/tomcat-redis-session-manager.

The `tomcat-redis-session-manager-2.0-tomcat-8.jar` copied to `tomcat/lib` comes from this repository.

 Tomcat 8 is still recent, and time is required for peripheral tools to follow releases. We don't provide `tomcat-redis-session-manager-2.0-tomcat-8.jar` for production use.

Viewing/flushing sessions in Redis

In the main installation directory for Redis, an executable for a command line tool (`Cli`) can be found. This executable can be launched from the command:

```
$ src/redis-cli
```

Or:

```
$ redis-cli.exe
```

This executable gives access to the Redis console. From there, for example, the `KEY *` command lists all the active sessions:

```
127.0.0.1:6379> keys *
1) "spring:session:sessions:4f39ce3-63b3-4e17-b1c4-5e1ed96fb021"
2) "spring:session:expirations:1418772300000"
```

The `FLUSHALL` command clears all the active sessions:

```
redis 127.0.0.1:6379> FLUSHALL
OK
```

 Discover the Redis client language with their online tutorial accessible at `http://try.redis.io`.

securityContextPersistenceFilter

We make use of this filter in the `cloudstreetmarket-websocket` Spring Security filter chain. Its role consists of injecting an external Spring Security context into a `SecurityContextHolder` from the configured `SecurityContextRepository`:

```
<bean id="securityContextPersistenceFilter"
  class="org.sfw.security.web.context.SecurityContextPersistence
    Filter">
    <constructor-arg name="repo"
      ref="httpSessionSecurityContextRepo" />
</bean>

<bean id="httpSessionSecurityContextRepo"
  class='org.sfw.security.web.context.HttpSessionSecurityContext
    Repository'>
    <property name='allowSessionCreation' value='false' />
</bean>
```

This filter interacts with `SecurityContextRepository` to persist the context once the filter chain has been completed. Combined with Spring Session, this filter is very useful when you need to reuse an authentication that has been performed in another component (another web app in our case).

After this point, we have also been able to declare a `global-method-security` element (of the Spring Security namespace) that allows us to make use of `@PreAuthorize` annotations in `@MessageMapping` annotated methods (our message handling methods)::

```
<global-method-security secured-annotations="enabled" pre-post-
annotations="enabled" />
```

AbstractSessionWebSocketMessageBrokerConfigurer

This is a long title. We have used this abstract class to give our `WebSocketConfig` the ability to:

▶ Ensure sessions are kept alive on incoming web socket messages

▶ Ensure that WebSocket sessions are destroyed when session terminate

AbstractSecurityWebSocketMessageBrokerConfigurer

In a similar fashion, this abstract class provides authorization capabilities to our `WebSocketSecurityConfig` bean. Thanks to it, the `WebSocketSecurityConfig` bean now controls the destinations that are allowed for incoming messages.

There's more...

Spring Session

Once again, we recommend the Spring reference document on Spring Session, which is very well done. Please check it out:

```
http://docs.spring.io/spring-session/docs/current/reference/html5
```

Apache HTTP proxy extra configuration

The few lines added to `httpd.conf` serve the purpose of rewriting the WebSocket scheme to ws during the WebSocket handshake. Not doing this causes SockJS to fall back to its **XHR** options (one WebSocket emulation).

Spring Data Redis

Also, we recommend that you read more about the Spring Data Redis project (in its reference document):

```
http://docs.spring.io/spring-data/data-redis/docs/current/reference/
html
```

See also

- **Deep-dive into Spring WebSockets** by Sergi Almar: This is the presentation that occurred at SpringOne2GX 2014:

  ```
  http://www.slideshare.net/sergialmar/websockets-with-spring-4
  ```

- **Spring-websocket-portfolio, showcase application**: We must also highlight the Spring WebSocket showcase application from Rossen Stoyanchev:

  ```
  https://github.com/rstoyanchev/spring-websocket-portfolio
  ```

9

Testing and Troubleshooting

With the following listed recipes, this chapter introduces a set of common practices for maintaining, debugging, and improving an application state:

- ▶ Automating Database Migrations with Flyway
- ▶ Unit testing with Mockito and Maven Surefire
- ▶ Integration testing with Cargo, Rest-assured, and Maven Failsafe
- ▶ Injecting Spring Bean in Integration tests
- ▶ Modern application Logging with Log4j2

Introduction

As we are now approaching the end of this journey, we must see how to consolidate the work. In the real world, tests must be written before a feature is developed (or at least at the same time). Writing automated tests in software development conveys a massive confidence about the application state. It is the best way of ensuring that nothing has been forgotten. Having a system that has the ability to test itself, with the help of modern continuous integration tools, ensures that features will not be damaged at any time.

Manual testing through UI cannot be trusted to cover every single edge case that a developer has to think about. It is the responsibility of the developer to secure all the breaches and to cover all the possible paths, and this is a big responsibility.

Our developer job is an amazing job. The perpetual technology enhancement sets an incomparable pace for every one of us—to stay in the race, to respond to the market, and sometimes to lead the market.

Our job is made of long hours of intense focus, search for information, design, redesign, and so on. Writing tests brings a healthy stability in the cycle. It allows us to finish our day happier with the features we develop, even weeks and months later.

Automating Database Migrations with FlyWay

In the delivery life cycle, maintaining databases across versions and multiple environments can be a real headache. Flyway is an assertive protection against the entropy that schema changes can induce. Managing and automating migrations, Flyway stands as a tremendously valuable asset for software makers.

Getting ready

In this recipe, we review the Flyway configuration. We especially review its integration in to Maven. This will get every build to upgrade (if necessary) the corresponding database so that it matches the expectation level.

How to do it...

1. From the **Git Perspective** in Eclipse, checkout the latest version of the branch `v9.x.x`.

2. In the `/app` directory of your workspace, the `cloudstreetmarket.properties` file has been updated. Also, one extra `db/migration` directory shows up with a `Migration-1_0__init.sql` file inside, as well as a new `/logs` directory.

3. Please do reflect all these changes to the app directory located in your OS user `home` directory: `<home-directory>/app`.

4. Also ensure that your **MySQL Server** is running.

5. Run the **Maven clean** and **Maven install** commands on the `zipcloud-parent` project (right-click on the project **Run as...** | **Maven Clean** and then **Run as...** | **Maven Install**).

6. Now, run the **Maven clean** and **Maven install** commands on the `cloudstreetmarket-parent` project.

7. At the top of the stack trace (at the package Maven phase), you should see the following logs:

```
[INFO] ------------------------------------------------------------------
[INFO] Building CloudStreetMarket Parent 0.0.1-SNAPSHOT
[INFO] ------------------------------------------------------------------
[INFO]
[INFO] --- maven-enforcer-plugin:1.3.1:enforce (enforce) @ cloudstreetmarket-parent ---
[INFO]
[INFO] --- flyway-maven-plugin:2.3.1:migrate (package) @ cloudstreetmarket-parent ---
[INFO] Current version of schema `csm`: 0
[INFO] Migrating schema `csm` to version 1.0
[INFO] Successfully applied 1 migration to schema `csm` (execution time 00:08.544s).
[INFO]
[INFO] --- maven-install-plugin:2.4:install (default-install) @ cloudstreetmarket-parent ---
```

8. At this stage, the database should have been reset to match a standard state of structure and data.

9. If you rerun the build again, you should now see the following logs:

```
[INFO] ------------------------------------------------------------------
[INFO] Building CloudStreetMarket Parent 0.0.1-SNAPSHOT
[INFO] ------------------------------------------------------------------
[INFO]
[INFO] --- maven-enforcer-plugin:1.3.1:enforce (enforce) @ cloudstreetmarket-parent ---
[INFO]
[INFO] --- flyway-maven-plugin:2.3.1:migrate (package) @ cloudstreetmarket-parent ---
[INFO] Current version of schema `csm`: 1.0
[INFO] Schema `csm` is up to date. No migration necessary.
[INFO]
[INFO] --- maven-install-plugin:2.4:install (default-install) @ cloudstreetmarket-parent ---
[INFO] Installing C:\Users\abretet\perso\git\cloudstreetmarket.com\cloudstreetmarket-parent\pom.xml
[INFO]
```

10. In the parent `pom.xml` (in `cloudstreetmarket-parent`), you can notice a new plugin definition:

```xml
<plugin>
    <groupId>com.googlecode.flyway</groupId>
    <artifactId>flyway-maven-plugin</artifactId>
    <version>2.3.1</version>
    <inherited>false</inherited>
    <executions>
        <execution>
        <id>package</id>
        <goals>
        <goal>migrate</goal>
        </goals>
        </execution>
    </executions>
    <configuration>
```

```
<driver>${database.driver}</driver>
<url>${database.url}</url>
<serverId>${database.serverId}</serverId>
<schemas>
  <schema>${database.name}</schema>
  </schemas>
<locations>
  <location>
    filesystem:${user.home}/app/db/migration
    </location>
  </locations>
  <initOnMigrate>true</initOnMigrate>
    <sqlMigrationPrefix>Migration-</sqlMigrationPrefix>
    <placeholderPrefix>#[</placeholderPrefix>
    <placeholderSuffix>]</placeholderSuffix>
    placeholderReplacement>true</placeholderReplacement>
    <placeholders>
    <db.name>${database.name}</db.name>
    </placeholders>
</configuration>
<dependencies>
    <dependency>
    <groupId>mysql</groupId>
    <artifactId>mysql-connector-java</artifactId>
    <version>5.1.6</version>
    </dependency>
</dependencies>
</plugin>
```

11. A few variables (for example, `${database.driver}`) used in this definition correspond to default properties, set at the top level of this `pom.xml`:

```
<database.name>csm</database.name>
<database.driver>com.mysql.jdbc.Driver</database.driver>
<database.url>jdbc:mysql://localhost</database.url>
<database.serverId>csm_db</database.serverId>
```

12. The `database.serverId` must match a new `Server` entry in the Maven `settings.xml` file (described in the next point).

13. Edit the Maven `settings.xml` file (that you must have created in *Chapter 1, Setup Routine for an Enterprise Spring Application*) located at `<home-directory>/.m2/settings.xml`. Add somewhere in the root node the following block:

```
<servers>
    <server>
    <id>csm_db</id>
    <username>csm_tech</username>
```

```
      <password>csmDB1$55</password>
      </server>
   </servers>
```

14. In the parent pom.xml (in cloudstreetmarket-parent), a new Profile has been added to optionally override the default properties (of this pom.xml):

```
<profiles>
   <profile>
   <id>flyway-integration</id>
   <properties>
   <database.name>csm_integration</database.name>
   <database.driver>com.mysql.jdbc.Driver</database.driver>
   <database.url>jdbc:mysql://localhost</database.url>
   <database.serverId>csm_db</database.serverId>
   </properties>
   </profile>
</profiles>
```

 Running Maven Clean Install with the csm_integration profile (mvn clean install -Pcsm_integration) would upgrade in this case, if necessary, a csm_integration database.

How it works...

Flyway is a database versioning and migration tool licensed Apache v2 (free software). It is a registered trademark of the company Boxfuse GmbH.

Flyway is not the only product in this category but is widely present in the industry for its simplicity and easy configuration. The migration scripts can be written in plain old SQL and many providers are supported. From classical RDBMS (Oracle, MySQL, SQL Server, and so on) to in-memory DB (HSQLDB, solidDB, and so on), and even cloud-based solutions (AWS Redshift, SQL Azure, and so on).

A limited number of commands

Flyway provides the six following commands for reporting and operation purposes.

Migrate

The Migrate command is the goal we have integrated to the Maven package phase. It looks up the classpath or the filesystem for potential migrations to be executed. Several locations (script repositories) can be configured. In the Flyway Maven plugin, these locations are defined in the root configuration node. Patterns are set up to retain specific filenames.

Clean

The `Clean` command restores pristine a database schema. All the objects (tables, views, functions, and so on) are dropped with this command.

Info

The `Info` command provides feedback about the current state and the migration history of a given schema. If you have a look into your local MySQL server, in the `csm` schema, you will notice that a metadata table has been created with the name `schema_version`. Flyway uses the following table to compare the script repository state with the database state and to fill the gaps.

version	description	script	installed on	success
0	`<< Flyway Schema Creation >>`	`'csm'`	12/11/2015 18:11	1
1	`drop and create`	`/Migration-1_0__ drop_and_create.sql`	12/11/2015 18:11	1

The `Info` command basically prints out this table as a report.

Validate

The `Validate` command can be useful to ensure that the migrations executed on a database actually correspond to the scripts currently present in the repositories.

Baseline

The `Baseline` command can be used when we have an existing database that hasn't been managed yet by Flyway. A Baseline version is created to tag the state of this database and to make it ready to live with upcoming versions. Versions prior to this Baseline will simply be ignored.

Repair

The `Repair` command can clean up a corrupted state of the metadata table. To do that, Flyway removes the failed migration entries and resets the stored checksums to match the scripts checksums.

About Flyway Maven plugin

The Flyway Maven plugin provides the interface for Maven to control the Flyway program. Our configuration of the plugin has been the following:

```
<plugin>
    <groupId>com.googlecode.flyway</groupId>
    <artifactId>flyway-maven-plugin</artifactId>
    <version>2.3.1</version>
    <inherited>false</inherited>
    <executions>
```

```
    <execution>
      <id>package</id>
      <goals>
        <goal>migrate</goal>
      </goals>
    </execution>
  </executions>
  <configuration>
    <driver>${database.driver}</driver>
<url>${database.url}</url>
<serverId>${database.serverId}</serverId>
<schemas>
    <schema>${database.name}</schema>
</schemas>
<locations>
  <location>
      filesystem:${user.home}/app/db/migration
  </location>
  </locations>
<initOnMigrate>true</initOnMigrate>
  <sqlMigrationPrefix>Migration-</sqlMigrationPrefix>
  <placeholderPrefix>#[</placeholderPrefix>
  <placeholderSuffix>]</placeholderSuffix>
  <placeholderReplacement>true</placeholderReplacement>
  <placeholders>
  <db.name>${database.name}</db.name>
  </placeholders>
  </configuration>
  </plugin>
```

As usual with Maven plugins, the executions section allows the binding of Maven phases to one or more Goals of the plugin. For Flyway Maven plugin, the goals are the Flyway commands presented previously. We tell Maven when to consider the plugin and what to invoke in this plugin.

Our `configuration` section presents a few parameters checked during migrations. For example, the `locations` specifies migration repositories to be scanned recursively (they can start with `classpath:` or `filesystem:`). The `schemas` defines the list of schemas managed by Flyway for the whole set of migrations. The first schema will be the default one across migrations.

An interesting feature is the ability to use variables in migration scripts so that these scripts can be used as template for multiple environments. Variable names are defined with `placeholders`, and the way variables are identified in scripts is configurable with `placeholderPrefix` and `placeholderSuffix`.

The whole list of configuration parameters can be found at

`http://flywaydb.org/documentation/maven/migrate.html`.

There is more...

The official documentation

Flyway is well-documented and actively supported by its community. Read more about the product online at http://flywaydb.org.

You can also follow or contribute to the project through the GitHub repository

at `https://github.com/flyway/flyway`.

See also

> ► **Liquibase**: The main Flyway competitor is probably Liquibase. Liquibase doesn't use plain SQL for its scripts; it has instead its own multirepresentation DSL. For more information, visit:
>
> `http://www.liquibase.org`.

Unit testing with Mockito and Maven Surefire

Unit Tests are useful to keep an eye on the components' implementation. The legacy philosophy of Spring promotes reusable components application-wide. The core implementations of these components may either alter states (states of transitory objects) or trigger interactions with other components.

Using Mocks in Unit Tests specifically assesses the **behavior** of component's methods in regard to other components. When the developer gets used to Mocks, it is amazing to see how much the design becomes influenced toward the use of different layers and logic externalization. Similarly, object names and method names are given more importance. Because they summarize something that is happening elsewhere, Mocks save the energy of the next developer that will have to operate in the area of code.

Developing Unit Tests is by definition an Enterprise policy. As the percentage of code covered by tests can easily reflect the maturity of a product, this code-coverage rate is also becoming a standard reference to assess companies in regard to their products. It must also be noted that companies practicing code reviews as a development process find valuable insights from Pull Requests. When Pull Requests highlight behavioral changes through tests, the impact of potential changes becomes clear faster.

How to do it...

1. Rerun a `Maven Install` on the `cloudstreetmarket-parent` project as in the previous recipe. When the build process comes to build the core module, you should see the following logs that suggest the execution of unit tests during the **test** phase (between **compile** and **package**):

```
[INFO] --- maven-surefire-plugin:2.4.2:test (default-test) @ cloudstreetmarket-core ---
[INFO] Surefire report directory: C:\Users\abretet\perso\git\cloudstreetmarket.com\cloudstreetmar

-------------------------------------------------
 T E S T S
-------------------------------------------------
Running edu.zipcloud.cloudstreetmarket.core.converters.IdentifiableToIdConverterTest
Tests run: 23, Failures: 0, Errors: 0, Skipped: 0, Time elapsed: 0.039 sec
Running edu.zipcloud.cloudstreetmarket.core.converters.YahooQuoteToIndexConverterTest
Tests run: 2, Failures: 0, Errors: 0, Skipped: 0, Time elapsed: 0.142 sec
Running edu.zipcloud.cloudstreetmarket.core.converters.YahooQuoteToStockQuoteConverterTest
Tests run: 1, Failures: 0, Errors: 0, Skipped: 0, Time elapsed: 0.007 sec
Running edu.zipcloud.cloudstreetmarket.core.services.CommunityServiceImplTest
Tests run: 49, Failures: 0, Errors: 0, Skipped: 0, Time elapsed: 0.199 sec
Running edu.zipcloud.cloudstreetmarket.core.converters.YahooQuoteToCurrencyExchangeConverterTest
Tests run: 2, Failures: 0, Errors: 0, Skipped: 0, Time elapsed: 0.009 sec
Running edu.zipcloud.cloudstreetmarket.core.converters.YahooQuoteToStockProductConverterTest
Tests run: 2, Failures: 0, Errors: 0, Skipped: 0, Time elapsed: 0.01 sec

Results :

Tests run: 79, Failures: 0, Errors: 0, Skipped: 0
```

2. Those tests can be found in the `cloudstreetmarket-core` module, specifically in the `src/test/java` source folder:

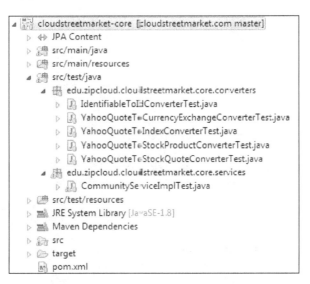

Both unit tests and integration tests use JUnit:

```xml
<dependency>
        <groupId>junit</groupId>
        <artifactId>junit</artifactId>
        <version>4.9</version>
</dependency>
```

3. JUnit is natively supported by Eclipse IDE, and this last one offers handles to **Run** and **Debug** tests from a class or a method outside Maven:

4. A very simple JUnit test class is `IdentifiableToIdConverterTest` (see the following code). This class asserts that all the registered Entities can be converted by `IdentifiableToIdConverter` for being `Identifiable` implementations (remember HATEOAS:):

```java
import static org.junit.Assert.*;
import org.junit.Test;
import edu.zipcloud.cloudstreetmarket.core.entities.*;

public class IdentifiableToIdConverterTest {

    private IdentifiableToIdConverter converter;

    @Test
    public void canConvertChartStock(){
        converter = new
            IdentifiableToIdConverter(ChartStock.class);
        assertTrue(converter.canConvert(ChartStock.class));
    }

    @Test
    public void canConvertAction(){
        converter = new
            IdentifiableToIdConverter(Action.class);
```

```
        assertTrue(converter.canConvert(Action.class));
    }
}
```

5. More advanced unit tests use the Mockito library. For instance, in the following
YahooQuoteToCurrencyExchangeConverterTest:

```
@RunWith(MockitoJUnitRunner.class)
public class YahooQuoteToCurrencyExchangeConverterTest {
    @InjectMocks
    private YahooQuoteToCurrencyExchangeConverter
            converter;
    @Mock
    private CurrencyExchangeRepository
        currencyExchangeRepository;
    @Test
    public void transferCriticalData(){
        when(currencyExchangeRepository.findOne(
        any(String.class))
        )
        .thenReturn(new CurrencyExchange("WHATEVER_ID""));
        CurrencyExchange currencyExchange =
            converter.convert(buildYahooQuoteInstance());
        assertEquals("WHATEVER_ID"",currencyExchange.getId());
        assertEquals("USDGBP=X"", currencyExchange.getName());
        assertEquals(BigDecimal.valueOf(10),
            currencyExchange.getEid());
        ...
        assertEquals(BigDecimal.valueOf(17),
        currencyExchange.getOpen());
        verify(currencyExchangeRepository, times(1))
            .findOne(any(String.class));
    }
    ...
}
```

Here, the highlighted transferCriticalData() test gets an instance of
YahooQuoteToCurrencyExchangeConverter that is not initialized with a real
@Autowired CurrencyExchangeRepository but instead with a **Mock**. The
converter gets its convert() method invoked with a YahooQuote instance.

The Mock is told to return a specific CurrencyExchange instance
when its findOne(String s) method is called inside convert().
Then, the returned currencyExchange object is assessed field by
field to ensure they are matching their individual expectations.

6. The following Maven dependency to Mockito has been added across the different modules:

```
<dependency>
  <groupId>org.mockito</groupId>
  <artifactId>mockito-all</artifactId>
  <version>1.9.5<version>
</dependency>
```

7. A more extended use of Mockito for unit tests can be found in `CommunityServiceImplTest`. For example, in the following example, the `registerUser_generatePasswordAndEncodeIt` test makes use of the `ArgumentCaptor`:

```
@Test
public void registerUser_generatesPasswordAndEncodesIt() {
  when(communityServiceHelper.generatePassword())
    .thenReturn("newPassword");
  when(passwordEncoder.encode("newPassword"))
    .thenReturn("newPasswordEncoded");
  ArgumentCaptor<User>userArgumentCaptor =
    ArgumentCaptor.forClass(User.class);
  userA.setPassword(null);
  communityServiceImpl.registerUser(userA);
  verify(userRepository, times(1))
    .save(userArgumentCaptor.capture());
  verify(passwordEncoder, times(1))
    .encode("newPassword");
  String capturedGeneratedPassword =
    userArgumentCaptor.getValue().getPassword();
  assertEquals("newPasswordEncoded"
    ,
    capturedGeneratedPassword);
}
```

How it works...

@Test annotation

The `@Test` annotation must be placed on public void methods so that JUnit considers them as test cases. An exception thrown within one of these methods will be considered as a test failure. Consequently, an execution without any exception thrown represents a success.

The `@Test` annotation can be customized, passing the following two optional arguments.

The expected and timeout arguments

An **expected** parameter on an `@Test` annotation specifies that the test is expected to throw a specific type of exception to be successful. When a different Type of exception is thrown or when no exception is thrown at all, JUnit must consider the execution as a failure. When a test case is provided a **timeout** parameter in its `@Test` annotation, this test will fail when the execution lasts more than the indicated time.

The @RunWith annotation

As introduced in the recipe, the `@RunWith` annotation permits the use of external test runners (instead of the default `BlockJUnit4ClassRunner` coming with JUnit). By the way, a declarative technique for specifying the default JUnit runner could be to get `@RunWith` targeting `JUnit4.class` like so: `@RunWith(JUnit4.class)`.

> *A runner runs tests and notifies a* `RunNotifier` *of significant events as it does so.*

> *JUnit.org Javadoc*

A custom `Runner` must implement abstract methods from `org.junit.runner.Runner` such as `run(RunNotifier notifier)` and `getDescription()`. It must also follow up on core JUnit functions, driving for example, the test execution flow. JUnit has a set of annotations such as `@BeforeClass`, `@Before`, `@After`, and `@AfterClass` natively handled by `org.junit.runner.ParentRunner`. We are going to visit these annotations next.

@Before and @After annotations

In test classes that contains several test cases, it is a good practice to try making the test logic as clear as possible. From this perspective, variable initialization and context reinitialization are operations that people often attempt to externalize for reusability. `@Before` annotations can be defined on `public void` methods to get them executed by the Runner before **every single test**. Similarly, `@After` annotations mark the `public void` method again to be executed after **each test** (usually for cleanup resources or destroying a context).

For information, on inheritance, `@Before` methods of parent classes will be run before those of the current class. Similarly, `@After` methods declared in superclasses will be run after those of the current class.

Another interesting point from the Javadoc specifies that **all** `@After` methods are guaranteed to run, **even if** a `@Before` or a `@Test` annotated method throws an exception.

@BeforeClass and @AfterClass annotations

The `@BeforeClass` and `@AfterClass` annotations can be applied to **public static void** methods. `@BeforeClass` causes a method to be run **once** in the test life cycle. The method will be run before any other `@Test` or `@Before` annotated methods.

A method annotated @AfterClass is guaranteed to be run **once** after all tests and also after all @BeforeClass, @Before, or @After annotated methods even if one of them throws an exception.

@BeforeClass and @AfterClass are valuable tools for handling performance-consuming operations related to the preparation of test context (database connection management and pre/post business treatments).

For information, on inheritance, @BeforeClass annotated methods in superclasses will be executed **before** the ones of the current class, and @AfterClass annotated methods in the superclasses will be executed **after** those of the current class.

Using Mockito

Mockito is an Open Source testing framework that supports Test-Driven Developments and Behavior-Driven developments. It permits the creation of double objects (Mock objects) and helps in isolating the system under test.

MockitoJUnitRunner

We have been talking about custom runners. The MockitoJUnitRunner is a bit particular in the way that it implements a decoration pattern around the default JUnitRunner.

Such design makes optional the use of this runner (all the provided services could also be implemented declaratively with Mockito).

The MockitoJUnitRunner automatically initializes @Mock annotated dependencies (this saves us a call to MockitoAnnotations.initMocks(this), in a @Before annotated method for example).

```
initMocks(java.lang.Object testClass)
```

Initializes objects annotated with Mockito annotations for given testClass: @Mock

Javadoc

The MockitoJUnitRunner also validates the way we implement the framework, after each test method, by invoking Mockito.validateMockitoUsage().This validation assertively gets us to make an optimal use of the library with the help of explicit error outputs.

The transferCriticalData example

The system under test is the YahooQuoteToCurrencyExchangeConverter. The @InjectMocks annotation tells Mockito to perform injection of dependencies (constructor injection, property setter, or field injection) on the targeted converter using initialized Mocks before each test.

The `Mockito.when(T methodCall)` method, coupled with `thenReturn(T value)` allows the definition of a fake `CurrencyExchange` returned object when a call to `currencyExchangeRepository.findOne` will actually be made inside the `converter.convert(...)` tested method.

The `Mockito verify` method with `verify(currencyExchangeRepository, times(1)).findOne(any(String.class))` tells Mockito to validate how the tested `convert` method has interacted with the Mock(s). In the following example, we want the `convert` method to have called the repository only once.

The registerUser example

More specifically in the `registerUser_generatesPasswordAndEncodesIt` test, we make use of a `MockitoArgumentCaptor` to manually perform deeper analyses on the object that a mocked method has been called with.

A `MockitoArgumentCaptor` is useful when we don't have an intermediate layer and when results are reused to invoke other methods.

More introspection tools than the superficial (but still very useful) Type checking can be required (for example, `any(String.class)`). An `ArgumentCaptor` as a solution is used with extra local variables in test methods.

Remember that local variables and transitory states in implementation methods will always increase the complexity of their related tests. Shorter, explicit, and cohesive methods are always better options.

There is more...

About Mockito

We advise the Mockito's Javadoc that is very well done and full of practical examples

```
http://docs.mockito.googlecode.com/hg/org/mockito/Mockito.html
```

JUnit Rules

We didn't cover JUnit Rules in any way so far. JUnit offers `@Rule` annotations that can be applied on test-class fields to abstract recurring business-specific preparations. It is often used to prepare test context objects (fixtures).

```
http://www.codeaffine.com/2012/09/24/junit-rules
```

```
http://junit.org/apidocs/org/junit/Rule.html
```

See also

> ▸ **Code coverage, JaCoCo**: JaCoCo is a library used to help maintain and increase the percentage of code covered by tests in applications; it is available at: `http://eclemma.org/jacoco`.

> ▸ Read more about JaCoCo Maven plugin at:
> `http://eclemma.org/jacoco/trunk/doc/maven.html`

Integration testing with Cargo, Rest-assured, and Maven failsafe

Integration Tests are as important as unit tests. They validate a feature from a higher level, and involve more components or layers at the same time. Integration tests (IT tests) are given more importance when an environment needs to evolve fast. Design processes often require iterations, and unit tests sometimes seriously impact our ability to refactor, while higher level testing is less impacted comparatively.

Getting ready

This recipe shows how to develop automated IT tests that focus on Spring MVC web services. Such IT Tests are not behavioral tests as they don't assess the user interface at all. To test behaviors, an even higher testing level would be necessary, simulating the User journey through the application interface.

We will configure the Cargo Maven Plugin to stand up a test environment as part of the pre-integration-test Maven phase. On the integration-test phase, we will get the Maven failsafe plugin to execute our IT Tests. Those IT Tests will make use of the REST-assured library to run HTTP requests against the test environment and assert the HTTP responses.

How to do it...

1. We have designed Integration tests in the `cloudstreetmarket-api` module. These tests are intended to test the API controller methods.

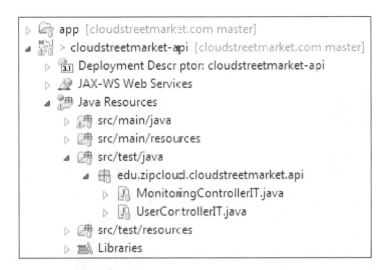

2. The great Rest-assured library comes with the following Maven dependency:

```xml
<dependency>
  <groupId>com.jayway.restassured</groupId>
  <artifactId>rest-assured</artifactId>
  <version>2.7.0</version>
</dependency>
```

3. A typical example of an IT Test using REST-assured would be the following `UserControllerIT.createUserBasicAuth()`:

```java
public class UserControllerIT extends
  AbstractCommonTestUser{
  private static User userA;
  @Before
  public void before(){
    userA = new User.Builder()
      .withId(generateUserName())
      .withEmail(generateEmail())
      .withCurrency(SupportedCurrency.USD)
      .withPassword(generatePassword())
      .withLanguage(SupportedLanguage.EN)
      .withProfileImg(DEFAULT_IMG_PATH)
      .build();
  }
  @Test
  public void createUserBasicAuth(){
    Response responseCreateUser = given()
      .contentType("application/json;charset=UTF-8")
      .accept("application/json"")
```

```
            .body(userA)
            .expect
            .when()
            .post(getHost() + CONTEXT_PATH + "/users");
    String location =
            responseCreateUser.getHeader("Location");
    assertNotNull(location);
    Response responseGetUser = given()
            .expect().log().ifError()
            .statusCode(HttpStatus.SC_OK)
            .when()
            .get(getHost() + CONTEXT_PATH + location +
                    JSON_SUFFIX);
      UserDTO userADTO =
        deserialize(responseGetUser.getBody().asString());
      assertEquals(userA.getId(), userADTO.getId());
      assertEquals(userA.getLanguage().name(),
      userADTO.getLanguage());
      assertEquals(HIDDEN_FIELD, userADTO.getEmail());
      assertEquals(HIDDEN_FIELD, userADTO.getPassword());
      assertNull(userA.getBalance());
   }
}
```

4. Because they take longer to execute, we wanted to decouple the IT Tests execution from the main Maven life cycle. We have associated those IT Tests to a Maven profile named `integration`.

> Maven profiles offer the possibility to optionally enrich a Maven build with extra life cycle bindings. For instance, our integration profile is activated passing this profile id as `Profile` argument in the usual command:
>
> ```
> $ mvn clean install -P integration
> ```

5. For our API IT tests, we have located the profile-specific configuration in the `cloudstreetmarket-api pom.xml` file:

```xml
<profiles>
  <profile>
  <id>integration</id>
  <build>
  <plugins>
    <plugin>
      <groupId>org.apache.maven.plugins</groupId>
      <artifactId>maven-failsafe-plugin</artifactId>
```

```xml
            <version>2.12.4</version>
            <configuration>
            <includes>
              <include>**/*IT.java</include>
            </includes>
            <excludes>
              <exclude>**/*Test.java</exclude>
            </excludes>
        </configuration>
        <executions>
            <execution>
              <id>integration-test</id>
              <goals>
                <goal>integration-test</goal>
              </goals>
            </execution>
            <execution>
              <id>verify</id>
              <goals><goal>verify</goal></goals>
            </execution>
        </executions>
    </plugin>
    <plugin>
     <groupId>org.codehaus.cargo</groupId>
     <artifactId>cargo-maven2-plugin</artifactId>
     <version>1.4.16</version>
        <configuration>
        <wait>false</wait>
        <container>
        <containerId>tomcat8x</containerId>
              <home>${CATALINA_HOME}</home>
        <logLevel>warn</logLevel>
        </container>
        <deployer/>
        <type>existing</type>
        <deployables>
        <deployable>
        <groupId>edu.zc.csm</groupId>
        <artifactId>cloudstreetmarket-api</artifactId>
        <type>war</type>
          <properties>
            <context>api</context>
          </properties>
        </deployable>
```

```
      </deployables>
    </configuration>
    <executions>
      <execution>
        <id>start-container</id>
        <phase>pre-integration-test</phase>
        <goals>
         <goal>start</goal>
         <goal>deploy</goal>
        </goals>
      </execution>
      <execution>
        <id>stop-container</id>
        <phase>post-integration-test</phase>
        <goals>
          <goal>undeploy</goal>
          <goal>stop</goal>
        </goals>
          </execution>
        </executions>
      </plugin>
    </plugins>
    </build>
    </profile>
</profiles>
```

6. Before attempting to run them on your machine, check that you have a **CATALINA_ HOME** environment variable pointing to your Tomcat directory. If not, you must create it. The variable to set should be the following (if you have followed *Chapter 1, Setup Routine for an Enterprise Spring Application*):

    ❑   `C:\tomcat8`: on MS Windows

    ❑   `/home/usr/{system.username}/tomcat8`: on Linux

    ❑   `/Users/{system.username}/tomcat8`: on Mac OS X

7. Also, ensure that Apache HTTP, Redis, and MySQL are up and running on your local machine (see previous chapter if you have skipped it).

8. When ready:

    ❑   either execute the following Maven command in your Terminal (if you have the Maven directory in your path):

        mvn clean verify -P integration

□ or create a shortcut for this custom build in your Eclipse IDE from the **Run | Run Configurations ..** menu. The Build configuration to create is the following:

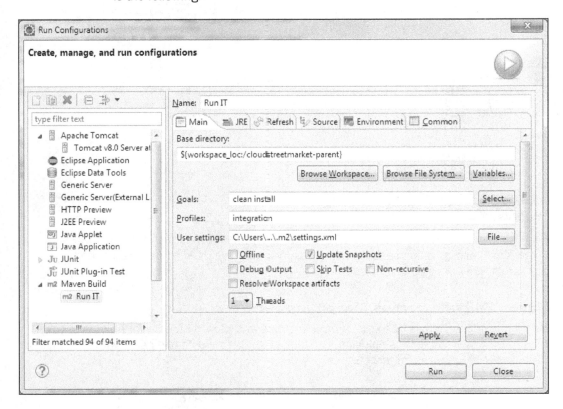

9. Running this command (or shortcut) should:

 1. deploy the **api.war** to the local Tomcat Server

 2. start the local Tomcat

 3. execute the test classes matching the **/*IT.java pattern

If all the tests pass, you should see the [INFO] BUILD SUCCESS message.

10. In between, when the build comes to the API, you should see the following bit of stack trace suggesting the successful execution of our IT tests:

```
[INFO] --- maven-failsafe-plugin:2.12.4:integration-test (integration-test) @ cloudstreetmarket-api
[INFO] Failsafe report directory: C:\ ... \target\failsafe-reports

- - - - - - - - - - - - - - - - - - - - - - - - - - - - - - - - - - - - - - - -
 T E S T S
- - - - - - - - - - - - - - - - - - - - - - - - - - - - - - - - - - - - - - - -
Running edu.zipcloud.cloudstreetmarket.api.MonitoringControllerIT
Tests run: 3, Failures: 0, Errors: 0, Skipped: 0, Time elapsed: 3.503 sec
Running edu.zipcloud.cloudstreetmarket.api.UserControllerIT
Tests run: 7, Failures: 0, Errors: 0, Skipped: 0, Time elapsed: 3.533 sec

Results :

Tests run: 10, Failures: 0, Errors: 0, Skipped: 0
```

How it works...

We will explain in this section why we have introduced the Maven failsafe plugin, how the Cargo Plugin configuration satisfies our needs, how we have used REST-assured, and how useful this REST-assured library is.

Maven Failsafe versus Maven Surefire

We are using Maven failsafe to run Integration tests and Maven Surefire for unit tests. This is a standard way of using these plugins. The following table reflects this point, with the Plugins' default naming patterns for test classes:

	Maven Surefire	Maven Failsafe

Default tests inclusion patterns	`**/Test*.java`
	`**/*Test.java`
	`**/*TestCase.java`
		`**/IT*.java`
		`**/*IT.java`
		`**/*ITCase.java`

Default output directory	`${basedir}/target/surefire-reports`	`${basedir}/target/failsafe-reports`

Bound to build phase	`test`	`pre-integration-test`
		`integration-test`
		`post-integration-test`
		`verify`

For Maven Failsafe, you can see that our overridden pattern inclusion/exclusion was optional. About the binding to Maven build phases, we have chosen to trigger the execution of our integration tests on the `integration-test` and `verify` phases.

Code Cargo

Cargo is a lightweight library that offers standard API for operating several supported containers (Servlet and JEE containers). Examples of covered API operations are artifacts' deployments, remote deployments and container start/stop. When used through Maven, Ant, or Gradle, it is mostly used for its ability to provide support to Integration Tests but can also serve other scopes.

Cargo Maven Plugin

We have used Cargo through its Maven plugin `org.codehaus.cargo:cargo-maven2-plugin` to automatically prepare an integration environment that we can run integration tests against. After the integration tests, we expect this environment to shut down.

Binding to Maven phases

The following executions have been declared as part of the `cargo-maven2-plugin` configuration::

```xml
<executions>
  <execution>
    <id>start-container</id>
    <phase>pre-integration-test</phase>
    <goals>
      <goal>start</goal>
    <goal>deploy</goal>
    </goals>
  </execution>
  <execution>
        <id>stop-container</id>
    <phase>post-integration-test</phase>
      <goals>
      <goal>undeploy</goal>
      <goal>stop</goal>
        </goals>
  </execution>
</executions>
```

Let's visit what happens when the `mvn install` command is executed.

The `install` is a phase of the default Maven life cycle. As explained in *Chapter 1, Setup Routine for an Enterprise Spring Application*, the default life cycle has 23 build phases from `validate` to `deploy`. The `install` phase is the 22nd, so 22 phases are checked to see whether there are plugin goals that could be attached to them.

Here, the `pre-integration-test` phase (that appears in the default life cycle between `validate` and `install`) will trigger the processes that are located under the `start` and `deploy` goals of our maven Cargo plugin. It is the same logic with `post-integration-test` triggers the `undeploy` and `stop` goals.

Before the IT tests execution, we start and deploy the Tomcat server. These IT tests are processed with Maven failsafe in the `integration-test` phase. Finally, the Tomcat server is undeployed and stopped.

IT Tests can also be executed with the `verify` phase (if the server is started out of the default Maven life cycle).

Using an existing Tomcat instance

In the Cargo Maven plugin configuration, we are targeting an existing instance of Tomcat. Our application is currently depending upon MySQL, Redis, Apache HTTP, and a custom session management. We have decided that the IT Tests execution will be required to be run in a proper integration environment.

Without all these dependencies, we would have got Cargo to download a Tomcat 8 instance.

Rest assured

REST-assured is an open source library licensed Apache v2 and supported by the company Jayway. It is written with Groovy and allows making HTTP requests and validating JSON or XML responses through its unique functional DSL that drastically simplify the tests of REST services.

Static imports

To effectively use REST-assured, the documentation recommends adding static imports of the following packages:

- `com.jayway.restassured.RestAssured.*`
- `com.jayway.restassured.matcher.RestAssuredMatchers.*`
- `org.hamcrest.Matchers.*`

A Given, When, Then approach

To understand the basics of the REST-assured DSL, let's consider one of our tests (in `UserControllerIT`) that provides a short overview of REST-assured usage:

```
@Test
public void createUserBasicAuthAjax(){
  Response response = given()
  .header("X-Requested-With", "XMLHttpRequest")
  .contentType("application/json;charset=UTF-8")
  .accept("application/json\"")
  .body(userA)
  .when()
```

```
        .post(getHost() + CONTEXT_PATH + "/users");
        assertNotNull(response.getHeader("Location"));
    }
```

The `given` part of the statement is the HTTP Request specification. With REST-assured, some request headers like `Content-Type` or `Accept` can be defined in an intuitive way with `contentType(...)` and `accept(...)`. Other **headers** can be reached with the generic `.header(...)`. Request parameters and authentication can also be defined in a same fashion.

For `POST` and `PUT` requests, it is necessary to pass a body to the request. This `body` can either be plain JSON or XML or directly the Java object (as we did here). This `body`, as a Java object, will be converted by the library depending upon the `content-type` defined in the specification (JSON or XML).

After the HTTP Request specification, the `when()` statement provides information about the actual HTTP method and destination.

At this stage, the returned object allows us either to define expectations from a `then()` block or, as we did here, to retrieve the `Response` object from where constraints can be defined separately. In our test case, the `Location` header of the `Response` is expected to be filled.

There is more...

More information can be found at the following Cargo and REST-assured respective documentations:

About Cargo

For more information about the product and its integration with third-party systems, refer to `https://codehaus-cargo.github.io/cargo/Home.html`.

More REST-assured examples

For more examples, the REST-assured online Wiki provides plenty:

`https://github.com/jayway/rest-assured/wiki/Usage`

Injecting Spring Beans into integration tests

This recipe is an example of how to inject Spring managed beans into integration test classes. Even for IT tests, whose first objective is to assess the backend as a blackbox, it is sometimes necessary to reach out technical objects from the intermediate layer.

Getting ready

We will see how to reuse an instance of a Spring managed `datasource` to be injected in our test class. This `datasource` will help us to build an instance of `jdbcTemplate`. From this `jdbcTemplate`, we will query the database and simulate/validate processes that couldn't be tested otherwise.

How to do it...

1. We have `@Autowired` a `dataSource` SpringBean in our `UserControllerIT` test. This bean is defined in the test-specific Spring configuration file (`spring-context-api-test.xml`) resources directory (`cloudstreetmarket-api`):

```
⊿ 📁 > cloudstreetmarket-api [cloudstreetmarket.com master]
   ▷ 📋 Deployment Descriptor: cloudstreetmarket-api
   ▷ 📄 JAX-WS Web Services
   ⊿ 📁 Java Resources
      ▷ 📁 src/main/java
      ▷ 📁 src/main/resources
      ▷ 📁 > src/test/java
      ⊿ 📁 > src/test/resources
            📄 > spring-context-api-test.xml
      ▷ 📚 Libraries
```

```xml
<context:property-placeholderlocation="
  file:${user.home}/app/cloudstreetmarket.properties""/>
<bean id="dataSource"
  class="org.apache.commons.dbcp2.BasicDataSource"
  destroy-method="close"">
  <property name="driverClassName"">
     <value>com.mysql.jdbc.Driver</value>
  </property>
  <property name="url"">
     <value>${db.connection.url}</value>
  </property>
<property name="username"">
  <value>${db.user.name}</value>
</property>
<property name="password"">
  <value>${db.user.passsword}</value>
</property>
<property name="defaultReadOnly">
  <value>false</value>
</property>
</bean>
```

A `jdbcTemplate` instance is created in the `UserControllerIT` class from the `@Autowired dataSource` bean:

```
@Autowired
private JdbcTemplate jdbcTemplate;
@Autowired
public void setDataSource(DataSource dataSource) {
    this.jdbcTemplate = new JdbcTemplate(dataSource);
}
```

2. We use `jdbcTemplate` to insert and delete `Social Connections` directly in the database (see *Chapter 5, Authenticating with Spring MVCA*). This allows us to bypass and simulate a successful user OAuth2 authentication flow (that normally happens through the web browser).

   For deleting social connections, we have created the following private method that is called as needed by the test(s:):

```
private void deleteConnection(String spi, String id) {
    this.jdbcTemplate.update("delete from userconnection
            where providerUserId = ? and userId = '?'", new
                Object[] {spi, id});
}
```

3. At the very top of the `UserControllerIT` class, the following two annotations can be noticed:

   □ `@RunWith(SpringJUnit4ClassRunner.class)` tells JUnit to run with a custom extension of JUnit (`SpringJUnit4ClassRunner`) that supports the Spring `TestContext` Framework.

   □ `@ContextConfiguration("classpath:spring-context-api-test.xml")` specifies where and how to load and configure the Spring application context:

```
@RunWith(SpringJUnit4ClassRunner.class)
@ContextConfiguration("classpath:spring-context-api-
    test.xml"")
public class UserControllerIT extends
    AbstractCommonTestUser{
private static User userA;
private static User userB;

...
}
```

How it works...

SpringJUnit4ClassRunner

In its design, the `SpringJUnit4ClassRunner` is a direct subclass of the JUnit's `BlockJUnit4ClassRunner`. `SpringJUnit4ClassRunner` that initializes when a `TestContextManager` is loaded. A `TestContextManager` manages the life cycle of a `TestContext` and can also reflect test events to the registered `TestExecutionListeners` (from `@BeforeClass`, `@AfterClass`, `@Before`, and `@After` annotations).

By loading a Spring context, the `SpringJUnit4ClassRunner` Spring context, `SpringJUnit4ClassRunner` enables the possibility use Spring managed beans in test classes. The `SpringJUnit4ClassRunner` also supports a set of annotations (either from JUnit or from Spring test) that can be used in test classes. The use of these annotations can be trusted for subsequently providing suitable life cycle management to context-defined objects.

Those annotations are `@Test` (with its `expected` and `timeout` annotation parameters), `@Timed`, `@Repeat`, `@Ignore`, `@ProfileValueSourceConfiguration`, and `@IfProfileValue`.

The @ContextConfiguration annotation

This class-level annotation is specific to Spring Test. It defines how and where to load a Spring Context for the test class.

Our definition in the recipe targets a specific Spring XML configuration file `@ContextConfiguration("classpath:spring-context-api-test.xml")`.

However, since Spring 3.1 the contexts can be defined programmatically, `@ContextConfiguration` can also target configuration classes as follows:

```
@ContextConfiguration(classes={AnnotationConfig.class,
        WebSocketConfig.class})
```

As shown in the following snippet, both declaration types can be combined in the same annotation:

```
@ContextConfiguration(classes={AnnotationConfig.class,
  WebSocketConfig.class}, locations={"classpath:spring-context-api-
  test.xml"})
```

There is more...

We will see more in this section about the Spring JdbcTemplate that has been used for test purposes.

JdbcTemplate

In *Chapter 1, Setup Routine for an Enterprise Spring Application*, we have introduced the different modules that make the Spring Framework what it is today. One group of modules is **Data Access and Integration**. This group contains the JDBC, ORM, OXM, JMS, and transactions modules.

The `JdbcTemplate` is a key-class part of the Spring JDBC core package. It reliably allows performing of database operations with straightforward utility methods and also provides an abstraction for big chunks of boilerplate code. Once more, this tool saves us time and offers patterns to design quality products.

Abstraction of boilerplate logic

Let's consider as an example the method in our test class that deletes connections:

```
jdbcTemplate.update("delete from userconnection where
  providerUserId = ? and userId = "?", new Object[] {spi, id});
```

Using `jdbcTemplate`, deleting a database element is a one-line instruction. It creates a `PreparedStatement` under the hood, chooses the right Type, depending upon the arguments we actually pass as values, and it manages the database connection for us, making sure to close this connection whatever happens.

The `jdbcTemplate.update` method has been designed to issue a single SQL update operation. It can be used for inserts, updates, and also deletes.

As often in Spring, `jdbcTemplate` also transforms the produced checked exceptions (if any) into unchecked exceptions. Here, the potential `SQLExceptions` would be wrapped in a `RuntimeException`.

Extraction of auto-generated IDs

The `jdbcTemplate.update` method also offers other argument Types:

```
jdbcTemplate.update(final PreparedStatementCreator psc, final
  KeyHolder generatedKeyHolder);
```

In the case of an insert, this method can be called when needed to read and potentially reuse the generated ID (which is unknown before the query execution).

In our example, if we would have wanted to reuse the generated connection IDs when inserting new connections, we would have done it as follows:

```
KeyHolder keyHolder = new GeneratedKeyHolder();
jdbcTemplate.update(
  new PreparedStatementCreator() {
    public PreparedStatement createPreparedStatement(Connection
    connection) throws SQLException {
```

```
PreparedStatement ps =
  connection.prepareStatement("insert into
  userconnection (accessToken, ... , secret, userId )
  values (?, ?, ... , ?, ?)", new String[] {"id""});
ps.setString(1, generateGuid());
ps.setDate(2, new Date(System.currentTimeMillis()));
...
return ps;
}
}, keyHolder);
Long Id = keyHolder.getKey().longValue();
```

But we didn't specifically require such a use case.

Modern application Logging with Log4j2

After 20 years of evolution in the Java ecosystem, the ways of Logging have seen different strategies, trends, and architectures. Nowadays, several Logging frameworks can be found among the used third-party dependencies. We must support them all to debug an application or to trace runtime events.

Getting ready

This recipe provides a future-proof implementation of Log4j2 for the CloudStreet Market application. It requires several Maven dependencies to be added to our modules. As a solution, it can appear quite complicated, but in reality the amount of Logging frameworks to support is limited, and the logic behind a Log4j2 migration is fairly straightforward.

How to do it...

1. The following Maven dependencies have been added to the dependency-management section of the parent-module (cloudstreetmarket-parent):

    ```
    <!-- Logging dependencies -->
    <dependency>
      <groupId>org.apache.logging.log4j</groupId>
      <artifactId>log4j-api</artifactId>
      <version>2.4.1</version>
    </dependency>
    <dependency>
      <groupId>org.apache.logging.log4j</groupId>
      <artifactId>log4j-core</artifactId>
      <version>2.4.1</version>
    </dependency>
    ```

```xml
<dependency>
  <groupId>org.apache.logging.log4j</groupId>
  <artifactId>log4j-slf4j-impl</artifactId>
  <version>2.4.1</version>
</dependency>
<dependency>
  <groupId>org.apache.logging.log4j</groupId>
  <artifactId>log4j-1.2-api</artifactId>
  <version>2.4.1</version>
</dependency>
<dependency>
  <groupId>org.apache.logging.log4j</groupId>
  <artifactId>log4j-jcl</artifactId>
  <version>2.4.1</version>
  </dependency>
<dependency>
  <groupId>org.apache.logging.log4j</groupId>
  <artifactId>log4j-web</artifactId>
    <scope>runtime</scope>
  <version>2.4.1</version>
</dependency>
<dependency>
  <groupId>org.slf4j</groupId>
  artifactId>slf4j-api</artifactId>
  <version>${slf4j.version}</version>
</dependency>
```

The last dependency-management, `org.slf4j`, allows us to make sure one single version of `slf4j` will be used everywhere.

2. In the `api`, `ws`, and `core` modules, the following dependencies have then been added: `log4j-api`, `log4j-core`, `log4j-slf4j-impl`, `log4j-1.2-api`, and `log4j-jcl`..

3. In the web modules (`api`, `ws`, and `webapp`), `log4j-web` has been added..

4. Notice that `slf4j-api` has only been added for dependency management.

5. Start the Tomcat Server with **the extra JVM argument**:

   `-Dlog4j.configurationFile=<home-directory>\app\log4j2.xml`.

Replace `<home-directory>` with the path you actually use on your machine.

6. The app directory in the user home now contains the `log4j2` configuration file:

```xml
<?xml version="1.0" encoding="UTF-8"?>
<Configuration status="OFF" monitorInterval="30">
<Appenders
  <Console name="Console" target="SYSTEM_OUT">
    <PatternLayout pattern"="%d{HH:mm:ss.SSS} %-5level
      %logger{36} - %msg%n""/>
  </Console>
  <RollingFile name="FileAppender" fileName="
        ${sys:user.home}/app/logs/cloudstreetmarket.log"
        filePattern="
        ${sys:user.home}/app/logs/${date:yyyy-
        MM}/cloudstreetmarket-%d{MM-dd-yyyy}-
        %i.log.gz">
    <PatternLayout>
      <Pattern>%d %p %C{1} %m%n</Pattern>
    </PatternLayout>
    <Policies>
      <TimeBasedTriggeringPolicy />
      <SizeBasedTriggeringPolicy size="250 MB"/>
    </Policies>
  </RollingFile>
</Appenders>
<Loggers>
  <Logger name="edu.zipcloud" level="INFO"/>
  <Logger name="org.apache.catalina" level="ERROR"/>
  <Logger name="org.springframework.amqp"
    level="ERROR"/>
  <Logger name="org.springframework.security"
    level="ERROR"/>

  <Root level="WARN">
    <AppenderRef ref="Console"/>
  <AppenderRef ref="FileAppender"/>
  </Root>
</Loggers>
</Configuration>
```

7. As a fall back option, a `log4j2.xml` file is also present in the classpath (`src/main/resources`) of every single module.

8. A couple of log instructions have been placed in different classes to trace the user journey.

Log instructions in `SignInAdapterImpl`:

```java
    import org.apache.logging.log4j.LogManager;
import org.apache.logging.log4j.Logger;

@Transactional
public class SignInAdapterImpl implements SignInAdapter{
  private static final Logger logger =
    LogManager.getLogger(SignInAdapterImpl.class);
  ...
  public String signIn(String userId, Connection<?>
    connection, NativeWebRequest request) {
  ...
  communityService.signInUser(user);
  logger.info("User {} logs-in with OAuth2 account",
    user.getId());
  return view;
  }
}
```

Log instructions in `UsersController`:

```java
@RestController
@RequestMapping(value=USERS_PATH, produces={"application/xml",
"application/json"})
public class UsersController extends CloudstreetApiWCI{
  private static final Logger logger =
    LogManager.getLogger(UsersController.class);
  ...
  @RequestMapping(method=POST)
  @ResponseStatus(HttpStatus.CREATED)
  public void create(@Valid @RequestBody User user,
    @RequestHeader(value="api", required=false) String
      guid,
  @RequestHeader(value="OAuthProvider", required=false)
    String provider, HttpServletResponse response) throws
    IllegalAccessException-
      if(isNotBlank(guid))
      ...
      communityService.save(user);
      logger.info("User {} registers an OAuth2 account:
        "{}", user.getId() - guid);
      }
      else{
```

```
        user = communityService.createUser(user,
          ROLE_BASIC);

        ...

        logger.info("User registers a BASIC account"
          ",
          user.getId());
          }

        ...

      }

    ...

  }
```

9. Start your local Tomcat Server and navigate briefly through the application. As with the following example, you should be able to observe a trace of the customer activity in the aggregated file: `<home-directory>/apps/logs/cloudstreetmarket.log`:

```
2016-01-18 06:44:03,107 INFO SignInAdapterImpl User IMQRDBSFHTC5V37ZUMP5DJ7OYI logs in with OAUth2 account
2016-01-18 06:44:04,051 WARN ChartIndexController Resource not found: Chart for Index ^GDAXI
2016-01-18 06:44:16,481 INFO UsersController User marcus registers an OAuth2 account: IMQRDBSFHTC5V37ZUMP5
2016-01-18 06:44:27,199 INFO UserImageController User marcus uploads a new profile picture: fbed4828-26ef-
2016-01-18 06:44:51,278 INFO TransactionController User marcus buys 12 FB at 94.0 USD
2016-01-18 06:45:14,027 INFO UsersController User registers a BASIC account
2016-01-18 06:45:24,289 INFO LikeActionController User happy_face likes action id 280
2016-01-18 06:45:33,794 WARN ChartStockController Resource not found: Chart for ticker AMD
```

 With the `log4j2.xml` configuration we have made, the `cloudstreetmarket.log` files will automatically be zipped and categorized in directories as they reach 250 MB.

How it works...

We are mainly going to review in this section how Log4j2 has been set up to work along with the other Logging frameworks. The other parts of the configuration (not covered here) have been considered more intuitive.

Apache Log4j2 among other logging frameworks

Log4j1+ is dying as a project since it is not compatible any longer with Java 5+.

Log4j 2 has been built as a fork of the log4j codebase. In this perspective, it competes with the Logback project. Logback was initially the legitimate continuation of Log4j.

Log4j 2 actually implements many of the Logback's improvements but also fixes problems that are inherent to the Logback's architecture.

Logback provides great performance improvements, especially with multithreading. Comparatively, Log4j 2 offers similar performance.

The case of SLF4j

SLF4j is not a Logging framework as such; it is an abstraction layer that allows the user to plug in any logging system at deployment time.

SLF4j requires a SLF4j binding in the classpath. Examples of bindings are the following:

- `slf4j-log4j12-xxx.jar`: (log4j version 1.2),
- `slf4j-jdk14-xxx.jar`: (`java.util.logging` from the jdk 1.4),
- `slf4j-jcl-xxx.jar`: (Jakarta Commons Logging)
- `logback-classic-xxx.jar`.

It also often requires core libraries of the targeted Logging framework.

Migrating to log4j 2

Log4j2 does not offer backward compatibility for Log4j1+. It may sound like a problem because applications (like `CloudStreetMarket`) often use third-party libraries that embed their own logging framework. Spring core, for example, has a transitive dependency to Jakarta Commons Logging.

To solve this situation, Log4j 2 provides adapters guaranteeing that internal logs won't be lost and will be bridged to join the log4j 2 flow of logs. There are adapters pretty much for all the systems that may produce logs.

Log4j 2 API and Core

Log4j 2 comes with an API and an implementation. Both are required and come with the following dependencies:

```
<dependency>
    <groupId>org.apache.logging.log4j</groupId>
    <artifactId>log4j-api</artifactId>
    <version>2.4.1</version>
</dependency>
<dependency>
    <groupId>org.apache.logging.log4j</groupId>
    <artifactId>log4j-core</artifactId>
    <version>2.4.1</version>
</dependency>
```

Log4j 2 Adapters

As introduced earlier, a set of **Adapters** and **Bridges** are available to provide backward compatibility to our applications.

Log4j 1.x API Bridge

When transitive dependencies to Log4j 1+ are noticed in specific modules, the following bridge should be added:

```
<dependency>
  <groupId>org.apache.logging.log4j</groupId>
  <artifactId>log4j-1.2-api</artifactId>
  <version>2.4.1</version>
</dependency>
```

Apache Commons Logging Bridge

When transitive dependencies to Apache (Jakarta) Commons Logging are noticed in specific modules, the following bridge should be added:

```
<dependency>
  <groupId>org.apache.logging.log4j</groupId>
  <artifactId>log4j-jcl</artifactId>
  <version>2.4.1</version>
</dependency>
```

SLF4J Bridge

The same logic is applied to cover slf4j uses; the following bridge should be added:

```
<dependency>
  <groupId>org.apache.logging.log4j</groupId>
  <artifactId>log4j-slf4j-impl</artifactId>
  <version>2.4.1</version>
</dependency>
```

Java Util Logging Adapters

No transitive dependencies to `java.util.logging` have been noticed in our application, but if it would have been the case, we would have used the following bridge:

```
<dependency>
  <groupId>org.apache.logging.log4j</groupId>
  <artifactId>log4j-jul</artifactId>
  <version>2.4.1</version>
</dependency>
```

Web Servlet Support

The Apache Tomcat container has its own set of libraries that also produce logs. Adding the following dependency on web modules is a way to ensure that container logs are routed to the main Log4j2 pipeline.

```
<dependency>
  <groupId>org.apache.logging.log4j</groupId>
```

```
    <artifactId>log4j-web</artifactId>
    <version>2.4.1</version>
    <scope>runtime</scope>
</dependency>
```

Configuration files

The sixth step of this recipe details our log4j2 configuration. It is made of different and configurable `Appenders` (output channels basically). We are using the console and a file-based `Appender`, but Log4j 2 has a plugin-based architecture about `Appenders` that allows the use of external output channels if needed (SMTP, Printer, Database, and so on).

There is more...

As external sources of information, we point out the interesting Log4j2 auto-configuration which is made of a cascading lookup for configuration files, the official documentation, and an `Appender` for logging directly into Redis.

Automatic configuration

Log4j2 implements a cascading lookup in order to locate log4j2 configuration files. Starting from looking for a provided `log4j.configurationFile` system property, to `log4j2-test.xml` and `log4j2.xml` files in the classpath, the official documentation details all the followed waterfall steps. This documentation is available at:

```
https://logging.apache.org/log4j/2.x/manual/configuration.html
```

Official documentation

The official documentation is very well made and complete, and is available at

```
https://logging.apache.org/log4j/2.x.
```

Interesting Redis Appender implementation

The following address introduces an Apache licensed project that provides a Log4j2 **Appender** to log straight into Redis:

```
https://github.com/pavlobaron/log4j2redis
```

Index

Symbols

A

About Packt Publishing

Packt, pronounced 'packed', published its first book, *Mastering phpMyAdmin for Effective MySQL Management*, in April 2004, and subsequently continued to specialize in publishing highly focused books on specific technologies and solutions.

Our books and publications share the experiences of your fellow IT professionals in adapting and customizing today's systems, applications, and frameworks. Our solution-based books give you the knowledge and power to customize the software and technologies you're using to get the job done. Packt books are more specific and less general than the IT books you have seen in the past. Our unique business model allows us to bring you more focused information, giving you more of what you need to know, and less of what you don't.

Packt is a modern yet unique publishing company that focuses on producing quality, cutting-edge books for communities of developers, administrators, and newbies alike. For more information, please visit our website at www.packtpub.com.

About Packt Open Source

In 2010, Packt launched two new brands, Packt Open Source and Packt Enterprise, in order to continue its focus on specialization. This book is part of the Packt open source brand, home to books published on software built around open source licenses, and offering information to anybody from advanced developers to budding web designers. The Open Source brand also runs Packt's open source Royalty Scheme, by which Packt gives a royalty to each open source project about whose software a book is sold.

Writing for Packt

We welcome all inquiries from people who are interested in authoring. Book proposals should be sent to author@packtpub.com. If your book idea is still at an early stage and you would like to discuss it first before writing a formal book proposal, then please contact us; one of our commissioning editors will get in touch with you.

We're not just looking for published authors; if you have strong technical skills but no writing experience, our experienced editors can help you develop a writing career, or simply get some additional reward for your expertise.

Mastering Spring MVC 4

ISBN: 978-1-78398-238-7   Paperback: 320 pages

Gain expertise in designing real-world web applications using the Spring MVC framework

1. Design your own Spring web applications using tools such as Spring Boot and Spring Tool Suite.

2. Secure your developments with easy-to-write, reliable unit and end-to-end tests.

3. Deploy your application on the cloud for free and invite the whole world to see.

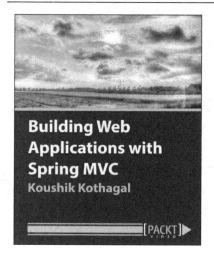

Building Web Applications with Spring MVC [Video]

ISBN: 978-1-78328-653-9   Duration: 03:13 hours

Build dynamic and powerful server-side web applications in Java using Spring MVC

1. Implement Spring MVC controllers that handle user requests, return HTML responses, and handle errors.

2. Provide locale and theme support for web applications as well as build sturdy RESTful web services.

3. A practical guide that demonstrates building Spring MVC applications using an example of an online e-commerce chocolate store.

Please check **www.PacktPub.com** for information on our titles

Spring Web Flow 2 Web Development

ISBN: 978-1-84719-542-5   Paperback: 200 pages

Master Spring's well-designed web frameworks to develop powerful web applications

1. Approach towards the Spring MVC framework with practical examples and code.

2. Bridge the gap between the popular web framework and the popular application framework.

3. Test applications that are developed with Spring Web Flow the above one is for Spring Web Flow 2 Web Development.

Spring Security 3.x Cookbook

ISBN: 978-1-78216-752-5   Paperback: 300 pages

Over 60 recipes to help you successfully safeguard your web applications with Spring Security

1. Learn about all the mandatory security measures for modern day applications using Spring Security.

2. Investigate different approaches to application level authentication and authorization.

3. Master how to mount security on applications used by developers and organizations.

Please check **www.PacktPub.com** for information on our titles